Ritual, Media, and Conflict

EDITED BY
RONALD L. GRIMES
UTE HÜSKEN
UDO SIMON
ERIC VENBRUX

OXFORD
UNIVERSITY PRESS

OXFORD
UNIVERSITY PRESS

Oxford University Press, Inc., publishes works that further
Oxford University's objective of excellence
in research, scholarship, and education.

Oxford   New York
Auckland   Cape Town   Dar es Salaam   Hong Kong   Karachi
Kuala Lumpur   Madrid   Melbourne   Mexico City   Nairobi
New Delhi   Shanghai   Taipei   Toronto

With offices in
Argentina   Austria   Brazil   Chile   Czech Republic   France   Greece
Guatemala   Hungary   Italy   Japan   Poland   Portugal   Singapore
South Korea   Switzerland   Thailand   Turkey   Ukraine   Vietnam

Copyright © 2011 by Oxford University Press, Inc.

Published by Oxford University Press, Inc.
198 Madison Avenue, New York, New York 10016

www.oup.com

Oxford is a registered trademark of Oxford University Press

All rights reserved. No part of this publication may be reproduced,
stored in a retrieval system, or transmitted, in any form or by any means,
electronic, mechanical, photocopying, recording, or otherwise,
without the prior permission of Oxford University Press.

Library of Congress Cataloging-in-Publication Data
Ritual, media, and conflict / edited by Ronald L. Grimes...[et al.].
    p. cm.
Includes bibliographical references and index.
ISBN 978-0-19-973523-5; 978-0-19-973554-9 (pbk.)
1. Rites and ceremonies. 2. Ritual. 3. Social conflict. 4. Culture conflict. 5. Mass media and culture.
6. Communication and culture. I. Grimes, Ronald L., 1943–
GN473.R55 2011
390′dc22   2010012913

9 8 7 6 5 4 3 2 1

Printed in the United States of America
on acid-free paper

Acknowledgments

The editors wish to thank two national agencies for funding Ritual, Media, and Conflict, the research project that led to this book: the Netherlands Organization for Scientific Research for awarding a generous Humanities Internationalization grant, and the Deutsche Forschungsgemeinschaft for funding collaboration through the SFB 619, The Dynamics of Ritual. We also thank Cynthia Read, Lisbeth Redfield, Karen Fisher, and Tamzen Benfield for their hard work on the volume.

Contents

Contributors, ix

1 Ritual, Media, and Conflict: An Introduction, 3
   Ronald L. Grimes

2 From Ritual Ground to Stage, 35
   Fletcher DuBois, Erik de Maaker, Karin Polit, and Marianne Riphagen

3 Insurgents and Icons, 63
   Anna-Karina Hermkens and Eric Venbrux

4 Ritual as a Source of Conflict, 93
   Robert Langer, Thomas Quartier, Udo Simon, Jan Snoek, and Gerard Wiegers

5 Place, Action, and Community in Internet Rituals, 133
   Marga Altena, Catrien Notermans, and Thomas Widlok

6 Contested Rituals in Virtual Worlds, 165
   Simone Heidbrink, Nadja Miczek, and Kerstin Radde-Antweiler

7 Media on the Ritual Battlefield, 189
   Ignace de Haes, Ute Hüsken, and Paul van der Velde

8 What's at Stake in Torture?, 223
   Werner Binder, Tom F. Driver, and Barry Stephenson

9 Refracting Ritual: An Upside-Down Perspective on
Ritual, Media, and Conflict, 255
Michael Houseman

Index, 285

Contributors

Marga Altena is a historian of visual culture working as a researcher, teacher, and publicist. Having completed her studies in art history and classical archaeology, Dr. Altena then specialized in the history of photography and film, especially the use of images by historians. Her PhD dissertation, written in the Netherlands at Radboud University Nijmegen, was titled "Visuele strategieën. Foto's en films van fabrieksarbeidsters in Nederland, 1890–1919" [Visual Strategies: Photos and Films of Female Factory Workers in the Netherlands, 1890–1919] (2003). She teaches gender history and visual culture at the Free University of Amsterdam and Radboud University, where she is employed as a research fellow at the Center for Thanatology investigating funerary films, television shows, and Weblogs as innovative death rituals. She is also engaged in a research project on the construction of ethnic differences in Dutch news media from 1886 to 1928.

Werner Binder received his MA with honors in 2006 after six years of studies in sociology, philosophy, and literature at the universities of Mannheim, Potsdam, and Berlin. His master's thesis on the relevance of ethnic and religious categories in the Turkish community in Germany was recently published as *Herkunft als Stigma, Emblem und Tabu* (2008). He is a junior lecturer and research assistant at the University of Konstanz, teaching courses in sociology and conducting research for his PhD project on the Abu Ghraib scandal. His interest in ritual stems from the comparative study of religions and is now informed by the writings of Emile Durkheim and contemporary studies in Durkheimian sociology. Other fields of interest are social and culture theory, hermeneutics and interpretation, visual sociology, and the sociology of morality. He currently works on the topics of violence, cultural trauma, iconicity, social performance, and public discourse.

Tom F. Driver, The Paul Tillich Professor of Theology and Culture Emeritus at Union Theological Seminary in New York, holds an MDiv in the study of theology and a PhD in English and Comparative Literature with a major in the history of theater and drama (Columbia University, 1957). His interest in ritual studies was born of twin concerns for theater and theology and nurtured by readings in anthropology. An avid photographer, he has often employed this medium in the documentation and analysis of ritual. His published books include *Romantic Quest and Modern Query: A History of the Modern Theater* (1970, 1980) and *Liberating Rites: Understanding the Transformative Power of Ritual* (2006; originally published as *The Magic of Ritual*, 1991). He was among the founders of the Ritual Studies Group of the American Academy of Religion. Today he represents the Rutgers Presbyterian Church in New York City on the Participating Members Council of the National Religious Campaign against Torture.

Fletcher DuBois is a full professor at National-Louis University in Chicago, in the National College of Education's Department of Educational Foundations, as well as its Department of Integrated Studies in Teaching, Technology and Inquiry. From 1996 to 2004 he was the academic director of the Heidelberg campus, coordinating NLU's MEd program, Interdisciplinary Studies in Curriculum and Instruction, in Germany, England, and Italy. Since 2003, he has been a guest research professor at the Department of Medical Psychology and is a member of the Ritual Dynamics Collaborative Research Center at the University of Heidelberg. Since 2006 he has coordinated a cooperative exchange project on critical media literacy with faculty and staff of NLU and the University of Heidelberg. He is also a professional singer-songwriter and recently had a novella accepted for publication by Hanser Publishing House.

Ronald L. Grimes is Professor Emeritus of Religion and Culture at Wilfrid Laurier University in Canada and held the Chair of Ritual Studies at Radboud University Nijmegen, the Netherlands, from 2005–2010. The fields of his interest include ritual studies, religion and the performing arts, field research in the study of religion, and indigenous religions in the Americas. Grimes is the author of several books on ritual, most recently, *Rite Out of Place: Ritual, Media, and the Arts* (2006). Among his other works are *Deeply into the Bone: Re-inventing Rites of Passage* (2000), *Readings in Ritual Studies* (1996), *Reading, Writing, and Ritualizing* (1993), *Ritual Criticism* (1990), and *Beginnings in Ritual Studies* (1982, 1994).

Ignace de Haes is public relations officer for the Faculties of Theology and Religious Studies at Radboud University Nijmegen. He holds a master's degree in the science of communication from the University of Amsterdam, as well as a master's degree in corporate communication from the University of Rotterdam. He wrote a thesis about media and human rights violations. He has worked in the media as a public relations officer for Mensen in Nood (Caritas, the Netherlands) and has accompanied television crews to disaster areas.

Simone Heidbrink is a junior researcher at the Institute of Religious Studies of the University of Heidelberg in Germany. After majoring in religious and Japanese studies at the universities of Heidelberg and Nara, Japan, she received her master's degree in 2005 and is now a member of the Ritual Dynamics Collaborative Research Center at the University of Heidelberg. Her doctoral research is on Emerging Church, a Christian liturgical reform movement that relies heavily on Web 2.0 Internet applications to distribute their views on Christianity, theology, and the role of rituals. She also studies Buddhism in Second Life from a transcultural, comparative perspective.

Anna-Karina Hermkens is an anthropologist and postdoctoral researcher at the Faculty of Religious Studies at Radboud University Nijmegen. Her fields of interest are material culture studies, gender, and religion and conflict. She is coeditor of *Moved by Mary* (2009). Her current research concerns the relation between religion, ritual, violence, and the female body in Papua New Guinea and Indonesia.

Michael Houseman is Professor of Religions of Black Africa (Ethnology) at the École Pratique des Hautes Études in Paris, France. He was trained in social anthropology at the University of Paris, Nanterre, and has done fieldwork in Cameroon, Benin, and French Guyana. He has published numerous articles on ritual, kinship, and social organization. Dr. Houseman is the editor of *Éprouver l'initiation* (2008) and, with Carlo Severi, author of *Naven or the Other Self: A Relational Approach to Ritual Action* (1998).

Ute Hüsken, Professor of Sanskrit at the University of Oslo, was educated as an Indian and Tibetan studies scholar and as a cultural anthropologist in Germany at the University of Göttingen. She teaches courses on religion in South Asia, Sanskrit, Pali, ancient and contemporary Buddhism, Hinduism, and Jainism. Her main fields of research are South Indian Hinduism, early Theravada Buddhism, and ritual studies. For five years Dr. Hüsken was a member of the executive committee of the Ritual Dynamics Collaborative Research Center at the University of Heidelberg. Since 2008 she has served as cochair of the steering committee of the Ritual Studies

Group of the American Academy of Religion. She is the editor of *When Rituals Go Wrong: Mistakes, Failure, and the Dynamics of Ritual* (2007) and coeditor of *Words and Deeds: Hindu and Buddhist Rituals in South Asia* (2005). Her book with DVD, *Vishnu's Children: Prenatal Lifecycle Rituals in South India*, was published in 2009.

Robert Langer, whose field is Islamic studies, has been a member of the Ritual Dynamics Collaborative Research Center since 2002 and an academic associate of a subproject studying the transfer of rituals within heterodox Muslim groups. He is affiliated with the University of Heidelberg's Department of Languages and Cultures of the Near East. He pursued Oriental studies and cultural anthropology at Heidelberg, receiving his MA in 2000. Additionally, he studied Arabic and Turkish at Damascus, Ankara, and Istanbul. From 2000 to 2002, he was a member of the Emmy Noether Research Group on Zoroastrian rituals at the Institute for Religious Studies, University of Heidelberg, where, after doing fieldwork in Iran in 2001, he completed his PhD (magna cum laude, Philosophy Faculty, Heidelberg, 2004). For this dissertation on the interaction of Muslim and Zoroastrian shrine worship in Iran, published as *Pîrân und Zeyâratgâh* (in the series Acta Iranica, no. 48, 2008), the Iranian Ministry of Culture awarded him the international research prize, Cultural Research of the Year 2002. His fields of research are anthropology, geography, and history of religion, especially in the Muslim world. He is now conducting fieldwork with Alevi and Yezidi groups in Turkey and Armenia, as well as among diaspora groups in Western Europe. Together with Michael Ursinus and Raoul Motika, he edited *Migration und Ritualtransfer* (2005), and together with Udo Simon, *The Dynamics of Orthodoxy and Heterodoxy* (a thematic issue of the journal *Die Welt des Islams*, no. 48, 2008).

Erik de Maaker is a lecturer and researcher at the Institute for Cultural Anthropology and Development Sociology of Leiden University in the Netherlands. His present research in South Asia is on religious conversions, the changing material and ritual dimensions of religious practices, and the politicization of ethnicity and indigenous identity. Using qualitative research methods along with video and photography, one of his specialties is visual anthropology. He has produced several ethnographic films and DVDs, among them *Teyyam: The Annual Visit of the God Vishnumurti* and *Ashes of Life, the Annual Rituals of Laboya* (1996). He has published articles such as "From the Songsarek Faith to Christianity: Religious Change and Cultural Continuity in West Garo Hills" in the journal *South Asia*. De Maaker was a postdoctoral research fellow at Radboud University Nijmegen, where he conducted research on contemporary mortuary practices in the Netherlands. He studied anthropology in Amsterdam and Leiden and wrote *Negotiating Life: Garo Death Rituals and the Transformation of Society*, a PhD dissertation on the mortuary rituals of a community in upland northeastern India.

Nadja Miczek is a postdoctoral researcher at the Institute of Religious Studies at the University of Lucerne, Switzerland. Her doctoral thesis, *Identities, Rituals, Media: A Qualitative Study on Constellations of Contemporary Religiosity* (2009), was written as a fellow of the Collaborative Research Center 619, Ritual Dynamics, at the University of Heidelberg. Her interests include the study of religions and rituals in virtual 3D environments, New Age religion, and the relation of religion to media and economics. Together with Simone Heidbrink she edited a special issue of the *Heidelberg Journal of Religions on the Internet* on "Aesthetics and the Sensual Dimension."

Catrien Notermans is an anthropologist working as a senior researcher and lecturer at the Department of Cultural Anthropology and Development Sociology at Radboud University Nijmegen. Her fields of interest include religion (African Christianity, witchcraft, Hinduism, material religion, pilgrimage) and kinship (polygyny, fosterage, transnational kin networks). Her regional expertise includes Cameroon, France, the Netherlands, and India. One of her articles, "Loss and Healing: A Marian Pilgrimage in Secular Dutch Society," appeared in *Ethnology* (2008). She is currently one of the project leaders of the international research program Gender, Nation, and Religious Diversity in Force at European Pilgrimage Sites, funded by NORFACE. As part of this program, she is conducting fieldwork on African migrants going to Marian pilgrimage sites in Western Europe.

Karin Polit has been a research fellow in the Ritual Dynamics Collaborative Research Center since 2005. Her main interests are in performance studies, visual anthropology, the anthropology of media, and medical anthropology. After studying anthropology in Germany and Australia, she conducted research in Indonesia, the Netherlands, and northern India. For her PhD dissertation, she conducted extensive research among the village women of Garhwal in the Indian region of the central Himalayas. Since then she has worked there with traditional medical practitioners and ritual specialists involved in ritual healing, as well as with traditional and new ritual performers of Garhwal and Uttarakhand. She is currently writing a book, including ethnographical material on DVD, on divine performances of northern India.

Thomas Quartier teaches ritual studies in the Faculty of Religious Studies of Radboud University Nijmegen, the Netherlands. He earned his PhD with a dissertation on contemporary Roman Catholic funeral rites in the Netherlands: *Bridging the Gaps: An Empirical Study of Catholic Funeral Rites* (2007). In addition to death rituals, he is interested in ritual dimensions of popular culture and new rituals in secular society. He is a member of the Refiguring Death Rites research group at Radboud University. Recent publications include "Personal Symbols in Roman

Catholic Funerals," *Mortality* 14, no. 2 (2009): 133–146; "Underground rituelen" in *Nieuwe religiositeit in Nederland* (2009); and "Rituelle Pendelbewegungen: Neue Trauerrituale im Niederländischen Kontext," in *Jaarboek voor liturgie-onderzoek / Yearbook for Liturgy-Research* 25 (2009): 185–205.

Kerstin Radde-Antweiler is an assistant professor at the Institute for the Scientific Study of Religions at the University of Bremen, Germany. She received her diploma in Protestant theology at the University of Heidelberg and finished her doctoral dissertation, "Ritual Design on the Internet: Reception and Invention of Magical Rituals of New Wiccan Groups," while she was a member of the Ritual Dynamics Collaborative Research Center at the University of Heidelberg. She has conducted research on wedding rituals in Second Life and edited a special issue on virtual-world research for *Online—Heidelberg Journal of Religions*.

Marianne Riphagen is a cultural anthropologist who received her MA, with honors, in 2005 from Radboud University Nijmegen, the Netherlands. Her MA thesis, based on fieldwork at an Indigenous Australian school on the Pitjantjatjara Lands, explored the relation between cultural values and educational results. At present, Marianne is employed by Radboud University as a junior researcher. Her PhD project is on photographic art created by Indigenous Australian artists. Combining art historical and anthropological approaches to art, she examines the ways in which photographs become meaningful and valuable through the cooperative activity of various actors within Australian and European art worlds. Her interest in ritual was first sparked when conducting fieldwork with young Indigenous artists in Melbourne.

Udo Simon studied history, Islamic studies, anthropology, and general linguistics at Mannheim and Heidelberg. Before becoming a member of the Ritual Dynamics Collaborative Research Center at the University of Heidelberg, he was a visiting professor of communication studies at the Faculty of Social and Cultural Studies at the University of Applied Sciences in Darmstadt, Germany. He teaches and conducts research at the Department of Languages and Cultures of the Near East in Heidelberg. His chief interests are Arabic studies, Islam, the sociology of religion, ritual studies, and migration studies. At present, he is investigating the ritual practices of Muslims living in Europe, especially the concept of ritual purity in Islam.

Jan Snoek is a member of the Institute for the Sciences of Religions of the University of Heidelberg, Germany. He studied the science of religion at the University of Leyden, in the Netherlands. His PhD thesis was titled "Initiations: A Methodological Approach to the Application of Classification and Definition Theory in the Study of Rituals" (1987). In 1996 he held the Théodore Verhaegen Chair in Freemasonry at the Institut d'Etude des Religions et de la Laicité at the Université Libre de Bruxelles and has been a guest lecturer at the universities of Tilburg, Leyden, and Göteborg. He is an honorary research fellow at the University of Wales, Lampeter, in the Department of Theology and Religious Studies. He specializes in methodology, ritual theories, and the historical development of Masonic rituals. Together with Michael Stausberg and Jens Kreinath, he edited the first volume of *Theorizing Rituals* (2006, 2007). He wrote "Defining 'Rituals,'" an article in the first volume and is one of the authors of the second volume, an annotated bibliography. His most recent publication is "Ritual Dynamics in the Independent United Order of Mechanics" (2008). Currently, he is writing two monographs: *The Adoption Rite* and *Transferring Masonic Rituals from Male to Mixed and Female Orders*.

Barry Stephenson holds a PhD in religious studies from the University of Calgary, Canada. His research deals with religion and literature, the arts, and ritual studies. He is author of *Veneration and Revolt: Hermann Hesse and Swabian Pietism* (2009) as well as several articles on ritual and performance. A steering committee member of the Ritual Studies Group of the American Academy of Religion, Dr. Stephenson is an independent scholar and university lecturer in religious studies. He is the author of *Performing the Reformation*, a study of Luther-themed festivity and pilgrimage in Wittenberg, Germany (2010).

Paul van der Velde studied Asian languages at the universities of Utrecht and Leiden in the Netherlands. He earned his PhD conducting research on religious experiences of the Hindu god Krishna and the aesthetics of Brajbhasha poetry. He is Professor of Asian Religions at Radboud University Nijmegen in the Netherlands, and his research concentrates on transformations of modern Buddhism, the interaction between psychotherapy and Buddhism, the art of modern Buddhism, and the role of biography in Buddhism and medieval Hinduism. Among his writings are "Navayana and Upaya: The Buddhist Dharma as a 'New Medicine,'" in M. G. T. Kwee, K. J. Gergen, and F. Koshikawa, eds., *Horizons in Buddhist Psychology* (2006) and "The Biography: 'Navayana' as the New Vehicle and Upaya," in P. S. Tian, Oei and Catherine So-Kum Tang, eds., *Current Research and Practices on Cognitive Behavior Therapy in Asia* (2007).

Eric Venbrux is Professor of Anthropology at Radboud University Nijmegen, the Netherlands, where he directs the research program Refiguring Death Rites: Post-Secular Material Religion in the Netherlands, funded by the Netherlands Organization for Scientific Research and the Centre for Thanatology. He has conducted anthropological fieldwork in Switzerland, Australia, and the Netherlands. Dr. Venbrux has published numerous articles on ritual, the visual and verbal arts, and material culture. He is the author of *A Death in the Tiwi Islands: Conflict, Ritual and Social Life in an Australian Aboriginal Community* (1995, 2009) and coeditor of various collections on art and ritual, including *Exploring World Art* (2006) and *Rituele creativiteit* (2008). He is working on a book on ritual change.

Thomas Widlok is an anthropologist trained at the London School of Economics and Political Science. He has carried out long-term ethnographic field research in Australia and southern Africa that has resulted in numerous publications including a monograph titled *Living on Mangetti: "Bushman" Autonomy and Namibia* (1999), two edited volumes, *Property and Equality* (2005, with Wolde Tadesse), and journal articles on the temporal dilemma of death in the *Journal de la Société des Océanistes* (2007). He has held teaching positions at the universities of London, Heidelberg, and Durham and currently holds a chair in anthropology at Radboud University Nijmegen. As a researcher, he has also been affiliated at the Max Planck Institute for Social Anthropology, the University of Cologne, and currently the Max Planck Institute for Psycholinguistics. His research interests include the relation between economics and religion, comparative hunter-gatherer studies, and the anthropology of space, place, and mobility.

Gerard Wiegers (PhD cum laude, Leiden University, 1991) is Professor of Religious Studies at the University of Amsterdam. Previously, he was Research Fellow of the Netherlands Academy of Arts and Sciences, 1992–1997; Associate Professor at Leiden University, 1997–2003; Professor of Comparative Religion and Islamic Studies at Radboud University Nijmegen, 2005–2009. His fields of interest are the relations between Islam and other religions; Islamic ethics; Islam on the Iberian Peninsula, North Africa, and Europe; ritual studies; and theory and method in the study of religions. He is a member of editorial boards for several series, including the Numen Book Series (Brill), New Religious Identities in the Western World (Peeters), and the Medieval and Early Modern Iberian World (Brill). His most recent monograph is *A Man of Three Worlds: Samuel Pallache, a Moroccan Jew in Catholic and Protestant Europe* (2007). In the field of comparative religious studies, his most recent book, written with Herman Beck, is *Religie in de Krant: Een eerste kennismaking met de godsdienstwetenschap* (2005).

Ritual, Media, and Conflict

1

Ritual, Media, and Conflict: An Introduction

Ronald L. Grimes

Rituals can provoke or escalate conflict. During the U.S.-led war in Iraq, suicide attacks, beheadings, and so-called surgical bombings were both ritualized and mediatized as strategies for legitimizing violence. Al Jazeera reported widespread outrage in the Middle East when Saddam Hussein was executed during Eid al-Adha, the holiest day of the year, a time when many Muslims, especially Sunnis, were making the hajj pilgrimage.[1] The execution ritual clearly conflicted with other rituals. Even in Europe and North America, where many supported the execution, smuggled video images of it were experienced as expressions of bad taste or bad judgment, since Saddam Hussein's apparent dignity seemed to undercut the image of him as a villain.

Rituals can also mediate conflict. South Africa's Truth and Reconciliation Commission (1995–2004) and Northern Ireland's Healing through Remembering Consultation (2001–present), and the Indian Residential Schools Truth and Reconciliation Commission of Canada (2009–present) have employed ritual as a means for fostering reconciliation in the aftermath of violent conflict.[2] In 1992, To Reflect and Trust, a ritualized form of storytelling initiated by Don Baron, brought together children of Holocaust survivors with children of Holocaust perpetrators. Currently, processes based on the Arab-Islamic practices of *sulh* (settlement) and *musalaha* (reconciliation) are emerging.

Anecdotal examples, however, are insufficient. There is a pressing need for case studies disclosing ritual's ambiguous role in public life. Even though ritualization marks the human life cycle and suffuses religious practice, existing research pays scant attention to ritual's capacity for mediating or provoking conflict. Although conflict is a normal aspect of human life, mass media technologies are changing the dynamics of conflict and shaping strategies for deploying rituals and ritualized processes in situations of conflict. Media representations have long been instrumental in establishing, maintaining, and challenging political and economic power, as well as in determining the nature of religious practice. More recently, online religious behavior, including online interreligious conflict, has become so pervasive that even practitioners of traditional rituals must now come to terms with the media-conditioned sensibilities of participants conscripted into the so-called war of images or risk being converted to ritually saturated game playing.

Ritual, Media, and Conflict emerged from a project funded by the Netherlands Organization for Scientific Research and the German Research Foundation. Grants from the two organizations facilitated two years of collaboration between the Faculty of Religious Studies at Radboud University Nijmegen in the Netherlands and the Ritual Dynamics Collaborative Research Center at the University of Heidelberg in Germany.

A group of twenty-four scholars set out to locate, describe, and explore cases in which media-driven rituals or ritually saturated media instigate, disseminate, or escalate conflict. Our aim was initial exploration rather than either sustained comparison or formal theory building, both of which we hope will develop in subsequent projects. The outcome is this book, each chapter multiauthored and built around global and local examples of ritualized, mediatized conflict. Growing out of international and interuniversity cooperation, this volume was written by teams that met face to face and online. Religious studies scholar Bruce Lincoln makes an observation that we share:

> Confronted with the disquieting reality of religious conflict, popular wisdom typically comforts itself with the ironist's refrain: "How sad to see wars in the name of religion, when all religions preach peace.".... In similar fashion, academic commentators often regard the religious side of conflicts like those in Sri Lanka or Northern Ireland as relatively unimportant or, alternatively, they deplore it as a debasement of all that is properly religious.... Their analyses rest on an understanding of what constitutes religion that is simultaneously idealized and impoverished: a "Protestant" view that takes beliefs and moral injunctions (such as those that normally inhibit conflict) to be the essence of the religious, while ignoring most other aspects that might be included. Preferable, in my opinion, is a model in which "religion" involves multiple components that can relate to one another in a variety of ways.[3]

Ritual is one such component, and it appears in every religion, as well as outside religion. Despite ritual's near-universal presence, scholars who study either media or conflict typically ignore or minimize religion, and they focus more on beliefs and ethics than rituals. Contrary to this practice, we focus on ritual. We collaborated less on the basis of our knowledge of either media or conflict than on our research into ritual. Although our disciplines and specializations vary, all of us study ritual of various types in geographically disparate places. Even though we take up a braid of three topics, one of them, ritual, is central.

In 2008, when we met to consider the first draft of this volume, it quickly became obvious that authors felt most comfortable in the warm nest of their case studies, the thicket of on-the-ground historical or ethnographic details to which much scholarly research is tethered. Our struggle was to discover the thread by which to string our patches together. We brainstormed questions and teased out theses. What claims might we make? We might, for example, state the obvious: Media document ritual. However, anyone who has ever pointed a camera at a ritual knows that cameras can also disrupt and, in the end, transform rituals. Similarly, we might argue that ritual resolves conflict, but doing so would provoke the obvious counterargument, ritual disguises conflict, thereby amplifying it.

Quickly, tentative, simple-sounding claims became complex. The task of formulating both a clear question and a substantive claim grew even more daunting when we mobilized all three concepts simultaneously. Consider the difficulties that arise when trying to argue either of these propositions: "Because media thrive on conflict, they are undermined by ritual," or "Ritual itself is a multimedium subject to all the manipulations and conflicts that characterize contemporary digital mass media."

We struggled with the temptation to reify, to talk as if ritual were a thing, which it is not. Rituals are events, not objects, and so we tried transposing nouns into verblike constructions: "Ritualizing media dulls the critical acumen of viewers" as well as, "Mediatizing ritual transforms it into a commodity, and commoditizing inevitably generates conflict." Other possibilities included, "Mediatizing conflict spreads it" and "Ritualizing conflict makes it intractable."

All these examples of possible claims are bald and unqualified, but we were not arguing their truth at this point, only exploring the range of claims we might advance in handling such a complex topic. When scholars develop actual, as distinct from hypothetical, arguments, we typically introduce historical and geographical qualifiers: "Interpreted in accordance with so-and-so's theory, the ritualizing of conflict A, in place B, at time C, rendered that conflict intractable." Scholars, confronted with overgeneralized claims, typically transform them into hyperqualified claims, in which case they are no longer universal, stated in the eternal now of the ethnographic present, but rather restricted to a historical period, tethered to a geographically locatable place, and treated as the outcome of a specific theoretical perspective.

The Ritual, Media, and Conflict Project aimed at cultivating a rich, collaborative environment that crossed interdisciplinary boundaries, thus avoiding excessive narrowness. Even so, here we were at the beginning, already struggling with extremes. At the unqualified, universalistic end of the spectrum, we risked claiming more than we could demonstrate. At the hyperqualified end, we risked merely stating the obvious.

After long discussions of authors' case studies, we agreed that all chapters should wrestle with a common question, initially formulated as: "What is it about ritual that, when it is mediatized, makes it especially generative of conflict?" Such a question would focus our inquiry squarely on ritual, but since it might also prompt the reply, "There is nothing special about ritual," we tried, "Is there something about ritual that, when it is mediatized, is especially conducive of conflict?" However, this version only required a yes or no response, not an argument line, so we entertained variants such as, "When ritual and media interact (either by the mediatizing of ritual or by the ritualizing of media), how do the patterns of conflict change?" This is probably the most productive version of the question, but we often lost sight of it. Since authors were allowed to work with other iterations of the question, and even to take issue with its presuppositions, it became obvious that the question was more of a touchstone than a hypothesis, which is to say, for better or worse our connection to the question became primarily ritualistic rather than strictly logical. Authors made a pilgrimage to the volume's guiding question but often could not provide a cogent, convincing answer to it.

In the discussions that eventuated in this book, there was a pronounced, recurrent tendency to deploy spatial metaphors for illustrating complex events. Events were "layered" top to bottom or else they had a "front" and "back" side. The implication was that there is a surface which, although visible, may not be the only, or most determinative, factor to consider. The utility of such metaphors is to signal to both writers and readers that social events are more complex than they appear and to warn that readers should not expect easy solutions.

Along with the usefulness of metaphors comes the temptation of using them to avoid the hard work of theorizing about how the whole—top plus bottom or front plus back—actually works. Is one cause and the other effect? Do they covary without either being the cause of the other? Are they both expressions of something else? So the question we ask of both ourselves and our readers is how it is possible to move from mobilizing metaphors with which to manage case studies to constructing models that explain them.

It is not only protracted or violent conflicts that cry out for explanation or resolution; so do more mundane conflicts and conflict avoidances that beset good-willed groups. We who participated in the Ritual, Media, and Conflict Project not only studied these topics but utilized media, ritualized our interactions, and engaged in conflict. As always, the backstage conflicts were revealing. The chapters of this book now constitute our group's front-stage zone, but our meetings constituted a backstage area, for which coffee breaks provided a kind of back backstage.

Before face-to-face meetings, when first drafts began arriving in inboxes, rarely was it obvious that one author in a chapter group had disagreed with another. The authors, it seemed, were more or less on the same page, diligently working toward a unified presentation of their findings. Since the cases were often divergent, many authors felt their primary obligation was to search out continuities and forge connections. Although multiple writing styles were sometimes evident in the chapters, editorial smoothing would soon erase the dissonance.

The group met for a writing retreat at the Soeterbeeck Study Center in the Netherlands.[4] As soon as we began to feel comfortable with one another in protracted face-to-face discussions, disagreements surfaced. Most disappeared rapidly after smoking out differing implicit definitions or ceasing to talk past each other. But some conflicts did not disappear so readily. They reappeared during breaks, sometimes driven by considerable heat, the shape of the disputes changing at each appearance. In the most heated conflict, a few declared that some kinds of writing should have no place in the book, specifically those that adopted a style of moral argumentation that they considered tacitly theological. This clash surfaced and resurfaced during the retreat. Another debate was methodological. It revolved around the question whether scholars are ever warranted in offering interpretations that run counter to those offered by ritual participants. Some despaired about the entire project, worrying whether a team of twenty-four scholars can ever write anything coherent and doubting whether anyone can ever arrive at a reliable conclusion on the basis of a handful of case studies. The fact that the chapters as they appear here are less reflexive than the discussions that helped produce them is a relief to some but a source of consternation to others.

Some of our scholarly conflicts are as ancient as Greek philosophy, and they recur throughout multiple disciplines, while others are more recent. Some have served as the engines of "culture wars," while others are mere squabbles that disappear in a few minutes. Such is the give and take of any investigative venture worth its salt. What we described as international scholarly collaboration on grant applications was just as surely a vigorous form of scholarly conflict, so it is important to remember what we told ourselves in the beginning: conflict is not necessarily bad.

In the beginning of the project, there was also considerable interest in a practical political question: can rituals help mediate conflict? Radio and television interviewers, along with government officials, had asked some of us this question.

Some asked it because their countries had witnessed religiously motivated violence, and they wondered whether civic rituals of reconciliation could be effective in shaping less violence-prone public attitudes. In the end, however, we concentrated on ritual as a factor in conflict rather as a means for resolving it. Although ritual may be a means for peacemaking or at least a means for expressing the hope that people can put an end to deadly strife, the scholars in this volume found that ritual does, in fact, mask or instigate conflict. The topic of ritualized peacemaking (along with our deferred comparative and theoretical treatments) must wait for other projects and books that might follow this initiatory gathering of specific cases. We first had to discover, and now we admit, publicly, our limitations.

Nevertheless, it is instructive to sneak a quick preview of what research on conflict mediation currently looks like. As a field both practical and academic, conflict mediation emerged out of American labor disputes, and came to be associated with Christian pacifism, especially its Quaker and Mennonite expressions. The field is now much broader than either labor disputes or the peacemaking efforts of these two denominations. Were it not for the role of ritual in South Africa's Truth and Reconciliation Commission and Ireland's Healing through Remembering,[5] it might have taken even longer for scholars to inquire whether rituals can mediate conflict, since neither the American labor movement nor these two religious traditions place much stock in ritual. In any case, as both a theory and a practice, conflict mediation is now being tested cross-culturally in the crucible of international and interreligious strife, but at least the question of ritual's role in conflict mediation is now being raised.

In discussing the application of conflict mediation models, George Irani and Nathan Funk construct a chart summarizing major differences between what they call Western/U.S.-based and traditional Arab-Islamic approaches.[6] Even though their typology oversimplifies, it nonetheless illustrates a pioneering approach to an important topic that we aspire to take up in future projects. The notion of ritual shows up twice, both on the Arab-Islamic side of the chart. Ritual appears not at all on the Western/U.S. side, creating the impression that the former is ritualistic while the latter is not.[7] But what if the left side were given a parallel title, say, Anglo Christian or Euroamerican Christian? Such a label might provoke readers to inquire whether there are unnoticed rituals or, if not, at least ritualized processes and symbolic resources that play out on the left side.

Irani and Funk's article describes Arab-Muslim rituals that include handshaking, coffee drinking, and meal sharing as constitutive gestures. Although these actions may not be labeled ritual in the West, they might well serve as the equivalents of ritual. Even if they are not rituals, they are actions that could be ritualized if someone felt a need for symbolic acts with which to mark conflict resolutions in the West. Even though the Western-modeled practice of conflict resolution may be more suffused by popular psychological practices (such as active listening) than by ritualistic ones, Western courtrooms, for instance, are marked by explicitly ceremonial posturing and gesturing. In short, the West lacks neither symbolic acts nor ritualized gestures that might be mobilized for—or regarded as conducive to—the purpose of conflict mediation.

Entertaining the notion of conflict mediation (not to mention conflict resolution) means grappling with the question of ritual efficacy. No one debates whether ritual can accompany trouble or reconciliation, but many debate whether ritual is capable of causing either. Ritual is so commonly regarded as either not working or as working only magically (which is to say, not at all) that one has to search far and wide for explanations of ritual efficacy.[8] Do healing rituals really work? Can symbolic acts effect reconciliation? If so, how? If not, why do people claim that they do? As much as magical efficacy might be desirable in the face of protracted, violent conflict, few believe in it. So when a group introduces, say, the practices of confronting accusers or making public confessions, and they perform these actions ritually, they are implicitly, if not overtly, assuming that such acts accomplish something. But what? And how? By what means might ritualizing reconciliation make it effective? And what are the liabilities of ritualized, as distinct from nonritualized, efforts at conflict mediation?

In any case, the point here is not to demonstrate that rituals can help bring about peace, only to note that considerable symbolic capital is being expended on the premise that they can, in which case scholars need to ask what such rituals are actually capable of doing.

Ritual: Definitions and Functions

Along with formulating questions that this volume could, or might, claim, authors wrestled with key terms. What counts as ritual? Which media? Is a book a medium? Is a flag? An elephant? What kinds of conflict matter? Although the web of connections among ritual, media, and conflict may not be readily apparent, the media-conflict nexus is obvious, since conflict is a staple of media. (As in law or sport, if conflict is not present, it must be contrived.) However, the ritual-media as well as the ritual-conflict connection remains opaque for most people, and ritual is the odd member of the triad. The public is not used to deploying the concept of ritual except perhaps to describe empty, redundant, or overtly religious acts, and if it is understood to be essentially religious, then ritual space is often imagined as a zone in which MP3 players, cell phones, and other electronic fads have no place. Such assumptions about ritual are mistaken, because ritual, along with every other aspect of human life, is now undergoing digitalization. For this reason, the views of ritual that emerge in the following chapters are both more complex and more interesting than stereotypical notions that ritual is conventionally nice or inescapably premodern.

Definitions of ritual, like perceptions of it, are colored by conflicting assumptions. Some scholars make ritual, by definition, religious; thus it is:

> [F]ormal behavior prescribed for occasions not given over to technological routine that have reference to beliefs in mystical beings or powers. (Victor and Edith Turner)[9]

> [C]onscious and voluntary, repetitious and stylized symbolic bodily actions that are centered on cosmic structures and/or sacred presences. (Evan Zuesse)[10]

> [A] stylized ceremonial in which persons related in various ways to the central actors, as well as these themselves, perform prescribed actions according to their secular roles; and that it is believed by the participants that these prescribed actions express and amend social relationships so as to secure general blessing, purification, protection, and prosperity for the persons involved in some mystical manner which is out of sensory control. (Max Gluckman)[11]

> [T]hose religious actions whose structural descriptions include a logical object and appeal to a culturally postulated superhuman agent's action somewhere within their overall structural description. (E. Thomas Lawson and Robert N. McCauley)[12]

However, many definitions circumvent the religious qualifier, mandating other qualities as definitive. Thus, ritual consists of:

> [A] culturally constructed system of symbolic communication. It is constituted of patterned and ordered sequences of words and acts, often expressed in multiple media, whose content and arrangement are characterized in varying degree by formality (conventionality), stereotypy (rigidity), condensation (fusion), and redundancy (repetition). (Stanley J. Tambiah)[13]

> [T]he performance of more or less invariant sequences of formal acts and utterances not entirely encoded by the performers. (Roy Rappaport)[14]

> Action is ritualized if the acts of which it is composed are constituted not by the intentions which the actor has in performing them, but by prior stipulation.... In adopting the ritual stance one accepts ... that in a very important sense, one will not be the author of one's acts. (Caroline Humphrey and James Laidlaw)[15]

> [Ritualization is] the adaptive formalization and canalization of motivated human activities so as to secure more effective communicatory ("signalling") function, reduction of intra-group damage, or better intra-group bonding (Julian Huxley)[16]

> [A] patterned, repetitive, and symbolic enactment of a cultural belief or value; its primary purpose is alignment of the belief system of the individual with that of society. (Robbie Davis-Floyd)[17]

> [C]ulturally defined sets of behavior. (Edmund Leach)[18]

By Leach's or Davis-Floyd's broad definition, virtually all human behavior is ritualistic, whereas by Tambiah's narrow one, seven or more criteria (depending on how you read the definition) must be met before an activity can be dubbed ritual.

The advantage of narrow definitions is that they are more adept at focusing research. As the number of qualifiers multiplies, it becomes easier to decide what is out of bounds, thus making the distinction between ritualistic and nonritualistic phenomena clearer. However, the connections between ritualistic and nonritualistic domains may be obscured by such definitions. Broader definitions are more adept at opening up the concept, but, because they include more, the boundaries between ritual and nonritualistic domains are fuzzy.

Reflecting on what is or is not ritual can be valuable, but it is not worth becoming interminably embroiled in definitional squabbles. Students of ritual typically carry on their work even though they have not resolved definitional ambiguities. Definitions, after all, are seldom the actual engines of research. Only in rare cases do scholars define the term *ritual* formally and then illustrate the methodological and theoretical consequences of carrying out research on the basis of this formal definition. Rather, definitions tend to rest in splendid isolation—a definition proposed at the beginning of a work is left without further reference or development.[19]

Some of the examples treated in this volume are about rituals as such while others focus on ritualization, that is, activities displaying fewer of the qualities normally associated with ritual. But whatever else it is, ritual is a kind of action, and it is enacted by agents, many of whom are human actors.[20] Even if there are divine actors in a ritual, scholars only know of their presence because someone says so or by way of a human who embodies a divine power by performing it. So there is no way around the most basic fact of ritual: embodied human beings enacting, or performing.

Another quality of ritual is its manner of bending time and space. Rituals often happen at special times in set-aside places. Since bodies are finite, existing in time and space, ritual of necessity transpires in a place and unfolds across time. Even if a ritual is said by practitioners to implicate realms beyond space and time, ritual actors are nevertheless space- and time-bound even as they claim to transcend time and space. Ritual is embodied, spatially bound, temporally constrained human activity even if ritual actors aspire to things of global, universal, or eternal significance.

However, such a statement claims nothing distinctive, since most human activity is embodied, spatially hedged, and temporally constrained. Is there some definitive quality about ritual that makes it distinctive? Probably not. There is no single characteristic that, alone, signals the presence of ritual, which is why these definitional reflections begin with the ordinary and obvious—bodies, action, space, time.

But one can go further. Ritual is usually prescribed and formalized; there are ways to do it, ways not to do it. If you do not do it the right way, you are not engaged in such-and-such a ritual, or you are not a proper person, or you do not have membership among this people. If you do not adhere to the prescribed ways, the event may not be a valid ritual, or if it is, it will not be effective; it will not work. A key metamessage of ritual activity is, "If you please, do things this way, not that way." To formalize an occasion is to elevate it, mark it as special or important. Ritual actors elevate actions to make them noticeable, different from the ordinary.

However, a problem arises in the process of making certain acts special. If one continues marking and re-marking an activity, the repetitiousness can itself render the action routine.[21] If formalization becomes pervasive, formality becomes increasingly nondistinctive, a new baseline against which counterformalization can push. Whereas embodiment, temporality, and spatiality are characteristic of human behavior, prescription and formality are less so. They do not show up so densely in other cultural activities, but they do appear, for instance, in dance, theater, and games, activities governed by forms and rules and thus akin to, but also different from, ritual.

A common assumption about rituals is that they are different insofar as they are repetitive. One does them over and over. However, sometimes rituals derive their force not from repetition but from their singularity, their rarity, so the idea of ritual should not be defined in a way that precludes either singularity or invention and improvisation. Some ritual traditions are more open to innovation than others;

a few even require it. So embedded within the prescribed, or formed, quality of ritual is the possibility for the creative, unformed, or emergent to arise. It is misleading, then, to identify ritual only with its repetitiveness and sameness, since these qualities constitute the background against which newness and difference appear all the more remarkable.

So far, I have characterized ritual as embodied, enacted, spatially rooted, temporally bound, prescribed, formalized, and repeated or singularized. Nothing on the list is so distinctive a characteristic as to be definitive of ritual, so rather than choose a strict, hard definition, the authors in this volume found that discussion and debate were better served by a family resemblance strategy.[22] Enumerating and discussing qualities of ritualized behavior is less restrictive than proposing formal definitions that require actions to be either ritual or not. The problem with this view is that it is blind to the fact that ritualization, like dramatization, goes on all the time. In everyday life, humans play roles, stage their behavior spatially, and segregate audiences (saying one thing to person A, another to person B). Theater is what happens when someone notices this quotidian fact and then compresses and performs a slice of it for an audience willing momentarily to suspend its disbelief in order to witness it. Similarly, a ritual is what happens when someone notices ordinary ritualization and then compresses, reframes, and enacts it. All human behavior is to some degree ritualized. Ritualizing is the activity of increasing the degree of this ritualization, and deritualizing is the act of decreasing it. An action that is merely repeated is less ritualized than an act that is both repeated and stylized. If an action is repeated, stylized, prescribed, and sacralized, it becomes more ritualistic.

There are differing kinds of ritualizing as well differing degrees of it. Actions differ in the ways they are ritualized. Action A is ritualized by being repeated, whereas action B is ritualized by being stylized. In creating this volume, we found it more fruitful to discuss kinds and degrees of ritualization than to debate whether or not an action qualifies as a ritual. We decided it was less important to identify the boundaries of the concepts (ritual, media, and conflict) than to describe their interactions.

Rituals are dynamic. Although they can appear static, in fact, they emerge, change, deteriorate, and fall into disuse. Ritualizing and deritualizing are not static opposites but social and historical processes in continual flux. During the attacks on New York's World Trade Center, ritual gestures were enacted by both the attackers and the attacked. Passengers aboard United Airlines flight 93 prayed. The scene of simultaneous, competing, cell phone-mediated prayers was later re-created for the feature film *United 93*.[23] Those who commandeered American Airlines flight 11 prepared themselves ritually, and hostages responded ritually. In the five pages of Arabic-language instructions found in Mohamed Atta's luggage the following passage appears:

> Perform the morning prayer in group and consider its rewards. While the taxi cab is taking you to the [airport], recite repeatedly the invocations to God (the boarding invocation, the invocation of the town, the invocation of the place, the other invocations). When you arrive and see the [airport], and get out of the taxicab, recite the invocation of the place. Wherever you go, recite the invocation of the place. When you step into the [airplane], and take your seat, recite the invocations and known supplications that we previously mentioned and keep busy with the repeated invocation of God.[24]

The document sketches details ranging from the shaving of excess hair and the application of perfume to leaving one's apartment in a state of ritual cleanliness. Even though some of the actions may not have looked to casual observers like ritual, they, in fact, were.

The ritualizing of 9/11 becomes even more complex if one takes media into account. The collapse of the towers, captured on video, was shown on television, a transformation that, perhaps, momentarily deritualized the scene; a documented collision is initially just a fact reported on the news. But soon the collision and collapse were being replayed. Not many called this repetitive watching and rewatching ritual, but the label became harder to avoid as the national anthem was played behind the scene or the flag superimposed over the top of it.

Eventually, International Agile Manufacturing forged tower debris into medallions stamped with an image of the New York City skyline. Dated September 11, the medallions bore the inscription, "God Bless America, United We Stand." On the back were the words, "In memory of those who perished." The medallions were advertised on television. For some the making of an icon out of tower rubble not only commemorated but also sacralized the event. For others, the sale desecrated the event.

Likely, however, the story of 9/11's ritualization and deritualization does not end even here. It is not difficult to imagine a day in the distant future when a child finds a grandparent's dusty medallion and tosses it nonchalantly into a garage sale bin. Thus, ritualizing escalates and cascades, but then deritualizing sets in. The process is dynamic; nothing ever is or is not a ritual, although any event can be ritualized or deritualized.

While definitional questions ask what ritual is, functional questions ask what rituals do. Scholarly answers to this second question polarize. Some say or imply, "Nothing, or almost nothing." In this view, rites are nonfunctional, weakly functional, maybe even dysfunctional.[25] Others argue, "A lot." One well-known anthropologist even argues that ritual is the foundational social act.[26] In such a view, rituals accomplish a variety of tasks, among them bonding groups, creating insiders and outsiders, retaining cultural memories, creating models for action, cultivating values, training bodies, inculcating attitudes, communicating information, forging conceptual and symbolic connections, and aiding social transformation. This is a generalized list, and some of the items bleed into others, but our aim here is less to inquire generally into ritual's many functions than to inquire about its interactions with media and conflict. Among ritual's possible functions regarding media and conflict are critiquing media, reinforcing media, transforming media, causing conflict, mediating conflict, and avoiding conflict.

Making lists is easy. The more difficult task is that of explaining in general (that is, theoretically) how ritual does what it does. If it structures things, how? If it is a structure, what kind? I once depicted ritual this way: "A ritual is a rope bridge of knotted symbols strung across an abyss. We make our crossings hoping the chasm will echo our festive sounds for a moment, as the bridge begins to sway from the rhythms of the dance."[27] Rituals, although potentially powerful, are also risky. Because rituals work by knotting things together, and because such bridging is imaginative, the whole edifice is perpetually in danger of collapsing. Even though rituals exercise power, doing the culturally necessary work of knotting parts into wholes, they also exhibit a characteristic fragility. This inherent weakness characterizes even ritual traditions laden with authority, texts, buildings, and other symbols of solidity.

Rituals are similar to plays insofar as they are constructions built on, or out of, ordinary life, but they are dissimilar inasmuch as theater announces its own fictionality, whereas ritual often denies or sequesters its. Viewed from the outside, other people's rituals may appear made-up or arbitrary. From the inside, however, ritual is experienced as correct, right, true, traditional, authorized, and believable. Because ritual is an especially vulnerable cultural activity, ritual traditions can grow fat with defensive structures—rationalizations, intractable hierarchies, theological mystifications, emotional double binds, moral evasions, and ensconced privileges. Defensive structures, then, can make it difficult to criticize a ritual. Criticism that is argumentative and direct may have little effect; thus indirect means become necessary. However, indirection is itself a ritual quality. As a result, launching ritual criticism—regardless of who does it or what its purpose is—may require that criticism itself becomes ritualized. In other words, ritual criticism is not so much antiritualistic as counterritualistic.

Ritual and Media

Icons span the domains of media and ritual. The term *icon* refers not only to tiny pictograms on computer desktops but also to ritually executed, liturgically venerated images of saints and divine beings. In ritual circumstances, icons do not merely refer or point to something; rather, they incarnate, or embody, it. Because the rights to use iconic photos shot by professional photojournalists are expensive, examples are not included here. However, look at "100 Photographs That Changed the World," visit World Press Photo,[28] or conduct a Google image search for either "The Falling Man" by Richard Drew (New York City, September 11, 2001) or "Tank Man" by Stuart Franklin, Jeff Widener, or Charlie Cole (June 5, 1989, Tiananmen Square).

Because three different photographers shot three widely viewed photos of a worker confronting a tank on Tiananmen Square, "Tank Man" precipitates a crucial question about iconicity: Who decides which version is canonical? The nearest thing to an official arbiter is World Press Photo. Founded in Amsterdam, since 1955 the foundation has chosen a photo of the year, in effect, dubbing it iconic. For a photojournalist to receive such a recognition is equivalent to a director receiving an academy award.

Marshall Poe, director of the Web site Mechanical Icon, argues that iconic photos are both indexes and icons. Following philosopher Charles Peirce, Poe defines indexes as signs produced by their referents; smoke is an index of fire. In Poe's view, the photo-photographed relation resembles the smoke-fire relation insofar as, "The image is mechanically produced by the interaction of light, the photographed object and the photographic plate."[29] In addition, Poe says, photos are icons, inasmuch as they resemble that to which they refer.

Photos, however, become iconic not only by resemblance but also by the power they exercise, thus their similarity to liturgical icons. An icon is any image that embodies itself in viewers with sufficient power that the viewers then echo, if not reproduce, it. Iconicity is attributed to photos that encapsulate a crucial historical moment in an especially compelling way, thereby becoming widely recognizable, shaping attitudes, and sometimes even determining political decisions or subsequent photographic practices.

In the documentary *Looking for an Icon*, Geoffrey Batchen, who teaches the history of photography, observes that echoes of Christian art often appear in iconic photos not so much because photographers decide to put them there but because their perceptions are conditioned by the compositional practices embedded in art history.[30] In the same documentary, Italian photographer-designer Oliviero Toscani remarks, "The church used religious icons to give expression to its power. Later on, art was put in the service of politics and put in the service of industry, in order to promote and sell products." Later, Toscani concludes, "So communication is an instrument of authority. And an authority that wants to assert its power has to create icons. That means that everyone who believes in an icon is a servant. We are servants of authority."[31]

Because icons threaten to buttress servitude, they engender not only veneration but also iconoclasm. Senior citizens in Glasgow produced a series of photos called *Iconic Moments of the Twentieth Century*.³² One picture shows a man with his pistol to the head of another senior, who is facing the camera. The picture is a parody, but it reinforces the iconicity of the original photo by asking viewers whether they recall Eddie Adams's 1968 picture of police chief Nguyen Ngoc Loan executing a Vietcong guerrilla during the Vietnam War.³³ Younger viewers may not get the seniors' allusion, in fact, might not even recognize the original photo if it were shown to them. The possibility of nonrecognition leads one to ask: if iconic images are neither universal nor eternal, what is the cultural and historical purview of an iconic photo? Iconicity is as much a function of contexts as it is of pictures themselves. Icons and iconic photos may be widely recognized, but they have a limited constituency as well as a life span. If someone tests us by naming some iconic photos, we may recognize a few, but not all of them, and even though we may recognize the photos themselves, we may not remember either the photographer or the situation.

The black and white photo in figure 1.1 and in color on the cover of this book is, I would say, borderline iconic. Taken on April 6, 2008, by Kaustav Bhattacharya, an amateur photographer, the picture elicited a large number of comments on Flickr.³⁴ It was widely linked to and reproduced, but it floated on a veritable sea of other pre-Olympic, torch-passing photos. Global Olympic torchbearing is itself a photographic-ceremonial occasion. Add to it confrontational protest actions—some of them spontaneously acted out and others deliberately staged to capture

FIGURE 1.1. "Olympic Torch Rally, London: Free Tibet Protest," photo by Kaustav Bhattacharya, © April 6, 2008, http://flickr.com/photos/astrolondon/.

media attention—and the event becomes doubly photogenic. Unlike, say, the situation with two iconic photos of the twenty-first century, "Falling Man" and "Tank Man," in which the photos were either one of a kind or one among a few, pre-Olympic photos were prolific, so no single photo, even a good one such as our cover photo, easily rises to iconic status.

The photographer himself says, "I'm neither in support of or against the whole 'free Tibet' argument. I think it's sad that the Olympic Games are being hijacked by political agendas. At the end of the day I'm just a photographer and I like to cover current affairs events in the city I live in. I went to this event and as I was walking around I noticed these people and thought it would make a great photo, however it's in no way reflective of my opinion on the Tibet issue."[35] Viewers often compliment the photographer, but only in a generic way: "Great photo," "wonderful," "stunning." Few viewers say what they think they are seeing, and the women are never identified. So, in the discussion of Bhattacharya's picture, the women become symbols of a cause rather than persons with names. The discussion, sometimes quite heated, is mainly around rather than about the photo. Despite Bhattacharya's aesthetic framing of his motives, most of the discussion of "Olympic Torch Rally, London: Free Tibet Protest" focuses on Chinese-Tibetan politics.

One can almost explain the photograph's iconicity merely by describing the picture. Its formal qualities appear consonant with the social qualities of the event. "Olympic Torch Rally" captures two women, standing, dripping wet, on the wall of a profusely spraying fountain at Trafalgar Square, London. During the Olympic torch-passing ceremony, they are protesting China's domination of Tibet. On the viewer's left, one woman, her right fist raised high, holds—almost wears—a Tibetan flag. The fountain is spraying with great vigor, as if issuing forth from the top of her head. The water's upward thrust echoes her raised arm, while the downward spillover from the fountain's upper bowl drenches both protesters. The other woman, on our right, is bending over, apparently reaching for the corner of the flag wrapped around her thighs and waist.

Because icons have been historically associated with the liturgical rites and contemplative practices of Orthodox Christianity, one might be tempted to think that icons enhance, even ensure, peaceful interactions. But, if that were ever true, the ubiquity of iconic photos now points in the opposite direction. Most of the pictures chosen for World Press Photo awards, for example, are embroiled in conflict, not nestled in the warm bed of peace. For liturgical insiders, rituals usually seem correct, right, and true, so it is easy to understand the entrenched assumption that ritual is, or should be, essentially peaceful, but scholars have long noted the persistent association of religion with violence.[36]

Just as the view of ritual as sacred, therefore peaceful, is severely disrupted by the examples in the chapters that follow, so is the assumption that media are exclusively electronic or always for the masses. *Media*, after all, is the plural of *medium*, but what counts as a medium? A sticky substance (for example, egg white) that binds color for artistic use? An adept who goes into trance to communicate with spirits? Here, of course, neither of those, but rather any means of communication that, metaphorically speaking, sits in a middle position, thereby linking two parties, is a medium. Like words spoken or images transmitted, objects, texts, places, and clothing are also media of communication insofar as they bear messages. If this broader understanding of media is accepted, the central problem is less that of defining terms than of distinguishing and relating various media. What happens to a picture when it is set alongside a text, and what happens to the text as well? Why do televisions seem out of place in one ritual but not in another? Is the textuality of text messaging the same as the textuality of a Koran passage or that of a textbook? Is a virtual wedding in Second Life as efficacious as an embodied wedding in "First Life" (this life)? If couples married in Second Life prefer to minimize the differences between Second and First Life, why do adolescent players of violent video games prefer to maximize the differences between on-screen and in-world violence?

A medium seldom remains isolated. Media tend to merge. Some claim that the world's first multimedia event occurred in the 1958 Brussels World Fair under the direction of Swiss-French architect Le Corbusier.[37] He directed *Poème électronique*, an eight-minute film, or "electronic poem," set to music by Edgard Varèse and piped through 425 speakers. Shown in the Philips Pavilion, a massive tentlike structure designed by Le Corbusier himself, the film was designed to interface with the ambient architecture, music, and art.

Others claim that the world's first multimedia event occurred in 1816, when the sinking of the *Medusa*, a French warship, was not only covered in books and news reports but also depicted on album covers and treated as the subject of oil paintings.[38]

Trying to adjudicate such competing claims leads to more questions: How many media are enough to warrant calling an event multimedia? Which kinds of media do we include? Since the study of one medium so regularly leads to the study of a related one, a single-medium event is more likely the exception than the rule. In this volume, we consider electronic mass media—television images, Internet pages, and newspaper columns—but we also pry open the concept of media to include texts, objects, buildings, even elephants.

If one opens up the idea of media sufficiently, even ritual itself can appear to be a primal multimedium. After all, what other kind of human activity has for so long integrated movement, music, art, oratory, architecture, and dance? There is, of course, no way of knowing what happened primordially. We can only imagine the origins and development of ritual. Maybe things evolved the other way around: the arts were being practiced separately and congealed into a kind of metamedium, ritual. The point is simply this: ritual and media are not necessarily two separate things that scholars must weld together by skilled erudition. Rather, they are interacting, overlapping processes. Here most authors have chosen not to collapse the two concepts but rather to study instances in which media exhibit ritualized dynamics or rituals exhibit characteristics we normally attribute to media.

What happens when a ritual is mediatized? The dynamics can shift in several ways, some obvious, some not. An obvious example is televising a presidential inauguration. Broadcasting Barak Obama's inauguration as U.S. president enabled many more people to witness the event, transposing an American civil ceremony into a global spectacle. However, televising it also disembodied it. Those who were not in Washington, DC, did not experience the smells on the street or feel the winter chill. Television "witnesses" neither saw nor heard the event but rather a representation of it, and representations are selective. Representations are points of view both literally and figuratively. Those who attended the inauguration were "really there," for sure, yet people who watched TV could observe Obama's facial expressions because of the multiple viewpoints made possible by the positioning of multiple cameras. Screen watchers saw more and saw it from more angles than those who saw the "real thing." Some attendees, after all, saw mainly the backs of other attendees' heads. There is another difference as well. Whereas a nontelevised inauguration ceremony might contain commodities, for instance, T-shirts sold before and after the event, a televised inauguration is a commodity, even if there are no commercials.

Consider how mediatized weddings have become. At one time in Western wedding history, photography was deemed an intrusion. Clergy often ruled it out as desecrating; some still do. However, hiring a videographer as well as a wedding photographer is becoming commonplace, and their documentation is sometimes supplemented by photos provided by friends and parents with cell-phone or throwaway cameras. As weddings become increasingly mediatized, the visual documentation of the ceremony no longer desacralizes but rather legitimates the event. Visual documentation certifies not only that a wedding happened but also that it counts for something. Shooting a wedding introduces another bit of torque as well. Those carrying cameras must split their attention between the machine in their hands and the actions that constitute the ceremony. Those on whom cameras dote become increasingly self-consciousness: "I'm having my picture taken. Is my hair combed?" The photographic or documentary heightening of a ritual event pushes it away from a liturgical sensibility and in the direction of a cinematic one.[39]

Now run the question in the other direction: what happens when media are ritualized? First, recall that ritualization and deritualization are fluctuating processes that occur in degrees. Also remember that calling an activity ritualized means simply that the qualities we associate with ritual begin to multiply.

Now consider this scene: the nightly news is, one might say, "lightly ritualized" by the sheer fact of its regular broadcast at, say, 6 P.M. In addition, there are the show's distinctive opening and closing formulas, the network's swirling logo, the arousing music, and the anchor's authoritative introduction. Let us say that this seemingly invariable opening scenario comforts a Canadian couple who, without fail, watch the news together, dinner plate on lap. She always hands him a filled plate (he serves her only if she is ill), and he always takes his milk glass two-thirds (not all the way) full. And it is his job, always, to clean up. The ritualization of this dinnertime scene is not only mediated through the tube but acted out in front of it. Since the ritualistic features of the whole news-watching event are now multiplying like rabbits, let us go further. Let us say that there has been a kidnapping by a terrorist. The couple begins watching apprehensively, because they have a grandson in the military. The masked terrorists are shown ritually humiliating a captured soldier, fortunately, not the grandson. The elderly couple breathes a sigh of relief, as the next news item begins to play out across the screen. This scene, explicitly ritualistic, is repeated every time there is a Canadian military death overseas: a few seconds of silence, the soldier's name, a photo, a flag-draped coffin slowly carried by surviving soldiers. This entire scene has now become a heavily ritualized media event, so much so that one can hardly resist calling it a ritual.

So far, I have talked more about ritualization than mediatization.[40] As we use the terms in this volume, they are parallel. Each refers to the process of increasing the extent to which something is pushed in the direction of socially recognizable ritual or media. No activity is a ritual, but any action can be ritualized. Similarly, anything can become a means, a medium, of communication, although we conventionally speak as if only certain institutions or events—newspapers, films, and Internet pages—are media. In this volume, we avoid using "mediation" as a synonym for "rendering in media form," since the former connotes something like "peacemaking" or "working toward compromise." Instead, we use "mediatization" to denote the process that includes both constructing and receiving communications by way of a medium.[41]

In one sense, perception itself is mediatized. (What the brain "sees"—actually, constructs—is not a wolf but the image of a wolf refracted through the lens of an eye.) Here, however, we are not talking about how the senses work but about the construction, distribution, marketing, and reception of media products, that is, the complex process whereby images or sounds are treated as representations of a subject. Not all representations are mediatizations. If you send a family member to a funeral that you cannot attend, that person is your representative but not a mediatized one. If however, you are ill and send a video of your lecture to a conference, that stand-in is mediatized. With these concepts in mind, we can now begin to frame hypotheses or questions, for instance: if mediatization escalates, does ritualization follow suit, or does ritualization decline? Do the two factors vary directly or inversely, or are they connected at all?

Ritual and Conflict

Religious studies scholar Bruce Lincoln defines conflict as "the situation that arises when rival interests can no longer be denied, deflected, negotiated, or contained by the structures and processes ordinarily competent to do so."[42] His definition would cover most of the examples studied in this volume. However, just as the authors broaden the scope of the notions of ritual and media, so we broaden, at least in theory, the range of the term *conflict*. We do so by including—at least in theory—all kinds of conflict: intrapsychic, interpersonal, political, interethnic, interreligious, and international. In actual practice, however, our research focuses on the upper end of the scale, situations in which conflict edges toward violence. We also intend to include varying degrees of conflict, from persistent disagreement through interpersonal abuse to globalized warfare. And we do not assume that conflict is necessarily bad any more than we assume that ritual is always good. Sometimes conflict, by revealing injustices, for example, can be an engine for change, and avoiding conflict can be as destructive as instigating it.

The most concentrated form of violent conflict is war, so it is worth asking what the ritual dimensions of war are. One possibility is articulated by Randall Collins, who writes, "Political violence is itself ritualistic; even warfare is not so much an effort at direct physical destruction as a symbolic use of violence in order to break the organizational solidarity of the opposing army. Armed violence between opposing forces is at one end of a continuum, in that it is a battle among opposing rituals, each striving to break the solidarity of the other."[43]

Building on Collins's insight, sociologist Philip Smith advances a strong claim—not that war is similar to ritual, or that one can look at war as if it were ritual, or that wars sometimes co-opt rituals, but that war is ritual.[44] On the basis of a Durkheimian theory of ritual, he studies the 1982 Falklands War between Great Britain and Argentina, criticizing the twin materialist assumptions that (a) major social events such as wars are driven only by economic and geopolitical forces, and (b) cultural processes such as ritual play only ancillary roles. In trying to overcome the stalemate between so-called hard (materialist) and soft (culturalist) ways of accounting for wars, Smith is not so much arguing against economic and political determinants as for the power of cultural ones. They too exercise force and are not mere mirrors reflecting what is "really" going on in other domains. He summarizes the core of his theory of ritual:

In religious ceremonies, the behaviors of the participants, and the collective understanding that proceedings are a "ritual," are predetermined to a large degree by rigid tradition and rules. In contrast, wars are full of contingent happenings at both the cultural and social structural levels, and in consequence, actions and understandings have to be improvised by the participants. Thus, the maintenance of the cultural motivations for war, as with any successful ritual, crucially depends upon the work of practitioners in maintaining a sacred/profane code. They must do two things for a war to become a ritual. Firstly, a cultural code embodying the sacred/profane distinction must be made the center of discourse. Secondly, "war" events must be accounted for as acceptable products of the code. In the first step the choice of code is accountable to events, and in the second, events are accountable to the codes produced by the encoding. If the sacred/profane code is shown to be the incorrect yardstick for evaluating events, or if events are held to contradict the code, the generative force of the sacred/profane distinction is lost, and the ritual motivations for fighting will evaporate (though of course instrumental motivations may remain). In consequence, much of the parole ["speech" as distinct from "grammar," langue] in the war can be seen, speaking ethnomethodologically, as accounting activity aimed at maintaining (or destroying) the ritual status.[45]

According to Smith, Prime Minister Margaret Thatcher's government ritualized the Falklands conflict by creating and maintaining a sacred/profane polarization that mobilized widely accepted British cultural values while assigning only vices to the other side (table 1.1). In Smith's theory, ritual is not a stylized, formalized event, for example, the blessing of troops, but rather the mobilization of cultural symbols in the service of a sacralized we/they dualism. Consequently, he does not quite

TABLE 1.1. Ritually Polarizing the Falklands War.

Sacred	Profane
British	Argentineans
Moral	Immoral
Democracy	Dictatorship
Free	Unfree
Liberators	Aggressors
Law abiding	Lawbreaking
Law enforcing	Criminals
Rational	Irrational
Strategic	Emotive

demonstrate that warfare itself is fought ritualistically, rather that a nation at war uses ritual to bolster support at home.[46]

Although Smith's account is useful for discussing war and ritual, it is only one way of theorizing the relationship, and it leaves four theoretical questions dangling: (1) Are any and all sacred/profane dualisms, by definition, ritualistic? (2) Can rituals be driven by some means other than a dualistic coding? (3) Do dualisms necessarily produce violence or war? (4) Does the deritualizing of contemporary warfare intensify or deintensify its violence?[47]

Other approaches to war and ritual are, of course, possible, especially if one taps the long history of theorizing about religion, violence, and sacrifice. An alternative approach to ritual and war based on Pierre Bourdieu's understanding of ritual, for example, might study the ways military organizations stylize men's bodies, thus inscribing taken-for-granted attitudes that make war seem normal. Alternatively, an approach based on Rene Girard's writings might treat ritual as a way of displacing unbounded retribution with "good" violence, as well as requiring consideration not only of media but of mediators, rivals whom we imitate because they stand between us and the objects of our desire.

The Chapters

In chapter 2, Fletcher DuBois, Erik de Maaker, Karin Polit, and Marianne Riphagen analyze cases illustrating the relationship between producing mediatized ritual forms and contesting claims about cultural identity, authenticity, and ownership. The authors track the ways ritual efficacy and emotional investment change when performances are reconfigured or moved to new places. The process of transposing traditional rituals into mediatized cultural expressions is frequently bound up with conflict. People use media to aestheticize rituals, that is, turn them into works of art, in order to transpose ritual knowledge into new settings and to declare themselves modern people distinct from seemingly superstitious traditions no longer deemed fit representations of themselves to the world. When rituals are turned into aesthetic forms that can be displayed to both insiders and outsiders, the display of these rituals demarcates ethnic groups and establishes supposedly authentic cultural identities, but these forms and boundaries are contested.

In the first case, Christian Bumbarra Thompson, an artist of Bidjara, German, Jewish, and English origins, transposes Bidjara ritual knowledge into a contemporary video and sculpture called *I Need You / You Need Me (The Fox)*. It presents Australian viewers with a contemporary reinterpretation of a bygone initiation ritual and in so doing evokes heated responses. The second case, that of the Garo of upland northeast India, does not provoke such heat. In 2006, Garo youth participated with Wangala dancing in the Republic Day Parade, a major annual celebration of the Indian state. Insertion into the parade required the Wangala dance to be abbreviated to fit the strict time frame and to be restyled to suit the taste of the all-India audience. In the third case, a local ritual tradition from Uttarakhand in north India provides the basis for an educational heritage piece performed on stages at the state and national levels to teach educated youth about their own traditions. However, backstage, after some of the performances, a deity appears, possessing young performers, making demands about traditional purity, and thus pressing the performances back in the direction of ritual.

"Insurgents and Icons," chapter 3, considers the use of ritual images as a tool for protest, war making, and peacemaking. Anna-Karina Hermkens and Eric Venbrux track the appropriation and circulation of two very different kinds of imagery. Their case studies show that mediatized ritual images can both instigate conflict and dampen it. First they examine media images of a protest action at Rome's Trevi Fountain, a tourist destination and pilgrimage site. Then they consider the deployment of images of the Virgin Mary on Bougainville in the Pacific. In both cases images are wielded in protest against oppression. Local actors, appropriating the power of these symbols, mobilize them in local media to mark their positions in war or conflict, thereby constellating divergent sentiments and practices. Simultaneously, global circulation of these images extends their range and transforms their dynamics. The images not only communicate messages, they also create structures of feeling and constellate communities of sentiment, what Arjun Appadurai calls "mass-mediated sodalities of worship and charisma."[48] The authors show that such images can communicate only certain kinds of messages. If they are used to convey deviant messages, causing a rupture in what is collectively known, accepted, performed, and felt, new conflicts arise.

Chapter 4, by Robert Langer, Thomas Quartier, Udo Simon, Jan Snoek, and Gerard Wiegers, analyzes four cases, asking: under what conditions do publicly mediatized rituals and ritualized practices become a source of conflict? In their first case, they show that as long as Freemasons kept their rituals secret, no conflicts developed. However, once pamphlets exposed imprecations in a ritual oath, implying that Freemasonry claimed sovereignty, conflict emerged, because sovereignty was a privilege that European states and churches regarded as their own exclusive prerogative. The second case shows that as the Muslim call to prayer is performed in public space by immigrants in present-day European countries, this act is interpreted by the majority as an attempt to achieve domination. By reporting on the conflict, the media transform local discussions about participation into national debates about cultural space. The third example traces the shifting identity boundaries created in contemporary Turkey by the display of Alevi rituals in the media. Major sources of conflict between Alevis and Sunnis are mediatized public events such as the *cem*, a standardized weekly communal ritual. The final case, that of the educational practices of American evangelicals, examines mediatized attempts to gain political influence in the United States. Ritually framed educational practices shown in the documentary *Jesus Camp* depict attempts to turn young children into an "army of God" trained to struggle against abortion, the theory of evolution, and homosexuality. The authors argue that their cases illustrate how conflicts over ritual are embedded in wider discourses that either reflect social tension or challenge political and religious authority. Such hidden "conflicts behind the conflicts," they observe, are frequently about hierarchy, power, and participation. Ritual, they claim, is a source of conflict precisely because of its being ritual, that is, a performative instrument for advancing identity claims, as well as a means of reproducing a group's values, social structures, and habitual practices.

The fifth chapter, "Place, Action, and Community in Internet Rituals," explores various Web sites in order to appreciate what the Internet adds to ritual practices, how it changes them, and what conflicts arise when existing rituals are transferred from physical space to cyberspace. In doing so, the authors engage Jonathan Z. Smith and Ronald L. Grimes regarding the place-bound nature of ritual. Thomas Widlok examines the function of Aboriginal smoking rituals as ways of belonging and reconciling. He argues that Web sites, because they invoke the bodily experience of ritual, are ultimately inseparable from the physical presence of the practitioners and the geographical places where rituals are performed. Catrien Notermans shows that the Lourdes Web site is not really a substitute for people's personal, tactile communication with the Marian shrine and with fellow pilgrims. Marga Altena illustrates how Weblogs of dying and bereaved people provide much needed recognition and contribute to the rediscovery, even reinvention, of spirituality. She claims that builders of Dutch Weblogs about death and mourning, as well as visitors to such sites, can find refuge and appreciation that they cannot find elsewhere. Through individually composed texts and images, people create innovative dying or death rituals, thereby helping transform professional funerary culture in the Netherlands.

Chapter 6 furthers the discussion of online rituals by examining their disruption within virtual worlds such as Second Life and other MMOGs (massively multiplayer online games). Simone Heidbrink, Nadja Miczek, and Kerstin Radde-Antweiler discuss negotiations concerning the emergence and resolution of ritual conflicts in three online environments. By interviewing online participants, the authors inquire into the relationship between offline and online identities, hoping to identify the triggers of conflict. Virtual worlds are fertile grounds for both traditional and emergent religions, including their rituals. However, the purposes of these new online environments are multiple and divergent, so they are subject to the interpretations of individual users of the spaces. In these supposedly playful game environments, multiple layers of conflict emerge among participants, public bystanders, and researchers studying these interactions. In the case of Second Life, where there is no predefined goal or purpose, rituals and their performance have played an important role for users since the online environment was first established. To the authors' surprise, these rituals seemed at first to be mere digital reconstructions of their offline counterparts; they were not especially "creative." The authors also discovered that participants engage in serious conflict over questions of ritual's authority, efficacy, and agency—issues that plague rituals in the offline world. However, the authors implicitly challenge approaches to ritual that are based on traditional offline examples.

Working with two case studies, Ignace de Haes, Ute Hüsken, and Paul van der Velde write about ritual in times of violent crisis. Chapter 7 is built around two examples, the toppling of the statue of Saddam Hussein in Baghdad on April 9, 2003, and the protests by monks and laity against the Junta in Myanmar, or Burma, during September 2007. The authors study the ways mediatization shapes conflict by affecting rituals. They argue that in times of national or international conflict, ritual and media are tools wielded to ensure that the dominant political and religious discourse will be embraced by the majority of a country's population. In investigating ritual's use in violent situations, and by studying the role of mass media, the authors show how rituals bring about social cohesion not only through inclusion but also through exclusion.

Drawing principally on the Abu Ghraib scandal and the photographs that helped precipitate it, Werner Binder, Tom F. Driver, and Barry Stephenson in chapter 8 discuss torture as a form of ritualization calculated to forge an enemy and consolidate absolute power. Torture, they show, bears similarities to forms of initiation, but it is actually a systematic elaboration of cruelty for political purposes. Following an introduction to the Abu Ghraib situation and an interpretation of two iconic photographs, the authors tender several propositions. To study torture as ritual, they argue, undercuts any view of torture as merely, or primarily, a technique of interrogation. Rather, it is a means of social control that transgresses the very rule of law that it supposedly upholds. Torture, they say, is a threat to all freedoms and to the health of the human heart and soul (or whatever makes us human). Assuming an explicitly ethical stance, the authors argue that concerted opposition to torture is not only possible but necessary, and opposition, they argue, can be successful only if supported by alternative liturgies aimed at building up the social body, what Victor Turner called *communitas*. To fight against state torture, the authors write, requires abandoning the illusion of an almighty state capable of protecting its citizens from every imaginable threat, including terrorism. There may be sensible ways to minimize the danger to societies from terrorism, but there can never be absolute security, only relative degrees of safety. Torture does not guarantee safety or even enhance security but merely traps citizens into believing in the illusion of a state capable of saving them from imaginary ticking bombs. To become cruel and inhumane, declare the authors, is a price too high to pay for such an illusion. In examining torture from a ritual studies perspective, they expose the dubious claim that torture is for intelligence gathering, and they conclude by offering readers a choice: human beings can ritualize cruel behavior and violence, or they can ritualize compassion and love.

The concluding response by Michael Houseman is not a mere polite afterword but rather a chapter in its own right. In the process of evaluating and teasing out the implications of preceding chapters, he forges his own unique understanding of ritual. What he dubs "identity-refracting" rituals are characterized by a high degree of self-consciousness, the use of immaterial props, and deliberative creativity, three characteristics less typical of canonical rituals. Houseman shows how understanding the dynamics of identify refraction might sharpen or further enlighten the views of ritual, media, and conflict proposed by other authors.

NOTES

1. "Saddam's Body in Tikrit for Burial," AlJazeera.Net, December 31, 2006, http://www.english.aljazeera.net/news/middleeast/2006/12/200852513501.

2. Healing through Remembering, http://www.healingthroughremembering.org/index.asp; Indian Residential Schools Truth and Reconciliation Commission, http://www.trc-cvr.ca/index_e.html.

3. Bruce Lincoln, "Conflict," in *Critical Terms for Religious Studies*, ed. Mark C. Taylor (Chicago: University of Chicago Press), 65.

4. Soeterbeeck Study Center of Radboud University Nijmegen, http://www.ru.nl/studiecentrumsoeterbeeck/vm_engels/history/.

5. The South African Truth and Reconciliation Commission, http://www.doj.gov.za/trc/; Northern Ireland's Healing through Remembering, Day of Private Reflection, www.healingthroughremembering.org/, as well as http://www.dayofreflection.com/.

6. George E. Irani and Nathan C. Funk, "Rituals of Reconciliation: Arab-Islamic Perspectives." Kroc Institute Occasional Paper #19, OP:2, 2000.

7. From as early as European colonizing expeditions, there was a stereotype of indigenous people as living a ritually saturated, therefore irrational, life, whereas Europeans, supposedly more rational, were comparatively free of rituals, especially those labeled magical.

8. The term's utility is disputed in religious studies and anthropology; see Daniel Lawrence O'Keefe, *Stolen Lightening: The Social Theory of Magic* (New York: Continuum, 1982); Robert Alan Segal, "Making the Myth-Ritualist Theory Scientific," *Religion* 30, no. 3 (2000). Among those who find the term *magic* useful, the word typically means "using symbolic means to achieve empirical ends." See Tom F. Driver, *Liberating Rites: Understanding the Transformative Power of Ritual* (Boulder, CO: Westview, 1998); Ronald L. Grimes, *Beginnings in Ritual Studies*, rev. ed. (Columbia: University of South Carolina Press, 1994), 48.

9. Victor W. Turner and Edith Turner, *Image and Pilgrimage in Christian Culture* (New York: Columbia University Press, 1978), 243.

10. Evan M. Zuesse, "Ritual," in *The Encyclopedia of Religion*, ed. Mircea Eliade (New York: Macmillan, 1987), 405.

11. Max Gluckman, "Les Rites de Passage," in *Essays on the Ritual of Social Relations*, ed. Max Gluckman (Manchester, UK: Manchester University Press, 1966), 24.

12. E. Thomas Lawson and Robert N. McCauley, *Rethinking Religion: Connecting Cognition and Culture* (Cambridge, UK: Cambridge University Press, 1990), 176.

13. Stanley J. Tambiah, "A Performative Approach to Ritual," *Proceedings of the British Academy* 65, no. 1979 (1981).

14. Roy A. Rappaport, *Ritual and Religion in the Making of Humanity* (Cambridge, UK: Cambridge University Press, 1999), 24.

15. Caroline Humphrey and James Laidlaw, *The Archetypal Actions of Ritual: A Theory of Ritual Illustrated by the Jain Rite of Worship* (Oxford: Clarendon, 1994), 97–98.

16. Julian Huxley, "A Discussion on Ritualization of Behaviour in Animals and Man," *Philosophical Transactions of the Royal Society of London, Series B*, 251 (1966).

17. Robbie E. Davis-Floyd, *Birth as an American Rite of Passage* (Berkeley: University of California Press, 1992), 229–234.

18. Edmond Leach, "Ritual," in *Encyclopedia of Social Sciences*, ed. David L. Sills (New York: Macmillan and Free Press, 1968), 13.

19. Some exceptions are Humphrey and Laidlaw, *The Archetypal Actions of Ritual*; Lawson and McCauley, *Rethinking Religion*.

20. Animals too engage in ritualization, although there is a debate over whether animal ritualization and human ritual are the same thing. In any case, the claim here is not that ritual is uniquely human, so we will not enter the debate. See Irenäus Eibl-Eibesfeldt, "Ritual and Ritualization from a Biological Perspective," in *Human Ethology: Claims and Limits of a New Discipline. Contributions to the Colloquium Sponsored by the Werner-Reimers-Stiftung*, ed. Mario Von Cranach, Klaus Foppa, Wolf Lepenies, and Detlev Ploog (Cambridge, UK Cambridge University Press; Paris: Editions de la Maison des Sciences de l'Homme, 1979); Erik Homburger Erikson, "Ontogeny of Ritualization in Man," in *Psychoanalysis: A General Psychology. Essays in Honor of Heinz Hartmann*, ed. Rudolph M. Lowenstein, Lottie M. Newman, Max Schur, and Albert J. Solnit (New York: International Universities Press, 1966); Huxley, "A Discussion on Ritualization of Behaviour in Animals and Man."

21. Harvey Whitehouse calls this the "tedium effect." See his *Modes of Religiosity: A Cognitive Theory of Religious Transmission* (New York: AltaMira, 2004), 98.

22. For an alternative polythetic strategy in defining ritual, see Jan Snoek, "Defining 'Rituals,'" in *Theorizing Rituals: Issues, Topics, Approaches, Concepts*, ed. Jens Kreinath, Jan Snoek, and Michael Stausberg (Leiden: Brill, 2006).

23. Tom Condon, reviewing the movie *United 93*, writes, "I was struck by the attention to prayer in the film.... The opening scene shows the terrorists praying for courage and strength. Much later in the film, the passengers pray in the face of danger. In an ironic way, terrorists and passengers are united in prayer. One scene cuts between passengers praying the Lord's Prayer and one of the hijackers mouthing a silent prayer." *Dominican Life USA*, http://www.domlife.org/moviereviews/United_93.htm.

24. Yuval Neriaa, David Roeb, Benjamin Beit-Hallahmicm, Hassan Mneimnehd, Alana Balabane, and Randall Marshall, "The Al Qaeda 9/11 Instructions: A Study in the Construction of Religious Martyrdom," *Religion* 35, no. 1 (2005), 3.

25. This is Catherine Bell's view. See Catherine M. Bell, *Ritual Theory, Ritual Practice* (Oxford: Oxford University Press, 1992), 105–106. For a critique of her view, see Ronald L. Grimes, "Performance Theory and the Study of Ritual," in *New Approaches to the Study of Religion*, ed. Peter Antes, Armin Geertz, and Randi Warne (Berlin: Verlag de Gruyter, 2004).

26. This is Roy Rappaport's view. See Rappaport, *Ritual and Religion in the Making of Humanity*. See also Ronald L. Grimes, "Ritual Theory and the Environment," in *Nature Performed: Environment, Culture, Performance*, ed. Bronislaw Szerszynski, Wallace Heim, and Clare Waterton (London: Blackwell, 2003), 39 ff.

27. Borrowed and modified slightly from Ronald L. Grimes, "The Lifeblood of Public Ritual," in *Celebration: Studies in Festivity and Ritual*, ed. Victor Turner (Washington, DC: Smithsonian Institute Press, 1982), 282.

28. "100 Photographs That Changed the World," *Life* and the *Digital Journalist*. http://www.digitaljournalist.org/issue0309/lm01.html; World Press Photo, http://www.worldpressphoto.org/.

29. Marshall Poe, "What Is a Mechanical Icon?," Mechanical Icon, http://mechanicalicon.com/whatis.html.

30. Hans Pool and Maaik Krijgsman, dirs. *Looking for an Icon*. 55 min., black and white, USA, 2007.

31. Quoted in a review of *Looking for an Icon*, CBC News, April 23, 2006, http://www.cbc.ca/correspondent/060423.html.

32. Henry VIII's Wives, "Iconic Moments of the Twentieth Century," http://h8w.net/work/im.html. For other refractions of the photo see "Covers and Citations," 1968, http://search.it.online.fr/covers/?m=1968.

33. The image is easily available on the Internet by conducting an image search using "Eddie Adams" and "Nguyen Ngoc" as search terms.

34. Kaustav Bhattacharya, "Olympic Torch Rally, London: Free Tibet Protest," http://www.flickr.com/photos/astrolondon/2396265240/.

35. Bhattacharya, "Olympic Torch Rally."

36. See, for example, Maurice E. F. Bloch, *From Blessing to Violence: History and Ideology in the Circumcision Ritual of the Merina of Madagascar*, ed. Jack Goody, Cambridge Studies in Social Anthropology, vol. 61 (Cambridge, UK: Cambridge University Press, 1986); Maurice M. Bloch, "The Presence of Violence in Religion," in *Why We Watch: The Attractions of Violent Entertainment*, ed. Jeffrey Goldstein (New York: Oxford University Press, 1998); Michael Cobb, *God Hates Fags: The Rhetorics of Religious Violence* (New York: New York University Press, 2006); Robert G. Hamerton-Kelly, ed., *Violent Origins: Walter Burkert, René Girard, and Jonathan Z. Smith on Ritual Killing and Cultural Formation* (Stanford, CA: Stanford University Press, 1987); Bruce Kapferer, *Legends of People, Myths of State: Violence, Intolerance, and Political Culture in Sri Lanka and Australia* (Washington, DC: Smithsonian Institute Press, 1988).

37. David Willoughby, "Le Corbusier: The Architect and the Brand," http://www.tokyoartbeat.com/tablog/entries.en/2007/04/le_corbusier_the_architect_and.html, April 5, 2007.

38. Ric Erickson, "Heatwave of the Week: Also Worldclass," *Café Metropole Paris*, http://www.metropoleparis.com/2006/1129/1129cafe.html?page=2. Another candidate for original multimedium might be Richard Wagner's "complete artwork" (*Gesamtkunstwerk*), that is, works combining the three performing arts (music, poetry, theater) with the three plastic arts (architecture, painting, sculpture). See Richard Wagner, *Das Kunstwerk der Zukunft* [*The Artwork of the Future*], 1849.

39. Ronald L. Grimes, *Rite out of Place: Ritual, Media, and the Arts* (New York: Oxford University Press, 2006).

40. For more on the term, see Winfried Schulz, "Reconstructing Mediatization as an Analytical Concept," *European Journal of Communication* 19, no. 1 (2004).

41. Because an older definition of *mediatization* is "to annex a principality into a larger state," some European scholars prefer the term *medialization*.

42. Lincoln, "Conflict," 65.

43. Randall Collins, "The Durkheimian Tradition in Conflict Sociology," in *Durkheimian Sociology: Cultural Studies* (Cambridge, UK: Cambridge University Press, 1988), 108.

44. Philip Smith, "Codes and Conflict: Toward a Theory of War as Ritual," *Theory and Society* 20, no. 1 (1991).

45. Smith, "Codes and Conflict," 108.

46. William Golding's novel, *Lord of the Flies*, as well as film renditions of this literary classic are graphic illustrations of ritualization in the service of violence. They, along with Bruno Bettelheim's *Symbolic Wounds*, demonstrate that deploying dualistically conceived symbols to identify scapegoats is not limited to politicians or military leaders. See Bruno Bettelheim, *Symbolic Wounds: Puberty Rites and the Envious Male*, rev. ed. (New York: Collier, 1954, 1962); *Lord of the Flies*, Peter Brook, dir., UK, 92 min., DVD, black and white, 1963; William Golding, *Lord of the Flies* (New York: Perigree, 1954, 2003); *Lord of the Flies*, Harry Hook, dir., USA, VHS, color, 1990.

47. Tom Driver argues that deritualization intensifies the violence; see Driver, *Liberating Rites*, chapter 3.

48. Arjun Appadurai, *Modernity at Large: Cultural Dimensions of Globalization* (Minneapolis: University of Minnesota Press, 1997), 8–9.

REFERENCES

Appadurai, Arjun. *Modernity at Large: Cultural Dimensions of Globalization*. Minneapolis: University of Minnesota Press, 1997.
Bell, Catherine M. *Ritual Theory, Ritual Practice*. Oxford: Oxford University Press, 1992.
Bettelheim, Bruno. *Symbolic Wounds: Puberty Rites and the Envious Male*, rev. ed. New York: Collier, 1962 (1954).
Bhattacharya, Kaustav. "Olympic Torch Rally, London: Free Tibet Protest," http://www.flickr.com/photos/astrolondon/2396265240/.
Bloch, Maurice E. F. *From Blessing to Violence: History and Ideology in the Circumcision Ritual of the Merina of Madagascar*, edited by Jack Goody. Cambridge Studies in Social Anthropology, vol. 61. Cambridge, UK: Cambridge University Press, 1986.

Bloch, Maurice M. "The Presence of Violence in Religion." In *Why We Watch: The Attractions of Violent Entertainment*, edited by Jeffrey Goldstein, 163–177. New York: Oxford University Press, 1998.

Brook, Peter, dir. *Lord of the Flies*. 92 min., DVD, black and white, UK, 1963.

Cobb, Michael. *God Hates Fags: The Rhetorics of Religious Violence*. New York: New York University Press, 2006.

Collins, Randall. "The Durkheimian Tradition in Conflict Sociology." In *Durkheimian Sociology: Cultural Studies*, edited by Jeffrey C. Alexander, 107–128. Cambridge, UK: Cambridge University Press, 1988.

Davis-Floyd, Robbie E. *Birth as an American Rite of Passage*. Berkeley: University of California Press, 1992.

Driver, Tom F. *Liberating Rites: Understanding the Transformative Power of Ritual*. Boulder, CO: Westview, 1998.

Eibl-Eibesfeldt, Irenäus. "Ritual and Ritualization from a Biological Perspective." In *Human Ethology: Claims and Limits of a New Discipline. Contributions to the Colloquium Sponsored by the Werner-Reimers-Stiftung*, edited by Mario Von Cranach, Klaus Foppa, Wolf Lepenies, and Detlev Ploog, 3–55. Cambridge, UK: Cambridge University Press; Paris: Editions de la Maison des Sciences de l'Homme, 1979.

Erikson, Erik Homburger. "Ontogeny of Ritualization in Man." In *Psychoanalysis: A General Psychology. Essays in Honor of Heinz Hartmann*, edited by Rudolph M. Lowenstein, Lottie M. Newman, Max Schur, and Albert J. Solnit, 601–621. New York: International Universities Press, 1966.

Gluckman, Max. "Les Rites de Passage." In *Essays on the Ritual of Social Relations*, edited by Max Gluckman, 1–52. Manchester, UK: Manchester University Press, 1966.

Golding, William. *Lord of the Flies*. New York: Perigree, 2003 (1954).

Grimes, Ronald L. *Beginnings in Ritual Studies*, rev. ed. Columbia: University of South Carolina Press, 1994.

———. "The Lifeblood of Public Ritual." In *Celebration: Studies in Festivity and Ritual*, edited by Victor Turner. Washington, DC: Smithsonian Institute Press, 1982.

———. "Performance Theory and the Study of Ritual." In *New Approaches to the Study of Religion*, edited by Peter Antes, Armin Geertz, and Randi Warne, 109–138. Berlin: Verlag de Gruyter, 2004.

———. *Rite out of Place: Ritual, Media, and the Arts*. New York: Oxford University Press, 2006.

———. "Ritual Theory and the Environment." In *Nature Performed: Environment, Culture, Performance*, edited by Bronislaw Szerszynski, Wallace Heim, and Clare Waterton, 31–45. London: Blackwell, 2003.

Hamerton-Kelly, Robert G., ed. *Violent Origins: Walter Burkert, René Girard, and Jonathan Z. Smith on Ritual Killing and Cultural Formation*. Stanford, CA: Stanford University Press, 1987.

Hook, Harry, dir. *Lord of the Flies*. VHS, color, USA, 1990.

Humphrey, Caroline, and James Laidlaw. *The Archetypal Actions of Ritual: A Theory of Ritual Illustrated by the Jain Rite of Worship*. Oxford: Clarendon, 1994.

Huxley, Julian. "A Discussion on Ritualization of Behaviour in Animals and Man." *Philosophical Transactions of the Royal Society of London, Series B* 251 (1966): 409–422.

Irani, George E., and Nathan C. Funk. "Rituals of Reconciliation: Arab-Islamic Perspectives." Kroc Institute Occasional Paper #19, OP: 2. 2000.
Kapferer, Bruce. *Legends of People, Myths of State: Violence, Intolerance, and Political Culture in Sri Lanka and Australia*. Washington, DC: Smithsonian Institute Press, 1988.
Lawson, E. Thomas, and Robert N. McCauley. *Rethinking Religion: Connecting Cognition and Culture*. Cambridge, UK: Cambridge University Press, 1990.
Leach, Edmond. "Ritual." In *Encyclopedia of Social Sciences*, edited by David L. Sills. New York: Macmillan and Free Press, 1968.
Lincoln, Bruce. "Conflict." In *Critical Terms for Religious Studies*, edited by Mark C. Taylor. Chicago: University of Chicago Press, 1998.
Neriaa, Yuval, David Roeb, Benjamin Beit-Hallahmicm, Hassan Mneimnehd, Alana Balabane, and Randall Marshall. "The Al Qaeda 9/11 Instructions: A Study in the Construction of Religious Martyrdom." *Religion* 35, no. 1 (2005): 1–11.
O'Keefe, Daniel Lawrence. *Stolen Lightening: The Social Theory of Magic*. New York: Continuum, 1982.
"100 Photographs That Changed the World." *Life* and the *Digital Journalist*. http://www.digitaljournalist.org/issue0309/lm01.html.
Poe, Marshall. "What Is a Mechanical Icon?" Mechanical Icon, http://mechanicalicon.com/whatis.html.
Pool, Hans, and Maaik Krijgsman, dirs. *Looking for an Icon*. 55 min., black and white, USA, 2007.
Rappaport, Roy A. *Ritual and Religion in the Making of Humanity*. Cambridge, UK: Cambridge University Press, 1999.
Schulz, Winfried. "Reconstructing Mediatization as an Analytical Concept." *European Journal of Communication* 19, no. 1 (2004): 87–101.
Segal, Robert Alan. "Making the Myth-Ritualist Theory Scientific." *Religion* 30, no. 3 (2000): 259–271.
Smith, Philip. "Codes and Conflict: Toward a Theory of War as Ritual." *Theory and Society* 20, no. 1 (1991): 103–138.
Snoek, Jan. "Defining 'Rituals.'" In *Theorizing Rituals: Issues, Topics, Approaches, Concepts*, edited by Jens Kreinath, Jan Snoek, and Michael Stausberg. Leiden: Brill, 2006.
Tambiah, Stanley J. "A Performative Approach to Ritual." *Proceedings of the British Academy* 65, no. 1979 (1981): 113–169.
Turner, Victor W., and Edith Turner. *Image and Pilgrimage in Christian Culture*. New York: Columbia University Press, 1978.
Whitehouse, Harvey. *Modes of Religiosity: A Cognitive Theory of Religious Transmission*. New York: AltaMira, 2004.
Zuesse, Evan M. "Ritual." In *The Encyclopedia of Religion*, edited by Mircea Eliade, 405–422. New York: Macmillan, 1987.

2

From Ritual Ground to Stage

Fletcher DuBois, Erik de Maaker,
Karin Polit, and Marianne Riphagen

The transformation and transfer of rituals or ritual elements from one performance environment to another can create conflicts, but these are not necessarily violent or even open and apparent. To explore how conflicts are connected to ritual transformation, we take a close look at the emotional involvements and proprietary investments that people have in ritual. In doing so, we frame three case studies with questions that clarify theoretical issues surrounding ritual conflict.

The first case is a video showing a white man adorning himself with a foxtail while getting dressed in a pair of pink lederhosen.[1] *I Need You/You Need Me (The Fox)* was created by Indigenous Australian artist Christian Thompson, who combines elements of Aboriginal ritual knowledge with non-Indigenous influences and styles. The artist describes his work as depicting a modern initiation rite. His assertion has provoked critical reactions. Why does an art video of a man turning into a fox conjure such heated responses?

Reformulating and transposing ritual performances do not necessarily provoke mixed feelings, as our second case shows. In South Asia, staged folk dances play an important role in displaying and defining social categories. The Garo, a community in upland northeast India, is represented at political rallies and state celebrations by Wangala folk dancing. In 2006, Garo youth engaged in Wangala dancing as a way of participating in the annual Republic Day Parade, a major celebration of the Indian state. Their participation was shown on national television and mentioned in the press. Insertion of Wangala dancing into the parade required the dance to be abbreviated and restyled. The dance performance had to fit the strict time frame of the parade and be tuned to the taste and expectations of the all-India audience to which the parade caters. Unlike the art video discussed in our first case, this reformatting did not spark critical reactions. No Garos argued against the inclusion of Wangala dancing in the Republic Day Parade, even though the parade is seen by a vocal Garo minority as an expression of political control over India's diverse populace. How can a ritual dance be altered and reinterpreted without arousing conflict? How does the significance of such a dance change when performances are shifted from one environment to another?

The third case study also delves into the consequences of a tradition shifted from one performance environment to another. In this instance, a local ritual tradition of Uttarakhand in north India becomes the basis for a theater piece performed as local heritage on state and national stages throughout India. The piece was also used to teach local youth about their own traditions, something they supposedly are not familiar with. One of the workshops for young people included screening of video footage that depicted the traditional ritual from which the theater piece is derived. Their teachers hoped to improve the young people's stage performance by showing this footage, but the instructional value of the video went well beyond the teachers' intentions. Besides showing the theatrical elements of the ritual event, the video included scenes of deity possession. In the group's subsequent performances, possession suddenly occurred, leaving the young performers with a strong sense of divine presence. What changed the young actors' attitude toward their own performance in such a way that a deity could appear on and off stage to possess them?

In each case study, mediatization plays a key role, often as the prime vehicle by which a ritual is presented, performed, or perceived. When ritual knowledge is utilized in a mediatized way and ritual actions are transferred, social conflict can easily occur. Most often the conflict is about the ownership of ritual, as well as access to, or gains from, ritual knowledge or experience. Because the mediatization of rituals often also includes economic gain or at least a rise in status, people less involved in this transfer often feel passed over. At the same time, ritually inspired events need a connection to the significance of the ritual events for their respective audiences to be able to appreciate the performance or presentation. Alas, in all three cases presented here, cultural performance is inspired by ritual heritage. What is telling about turning to ritual as inspiration for cultural performance is that, as soon as some people use ritual knowledge to produce art or other forms of representation, others, considering themselves experts on or proprietors of traditional ritual knowledge, object to the changing of the tradition. For them, to change is to desecrate. Of course, there are also instances in which the transfer or transformation of ritual is perfectly acceptable. We show that both responses are deeply connected with definitions of ritual ownership by outsiders and insiders. How do people become owners of a ritual practice? What happens to the sense of ownership when a ritual is transferred and transformed? Who profits from these changes, and how?

Gaining cultural, social, symbolic, or economic capital by transferring or transforming a ritual often leads some to conclude that rituals and other kinds of cultural performance lose value when commodified.[2] As soon as somebody earns money or profits from a performance, rituals are no longer valuable. This view, postulated by the Frankfurt School and promoted by Theodor Adorno, became popular in the latter half of the twentieth century.[3]

In performance studies, a similar view emerges from Richard Schechner's and Victor Turner's distinction between efficacy and entertainment.[4] They associate efficacy with ritual and entertainment with theater. For them, staging rituals signals a lack of commitment by performers, producers, and audiences. Consequently, such performances lack ritual significance; they may entertain but they are not efficacious. Turner and Schechner do not claim that either ritual or theater exists in a pure form. Any given performance of the one is alloyed by the other. They know that rituals can have entertaining elements and that theater can also be effective; nonetheless, ritual is by their definition more efficacious than theater. Both scholars imply that "traditional" rituals authentically bear the essence of a culture, whereas staged ones do not. We reject this view. The cases presented in this chapter show that the transformation of ritual into a commodified piece of art does not necessarily devalue it culturally, nor do the people involved understand such performances as less than efficacious. What forms, then, do ritual efficacy and emotional involvement take, as performances are reconfigured and shifted to new places?

Two aspects of ritual ownership and transformation guide our analysis. First, we look at how the ownership of ritual traditions is understood and how participants use their ritual traditions to serve their goals and aspirations. Second, following modern theories of performance,[5] we take a close look at the way people learn to become owners of a ritual practice, and how they acquire knowledge of a ritual, including its ostensibly correct performance or presentation. Doing so should help us understand the deeply felt, sometimes violent quarrels over ownership, performance, and rights to certain ritual traditions. Understanding notions of ownership held by ritual participants is immensely helpful in comprehending how rituals continue to be effective or acquire new efficacies even though performances change substantially. In the final analysis, we argue that shifts from ritual ground to artistic stage lead to shifts in the efficacy of rituals.

I Need You / You Need Me (The Fox)

Australian artist Christian Thompson was commissioned by the Centre for Contemporary Photography in Melbourne to create a photomedia work for the 2005 exhibition Black on White. This exhibition, which set out to show "photographs by Aboriginal artists representing non-Aboriginality,"[6] was built on developments in Indigenous Australian photomedia practices first begun in the 1980s, when artists increasingly took up the camera to reconfigure photographic representations of Aborigines by non-Aboriginal people.[7] Black on White, rather than exploring Indigenous representations of Aboriginality, endeavored to interrogate how Aboriginal photomedia artists "see the people and culture that surrounds them."[8]

Christian Bumbarra Thompson is an artist of Bidjara, German, Jewish, and English origins. The Bidjara Aboriginal people from whom he descends live in southwest Queensland. In response to Black on White's curatorial premise, he transposed Bidjara ritual knowledge into a contemporary work of art. *I Need You / You Need Me (The Fox)* is the first Indigenous work using video and sculpture to draw explicitly on Aboriginal ritual knowledge. The work presents a contemporary reinterpretation of a bygone initiation ritual. Thompson's reconfiguration of Bidjara ritual knowledge into what he regards as a contemporary initiation rite is not always accepted cross-culturally as authoritative. Non-Indigenous responses to *The Fox* highlight the kinds of interpretive disputes that erupt when ritual knowledge is transformed and transposed into new media such as artworks.

I Need You / You Need Me (The Fox) consists of a video and a sculptural installation. The video documents the performance of a white man dressing in a fox costume, including mask and tail, during which he increasingly embodies the fox, exhibiting animal-like behavior (see figures 2.1 and 2.2). The six-minute video also includes a brief, low-pitched noise. Thompson aestheticized, that is, embellished and enhanced, the performance by means of lighting, sound, and camera position. The sculptural installation accompanying the video consists of the shoes, garment, and fur that make up the fox costume.

When exhibited, each of the elements composing the sculpture is positioned on a shelf in close proximity to the *Fox* video. Thompson explains that his work is an interpretation of the Australian Aboriginal concept of Dreaming.[9] An aspect of Dreaming in a ceremonial context, he argues, is the incarnation of ancestral spirits by individual Aboriginal performers.[10] In the video, the young man symbolically transforms into an animal and, in the end, he acts like one. According to the artist, his work exemplifies the idea of emulating a spiritual ancestor as well as

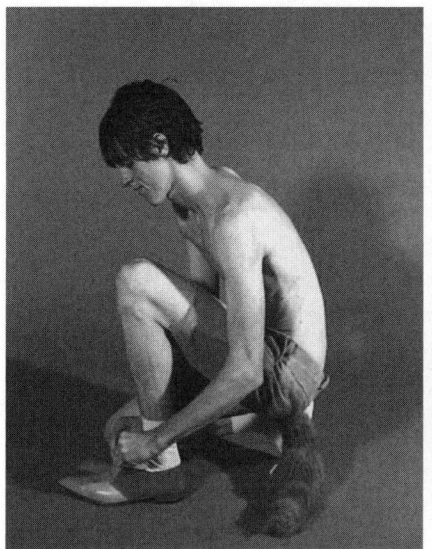

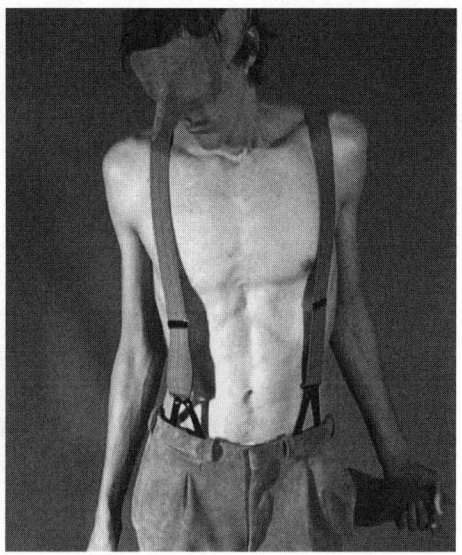

FIGURES 2.1 AND 2.2. *I Need You / You Need Me (The Fox)*, 2005, Christian Thompson. Frame captures courtesy of the artist and Gallery Gabrielle Pizzi.

symbolizing the transformation from boy to man. However, by using an animal such as the fox, which is not native to Australia, Thompson is presenting a white man's Dreaming. He says, "The video comes from my perspective as a Bidjara man. It is completely informed by Bidjara philosophies about art, incarnation and initiation."[11] At the same time, Thompson states that he employs "Western aesthetic and contemporary cultural references."[12]

The basis for *The Fox* is Thompson's knowledge of Bidjara initiation ceremonies imparted to him by his Aunt Carrie, known by the family as someone with an in-depth comprehension of their Bidjara heritage. When she passed away, Carrie gave each of her relatives an audiotape containing a story of importance to Bidjara people. The story that Thompson, the artist, received was part of an initiation.

Among the long-term detrimental effects of Australia's colonization by the British, which began in 1788, were enforced assimilation, disease, violence, and the involuntary removal of Aboriginal children from their families. Aboriginal people are still confronted with the loss of cultural knowledge and practices. Thompson illustrates this fact by a comment about his Bidjara forefathers: "My great-great-grandfather was the last person to be initiated, so he had traditional scars across his chest. After him, my great-grandfather and grandfather were not initiated."[13] While recognizing the destructive forces that have shaped his history, the artist draws on and revitalizes fragmented knowledge about Bidjara rituals and philosophies.[14] To construct a modern Bidjara initiation rite, Thompson uses the knowledge conveyed to him by Aunt Carrie's tape. The artist does not, however, want to expand on the contents of the taped narrative. Too often, he argues, Indigenous Australians are coerced into disclosing aspects of themselves and their cultural practices for Euro-American scientific and ethnographic studies. Resisting what he describes as "emotional striptease," Thompson only discloses that the account is part of "men's business."[15]

Besides drawing on Indigenous ritual knowledge, *The Fox* also references non-Indigenous practices and styles. Certain fashion elements allude to the artist's connection to his European background. For instance, the shoes, garments, and mask that make up the fox costume were made by first- and second-generation European immigrants in Melbourne. The pointy-tipped, hand-sewn shoes were crafted by the now-retired Italian-born shoemaker Rocco Buffalo, whose famous creations, which have their origin in Italian craft, are in high demand among artists and international pop stars. Furthermore, the combination of pants and suspenders resembles lederhosen, men's folkloric garments originating in the alpine regions of Germany, Austria, and Switzerland. Thompson has explained how working in Melbourne with handcraftspeople enabled him to strengthen relations with members of European minority communities with whom he shares a background, and whose experiences of displacement and discrimination resemble his own.[16]

The cultural references of Thompson's art epitomize interconnections between Aboriginal and non-Aboriginal identities, experiences, persons, and cultural practices in contemporary Australian society. *The Fox*'s importance lies in the fact that it represents an alternative vision to commonly assumed divisions by, for instance, opposing the expectation inherent in Black on White's curatorial premise that Aboriginal photomedia artists are separate from the "people and culture that surrounds them."[17] Rather than commenting on non-Indigenous Australians as somehow incommensurate with Aborigines, Thompson says, "I am white culture as much as I am Aboriginal culture."[18] Emphasizing both his European and Aboriginal heritages, the artist states that stringent distinctions between categories such as Indigenous and non-Indigenous are "really difficult, unless you are a fundamentalist as an Aboriginal person. My work is about the juxtaposition of those identities, not about the delineation of them."[19] *The Fox* provides a different conception of modern Indigenous lifeworlds, a conception that is only slowly gaining recognition in Australia.[20] Ultimately, the fox's Dreaming enacted in Thompson's work mirrors the artist's convictions. While the ritualized performance and the concept of the Dreaming reflect Indigenous philosophies, the Anglo-Saxon performer and the fox embody non-Indigenous elements. The identity of the fictional ancestral spirit is neither exclusively Indigenous nor non-Indigenous.

Building on Émile Durkheim's ideas, we argue that Thompson, by conceiving of the fox as a totemic being, asserts the existence of a group of people at once Indigenous and non-Indigenous. Durkheim's claim is that the totemic principle, or god of a clan, can be "nothing else than the clan itself, personified and represented to the imagination under the visible form of the animal or vegetable which serves as totem."[21]

Thompson's creation and interpretation of a modern Indigenous initiation rite has been challenged and critiqued in revealing ways. One consultant said the artist romanticizes Indigenous ritual practices.[22] According to this person, Thompson should only have engaged with Aboriginal initiation rites after extensive research. Questioning the depth of the arts practitioner's ritual knowledge, this consultant wonders whether Thompson has been initiated and whether he has witnessed Bidjara initiation ceremonies. She feels uncomfortable about the discrepancy between the artist's significations and the actual work of art, in which she cannot discern "Indigenous content." Her position evokes an argument articulated by Elizabeth Povinelli. This anthropologist has written extensively about the ways in which non-Indigenous Australian liberal values, discourses, knowledge systems, and socialities conflict with Indigenous self-definition. Povinelli contends that colonists long used the ability to conduct a ritual performance as the litmus test of Australian Aborigines' authenticity.[23] If Indigenous persons did not pass this colonial test, they were deemed degenerate and inauthentic. The consultant who was uneasy with *The Fox*'s claim to represent an initiation ritual has worked extensively with Indigenous Australians in the Northern Territory, and so it is fair to say that firsthand experience of ceremonial practices in Northern Australia informs her evaluation of Thompson's work.

A second group of viewers refrains from assessing *The Fox* based on any criterion of authenticity. Nevertheless, they contest Thompson's claim that the performance constitutes an Indigenous initiation rite. After watching the *Fox* video, one consultant argued that the work presents a model that dabbles with ritual rather than representing an actual initiation. Pointing to the performer who plays with mask and clothing, the consultant observed that this scene is really about an initial encounter with the ritual garments, when they are first tried on. While the moving image comes across as a play on the possible beginnings of a ritual, the *Fox* performance is actually cut off before the ceremony takes place.

These responses illustrate how Thompson's contemporary ritualizing conflicts with viewers' convictions and assumptions about Aborigines, as well as with their conceptions of the form and content of Indigenous ritual practices. This discord between the artist's intentions and viewers' interpretations is evidence of the artwork's potential to stir debate. However, the discord also reveals reservations regarding ritual innovation. The first consultant's interpretation reveals how implicit distinctions between authentic and inauthentic Aborigines underlie judgments about the authority with which an artist such as Thompson can speak about Indigenous ritual practices. The second interpretation demonstrates how definitions of ritual, or beliefs about what Aboriginal initiation rites ought to be, control and constrain the extent to which an Indigenous artist can reconfigure ritual knowledge to invent modern rites. What Thompson considers a signification of modern life is challenged by non-Indigenous viewers concerned about the veracity of his construction.

Performing the Garo Nation?

January 26, 2008, the fifty-eighth Republic Day, was celebrated under a crisp blue Delhi winter sky. Political and military leaders, as well as a crowd of thousands, cheered an immaculately performed parade meant to display the military might and cultural diversity of India as a nation. In addition to polished combat tanks, stern-looking soldiers, and floats for each of the States and Union Territories, the parade included a children's pageant. One of the groups in the pageant consisted of more than a hundred college students from the northeast Indian Garo community. Dressed in bright clothes, wearing ornamental jewelry, and with feathers in their hair, the Garo students submitted to the expectations of the general Indian audience about tribal people as exotic and "other." The choreographers of the parade had calculated that the group could stop for two minutes and fifteen seconds in front of the Indian president to deliver a Wangala dance performance crafted precisely to fit the time slot. The choreographers had revamped and modernized the dance to ensure that it would meet the expectations of an urban, moviegoing audience. The performance was shown on national television as a part of the live broadcast of Republic Day. It was featured in other news media as well. The next day, the front page of the national daily, *The Hindu*, carried a large color photograph of the Wangala dance performance bearing the caption, "Showcasing Culture" (figure 2.3).[24] But what culture was being showcased for the eyes of the nation? How did the performance of the Wangala dance at Republic Day relate to other settings in which this dance is, or has been, performed?

The Garo are a minority community of about 850,000, about two-thirds of whom live in the northeastern state of Meghalaya. In Meghalaya, performances of Wangala dancing have over the last couple of decades gained public prominence. Whenever a government department, cultural organization, or political group hosts an event at which "Garo culture" needs to be represented, Wangala dancing plays a prominent role. On such occasions, a group of villagers or students is paid

FIGURE 2.3. The lead article on the front page of the national daily, *The Hindu*, reporting on the 2008 Republic Day celebrations (© The Hindu).

to perform in front of an audience. These kinds of performances are often covered in the regional press, usually accompanied by a photograph showing the dancers with their typical ornaments and dress. Images of Wangala dancing or Garos in Wangala attire are increasingly popular as illustrations for calendars produced by cultural or political organizations wanting to identify themselves as Garo. In addition, Wangala dancing features on popular photo- and video-sharing Internet sites.[25] All these are relatively novel ways in which Wangala dancing is performed and mediated.

Historically, Wangala dancing was but one element of a much more elaborate postharvest festival that played, and plays, a crucial role in the community religion of the Ambeng Garo, numerically and politically the most dominant section of the Garo community. According to scholarly accounts, including ethnographic sources, the Wangala festival is the most important of a series of annual rituals enabling people to advance the growth of crops and to create the conditions under which they can reap and consume the harvest.[26] Wangala is celebrated in the month of October after dry rice has been taken in from the swiddens.[27]

When the starting date is decided by the head of the village, adherents of the Garo community religion celebrate Wangala at the village level. At the start of the festival, families make offerings in their fields. In the house of the village head this offering is followed by a joint sacrifice and omen reading regarding crops in the year to come. Subsequently, a shaman chants the myth of creation as he dances, with many others, from inside the village headman's house onto the courtyard in front of it. There, a variety of dances is performed, in the course of which the deities are fed cooked rice (figure 2.4).

Among Garos, Wangala celebrations are less reputed for their sacrificial and predictive elements than for dancing, socializing, and most of all copious drinking of home-brewed rice beer. The last consumes the largest share of time and resources. Celebrating Wangala includes making the rounds of all the families involved with the community religion that reside in a particular village. One after the other, these families host a group of villagers, some of whom carry the drums used for the Wangala dancing. Whoever wants the group to visit them provides at least one vessel of rice beer. Each host is also expected to feed the visitors; the more abundant the better. People play music and sing. Most joke and tease each other seemingly without end. In the courtyard, near the house of the host, people dance to the rhythm of the drums. The celebration lasts several days, if not a week, continuing day and night. It also reputedly allows for unusually free interaction between unmarried men and women, preparing the ground for the marriage season that is soon to follow. The partying is open to visitors, not just people from the village, but other Garos and anyone else who shows up. Those who take part in the celebration are

FIGURE 2.4. Wangala dancing in a Garo village.

actively encouraged, even expected, to join in the dancing. The movements and steps are relatively easy to learn, allowing the participation of all. Consequently, dancing is a way to engage all who are present, and it contributes significantly to the creation of a Wangala sense of *communitas*.[28]

Going by ethnographic sources as well as what people say, it seems likely that Wangala has long been an important festival for the Ambeng Garo. But it is unlikely that Wangala enjoyed the same kind of prominence among other Garo subgroups, if they celebrated it at all. Historically, the various Garo subgroups adhered to broadly the same kinship model and mostly spoke one or the other dialect of Garo, but in other spheres of life there was considerable variation. Gradually, over the past century, a shared Garo identity has developed. In this process, Wangala dancing has emerged as a crucial unifying symbol.

It may come as a surprise that a dance from a celebration that is very important to the community religion has become a vital representation of Garo culture, since the vast majority of the Garos are Christians. Conversions began by the middle of the nineteenth century, when Australian missionaries introduced Christianity. Initially, Christianity was confined to an urban educated elite, and most Garo did not convert until the 1960s and 1970s. Conversion implied a prohibition against consulting or worshipping, thus acknowledging, deities associated with the Garo community religion. At least as important was a ban on the consumption of rice beer, probably due to its strong association with the community religion's rituals. In the few villages where people still celebrate Wangala, Christian families do not participate. In towns where the Garo community religion is in many ways a mere memory of a past way of life, village-style Wangala celebrations are altogether absent. Most Christian Garos are aware of such celebrations by way of locally made documentary films, most of which are sanctioned by the regional division of the state broadcasting corporation.

In Christian contexts, non-Christian deities are frequently referred to as "demons" or "devils," and many preachers maintain that all adherents of the community religion will eventually "burn in hell." This demonization of the community religion makes it difficult for Christian Garo to perceive their cultural present as a continuation of their past. Christian Garos tend to look at people who are continuing to practice the Garo community religion as oriented toward the past, an attitude that creates a structural inequality among these two catagories. This inequality resonates in other dimensions of life as well. People who practice the community religion are usually poor, having limited access to resources of the state, while town Garos (Christians) are, by comparison, not only relatively rich but also privileged in accessing political power.

Staged and mediatized performances of Wangala dancing connect the present to the past and the rural poor to the urban-educated rich. This unifying role is explicit in the Hundred Drums Wangala Festival organized annually by the government of the state of Meghalaya. At this festival ten dancing troupes compete. About half are made up of villagers; the rest feature college students. Performances are judged by a jury consisting of the urban elite such as local scholars and high-ranking civil servants. The festival attracts thousands and is one of the only events celebrated jointly by both adherents of the community religion and Christian Garo. The competition is usually won by people practicing the community religion, since "their sense of rhythm is much better than that of the students," as a prominent Garo folklorist and historian remarked.[29] Wangala dancing continues to be experienced as the prerogative of Garos practicing the community religion, whose performances the college students imitate. As one of the coaches involved with the preparations for the Republic Day Parade remarked about the educational value of college students learning Wangala dancing, "Wangala dancing is something of the non-Christians, but for the students it is important to get an idea how our ancestors engaged in merrymaking."[30]

(Re)Producing Cultural Heritage?

Once again, Dehra Dun is hosting the yearly national heritage festival, Virasat. For ten days, artists from the whole country will perform on the stage, presenting a well-disposed audience with the beautiful and unique heritage of India. Every evening starts with the performance of a local group, placing the heritage of Uttarakhand at the center of attention with the aim of creating feelings of pride and unity among Uttarakhandis in the audience. Tonight is supposed to start with the performance of Burhdeva, the local trickster god, famous for his wit and political satire. The festival ground is slowly filling up, and many of the visitors are still strolling through the handicraft stalls that surround the stage. Then, just as the sun is setting, speakers announce the performance of one of Garhwal's richest traditions, that of Burhdeva. To the beating of traditional drums and playing of a harmonium, a procession of people carrying a long pole with a golden mask representing the local deity Jakh makes its way through the crowd. Drums are beating the traditional sound of the god. Once the performers reach the stage, more instruments join, and a wild-looking man, his face obscured by a mask of black hair, starts dancing on the stage. His dance is vulgar. He jumps and jerks, making scary noises and stumbling across the stage looking wildly at musicians and audience. Then the music stops and the man starts abusing the audience, joking about local politicians and the bard's singing. The man is Narad, or Burhdev, the gods' messenger on earth. He is the master of ceremonies, performer of his own story, and audience for the other gods who will soon appear one after the other on stage.

So go staged performances of the ritual-theatrical tradition belonging to the deities Jakh and Chandikah of Chamoli Garhwal. Usually, this kind of performance happens in a village square in honor of the god, who is on pilgrimage through the villages of his disciples. For six or nine months he (or she if the god is Chandikah) and his entourage reside in a different village every other day. Low-caste musicians traveling with them are the owners of the drums, and they possess knowledge of the songs that bring the gods down to dance. The entourage also carries old wooden masks that are thought to contain the spirit of the gods. Every night during the pilgrimage eighteen masks need to be danced.

Narad, the trickster god, is the most important deity of the show. During a night's performance, he makes fun of what happened in the villages they have passed. He remarks on the generosity, or stinginess, of former hosts. He makes fun of one village's women and another's men, remarks about the many cats in one village, and people's strange habits in another. Every night, Narad's performer produces a new satire about Chamoli's villages, villagers, and local politicians. What he says is put on his tongue by a deity, the spirit of Narad. The person wearing Narad's mask becomes Narad. Narad not only reports on this year's pilgrimage, he also performs his own story. A deity born as a human, he has to go through all the phases that a Garhwali peasant passes through in his lifetime. For example, he needs to plow fields, get married, and raise children. On his way through life he meets many obstacles, fights with the *pandit*, quarrels with his bride's father, and dances with his wives. His tasks in the performance do not stop here. Narad is also master of ceremonies, watching carefully as the other deities dance before him. A full performance lasts all night, from sunset to sunrise, and the audience, once settled in, is advised not to leave the performance ground, as the presence of all the deities draws the attention of dangerous spirit beings that crawl closer in the dark, waiting for an innocent to leave the safety of lights and other human beings in order to attack.

In the context of a deity's procession, the masks are danced to honor the gods, to bless the land, and to entertain and inform the villagers. When Jakh is on pilgrimage, the performance needs to take place whether there is an audience or not. Until recently, the tradition was known only to the disciples of the deities to whom Narad's performance belongs. While the tradition is associated with the deities Jakh and Chandikah, the knowledge of the full stories, music, and dances that make the gods appear belongs to the low-caste bards and is handed down through one family. Because the music and rhythms that please and appease the spirits are deeply connected to the drums, higher-caste people, until very recently, would not have thought of playing this music. Roles in the performance are strictly divided according to caste hierarchies. The higher-caste people dance and take care of the god's insignia, masks, pole, and shrine, while the lower-caste bards are responsible for the appearance and control of deities. Without their drums and singing, the gods will not appear.

This tradition has recently been discovered by the intellectual elite of the region, who are mostly of high-caste origin and who have studied the tradition. With the help of modern media technology, they have been able to record the songs and produce videos of the performance. These recordings in turn have enabled them to write down the songs and music and learn to perform it themselves. A stage version was created for performance during local fairs, regional heritage festivals, and nationwide theater festivals in India. The theater groups formed were modern in the sense that they rejected caste hierarchies and the exclusion of women from the performance. Most musicians were high caste. Young girls danced on the stage, and low-caste people were involved in dancing. What was important to them was what they considered artistically valuable and unique to their region—the satire, the music, and the costumes.

Burhdeva has become a tradition representing the outstanding artistic skill and local color of Uttarakhand. The stage version was supposed to save the tradition from disappearance. Therefore, the makers of this version have also begun giving workshops to communities and schools so the young and educated people of the region can learn the songs and myths, perform the play, and, in the process, embody traditional movements. The hope is that young people will then get a sense of the traditions of their own region that are similar, yet superior, to the experience of the villagers who grow up with the village version of the performances.

The stage performance described in the beginning of this case study was enacted by a group of young people from the small market town of Gopeshwar in the center of Chamoli. Gopeshwar lies also in the center of the area where Burhdeva's tradition is performed in divine processions. Nearly every year, different forms of Jakh or Chandikah travel through this region with performances happening in many nearby villages. On ritually important days, local film teams, along with television and radio journalists, usually appear to report on the event.

One of the filmmakers produced a video of the day's and night's ritual events. He happened to be the brother-in-law of the local schoolteacher directing the Burhdeva play for the group of young people from Gopeshwar. The two decided to show the video to the group in order to improve their performance on stage. During their next performance, unexpected changes happened. The performer of Narad claimed to have been possessed by the real Burhdeva while performing. Having felt the god's power come over him while he was on stage, his performance had not been that of an actor, but that of a god. He had felt the power of the god in him, just like the village performers do when they put on the god's mask. Then, after the performance, backstage, one of the young actors started shaking wildly, dancing in the way a person does when possessed by a god. Dancing toward the teacher, he demanded that the god be honored and that the low-caste members of the group be excluded. The teacher said that similar scenes happened several times at different places where the students performed the play after they had seen the video. The possession became more and more violent and the demands more and more discriminatory against the low-caste members of the group until the teacher decided not to perform the play again.

Ritual "Owners": Commodification, Expectation, and Aspiration

In their influential study *The Archetypal Actions of Ritual*, Caroline Humphrey and James Laidlaw postulated that ritual acts have no intrinsic or socially enforced meaning.[31] Rather, ritual action is institutionalized action, the importance of which lies in what they call "ritual commitment."[32] According to Humphrey and Laidlaw, ritualized actions are, like nonritualized actions such as promising and thanking, socially and culturally institutionalized. The difference between ritualized and other action is that by acting with ritual commitment, one simultaneously authors one's actions, in the sense that the action is done in order to do ritual and gives up authorship in the sense that ritual actions have to be done a certain way; if they are not, the action is not ritual. A tourist who happens to put a flower on a Jain shrine has not performed a ritual act, because he or she did not do it as a ritual, but somebody who puts a flower down with ritual commitment, that is, with the intention to do *puja*,[33] performs a ritual act even if he or she does not know the name or meaning of the action. Humphrey and Laidlaw claim that the identity of a ritual does not depend on intentionality. A ritual action does not need to carry a certain meaning shared by a ritual community, but the action performed is still intentional in the sense that it is done with the intention to do *puja*. In other words, according to Humphrey and Laidlaw, people mimic an idea of what a ritual should look like.

While Humphrey and Laidlaw make it explicit that their theory concentrates on liturgical rituals, their ideas of ritual commitment and intentionality can be fruitfully applied to the practices that appear in our cases, which suggest that practitioners, performers, and audiences need not agree on the meaning of a ritual in order to agree that a ritual is important. It is important that participants consider their ritual important but not that they agree upon, or even know, the meanings of their actions.[34] By agreeing that a ritual is crucial, people define themselves as part of a group whose members share the experience and knowledge of that event, thus positioning themselves as its "owners." Therefore, changing a ritual in order to present it either as a single person's creative innovation or as the common heritage of people who may not always have thought of themselves as a unit is risky. Our three case studies suggest that ritual knowledge determines group membership. When Christian Thompson exerts ownership over the ritual knowledge passed on to him by his aunt, he places himself in a tradition that belongs specifically to Aboriginal Australia. However, his assertion that *The Fox* presents an initiation ritual incites controversy, because there is no shared agreement about the ritual importance of *The Fox*. On the other hand, in Uttarakhand the young people were stirred only when they realized that they were violating the rules of ritual commitment by performing a ritual onstage as if it were a piece of theater art. In that sense they acted like the tourist who puts down a flower in front of a shrine for aesthetic or romantic reasons. The video, however, reconnected their actions on stage with their sense of their own ritual heritage. Therefore their actions onstage changed.

The three case studies show that alterations of ritual practices into performance or art, changes made to meet the expectations of a specific audience, and commodifications of rituals all imply statements about who people are or wish to become. The Indigenous artist clearly understands himself to be the owner of a certain piece of ritual knowledge and thinks it fit to use that knowledge in his art. However, his creative use of ritual and his claim to have constructed a new form of initiation ritual clash with the expectations and convictions of his audience. In claiming to have created a new initiation ritual, Thompson, an individual, makes a statement to a community of Indigenous and non-Indigenous people. In doing so, he transgresses one of the unwritten rules of ritual—individuals cannot, or should not, change ritual practices. The two Indian case studies, however, show that altering a ritual performance to fit the aesthetic demands of a stage does not necessarily lead to dispute.

The appropriation of ritual practices for artistic purposes conveys a message about artists and performers. The artist of Australian Aboriginal origin claims that he identifies not only with his Aboriginal but also with his European and Australian origins. Two different Indian communities perform themselves on the heritage stages of India. Putting ritual performances on stages cleared of "superstition" declares each group's unity as well as its modernity. Such performances condense what they consider the essence and beauty of "their tradition," a deeply rooted pan-Indian idea facilitating simultaneous identification with and differentiation from others. In all three case studies, we are confronted with what Appadurai calls "intentional cultural reproduction."[35]

In the course of becoming intentional reproductions of culture, the performances may seem no longer to be ritual practices. Rather, they became ritually informed art forms and statements of belonging to a particular social milieu. Thompson makes a statement about himself as an artist of international standing; Garo dancers present themselves as representatives of a specific community while they are at the same time modern Indian subjects; and the Garhwali producers of traditional theater see themselves as part of a global community of theater lovers.

The aesthetic transformations described in our three case studies have a similar dynamic. In all three instances, changes in ritual traditions function as statements about what those engaged in the performances wish to be. People perform themselves and their role in the world. According to Bourdieu, aesthetic understanding is part of a person's habitus, one's habitual way of being in the world. Understanding what is aesthetic and what is not—in other words, taste—depends more on cultural and social background than objectivity. Christiane Brosius, a visual and media anthropologist, claims that aesthetic values are shared worldwide among people of a certain class.[36] Taking the examples of the new Indian middle class in India, London, New York, or any other megacity on the globe, she argues that a certain shared understanding of aesthetic values in ritual practice, performance, and everyday life distinguishes those who are middle class from those who are not. These are no fixed states. If a group or an individual person wishes to claim membership in a certain class or group, aesthetics play an important role and can be used to underline this claim. It is in this sense that we consider the changes in ritual aesthetics in all three case studies as part of the performance of what people want to be or become.

Christian Thompson wants to clarify that he, like most contemporary Indigenous Australians, is of many heritages. The Indian performers enact their modernity on stage. In performing their heritage the way they do, objectifying and aestheticizing their traditions, the young performers claim to be modern and yet distinct from Western modernity. They claim to be modern Indians who maintain important values without being backward and superstitious. The young people of Uttarakhand consider themselves modern, not needing justification by way of old traditions. On the contrary, they perceive professionalization and aestheticization as a violation of their roots. Thus, these youngsters turn back to what their teacher wants to deny, reintroducing divinity back into the tradition. In their view, the divinity does not allow herself to be excluded from the ritual performances.

Our argument runs contrary to those claiming that recent changes in ritual weaken or destroy tradition. During the past decades, much of the literature dealing with mediatization has argued that such changes are merely a commodification for tourists or consumers.[37] The owners of these traditions do not see it that way. In the first case study, an Indigenous Australian artist engages with ritual knowledge that, due to the detrimental effects of colonization, has become fragmented. In reaction to the destructive forces that have shaped Aboriginal histories, Thompson, like most Indigenous Australians today, reconfigures and revitalizes cultural forms from his past.[38]

Likewise, the demonization of animism that occurred after the introduction of Christianity among the Garo makes it difficult for Christian Garo to conceive of the present as a continuation of their cultural past. Staged performances of Wangala dancing have emerged in recent years as a cultural expression linking the present to the past. Staged events in new contexts enable Christian Garo as well as Garo audiences to connect with their cultural heritage today. Apart from newly created stage performances, Wangala dancing is now featured on calendars, the Internet, television, newspapers, and national stages such as those provided by the 2008 Republic Day Parade. In the third case study, the fear of religious disappearance is explicit. Wishing to keep their tradition alive among young educated Uttarakhandis, participants create the stage version. Local people do not see aesthetic transformation as commodification ultimately destroying their traditions but as tools enabling them creatively to include their ritual heritage in modern life. The two Indian case studies show that tradition has become a value in its own right.

The artists involved in these transitions are as much concerned with questions of authenticity as in the creative possibilities their rituals provide. These artists want to make sure that their performances are linked to but differentiated from earlier ritual, a combination that enables them to make statements of desire and community membership. The initiatory presentation by Christian Thompson's *Fox* video, for example, is an amalgam of Indigenous and non-Indigenous styles, knowledge, philosophies, and influences. Using the media of video and sculpture, Thompson has reworked an Indigenous ritual in its fragmented form into a form that he labels neither exclusively Indigenous nor non-Indigenous. *I Need You / You Need Me (The Fox)*, which portrays a twenty-first-century initiation ritual in an urban landscape, is intended to convey an alternative to the often articulated expectation that Aboriginal and non-Aboriginal peoples, cultures, and identities are largely incommensurable. Thompson remarks, "My family is really caught between traditional philosophies about life, but adopted Western ideologies as well. I feel that that has been a very defining point in my work and my life.... I have always seen myself as a fusion of many different influences. I have always felt connected with every part of my heritage. I have never denied anything."[39]

Similarly, Wangala dancing, performed and mediated in novel ways, is no longer exclusively attached to its roots in the elaborate Ambeng Garo postharvest village festivals. Today, dancers are paid to execute performances deemed Garo culture and treated as a symbol of unity.

Finally, the stage version of the Burhdeva performance in the central Himalayas, carried out during fairs, heritage festivals, and theater festivals, has come to represent the artistic skill and local color of the region. The local elite aspired to preserve what they deemed the core of their tradition, an aesthetic version of the divine performance. In their folklorized and modernized version, there was no place for the deity. The elite intended to create a link between what they understood to be their cultural heritage and what they wanted to be, part of a global modern intellectual community interested in the beauty of art and performance.

Our three case studies reveal how people perform their modernity while at the same time stressing their links to tradition. Aestheticization and commodification are processes of creativity instigated by individual brokers as well as by groups. These creative processes, generative of alternative modernities, are part of local discourses on global and traditional disadvantages and advantages, on people's hopes and fears. Aestheticized ritual practices are statements of intentional cultural reproduction that often, but not always, generate conflict.

Evaluating Ritual Performances

The aestheticization and mediatization of ritual traditions often creates controversy. At the same time, the presentation of ritual knowledge in new forms and new contexts also serves the cause of dialogue across differences. Wangala dancing, for instance, has become a unifying symbol, bringing together Christian and non-Christian Garo. Staged performances of this dance, such as the one performed at the Hundred Drums Wangala Festival, cross boundaries between the rural poor and urban, educated, wealthy Garo communities. Contemporary Wangala dancing produces affiliations between the Indian state and one of its minority groups. In the case of Indigenous Australian photomedia art, we have seen how Thompson challenges habitual distinctions between so-called Indigenous and non-Indigenous people. His use of the fox as a totemic being to represent a group of people at once Indigenous and non-Indigenous emphasizes interrelationships and simultaneously presents an argument for redefining the categories to which people belong.

Mediatized and aestheticized reinterpretations of ritual knowledge do not necessarily induce conflict; they sometimes feed into existing conflicts. The Indian state categorizes the Garo as a tribe. The term refers to a form of social organization that differs from that used by the majority of the population. One document published by the state defines tribes as people "known to dwell in compact areas, follow a community way of living, in harmony with nature, and have a uniqueness of culture, distinctive customs, traditions and beliefs which are simple, direct and non-acquisitive by nature."[40]

This definition carries with it an assumption that tribal people are especially vulnerable, requiring the state to take protective measures. Categorizing the Garo as a tribe has brought important economic, administrative, judicial, and educational benefits. In Meghalaya, the Indian state in which the majority of the Garo reside, tribal people are exempt from paying income tax. A substantial share of government jobs are reserved for Garos, as are seats in schools and colleges. Elsewhere in India, other tribes enjoy comparable benefits. These are of such magnitude that groups not categorized as tribal make an effort to match the criteria set by the Indian state so they can qualify for such benefits.

A religion such as Garo animism, which Wangala dancing continues to be associated with, is, in popular Indian perception, derived from time immemorial, suggesting that the Garo are a community indigenous to the subcontinent. The presence of such indigenous groups is assumed to have preceded the arrival of people who later settled the area. These sorts of associations render performances and mediatizations of Wangala dancing fit to support the projects of politically and culturally vocal Garo groups, such as student unions and political parties. These groups advance far-reaching claims about regional autonomy based on the assumption that the Garo were the area's "original" people. It is an issue that can generate bitter conflict fought both inside and outside of politics. Brochures and calendars of politically active groups favor photographs of Wangala dancing, substantiating the presumed primordial connections of the Garo to the area in which they are a majority community. However, with the inclusion of Wangala dancing in the Republic Day Parade, the Indian state appeals to the symbolic value of Wangala dancing as well. Rather than supporting a secessionist agenda, the dance performance is used to display the loyalty of a community to the Indian state.

In the case of the Burhdeva performances in the Indian Himalayas, similar conflicts over resources and the construction of national and regional identities are involved. In addition, a clash of generations results in a different kind of conflict. Recall the schoolteacher who taught the modern version of the performance to a group of local young people. After a few performances, members of the group started to feel the presence of the deity. Backstage a discourse erupted, becoming increasingly violent and discriminating toward the lower-caste members of the group. What had happened? Several groups of young Garhwalis had learned and performed this play on previous occasions. Some had claimed to have felt the powers of the gods, but they had never been possessed, nor did the deity demand that the rules of purity be reinstated. What was different this time? The schoolteacher happened to be a relative of the professional filmmaker who had made a video during one of the village performances. After the group had gone through the first workshop with the creators of the Burhdeva play, the schoolteacher played these videotapes to his group members. He had wanted them to see how the performance looked in the village so that they could perform even more authentically on stage. However, when the young actors saw that video, things got out of hand. Watching villagers only thirty kilometers away worshipping the deities fundamentally altered the young people's understanding of the performance. Somehow, something that had earlier been experienced as play suddenly became real in the sense that the youth realized the deity was indeed present. While they were all from the region and proud of the region's opportunities for schooling and higher education, ritual traditions were not as present in their daily lives as they are in the life of a Garhwali villager. However, many deities travel through the region, stopping in Gopeshwar. During these stops, people are often possessed by deities. Thus, the schoolteacher's students easily grasped what they had seen on the video. The schoolteacher had intended the staged play to be a purely aesthetic version of the performance, void of any "superstitious" acts such as possession. Consequently, the staged version was not effective in transferring the understanding that the tradition was deeply embedded in the religious traditions of the region. The video, however, readily conveyed this message. The video also brought conflicts to the fore that had until then been hidden under the cloak of education and the wish to be distinguished men and women. The possibility of divine intervention reintroduced caste discrimination into the group at the same time as it articulated a critique of those who wanted to change the tradition and, by implication, its people.

In our view, the ascription of meaning and value to staged performances and visual art[41] depends on viewing contexts and people's expectations, along with their gender, class, ethnic origin, sexuality, and religion.[42] When evaluating performances, people accept some deviations from what they consider the normative form of a ritual. However, they may also feel that there is a boundary, sometimes visible, sometimes not, that should never be crossed. While some ritual practices may be changed and adapted, other things simply should never be done, and if they are, the performance ceases to be part of what people consider tradition, and their disapproval is all but assured. This disapproval results partially from the fact that people's sense for ritual is acquired through embodied learning. Religious studies scholar Catherine Bell argues that bodies are shaped and changed through ritual practice.[43] In her view and ours, one's sense of ritual is embodied, and it develops over time. Ritual has the power to produce changes and is not merely an expression of personal dispositions. She writes, "The ritualized body has a sense of ritual that produces a certain sociocultural situation that the ritualized body can somehow dominate."[44] Body and cultural space are intimately related. As Bell puts it, "Space and time are redefined through the physical movements of bodies projecting organizing schemes on the space-time environment on the one hand while reabsorbing these schemes as the nature of reality on the other."[45]

The young students staging a performance in the Himalayas had an embodied sense of ritual that seemed initially to prevent their connecting the "purified" stage version with traditional religious sentiments. Alternatively, perhaps their traditionally embodied sense of ritual was so strong that the students were unable to accept a merely folklorized version of the ritual. In either case, their watching the video created a powerful connection. The mediatized ritual ignited possession, and because the conflicts were of a ritual nature, they were played out in a ritualistic manner, through possession.

Because ritual knowledge is physical as well as intellectual, it is difficult to process drastic changes quickly, thus people's strong, angry reactions to rapid, drastic change. Disapproval is evident in the resistance of young Garhwalis to the schoolteacher's revision of the Burhdeva performance. Similarly, significant artistic adaptation of ritual traditions in the case of Christian Thompson's *Fox* video leads to harsh criticism, which ultimately questions the authenticity of the artist's ritual knowledge.

Rituals have aesthetic aspects, and vice versa: aesthetic performances have ritual aspects. Both aspects matter. Some ritual performances become signifiers for national or regional identities, while others are regarded as inauthentic performances by people not considered the true owners or conveyers of tradition. The aesthetics of possession and wild ecstasy, for instance, do not promote pristine, nostalgic feelings. When a ritual shifts from a traditional ritual ground to a modern or public stage, several things happen at once. Not only does the relationship between audience and performers change, elevating a ritual's aesthetic dimensions, it transforms from the everyday to something special. This heightening makes the performance modern and mainstream, but this aestheticized stage presentation also inhibits the participation of deities, thus calling into question the ritual commitments of producers, performers, and audience members.[46] Hence, we argue with religious studies scholars Ron Williams and James Boyd, "a change in the aesthetic representation of a ritual may include a change in the efficacy of the performance."[47]

Wangala dancing, when presented as a staged performance representing a state or region, apparently does not heal, make fertile, or bless the people who perform and watch. However, people still perceive staged performances as connected to the ritual traditions that lie behind them. Because people do not clearly distinguish between ritual ground and theatrical stage, they struggle to understand the kind of efficacy exerted by ritual performances.

Considering the broad variations in our three case studies, what unites them? One thing is the central importance of aesthetically framed bodily movement.

Quick motions by a performer-artist recorded on video evoke an animal spirit initiation. A three-minute dance performance paraded before political authorities signifies a whole cultural tradition. The staged re-creation of a nightlong ritual summons the gods through masks and music. All three cases contain rehearsed, repeatable, temporally compressed, electronically mediated movement produced for the sake of artistic performance.

Another commonality is the fact that each case exhibits a shift in expectations about efficacy when rituals shift from one geographical or cultural context to another. One must always ask, efficacious for whom? From whose perspective? The teacher-director had a different notion of what counts as a successful result than did his students swept up in possession by the divinity. Likewise, the expectation that the dancing team would enable Garo Christians to understand their historical tradition of merrymaking is one that only partially represents the culture of the dance troupe. Efficacy is partly, but not only, in the eye of the beholder, and it is based on complex factors that shape people's expectations and experiences. These manifold perceptions and goals are fertile grounds for conflict.

NOTES

1. Marianne Riphagen (coauthor of this chapter) has collaborated with urban-based Indigenous Australian artists for several years. Her work with four artists, Christian Thompson, Brook Andrew, Darren Siwes, and Dianne Jones, will result in a PhD thesis about the construction of meaning and value for Indigenous Australian photomedia art within institutional art worlds. This research project, completed in 2010, was sponsored by the Australian Department of Education, Science and Training (today known as the Department of Education, Employment and Workplace Relations) as well as by the Netherlands Organization for Scientific Research (NWO/MAGW).

2. For a lengthy discussion on capital, see Pierre Bourdieu, *The Logic of Practice* (Cambridge: Polity Press, 1990).

3. The Frankfurt School came into existence in the mid-1920s as an association of left-wing intellectuals grouped around the Institute for Social Research in Frankfurt. It comprises sociologists, psychologists, political scientists, literary critics, philosophers, and economists, of whom Walter Benjamin, Jürgen Habermas, Theodor Adorno, and Leo Lowenthal are the main figures. An engagement with critical theory, most importantly Kantian critical philosophy and the Marxian tradition of ideological critique, unites these scholars. Theodor Adorno (1903–1969), leading figure of the Frankfurt School, is considered one of Germany's most influential philosophers and social critics after World War II. Adorno critiqued contemporary Western society and wrote about, among other things, existential philosophy, aesthetic theory, music criticism, and sociology.

4. See Richard Schechner, *Between Theatre and Anthropology* (Philadelphia: University of Pennsylvania Press, 1985); Victor Turner, *From Ritual to Theatre: The Human Seriousness of Play* (New York: PAJ, 1985); Victor Turner, *The Anthropology of Performance* (New York: PAJ, 1986).

5. See for example Diane Taylor, *The Archive and the Repertoire* (Durham, NC: Duke University Press, 2006).

6. Centre for Contemporary Photography, *Black on White: An Exhibition of Photographs by Aboriginal Artists Representing Non-Aboriginality* (Melbourne: Centre for Contemporary Photography, 2005), n.p.

7. Kelly Gellatly, "Is There an Aboriginal Photography?" in *The Oxford Companion to Aboriginal Art and Culture*, eds. Sylvia Kleinert and Margo Neale (Oxford: Oxford University Press, 2000), 286.

8. Centre for Contemporary Photography, *Black on White*, n.p.

9. Christian Thompson, personal conversation with author, May 2, 2006.

10. Centre for Contemporary Photography, *Black on White*, n.p.

11. Christian Thompson, personal conversation with author, June 6, 2006.

12. Thompson, June 6, 2006.

13. Thompson, April 18, 2006.

14. Robert Tonkinson, "The Pragmatics and Politics of Aboriginal Tradition and Identity in Australia," *Journal de la Societe des Oceanistes* 109, no. 2 (1999): 133–147.

15. Thompson, February 11, 2009.

16. Thompson, June 6, 2006.

17. Centre for Contemporary Photography, *Black on White*, n.p.

18. Thompson, June 6, 2006.

19. Thompson, June 6, 2006.

20. Marianne Riphagen, "Black on White: Or Varying Shades of Grey? Indigenous Australian Photo-media Artists and the 'Making of' Aboriginality," *Australian Aboriginal Studies* no. 1 (2008): 78–89.

21. Émile Durkheim, *The Elementary Forms of the Religious Life*, trans. Joseph Ward Swain (New York: Macmillan, 1915), 206.

22. The author showed *The Fox* as part of the delivery of a research paper, on September 4, 2006, at the Australian Institute of Aboriginal and Torres Strait Islander Studies (AIATSIS) in Canberra, Australia. Furthermore, she presented this work of art to academics in private sessions to gain insight into the range of interpretations ascribed to *The Fox*. The responses described in this chapter derive from these occasions. To protect the privacy of those who have commented on *The Fox*, no proper names are used.

23. Elizabeth Povinelli, *The Power, History, and Culture of Aboriginal Action* (Chicago: University of Chicago Press, 1994), 74.

24. Devesh K. Pandey, "Military Might, Cultural Heritage on Display at Republic Day Parade," *The Hindu*, January 27, 2008, Delhi city edition.

25. On YouTube, see http://nl.youtube.com/results?search_query=wangala&search_type=&aq=f. To search Google Video, go to http://video.google.com/videosearch?q=Wangala&emb=0&;aq=f#. For Flickr, see http://www.flickr.com/search/?q=wangala.

26. For example, see Robbins Burling, *Rengsanggri: Family and Kinship in a Garo Village* (Philadelphia: University of Philadelphia Press, 1963); Alan Playfair, *The Garos* (Gauhati: United Publishers, 1975); Milton S. Sangma, *History and Culture of the Garos* (New Delhi: Books Today, 1981). Erik de Maaker (coauthor of this chapter) has done extensive fieldwork among the Garo of Meghalaya, which resulted in the PhD thesis,

Negotiating Life (Leiden University). The research project was sponsored by the Netherlands Foundation for the Advancement of Tropical Research (NWO/WOTRO) as well as the Indian Council for Cultural Relations.

27. Dry rice is cultivated on swiddens. Until a couple of decades ago it appears to have been the major staple crop. In recent decades, the yields have fallen dramatically due to degradation of the soil, but it is also likely that the rains in the region have become less frequent and less intense.

28. Victor Turner, *The Ritual Process: Structure and Anti-structure* (Chicago: Aldine, 1969).

29. Professor Milton Sangma, personal conversation, fall 1999.

30. Conversation with one of the coaches of the Garo students performing at the Republic Day Parade, January 2008.

31. Caroline Humphrey and James Laidlaw, *The Archetypal Actions of Ritual: A Theory of Ritual Illustrated by the Jain Rite of Worship* (Oxford: Clarendon Press, 1994).

32. Humphrey and Laidlaw, *The Archetypal Actions of Ritual*, 97–100.

33. *Puja* is a general term for any kind of worship for Jains, Hindus, and Buddhists alike.

34. Stanley Tambiah put this idea nicely into words: "I am persuaded that human beings everywhere commonly structure certain events which they consider important in a similar way, events which we can recognize as ritual, and that there are good reasons why they should do so." Stanley Tambiah, *Culture, Thought, and Social Action: An Anthropological Perspective* (London: Harvard University Press, 1985), 125.

35. Arjun Appadurai, *Modernity at Large: Cultural Dimensions of Globalization* (Minneapolis: University of Minnesota Press, 1996).

36. Christiane Brosius, *India Shining: Cosmopolitan Pleasures of India's New Middle Classes* (New Delhi: Routledge, 2009).

37. For a lengthy discussion, see Ute Hüsken and Christiane Brosius, eds., *Ritual Matters* (New Delhi: Routledge, 2009).

38. Tonkinson, "The Pragmatics and Politics of Aboriginal Tradition and Identity in Australia," 133–147.

39. Christian Thompson, personal conversation with author, April 18, 2006.

40. Ministry for Tribal Affairs, draft for *A National Tribal Policy* (published online by the Ministry for Tribal Affairs, most probably 2004).

41. Dereck Prize and Liz Wells, "Thinking about Photography: Debates, Historically and Now," in *Photography: A Critical Introduction*, ed. Liz Wells (New York: Routledge, 2004), 9–64.

42. Graham Clarke, *The Photograph* (Oxford: Oxford University Press, 1997), 27.

43. Catherine Bell, *Ritual Theory, Ritual Practice* (New York: Oxford University Press, 1992).

44. Bell, *Ritual Theory, Ritual Practice*, 98.

45. Bell, *Ritual Theory, Ritual Practice*, 99.

46. For more on the idea of ritual commitment, see Humphrey and Laidlaw, *The Archetypal Actions of Ritual*.

47. Ron G. Williams and James W. Boyd, "Aesthetics," in *Theorizing Rituals: Topics, Approaches, Concepts*, ed. Jens Kreinath, Michael Stausberg, and Jan Snoek (Leiden: Brill, 2006), 298.

REFERENCES

Appadurai, Arjun. *Modernity at Large: Cultural Dimensions of Globalization*. Minneapolis: University of Minnesota Press, 1996.
Barthes, Roland. "Rhetoric of the Image." In *The Photography Reader*, edited by Liz Wells, 114–125. New York: Routledge, 2003.
Becker, Howard. *Art Worlds*. Berkeley: University of California Press, 1982.
Bell, Catherine. *Ritual Theory, Ritual Practice*. New York: Oxford University Press, 1992.
Bourdieu, Pierre. *The Logic of Practice*. Cambridge: Polity Press, 1990.
Brosius, Christiane. *India Shining: Cosmopolitan Pleasures of India's New Middle Classes*. New Delhi: Routledge, 2009.
Burling, Robbins. *Rengsanggri: Family and Kinship in a Garo Village*. Philadelphia: University of Philadelphia Press, 1963.
Centre for Contemporary Photography. *Black on White: An Exhibition of Photographs by Aboriginal Artists Representing Non-Aboriginality*. Melbourne: Centre for Contemporary Photography, 2005.
Clarke, Graham. *The Photograph*. Oxford: Oxford University Press, 1997.
Durkheim, Émile. *The Elementary Forms of the Religious Life*, trans. Joseph Ward Swain. New York: Macmillan, 1915.
Gellatly, Kelly. "Is There an Aboriginal Photography?" In *The Oxford Companion to Aboriginal Art and Culture*, edited by Sylvia Kleinert and Margo Neale, 284–291. Oxford: Oxford University Press, 2000.
Humphrey, Caroline, and James Laidlaw. *The Archetypal Actions of Ritual: A Theory of Ritual Illustrated by the Jain Rite of Worship*. Oxford: Clarendon Press, 1994.
Hüsken, Ute, and Christiane Brosius, ed. *Ritual Matters*. New Delhi: Routledge, 2009.
Kapferer, Bruce. *The Feast of the Sorcerer: Practices of Consciousness and Power*. Chicago: University of Chicago Press, 1997.
Pandey, Devesh K. "Military Might, Cultural Heritage on Display at Republic Day Parade." *The Hindu*, January 27, 2008, Delhi city edition.
Playfair, Alan. *The Garos*. Gauhati: United Publishers, 1975.
Povinelli, Elizabeth. *The Power, History, and Culture of Aboriginal Action*. Chicago: University of Chicago Press, 1994.
Prize, Dereck, and Liz Wells. "Thinking about Photography: Debates, Historically and Now." In *Photography: A Critical Introduction*, edited by Liz Wells, 9–64. New York: Routledge, 2004.
Riphagen, Marianne. "Black on White: Or Varying Shades of Grey? Indigenous Australian Photo-media Artists and the 'Making of' Aboriginality." *Australian Aboriginal Studies* no. 1 (2008): 78–89.
Sangma, Milton S. *History and Culture of the Garos*. New Delhi: Books Today, 1981.
Schechner, Richard. *Between Theatre and Anthropology*. Philadelphia: University of Pennsylvania Press, 1985.
Tambiah, Stanley. *Culture, Thought, and Social Action: An Anthropological Perspective*. London: Harvard University Press, 1985.
Taylor, Diane. *The Archive and the Repertoire*. Durham, NC: Duke University Press, 2006.

Tonkinson, Robert. "The Pragmatics and Politics of Aboriginal Tradition Australia." *Journal de la Societe des Oceanistes* 109, no. 2 (1999): 133–

Turner, Victor. *The Anthropology of Performance*. New York: PAJ, 1986.

———. *From Ritual to Theatre: The Human Seriousness of Play*. New Yo

———. *The Ritual Process: Structure and Anti-structure*. Chicago: Aldine

Williams, Ron G., and James W. Boyd. "Aesthetics." In *Theorizing Rituals Approaches, Concepts*, edited by Jens Kreinath, Michael Stausberg, a 285–306. Leiden: Brill, 2006.

3

Insurgents and Icons

Anna-Karina Hermkens and Eric Venbrux

People sometimes resort to violence when a familiar ritual or sacred image is disturbed or attacked. The threats following the publication of Danish cartoons depicting the prophet Muhammad are examples of such a response.[1] The usual way of explaining this kind of outrage is to treat it as intrinsic to religious identity and assume that people respond violently when their religious beliefs are attacked.[2] Our approach focuses less on beliefs than on practices, specifically on ritual practices and media practices. To that end, we wrestle with several questions: How are rituals related to mediatized global icons deployed in acts of protest? And how may such fights with rituals lead to both internal and external conflict?

According to Alan Klima, "A great deal of what has come to be common sense about the representation of graphic violence in modern mass media could benefit from fundamental reconsideration."[3] While acknowledging the global underpinnings of this new era, one in which images matter, Klima notes that conventional analysis of images tends to follow "the narrative principles of modernity discourse," thereby failing to see how images are implicated in the process. Consequently, he argues, analysis itself has become "closely tied to mass media's own project."[4] As an antidote, Klima argues for "a very different economy from that of the media images circulating over the surface of the globe,"[5] an economy that stresses the mutability of global and local technologies of imaging. Drawing on the imagery of Buddhist funeral rituals and meditation, and predicated on cyclical violent conflict, he shows the social and cultural embeddedness of Thai political ritual, showing that local events go well beyond the media and cannot be attributed solely to a historical agency called modernity. He does not deny mass media's importance to people all over the world but tries rather to answer a significant question: "How could the media be divested of 'real life,' when the media is, to some extent, our life?"[6] For him, real life and media are not separate from one another; for one thing, without resonance in local life worlds, media imagery cannot be a political resource.

Here, Hermkens focuses on images of the Virgin Mary in Bougainville, Papua New Guinea, and Venbrux, on images of the Trevi Fountain in Rome, Italy. Following Arjun Appadurai, we argue that such images both evoke and require "mass-mediated sodalities of worship and charisma."[7] Images of Mary and Trevi Fountain become the occasions for charismatically inspired parachurch organizations. The sodalities in Rome will not allow images of Trevi to be used for conveying deviant messages that might cause a rupture in what is collectively known, performed, and anticipated. As a result of both deviance and the attempts of sodalities to control it, conflicts arise. Drawing the attention of wider audiences, the images we examine are used as symbolic vehicles that empower local actors to mark their positions in conflict or war. They allow political actors to appropriate the images' power for their own use.

These case studies highlight another feature of mediatized ritual imagery, namely, the interaction of local meanings and imagining practices with ritual. The ritual dynamics of conflict are often overlooked in the literature, which focuses mainly on divergent interpretations and conflicts of interest.[8] By contrast, the cases in this chapter focus on the local appropriation of global ritual imagery to empower particular actors or agents.

Bougainville is an island and autonomous province of Papua New Guinea in the Pacific, where the Virgin Mary—a figure who is institutionalized in religious practices and rituals worldwide—was appropriated locally and conflated with traditional beliefs and practices. During the secessionist war of 1988–1998, these beliefs and practices gained momentum, as localized forms of Catholicism, especially concerning Mary, had considerable impact on the conflict and how it was resolved. Yet surprisingly, religion is virtually absent from studies of the conflict; most of the analyses emphasize neocolonial power relations and political economy.[9] However, we argue that Mary and her imagery were appropriated into local secessionist protests and violent practices of resistance, as well as into local peace efforts. For the Bougainville Revolutionary Army (BRA), as the "rebels," or secessionist movement, called themselves, Mary was central to their fight for independence from Papua New Guinea. Indeed, the ritual image of the Virgin Mary, or Mama Maria as she is called locally, and her appropriation by the BRA legitimated their secessionist warfare, turning it into a holy war. This image of Mary and the rituals associated with her, especially praying the rosary and performing a pilgrimage, evoked local and global protests. Local protests came from the Bougainville Catholic Church as well as from Seventh-Day Adventists, who were blamed for demolishing several statues of Mary. Global protests of the BRA's appropriation of Mary included Dutch Christians who responded to an article in the Dutch newspaper *Trouw*, which covered the role of Mary in Bougainville. They objected strongly to her being "used" in relation to violence. Other commentators objected to what they regarded as the "worship" of Mary by saying that only God deserves worship.[10] This brief example illustrates how global Marian imagery is appropriated in a local fight, thereby stirring up both internal conflict between Catholics and external conflict between Catholics and non-Catholics.[11] The example also shows how mediatization can stir up transnational debates about the proper ritual use of Mary.

Our second example is the "sacrilege" of the famous Trevi Fountain in Rome that occurred when an activist turned its waters red, making it look like blood, on October 19, 2007 (see figure 3.1). Once news of the outrageous act hit the world media, its purposeful irreverence toward this hallowed place became a powerful instrument in a local cultural fight closely tied to a whole stream of political undercurrents in Italy. The attack on Trevi protested the millions spent on media events and advertising to promote the "lackluster" Rome Film Festival. The world-famous

FIGURE 3.1. Tourists photographing the red-dyed Trevi Fountain in Rome (photo: Gregorio Borgia/AP, printed with permission).

fountain, by contrast, offers free publicity. Trevi is a major tourist attraction; thousands of visitors ritually toss coins into the fountain. Not surprisingly, then, the assault on this cultural heritage site and its related commercial interests shocked media pundits and power holders in the Eternal City. Although symbolic, the act was perceived as inflicting tremendous damage on Rome's money-generating image in the world. The gesture was also meant to imply that Italy itself was degenerating. Authorities responded by dispatching police to the scene to investigate the crime. Celebrities, too, spoke out. The violation of Rome's sacred image enraged actress Anita Ekberg, whose nightly splashing in the waters of Trevi in Fellini's *La Dolce Vita* had made both her and the fountain famous. Indeed, this 1960 film scene had become part of the collective memory of movie fans around the globe. The artist-activist who threw red dye into the fountain drew on this well-known cinematic imagery, along with the traditional tourist imagery of offering coins. In addition, coloring Trevi's waters blood red alluded to the fact that the Rome Film Festival featured prominent images of rolled-out red carpet on its posters. The red carpet, of course, refers to the glamor and glitter of film premieres and festival openings, a ritualized affair that, in the view of the protesters, masked the shallow nature of the films being shown—films having "no depth, no color"—and highlighted the waste of money, to the detriment of local artists.

Marketers were quick to turn the subversive act into a unique selling point: the red Trevi was the lifeblood of Rome, proof that the city was still very much alive and a source of creativity. As one commentator noted, photographs of the blood-red fountain, unlike the film festival, had made a splash worldwide, thereby placing Rome in the spotlight for free.[12] Ironically, then there were succeeding waves of appropriation. By appropriating the activist's ritual gesture of protest, marketers succeeded in diverting the media coverage into support for Rome's vested interests. At the same time, all this local conflict gained global attention by means of widespread media coverage.

Mary and Trevi Fountain

What do Mary and Trevi Fountain have in common? At first sight, they seem wholly incommensurate. Both case studies illustrate how conflicts make use of media in such a way that the local interacts with the global and ritualization with mediatization. Mary, the mother of Jesus, in whom Catholics all over the world put their faith, is variously considered a saint, holy virgin, holy mother, mother of God, and mediatrix. Trevi Fountain, on the other hand, is an architectural centerpiece of Rome. The figure of Mary is related to religious belief, while Trevi Fountain is part of Rome's material culture, and it dates to the pre-Christian legend of the virgin who discovered its water source. People make pilgrimages to the famous fountain, which is close to the Vatican, headquarters of international Catholicism, while in remote Bougainville, people move Mary around by transporting statues and images, that is, material representations, of the Virgin. Nevertheless, what Mary and the fountain have in common is that they are both ritualized and mediatized icons that convey particular messages and sentiments. Mary is a globally recognized religious icon, while Trevi Fountain is a predominantly local and national one. Both are representative symbols that stand for particular values and identities whose meanings are mediated through capturing, materializing, and circulating particular properties.

Mary and her virtues are manifested in various ways: through apparitions at particular places and representation of her in texts, images, statues, and on the Internet, as well as in related rituals such as praying the rosary. This manifold materiality means that Mary, in effect, circulates around the globe, mediating her particular meanings and values. Whereas the geographical space of Trevi Fountain is fixed, media coverage guarantees that the fountain and its associated rituals are circulating around the globe while simultaneously being internalized and expressed in Roman culture. Materiality and mobility thus allow images of Mary and the fountain to cross contexts,[13] linking specific localities with the global. Marian devotees may express their dedication on local, national, and international levels, but people's experiences of Mary are affected by the interplay between the local and the global. Thus through the transnational use of Mary's images and related rituals, people become interconnected. Each image or devotional act stands not only for Mary but also for the connection between her devotees and nondevotees, as the Dutch protest against Mary's deployment in Bougainville's secessionist struggle suggests.

Representations of Trevi Fountain illustrate the importance of photography, video, film, television, print media, and the Internet in conveying information and thereby connecting the local with the global. All over the world, private photo albums, homemade videos, and clips on YouTube show people engaged in a cointossing ritual at Trevi. The worldwide coverage of a sensational "sacrilege" connected communities of Trevi protagonists who protested the interference.

Considering that icons represent values and identities that are variously mediated through rituals as well as televised images, the dual properties of Mary and Trevi Fountain as both mediator and mediatized come to the fore. Yet, according to Ronald L. Grimes's critique of Jonathan Z. Smith's theory of ritual space, casting ritual as both mediator and party in need of mediation constitutes a contradiction.[14] Catherine Bell makes a similar complaint when she argues that this contradiction is typical of many, if not most, theories of ritual.[15] But why should this dual property of rituals or icons be contradictory and problematic? Or, to repeat Klima's question, "How could the media be divested of 'real life,' when the media is, to some extent, our life?"[16] According to William Mazzarella, a medium is

> a material framework, both enabling and constraining, for a given set of social practices. In this guise a medium is both dynamic and largely taken for granted. However, a medium is also a reflexive and reifying technology. It makes society imaginable and intelligible to itself in the form of external representations. Inseparable from the movement of social life and yet removed from it, a medium is thus at once obvious and strange, indispensable and uncanny, intimate and distant.[17]

Given this description, icons and rituals themselves could be regarded as media. Like radio and television, icons and rituals are interpreted and reflected upon, either during or after a ritual's performance. According to Grimes, this reflection is not always and everywhere part of ritual,[18] but it does become so when rituals are mediated and circulated outside their local context of performance.[19] In fact, we argue that contesting particular rituals or icons stems from reflecting on their particular appropriation and subsequent mediation. As Klima argues, "The powerful potential in media-reproducibility . . . far from excluding the 'real presence' of bodies and feelings, heightens awareness of them."[20] Moreover, like any other media, icons and rituals "constrain the control and dissemination of information in particular ways."[21]

The figure of Mary not only conveys messages to devotees who pray in front of her image or visit her shrines but also communicates at a distance by way of newspaper clippings and the Internet. For many believers, Mary serves as a mediator between human beings and God. Moreover, being an essential, albeit contested, part of the Catholic faith, she makes the greater Catholic religious community imaginable and intelligible to itself. Emerging from religious, social, and historical contexts that shaped both her formal and material properties, the figure of the Virgin recursively remediates each new social context in which she becomes relevant, "often at great spatial and temporal removes from [her] origins."[22] She is considered the mother of Jesus, the mother of God, queen of heaven, as well as co-redemptrix. She represents and mediates values such as humility, patience, obedience, and faith. Female believers, in particular, are expected to internalize the values mediated through Mary's imagery. Not only does Mary prompt women to reflect upon their lives, they are also encouraged to transform themselves in light of what Mary represents to them.[23]

Trevi Fountain represents Rome and its particular cultural heritage and is also intimately connected to Roman citizenship. The Acqua Vergine, which supplies the fountain, dates from antiquity, and the aquaduct itself was completed in 19 B.C.E. Legend has it that a virgin showed the water source to Agrippa's soldiers, hence the name of the aqueduct, Acqua Vergine. Furthermore, the name refers to the water's purity—"the clearest and most healthful of all the waters brought to Rome," but it was the story of the virgin that gained greatest currency. A plaque at the fountain installed in the eighteenth century shows the legendary scene of its discovery by the virgin.[24] Work on the present fountain, which was designed by Nicola Salvi, commenced in 1732 and took some thirty years to complete. The ruling popes and the general public—at least those who purchased lottery tickets—supplied money for the project. According to Cooke, "The Fountain of Trevi has generally appealed to all levels of taste and education, and the process of building by continual referendum to public opinion in part explains its success."[25] An additional reason might be that Salvi worked along the lines of his theatrical designs for festivals.[26] The monumental fountain is located in such a way that it takes visitors by surprise. It is an architectural setting that possesses, as Zucker remarks, a "grandiose stage effect."[27]

The semisacred waters in the basin received offerings long before Anita Ekberg first appeared on the scene. The ritual gesture of flipping a coin over the left shoulder into the water has probably been performed at the Fountain of Trevi for over two centuries. Guides relate the story that the good-luck ritual will bring visitors back to Rome one day. Performing the offering twice is good for meeting a Roman beauty, and the male tourist who makes the gesture three times can even expect to marry her. Nowadays coins valued at 3,000 euro are thrown into the basin every day. The accumulated money is distributed as charity to Rome's needy.[28]

The imagery of the baroque fountain has been widely disseminated by way of souvenirs, picture postcards, photographs, and other media. "Rome is a leading actor in Fellini's *La Dolce Vita* (1960).... Marcello Mastroianni and Anita Ekberg romp in Trevi Fountain, and are caught unawares when the cleaning crew turns off the jets."[29] Film aficionados agree that the Trevi scene captures Rome best.[30] The film script makes clear that the character Sylvia, played by Anita Ekberg, was "a woman with the body of a sex queen and the emotions of a little girl."[31] The pope, who had a private screening of the film, considered the scene appalling. The Vatican paper *L'Osservatore Romano* expressed horror at the scandalous film with an article headed "Basta!" Federico Fellini, the director, ran the risk of being excommunicated.[32] Yet Fellini deftly uses Catholic idiom to refer to the sacrament of baptism. In the film script, Marcello Mastroianni hesitates to step into the water, "But her naturalness, her total abandon to sensual delight, pulls on him. He sees her as the figure of Eve, fresh and unspoiled in a decadent and sophisticated world." When Marcello finally enters the water, this Eve, played by Ekberg, takes a handful of falling water and, "letting the drops fall like a blessing" over his head, she baptizes him. As Salerno points out, the water is a "symbol for regeneration and rebirth through purification."[33]

In 1994, to celebrate the centennial of cinema, the city of Rome projected *La Dolce Vita* on the water of Trevi Fountain. To facilitate the showing, the statues were covered in black.[34] For the Romans, the fountain thus illuminated by the legendary film scene contained holy water that acted as a screen for the iconic imagery.

Mediatization can be a matter of great intimacy: "It is the process by which the self recognizes itself by returning to itself, renewed and once removed."[35] In addition, it is also a public matter, as the mediatized icons of Mary and Trevi Fountain oscillate between private lives and collective space. The people of Rome incorporate the fountain and its associated rituals into their private experiences and into their definition of what it means to be Roman, thus inverting Michael Herzfeld's concept of cultural intimacy, "the recognition of those aspects of a cultural identity that are considered a source of external embarrassment but nevertheless provide insiders with their assurance of common sociality."[36] Here, we focus upon icons that are far from embarrassing; on the contrary, they are used by insiders to express national or religious traits that provide them with pride and strength.

The depth of cultural intimacy associated with these icons and their mediatization exposes a division between official ecclesiastical and national models, on the one hand, and the lived experience of ordinary believers and citizens, on the other. As with any medium, both the content and form of Mary and Trevi Fountain are scrutinized and controlled. The Catholic Church has repeatedly tried to control Mary's growing power and dominance in believers' religious experiences and ritual practices. This tension between private and official, between believers and citizens, sprang to the fore when Mary was appropriated by secessionists in Bougainville and when red dye was tossed into Trevi Fountain. To understand why these mediatizations led to such conflict, it is necessary to analyze the circulation and appropriation of these icons.

Mary and the Rosary in the Bougainville Conflict

To understand the mediating capacities of ritual, we turn first to the political use of religious imagery and rituals in violent acts of resistance and in peaceful reconciliation. Bougainville is a relatively small island group in the South Pacific, consisting of two main islands, Buka (roughly fifty kilometers long) in the north and, separated by a small sea channel, Bougainville Island (approximately two hundred kilometers long) in the south. In addition, there are many small islands and atolls (see figure 3.2).

Today, after almost ten years of civil conflict, Bougainville is an autonomous province of Papua New Guinea. From 1989 until the end of the 1990s, though, the

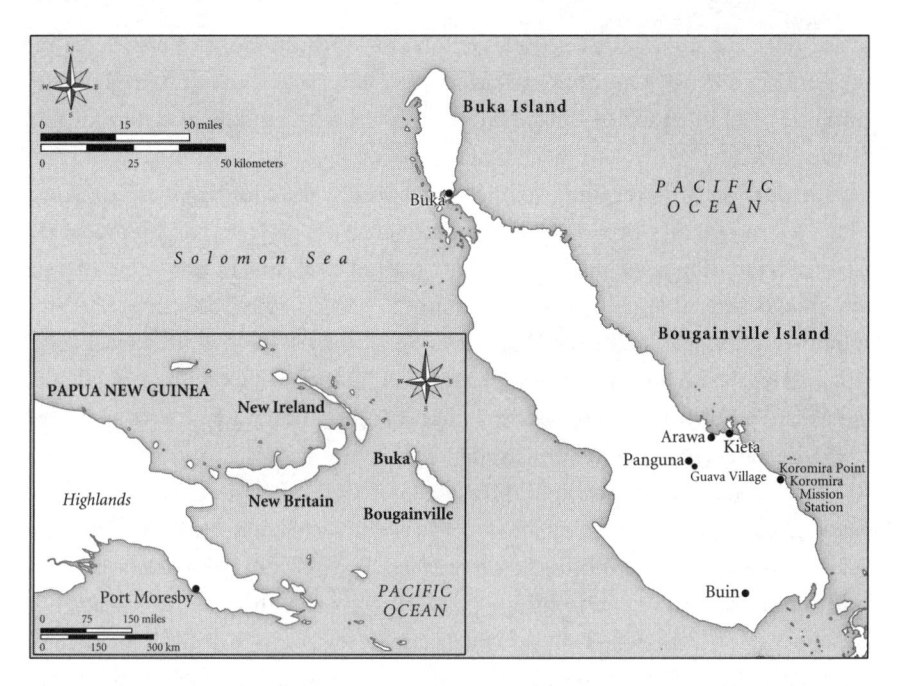

FIGURE 3.2. Buka and Bougainville Islands.

people of Bougainville were immersed in vicious warfare. Major actors in this war were the BRA and the secessionist movement of Me'ekamui,[37] whose fight for justice and independence often led to brutal encounters with the Papua New Guinea Defence Force and the Bougainville Resistance Forces. The latter consisted of Bougainvilleans who sided with the Papua New Guinea government because they opposed the BRA's political and military actions, especially their instigating anarchy and violence. While the Papua New Guinea government tried to prevent political fragmentation of its nation-state, according to the secessionists, the government was trying to control Bougainville's natural resources, especially what was then the world's largest copper mining venture near Panguna village in the Crown Prince Ranges of central Bougainville.

Led by former mine employer Francis Ona, a group of landowners demanded compensation for past damage to their land and the environment.[38] Francis Ona and his group—initially called Rambos because they modeled themselves after the protagonist of the popular Sylvester Stallone action film—became known as the Bougainville Revolutionary Army or BRA. When the mining company refused to meet their terms, the group sabotaged a power line pylon, cutting off power to the Panguna mine.[39] This militant action in November 1988 was followed by others that effectively shut down mining operations. These acts of sabotage triggered a severe response from the Papua New Guinea government, which, after sending a police riot squad, mobilized its defense forces to protect the mine and bring the BRA under control.[40] One of the government's tactics in this power struggle was to enforce a total blockade of Bougainville, prohibiting the inflow of economic and medical aid.

To deal with the ensuing hardships, people looked for spiritual guidance, which led to at least one unintended consequence of the crisis and blockade: the establishment of new religious movements. Catholicism and, in particular, Marian movements such as Our Lady of Mercy and the Marian Mercy Movement became extremely popular.[41] Moreover, Marian images, statues, biblical texts, and other religious regalia became mediators of religious affiliation between Bougainville and the wider world as, for example, when images and statues of Mary were smuggled in via the independent Solomon Islands.

Marianism was important to those who initiated the crisis. Ona believed that devotion to Mary would draw faithful leaders who were connected with Bougainville's land and lore, especially the perception of the island as *Me'ekamui*, a holy land where God lives close to his people. But to retrieve this holiness, which had been lost due to foreign, that is, Australian, intervention and the "destructive" presence of Papua New Guinean immigrants, the Bougainville people, including its leaders, would have to become holy. In Ona's vision of *Me'ekamui*, the veneration of Mary would provide the power, means, and guidance to purify both the people and land.

As recounted by the now retired Dutch bishop of Bougainville, Henk Kronenberg, Ona daily addressed a statue of Mary to seek her advice.[42] Only if he received an affirmative message from her would he carry out his plans for the day. As a token of his devotion to Mary, Ona also initiated the Marian Mercy Mission. Its members have a unique way of saying the rosary, and they regularly engage in fasting and prayer. Father Bernard Unabali, a Bougainvillean Catholic priest in Arawa, described it as a very strong movement with a strong moral emphasis urging the conversion of all Bougainvilleans.[43] The Marian movement's association with Ona and the secessionist struggle entailed not only spiritual aspects but also political and nationalistic ones. This interplay between Marianism and the island's secessionist struggle benefited from the way members of Ona's BRA conceptualized their fight. As explained by ex-combatant and chaplain Albert Natee:

> Francis Ona said this land must become holy again, *Me'ekamui*. We prayed to God and he gave us strength. This directed us to engage in a clean battle. We were fighting for our rights, to get rid of all these bad companies and their effects. All BRA and all Bougainvilleans—everybody practiced this holiness. We had to stay with the Church. Our spirits had

to be holy, so God would get rid of Satan [the mining companies]. We had to stay holy to get rid of it. And God helped us. How? His power worked through the rosary.[44]

Natee's explanation reveals how members of the BRA saw themselves as waging a holy war under Mary's protection in order to restore the Holy Nation of Bougainville. Natee's explanation also shows how the Catholic emblem of the rosary came to serve both nationalistic and religious ends. As expressed by Natee (see figure 3.3), being holy and becoming one was achieved through the ritual of individual and collective prayer:

> Before we would go on patrol or go into battle, we would pray the three most powerful decades: The Lord's Prayer and three Hail Marys. This we did collectively, as a group. The mysteries we would pray in private. We would pray for protection and for guidance. I would get them [the BRA] all together and read Bible passages and explain how to stay holy in combat. We stayed holy by not gossiping, not swearing, and not getting angry. When somebody caused trouble in the camp, we would send him away. We had to stay holy! As a group we should stay holy, and one man could not be allowed to destroy this. He would have to make some kind

FIGURE 3.3. Albert Natee's home altar showing a newspaper clipping of him and his fellow BRA combatants together with various religious objects such as images and statues of Jesus and Mary, as well as prayer booklets and several rosaries.

of sacrifice and could return after some weeks. He had to apologize to God, to us, to those whom he had wronged. If he refused, he would jeopardize our safety. God will not protect us when we have done wrong. Also, when I die, I must go to heaven. So before and during the battles, I had to stay holy so that in case I got shot, I would go straight to heaven.[45]

The emphasis on experiencing a personal call to holiness is a central notion in Catholicism. All people are called to be holy.[46] This conviction implies that one should strive to receive the grace of God. Everyone within the church should live holy lives and spread holiness to others. Holiness is not merely a state of being but also an obligation, "whereby Christians should strive for a full Christian life, imitating Christ, the Son of God, who gave his life for God and for his neighbor."[47] The ritual of praying, either individually or in a group, is considered a way of obtaining God's grace and holiness.

As expressed by former BRA member Natee, praying purifies one's soul, redeems one's sins, and enables one to conduct "a clean fight." Thus, the ritual of praying, he believes, effectively leads to individual and collective purification. In addition to this ritual preparation before fighting, soldiers of the BRA also used the holy power of religious regalia in combat. By carrying blessed rosary beads as well as small statues of Mary while fighting their enemies, the insurgents transformed their warfare into a holy fight conceptualized in terms of good versus evil.

Fighting in ritual regalia also had disadvantages. According to several ex-BRA soldiers, the rosary beads not only ensured the soldiers would wage a clean fight but also would protect them from getting hurt. At the same time, however, they could not wear the rosary around their necks because Mary's power would be too strong and block their machine guns. As the mother of all people, Mary would not allow any of her children to be killed. To mitigate the effects of exposing this much power, BRA soldiers would instead tuck their rosary beads in their pockets.[48]

While parts of Mary's powers were appropriated to fight a clean and holy fight, they were also put to work making peace. Mary is believed to have given courage and strength to Bougainville women to fight for peace. Bougainville women are renowned for being actively involved in the ending of violence,[49] but it is less known that Marian devotion played an important role in women's actions. As narrated by Catholic women involved in the peace process, mothers were standing on the front lines, praying and clasping the rosary in their hands in an attempt to stop the shooting. According to these women, Mary and the rosary gave them strength to intervene, thereby enabling them to facilitate the ending of the crisis. This fighting with rituals to obtain peace becomes especially salient in light of a Marian pilgrimage to Ona's hideout in the Panguna Mountains. According to many, Mary, in the form of a statue of Fatima, persuaded Francis Ona to stop fighting.

(Mis)Appropriating Marian Pilgrimage

In 1997, after almost nine years of violent conflict, an economic blockade, and several failed peace negotiations, hope of obtaining a truce arose again when formal negotiations between the conflicting parties resumed in July of that year.[50] Beginning on July 13, concurrent with the negotiations, was a five-day pilgrimage with the International Pilgrim Virgin Statue of Our Lady of Fatima. David Morgan describes how the Fatima statue was consecrated in the United States for the purpose of teaching people about Christianity and converting them to it.[51] It is transported around the world in itinerant ministry by Carl Malburg: "If millions have made pilgrimage to the Shrine of Our Lady of Fatima in Portugal, built on the site of the apparition, Malburg's work is to serve Our Lady by making her likeness a traveler or pilgrim to many millions more."[52] This statue is an apt representation of the transnational character of Marianism. Its local pilgrimage in Bougainville shows how different aspects of Fatima's worldwide mission were appropriated by various actors to serve both religious and political agendas.

As intended by the local Papua New Guinea and Bougainville custodians and organizers of the pilgrimage—Father Zdzislaw Mlak, a Polish Divine Word (SVD) missionary, and Father John Koran, a Marist from Buka—Fatima's mission in Bougainville was to send a message of peace to BRA leader Francis Ona, who was refusing to participate in peace negotiations. This message was communicated and simultaneously filmed (but never broadcast)[53] by bringing the statue up the central

FIGURE 3.4. In front of the International Pilgrim Virgin Statue of Fatima in Guava village in 1997, Francis Ona consecrates Bougainville in Mary's name and promises to work toward peace (image from the film *Pilgrim of Peace*, courtesy of its maker, Fr. Zdzislaw Mlak).

mountain range to Guava village (see figure 3.4), the almost impenetrable hideout of Ona and his followers:

> When we brought the statue in with candlelight, the entire Catholic population of the Panguna area welcomed us. We were really welcomed! We were welcomed by the Marian Mercy Mission and had Mass in Guava village. The statue was placed in front of the chapel and groups of people came to pray to her, praying for her intercession. It was the first thing coming into Guava since the war. Everything, all prayers and all intentions were focused on peace. Praying and hoping Mary would bring it. During Mass, Francis Ona came with the solution to achieve peace for Bougainville [promising peace to Mary and consecrating the island of Bougainville in the name of Mary]. Everybody wanted this.
>
> In the morning, we had Mass again. After Mass, Ona made a big prayer to bring peace to Bougainville. I prayed for the people in the free zone. After two nights in Guava we went back to Arawa town. The people there were worried that something might have happened to us. The same day, a helicopter took us to Buka Island, where an overnight praying session was held. Next morning, people held a procession all the way to the airport. A chartered plane came and took us with the statue to Lae and from there Father Koran and Father Mlak flew with the statue to Port Moresby. From there, it somehow went to Russia, I heard.[54]

According to the local organizers, the five-day pilgrimage of Fatima to Buka and Bougainville was about peace and reconciliation; its purpose was to "work toward peace" and to "help with the peace process."[55] The priests' quest was to bring peace to the people of Bougainville through the Fatima pilgrimage. Father Koran expressed it this way: "I think it was good that Mary went to Guava village. It soothed things and people identified with her. According to Father Mlak and me, this was the way to do it [reconciliation]: through praying the rosary."[56] Like his colleagues, Father Pisi was convinced of the positive impact of Fatima's "journey of peace," arguing that it marked a turning point in the crisis:

> As I look back, the pilgrimage was the starting process of peace.... The experiences of Ona's soldiers after his promises to Fatima were that the fighting stopped. Also the civil fight. People blamed and killed each other, and Papua New Guinea citizens were targeted. During the war, everything got blurred. Local resistance forces were fighting against the local Bougainville Revolutionary Army, who fought with the Papua New Guinea soldiers. After the statue came, it all stopped! It is the work of Mary. She brought this about. The starting point of peace was Ona's

statement: his commitment to this statue to seek peace. Even today, some say it was the statue that brought peace to Bougainville.[57]

Not everyone was convinced of Ona's good intentions. During the final years of the crisis, Ona faced considerable opposition, and many tired of his refusals to partake in the peace negotiations. The former bishop of Bougainville, Henk Kronenberg, recalls, "There was so much opposition in Bougainville to what was happening on top of the mountains that through this visit [of Fatima] others were offended."[58] Those outside the influence of Francis Ona felt they had endured most of the hardships of the crisis as targets of both the BRA and the Papua New Guinea army. When Fatima traveled to Francis Ona and Guava village instead of visiting them, people felt offended and neglected: why did Fatima visit the one who was responsible for the crisis?

Ambivalence was deepened by the fact that, according to the bishop, Francis Ona had used Fatima's coming as propaganda for the BRA. In the unbroadcast film, Ona addresses the Guava village community during a Mass. Standing in front of the Fatima statue, he consecrates Bougainville in name of Mary, while promising his audience to work toward peace.[59] By consecrating the Holy Island of Bougainville in the name of Mary, Fatima's pilgrimage effectively became part of Ona's political agenda to transform the island into a theocracy, ruled by Ona himself under the guidance of Mary and God, with the independent nation of Me'ekamui crowning him king of the Holy Island of Bougainville.[60] For Ona, mobilizing Mary and her associated rituals simultaneously legitimized his secessionist warfare and empowered his personal ambitions. While Ona's charismatic leadership abilities were limited,[61] Mary's popularity significantly increased support for his leadership position. Ona's establishment of the Marian Mercy Mission exemplifies how he made use of the power of Mary's imagery to generate sodalities based upon worship and charisma.

In Bougainville, Catholic rituals were not only a source of conflict among Catholics but also between Catholics and non-Catholics. Throughout the crisis, Catholic churches and their ritualistic emblems such as statues of Mary were attacked. At the Koromira Mission Station, people threw one statue of Mary into the water and shot at another. Almost all the informants spoken with blamed Seventh-Day Adventists for this iconoclasm. Regardless of what actually motivated such attacks, the aggression could be read as a strong "denial of the power of things to mediate divine actions."[62] Catholics consider the sacrament as well as related objects holy. Usually blessed by a priest, such holy objects include rosaries, crucifixes, and medals, as well as statues of Jesus, the saints, and Mary. Discussing images of Jesus and Mary, an informant exclaimed, "All these pictures are holy! You see it straight!"[63] The attacks on Mary's images were attempts at purification, actions aimed at creating what Bruno Latour describes as "entirely distinct ontological zones: that of human beings on the one hand; that of nonhumans on the other."[64]

For Francis Ona and the Bougainville Revolutionary Army, Mary and her associated rituals of praying and pilgrimage mediated divine intervention in the context of both war and peacemaking. As mediatrix, she was regarded as having the power to mediate between humans and God to receive the latter's blessing and support. At the same time, Mary was also deployed as a medium to convey conflicting messages and sentiments. In Ona's case, Mary mediated nationalistic sentiments and political ambitions, while for the organizers of Fatima's pilgrimage, Mary mediated peace and spiritual reconciliation. According to the bishop of Bougainville, Ona's appropriation of Mary and Marian rituals actually mediated deviant messages that stirred up local conflict by creating tensions among Catholics who opposed Ona's actions.

This intimate interplay between icon and ritual, mediator and mediation, message and conflict also comes to the fore in our study of Rome's Trevi Fountain.

Trevi Fountain: A Media-Savvy Operation Stirs Up Conflict

The media identified the alleged culprit in the dyeing of the fountain. Over the phone, Graziano Cecchini did not admit to the deed but only said, "Who knows?" Then he added, "If it had been me, wink wink, I'd say this had been a media-savvy operation in the face of a very gray society."[65] The man in question had picked the eighteenth-century fountain for a counterritualistic gesture that instantly became world news. Philosopher Gianni Vattimo's comment in the *Corriere della Sera* that "the cities have become greyish" ostensibly supported Cecchini's act of turning the waters of Trevi red.[66] In any case, the attention-grabbing gesture had immediate success thanks to Trevi's ritual value and symbolic status, both of which were familiar to people around the globe. The next day, the *New York Times* broke the news under the heading, "The Waters Run Red."[67] What waters? The colorful image of Trevi Fountain told the tale.[68] Of course by then readers were already seeing the photographs and video clips circulating wildly on the Internet.

The news also spread by word of mouth, an underestimated means of mass communication.[69] Take, for instance, what someone by the name of Miss Chiquita Breakcore reported on the site called the Cranky Professor: "I had lunch yesterday with a friend from Rome who went by the Trevi the other day during its brief red spell. He says he rather liked it—that it was a break from the (imagine the gesture) consistency that is Roma. When someone at the table asked if it was a Communist protester he laughed and reminded her that the Communists are too conservative now for anything this amusing."[70]

Others, however, were not amused. Italy's Minister of Culture, Francesco Rutelli, said the intervention was "an unacceptable and irresponsible act of vandalism." He called for a new antivandalism law to prevent the crime at Trevi Fountain from being committed again.[71] Actress Anita Ekberg said the act was "an offence to Rome's culture,"[72] and the mayor of Rome, Walter Veltroni, uttered words to the same effect.[73]

Actual harm to the monument would have been a disaster. When the news broke, concern about vandalism was foremost. It took a few days before the circumstances behind the rogue act were fully revealed. By then, the shock effect of the blood-colored waters had become a global sensation. Gradually, it became clear that the mediatized event was not just a stunt, but that a war of cultural politics was being waged behind the scenes.

Trevi has been a favorite destination since Anita Ekberg's famous bath in the fountain's eight-degree Celsius waters.[74] From the eighteenth century onward, tourists have been offering coins to Trevi, throwing them in the pure water hoping to return to Rome. The water runs into Rome from a source in the countryside; tourists also stream into Rome, to its landmark in the center of the city.

What accounts for the urge to flip a coin into the water? For one thing, the act seems hard to resist. People do not act in isolation. Whether motivated to throw coins into the water because they read about the act in a tourist guide or witness others doing so firsthand, coin tossers mimick each other. Michael Taussig shows how mimicking distant others is a means of appropriating their power.[75] Paul Stoller says that people divert appropriated power for use for their own purposes and for their own interests.[76] This kind of diversion occurred when a man turned Trevi blood red.

Many tourists to Rome perform the ritual act at Trevi Fountain as a secular one, with no god whatsoever in mind. They have been told that throwing a coin into the water over their shoulder will guarantee their return to the city one day in the future. When countless tourists perform the lucky gesture, they also enact a form of sympathetic magic. The practice of leaving a little of oneself behind creates a lasting tie to the place.

Places that are capable of evoking future memories or recollections of a memorable trip, creating what Nelson Graburn dubs a "sacred journey,"[77] are remarkable in their capacity to inspire people to invest coins. Throwing them into shallow water is an ambiguous kind of destruction. Once the gesture has been performed, and its ritual function fulfilled, the coins may be gathered up and taken away by unseen others for some good cause. When a coin has been ritually processed, it may be used for other purposes, not unlike a sacrificial animal that is eaten after being ritually killed. These offerings are nonverbal communications that imply an exchange. By means of the ritual gesture, a material object is transacted for something intangible.

The small material gift is transformed by the gesture, allowing the performers to tap into a metaphysical stream of grace.

The coins thrown into the water are, for some, tokens of respect for higher powers. From a Durkheimian perspective, the deity worshipped in ritual fashion is actually society itself, in this case a "gray society" momentarily rendered colorful by red dye. Coin tossing typically happens at liminal places such as the destinations of religious and secular pilgrimage. Those who perform the ritual gesture do so almost automatically, like passing on chain letters or legends and stories with irresistible plots. Like the image of Mary, the Trevi ritual is entangled with similar practices all over the world. Circulated in mass media, the image of Trevi Fountain strikes a chord with all who have performed such gestures, irrespective of location. The ritual links people to that imaginary place at which sacred waters evoke a sense of belonging.

In the gesture at Trevi, image, story, and overt actions are interrelated, seeming to follow a plot.[78] The activist, very aware that the place was special for many other people, performed the counterritualistic gesture of dropping red dye instead of a coin into the water of Trevi Fountain, thereby enacting "a play upon form," to use Mary Douglas's phrase.[79] This play also extended the famous Trevi scene in *La Dolce Vita*. An appropriation of that momentous event in film history by the activist required the performance to be filmed and the imagery disseminated.[80] On this location, with its "grandiose stage effect,"[81] security cameras registered the man's behavior. Most likely he knew the eye of a camera would make him into an instant movie star. Not only did the technical equipment at Trevi ensure a live recording, but also tourists filmed and photographed. After his disappearance, they turned to photographing the spectacular red-colored fountain. The counterritualistic act caused great upheaval, especially since it was feared that damage had been done to the marble statue of the sea deity, Neptune, who towers over the basin on his chariot. The dramatic event soon hit the airwaves when the news agency ANSA reported that a box of fliers found beside Trevi Fountain declared that a group called FTM Azione Futurista 2007 was claiming responsibility for the irreverent attack. The fliers revealed that the group had declared a fight against "everything and everyone with a spirit of healthy violence" and aimed to turn this "grey bourgeois society into a triumph of color."[82] Furthermore, the fliers explained that the red dye had been used to protest the Festa del Cinema, which, "at 15 million Euro was a little too expensive," as well as the whole film scene in Rome. The latter, according to the pamphlet, consisted of "four courtesans, an ugly old hen and a smurf."[83] While the red paint referred to the film festival's red carpet, the expression "an ugly old hen" (*una vecchia gallinaccia*) explains why Ekberg, once the alluring Eve of the famous film sequence, was infuriated.

The artist-activist targeted the fountain as a way of arguing that the funds squandered on glitzy films rightly belonged to Rome's needy artists. He could argue in this way because the coins thrown into the water of the Trevi went to the poor. What is more, Trevi had been appropriated before by the film industry at a time of prosperity. By the end of the 1950s, Italy's economy had miraculously recovered from the Second World War, and *La Dolce Vita*, first shown in the studios of Cinecittà, reflected the tone of the new era. The bath of a seductive Swedish actress, clad in the latest fashion, changed the image of Trevi Fountain forever.[84] At the time, however, the scene met with resistance as a scandalous profanation of the holy waters. Here was the "communist" Fellini creating an adorable Eve to compete with Rome's beloved Virgin Mary. On all accounts the Trevi scene was a sensation. The more that trespassing in the basin counted as vandalism, the more it made the performance immortal.

The "crime" of October 19, 2007, did as little harm to the fountain as Anita Ekberg's sensual splashing. As a matter of fact, no damage was incurred by the monument. The marble statue of Neptune on his chariot did not absorb the red paint. Within a day, the red was flushed out and a clear flow restored. Famous destinations are favorite targets of dissidents, in large part because of the publicity they guarantee. As Silvio Di Francia, who bore the responsibility for Rome's monuments, said to the media, "We are obviously in a city full of tourists so the gesture of an agitator is always a potential problem."[85] The question was, who would instigate such a deed? If indeed communists were now considered too conservative to commit such imaginative acts, then the agitator had to be of a different inclination. Clearly, the activist was targeting the old elite who dominate Rome's cultural life. For him, "the mummified grand cultural institutions" (*le grandi istituzioni culturali mummificate*)[86] are in decline, as the superfluous film fest showed. "You wanted just a red carpet—we want a city entirely in vermilion. We who are vulnerable, old, ill, students, workers, we come with vermilion to color your greyness," the text on the abandoned fliers announced.[87] The media were quick to learn that the culprit was "a 54-year-old unemployed painter." The *Guardian* reported that Rome's police had identified Graziano Cecchini and placed him "under investigation for allegedly damaging a historical or artistic building." According to a statement issued by the police, Cecchini was known as "an extreme-right sympathiser."[88]

Given that the fliers were signed "FTM Futurist Action 2007," the man could then be identified as a neofuturist. Futurism had emerged as an art movement at the beginning of the twentieth century that advocated "a violent break with the past."[89] Although it eventually got caught up with fascism under Mussolini, the movement's great inspiration, founder, and leader was Filippo Tommaso Marinetti or FTM. Now, at the beginning of another new century, the futurist sympathizer Cecchini also wanted to break with the past, which he did via his radical gesture at Trevi. As one scholar writes, "Futurism was deeply haunted by the problematic of decline."[90] In the words of media critic Gianlucca Nicoletti, the action at

Trevi could also be seen as a "dramatic representation of the decline of the country." The contrast with the dull film festival could not have been greater: "The real splash was the one made at a fountain."[91]

"The poet," according to the sixth principle of the founding manifesto of futurism, "must spend himself with ardor, splendor, and generosity."[92] Futurism's interest in fabrics and colors must have inspired its new poet, Cecchini, who told the media he had hid somewhere with Oliviero Toscani, the renowned photographer of the controversial United Colors of Benneton campaign.[93] In keeping with his style, Toscani made the following remark about Cecchini's gesture: "Rome that's still menstruating, Rome that has not entered menopause yet, can still have children, is still fertile."[94] The remark added to the insult already lobbed at the film diva. Meanwhile, Cecchini, in turn, cited Toscani's words concerning the blood-red fountain.[95]

"Once the indignation had died down we rediscovered the Fountain of Trevi thanks to that liquid," wrote Italian blogger Roberto D'Agostino.[96] Cecchini had had his fifteen minutes of fame. The neofuturist artist had acted according to the principles of futurist performance, as described in "The Synthetic Futurist Theatre: A Manifesto" by Filippo Tommaso Marinetti and others in 1915. Futurist theater is said to be "synthetic, that is, very brief. Grasping in a few minutes, a few words, and a few gestures innumerable situations, feelings, ideas, sensations, events, and symbols." The authors add, "For us, acts can even be *moments*; that is, they may last only a few seconds. With this essential and synthetic brevity, drama will hold its own in—and even win—the competition with cinema."[97]

Cecchini's very brief action was in line with the cited manifesto. His references to the red carpet of the Rome Film Festival and the iconic Trevi scene in *La Dolce Vita* underscored this aim. According to the fliers left behind, the goal of the artist-activist was to transform society. In "Avant-gardes and Totalitarianism," Tzvetan Todorov notes, "The Futurists recognized themselves in Mussolini and were pleased that he reserved an important role for cultural action in the fabrication of the new men. In this respect, Filippo Tommaso Marinetti, the Italian Futurist, resembled Mayakovsky, the Russian Futurist: both sought to place their talent at the service of the revolution. Fascism relied on artistic action to transform society, to make it a spectacle worthy of admiration."[98]

Il Duce thought that the project of "transforming Italians into new men" had failed, and hence Italy was to lose the war. "What I lacked was good material," he said not long before his death. The idea of "regeneration by violence" had to await a better time in the future.[99] The aesthetic aspects of ritual gestures, swift and theatrical, the futurists knew, can be most seductive.

While the media-savvy neofuturist may have chosen Trevi Fountain as the medium for his iconoclastic message, the simple gesture of dropping a coin into the

FIGURE 3.5. Tourists offering coins at Trevi Fountain (photo courtesy of Janneke Peelen).

water (see figure 3.5) continues to attract countless tourists to Rome who want to indicate with the ritual practice that they "have been there."

The Ritual Dynamics of Media and Conflict

Appropriation is the taking possession of objects, ideas, language, or practices, and assimilating them into the "visual rhetoric and vocabulary of one's own."[100] According to David Morgan, who discusses religious images in a missionary context, appropriated images "preserve the Christian identity of the exported source while adapting their form and use to the new, local context of the faith."[101] The Bougainville case shows that appropriation does not necessarily mean changing the image's original form but rather its ritual use and meaning, both of which accord with a local "technology of imagining," to use Alan Klima's phrase, that differs from the global circulation of Marian imagery.

The concept of circulation sets the appropriation of religious objects in a broader landscape.[102] If the materiality and mediation of icons such as Mary and Trevi Fountain permit them to circulate across contexts,[103] then by extension, we can follow the paths of circulation to trace the variations in meaning and styles of appropriation. We have shown how the circulation of religious objects, texts, narratives, videos, and other imagery link the local with the global. The transnational mediation of Mary transpires, for example, through the travels of the pilgrim statue of Our Lady of Fatima, which originated in Portugal, was relocated to the United States, appropriated by American devotees, and subsequently traveled to Papua New Guinea, where she was appropriated by the BRA, among others. From the perspective of her devotees, it was not they who appropriated Mary but the other way around. As Morgan states, "Fatima appropriates the world through her going on pilgrimage."[104] On the other hand, when pilgrims make the trek to Trevi in Rome, its quasi-religious imagery is spread via various secular media; everything from cameras to cell phones circulate Trevi's enduring power and charm.

Moreover, this circulation of imageries is crucial for establishing communities of belief and practice, as is shown in studies of mission histories and colonial encounters.[105] Our case studies demonstrate that even in contemporary contexts, the circulation of religious and ritual imageries is crucial to the processes of conversion and the establishment of religious, as well as secular, sodalities. At the same time, this circulation can also lead to contestation and violence between denominations and communities. In the words of David Morgan, images "help to organize human experience into an ordinary regime of order," but, at the same time, "they can also operate to subvert the ordinary as peoples encounter one another, their visual covenants clashing as their respective constructions of time, space and authority lock in ideological conflict."[106] Sacrilege of a ritual or ritual object amounts to an attack on values and beliefs. The holy waters of the Fountain of Trevi and the holy land of Bougainville are key resources, literally and symbolically. The long drawn-out war in Bougainville and the surprise attack on Trevi both were predicated on political contestation through symbolic means, ritual enactment, and media.

Public ritual is one of the primary ways in which the sacred is produced.[107] Public ritual such as that performed at Trevi Fountain gives people a shared language and practice revolving around a common heritage. Like religious rituals such as praying the rosary in front of Mary's image, Trevi's coin-tossing ritual provides participants with a sense of *communitas*. In addition, the infamous movie scene of "Eve" still has a "magical" appeal to film buffs. In both cases, the aesthetic aspects of ritual gestures are foregrounded, and their importance makes them easily transferable through a variety of visual media. In an instant, attention was drawn to the Holy City by the mass media's dissemination of the exploits of an activist-cum-artist tampering with a familiar ritual gesture at an iconic destination, while in the Catholic hinterland of Bougainville a conflict over land and resources cast in religious imagery and the media of veneration smoldered for years. Thus the entanglement of imagery and ritual heightens the potential of conflict to exacerbate as well as mediate.

NOTES

1. "Muhammad Cartoon Now Intensifies." BBC News Online, February 1, 2006, http://news.bbc.co.uk/2/hi/europe/4670370.stm; Thomas Buch-Andersen, "Denmark Row: The Power of Cartoons." BBC News Online, October 3, 2006, http://news.bbc.co.uk/2/hi/europe/5392786.stm.

2. Hector Avalos, *Fighting Words: The Origins of Religious Violence* (New York: Prometheus, 2005).

3. Alan Klima, *The Funeral Casino: Meditation, Massacre and Exchange with the Dead in Thailand* (Princeton: Princeton University Press, 2002), 156.

4. Klima, *The Funeral Casino*, 173.

5. Klima, *The Funeral Casino*, 11, 173.

6. Klima, *The Funeral Casino*, 197.

7. Arjun Appadurai, *Modernity at Large: Cultural Dimensions of Globalization* (Minneapolis: University of Minnesota Press, 1997), 8–9.

8. Marc Howard Ross, *The Management of Conflict: Interpretations and Interests in Comparative Perspective* (New Haven: Yale University Press, 1993).

9. Anthony Regan, *The Bougainville Conflict: Origins and Development, Main "Actors," and Strategies for Its Resolution* (Port Moresby: Faculty of Law, University of Papua New Guinea, 1996); Gerard A. Finin and Terence Wesley-Smith, "Coups, Conflicts and Crisis: The New Pacific Way?," *Race and Class* 42, no. 4 (2001): 1–16; Helen Ware, "Demography, Migration and Conflict in the Pacific," *Journal of Peace Research* 42, no. 4 (2005): 435–454.

10. Responses to Marc van Dijk, "Vergelijkend onderzoek / Maria heeft ook militaire talenten." *Trouw*, De Verdieping, September 23, 2006.

11. See also Patricia Spyer, "Fire without Smoke and Other Phantoms of Ambon's Violence: Media Effects, Agency, and the Work of Imagination," *Indonesia* 74 (2002): 1–16.

12. Elisabetta Povoledo, "Dye in Roman Fountain May Have Been Art," *International Herald Tribune*, October 23, 2007.

13. See also Webb Keane, *Christian Moderns: Freedom and Fetish in the Mission Encounter* (Berkeley: University of California Press, 2007), 311.

14. Ronald Grimes, "Jonathan Z. Smith's Theory of Ritual Space," *Religion* 29, no. 3 (1999): 263.

15. Catherine Bell, *Ritual Theory, Ritual Practice* (New York: Oxford University Press, 1992), 6. See also Grimes, "Jonathan Z. Smith's Theory of Ritual Space," 271, n. 8.

16. Klima, *The Funeral Casino*, 197.

17. William Mazzarella, "Culture, Globalization, Mediation," *Annual Review of Anthropology* 33 (2004): 346.

18. Grimes, "Jonathan Z. Smith's Theory of Ritual Space," 265.

19. Klima, reflecting on Thai Buddhist meditation, turns the tables by speaking of "a fundamental illusion of life itself, which cinema mimics." Klima, *The Funeral Casino*, 217, see also 169–230.

20. Klima, *The Funeral Casino*.

21. Mazzarella, "Culture, Globalization, Mediation," 358.

22. Mazzarella, "Culture, Globalization, Mediation," 358.

23. Anna-Karina Hermkens, "Josephine's Journey: Gender-Based Violence and Marian Devotion in Urban Papua New Guinea," *Oceania* 78, no. 2 (2008): 151–167.

24. Hereward Lester Cooke Jr., "Documents Relating to the Fountain of Trevi," *Art Bulletin* 38, no. 3 (1956): 149–150.

25. Cooke, "Documents Relating to the Fountain of Trevi," 172.

26. Cooke, "Documents Relating to the Fountain of Trevi," 157–158.

27. Paul Zucker, "Space and Movement in High Baroque City Planning," *Journal of the Society of Architectural Historians*, 14, no. 1 (1995): 13.

28. "Ce rite est probablement un prétexte inventé par le Vatican car les monnaies étaient au départ une contribution aux dépenses de nettoyage de la fontaine." Julien Neutres, "Le cinéma fait-il l'histoire? Le cas de 'la dolce vita,'" *Vingtième Siècle. Revue d'histoire*, 83 (2004): 55.

29. Michael Webb, "The City in Film," *Design Quarterly*, 136 (1987): 20–21. For the Trevi scene, see "La Dolce Vita: Trevi Fountain Scene" on YouTube at http://www.youtube.com/watch?v=GKN1T3K1idg.

30. "Rome, décor de cinéma inépuisable, présente dans ce film et particulièrement dans cette scène très symbolique tous les caractères du baroque et du cinéma de Fellini, de la démesure à l'effect de surprise, de l'exaltation du détail a l'exubérance des rondeurs, du goût pour la provocation à la présence du profane au sein sacré." Neutres, "Le cinéma fait-il l'histoire?," 55.

31. Nicholas A. Salerno, "La Dolce Vita or La Vita Nuova?," *College Composition and Communication* 14, no. 4 (1963): 224.

32. Neutres, "Le cinéma fait-il l'histoire?," 56.

33. Salerno, "La Dolce Vita or La Vita Nuova?," 224–225.

34. As Jean Neutres notes: "C'est dans ce bassin que se situe une pièce essentielle de l'imaginaire de cette ville." Neutres, "Le cinéma fait-il l'histoire?," 62.

35. Mazzarella, "Culture, Globalization, Mediation," 357.

36. Michael Herzfeld, *Cultural Intimacy: Social Poetics in the Nation-State*, 2nd ed. (New York: Routledge, 2005), 3.

37. *Me'ekamui* means holy land.

38. Regan, *The Bougainville Conflict*, 71.

39. Not only Ona and his followers were inspired by Rambo's one-man guerilla fight against his and America's enemies. T-shirts displaying photographs of Jean Claude van Damme, Bruce Lee, and other Rambo-like heroes are very popular in this part of the world, and many young men and boys dress themselves up Rambo-style, not only during the crisis, but also in the current postconflict situation.

40. See further Regan, *The Bougainville Conflict*; and Anna-Karina Hermkens, "The Holy War of Bougainville: The Power of Religion in Times of Crisis and Reconciliation," in *Powers: Religion as a Social and Spiritual Force*, ed. Meerten B. ter Borg and Jan Willem van Henten (New York: Fordham University Press, 2010).

41. Anna-Karina Hermkens, "Religion in War and Peace: Unravelling Mary's Intervention in the Bougainville Crisis," *Culture and Religion* 8, no. 3 (2007): 271–289; Hermkens, "The Holy War of Bougainville."

42. Interview with Bishop Kronenberg, Catholic Mission Station, Buka Island, 2005.

43. Interview with Fr. Unabali, Arawa, December 2005. In December 2009, Fr. Unabali became bishop of Bougainville.

44. Interview with Albert Natee, Koromira Mountains, 2005.

45. Interview with Albert Natee, Koromira Mountains, 2005.

46. Vatican Archives, "Lumen Gentium, Dogmatic Constitution on the Church Solemnly Promulgated by His Holiness Pope Paul VI on November 21, 1964," Chapter V, http://www.vatican.va/archive/hist_councils/ii_vatican_council/documents/vat-ii_const_19641121_lumen-gentium_en.html.

47. Vatican Archives, "Lumen Gentium."

48. Interview with former BRA members, Koromira Mountains, December 2005.

49. Marilyn Taleo Havini, "The Role of Bougainville Women in the War and Peace Process," in *Building Peace in Bougainville*, ed. Geoff Harris, Naihuwo Ahai, and Rebecca Spence (The Centre for Peace Studies, University of New England, Australia and the National Research Institute 1999), 39-43; Patrick Howley, *Breaking Spears and Mending Hearts: Peacemakers and Restorative Justice in Bougainville* (London: Federation Press, 2002), 163–166.

50. A slightly different version of this section appeared in Anna-Karina Hermkens, "Mary's Journeys through the Warscape of Bougainville," in *Moved by Mary: The Power of Pilgrimage in the Modern World*, ed. Anna-Karina Hermkens, Willy Jansen, and Catrien Notermans (Aldershot, UK: Ashgate, 2009), 74–77.

51. David Morgan, "Aura and the Inversion of Marian Pilgrimage: Fatima and Her Statues," in *Moved by Mary: The Power of Pilgrimage in the Modern World*, ed. Anna-Karina Hermkens, Willy Jansen, and Catrien Notermans (Aldershot, UK: Ashgate, 2009).

52. Morgan, "Aura and the Inversion of Marian Pilgrimage," 52.

53. Zdzislaw Mlak, *Pilgrim of Peace*, unreleased film (Port Moresby: Religious Television Association, 1997). Although the film was never broadcast, filming the pilgrimage and, in particular, Ona's reception of the statue and his address during the Mass effectively contributed to the importance of the event. Having a white (Polish) priest filming the event increased the significance of the pilgrimage and confirmed Ona's position as important. In fact, in this case one can argue that the making of moving images can be regarded as a ritual gesture marking the significance of an event.

54. Interview with Fr. Matthew Pisi, a diocesan priest from the Panguna mine area, Tunuru Mission Station, November 2005.

55. Interview with Fr. Koran, Buka, December 2005.

56. Interview with Fr. Koran, Buka, December 2005.

57. Interview with Fr. Pisi, Tunuru Mission Station, November 2005.

58. Correspondence with Bishop Kronenberg, 2007.

59. Mlak, *Pilgrim of Peace*.

60. On May 17, 2005, Ona proclaimed himself His Royal Highness King Francis Dominic Dateransy Domanaa, King of the Royal Kingdom of Me'ekamui. Ona's reign did not last long, as he passed away unexpectedly on July 24, 2005.

61. Hermkens, "The Holy War of Bougainville."

62. Keane, *Christian Moderns*, 60.

63. Interview with Peter Kira, Siriwai village, Bougainville Island, December 2005.

64. Bruno Latour in Keane, *Christian Moderns*, 76–77.
65. Povoledo, "Dye in Roman Fountain May Have Been Art."
66. Fabrizio Caccia, "La fontana in rosso? E' un'idea geniale degna di Andi Warhol," *Corriere della Sera*, October 23, 2007.
67. "The Waters Run Red," *New York Times*, October 20, 2007.
68. *Euronews* showed it on television "without comment," and a clip of the news item was uploaded onto YouTube.
69. See Wim Evers, "Informele openbaarmaking: Een studie naar de massacommunicatieve betekenis van onderlinge gesprekken," PhD diss., Radboud University Nijmegen, 1999.
70. "Turning the Trevi Fountain Red," The Cranky Professor, October 31, 2007, http://www.crankyprofessor.com/archives/001352.html.
71. "Minister Sees Red at Trevi Prank," BBC News Online, October 20, 2007, http://news.bbc.co.uk/2/hi/europe/7053908.stm.
72. Malcolm Moore, "'Artist' Dyes Rome's Trevi Fountain Red," *Telegraph*, October 22, 2007.
73. Caccia, "La fontana in rosso?"
74. Neutres, "Le cinéma fait-il l'histoire?," 55.
75. Michael Taussig, *Mimesis and Alterity: A Particular History of the Senses* (New York: Routledge, 1993).
76. Paul Stoller, *Embodying Colonial Memories* (New York: Routledge, 1995).
77. Nelson Graburn, "Tourism: The Sacred Journey," in *Hosts and Guests: The Anthropology of Tourism*, ed. Valene L. Smith (Philadelphia: University of Pennsylvania Press, 1989).
78. Eric Venbrux and Theo Meder, "The False Teeth in the Cod: A Legend in Context," *Contemporary Legend* 5 (1995): 115–131.
79. Mary Douglas, "Jokes," in *Implicit Meanings: Selected Essays in Anthropology* (London: Routledge, 1975).
80. See also the video clip "La fontana di Trevi si tinge di rosso" on YouTube: http://www.youtube.com/watch?v=4Y5rDhiB-m4.
81. Zucker, "Space and Movement in High Baroque City Planning," 13.
82. See Povoledo, "Dye in Roman Fountain May Have Been Art."
83. Ishita Sukhadwala, "Man Throws Red Dye into Trevi Fountain in Rome Denouncing Rome Film Festival," AHN (All Headline News), October 20, 2007, http://www.allheadlinenews.com/articles/7008891368 (accessed January 20, 2009).
84. Neutres, "Le cinéma fait-il l'histoire?," 53.
85. "Man Throws Bucket of Red Paint in Rome's Trevi Fountain," Yahoo! News, October 19, 2007. http://news.yahoo.com/s/ap_travel/20071019/ap_tr_ge/travel_brief_italy_trevi_fountain (accessed January 20, 2009).
86. Caccia, "La fontana in rosso?"
87. Sukhadwala, "Man Throws Red Dye into Trevi Fountain."
88. "Police Name Trevi Fountain Red Dye 'Vandal.'" *The Guardian*, October 23, 2007.
89. Povoledo, "Dye in Roman Fountain May Have Been Art."

90. Jeffrey T. Schnapp, "The Fabric of Modern Times," *Critical Inquiry* 24, no.1 (1997): 198.

91. Povoledo, "Dye in Roman Fountain May Have Been Art."

92. Schnapp, "The Fabric of Modern Times," 199.

93. Cecchini's words suggested that he hid out with Toscani from the police, but this was confirmed by neither Toscani nor the police in the subsequent media reports.

94. Elisabetta Povoledo, "Dye in the Trevi: Some Romans See Red, but Others Cry 'Art'!" *New York Times*, October 24, 2007.

95. Povoledo, "Dye in the Trevi."

96. Povoledo, "Dye in Roman Fountain May Have Been Art."

97. Filippo Tommaso Marinetti, Emilio Settimelli, and Bruno Corra (trans. Suzanne Cowan), "The Synthetic Futurist Theatre: A Manifesto," *Drama Review* 15, no. 1 (1970): 142–143.

98. Tzvetan Todorov, "Avant-gardes and Totalitarianism," *Daedalus* 136, no. 1 (2007): 58.

99. Todorov, "Avant-gardes and Totalitarianism," 58.

100. David Morgan, *The Sacred Gaze: Religious Visual Culture in Theory and Practice* (Berkeley: University of California Press, 2005), 157.

101. Morgan, *The Sacred Gaze*, 157.

102. See also George Marcus and Fred Myers, "The Traffic in Art and Culture: Introduction," in *The Traffic in Culture: Refiguring Art and Anthropology*, ed. George Marcus and Fred Myers (University of California Press, 1995), 34.

103. See also Keane, *Christian Moderns*, 311.

104. Morgan, "Aura and the Inversion of Marian Pilgrimage."

105. For example, Morgan, *The Sacred Gaze*, 147–187.

106. Morgan, *The Sacred Gaze*, 147.

107. Robert Wuthnow, *Producing the Sacred: An essay on Public Religion* (Urbana: University of Illinois Press, 1994), 125.

REFERENCES

Anderson, Benedict. *Imagined Communities*. London: Verso, 2006.
Appadurai, Arjun. *Modernity at Large: Cultural Dimensions of Globalization*. Minneapolis: University of Minnesota Press, 1997.
Avalos, Hector. *Fighting Words: The Origins of Religious Violence*. New York: Prometheus, 2005.
Bell, Catherine. *Ritual Theory, Ritual Practice*. New York: Oxford University Press, 1992.
Caccia, Fabrizio. "La fontana in rosso? E' un'idea geniale degna di Andi Warhol." *Corriere della Sera*, October 23, 2007. http://www.corriere.it/cronache/07_ottobre_23/fontana_provocazione_warhol_caccia.shtl.
Cooke, Hereward Lester, Jr. "Documents Relating to the Fountain of Trevi." *Art Bulletin* 38, no. 3 (1956): 149–153.
Degli-Esposti, Cristina. "Frederico Fellini's Intervista or the Neo-Baroque Creativity of the Analysand on Screen." *Italica* 73, no. 2 (1996): 157–172.

Douglas, Mary. "Jokes." In *Implicit Meanings: Selected Essays in Anthropology*. London: Routledge, 1975.

"E Fontana di Trevi diventa rossa." *Corriere della Sera*, October 19, 2007 (modified October 21, 2007). http://www.corriere.it/cronache/07_ottobre_19/fontana_trevi_rossa.shtml.

Evers, W. J. M. "Informele openbaarmaking: Een studie naar de massacommunicatieve betekenis van onderlinge gesprekken." PhD diss., Radboud University Nijmegen, 1999.

Finin, Gerard A., and Terence Wesley-Smith. "Coups, Conflicts and Crisis: The New Pacific Way?" *Race and Class* 42, no. 4 (2001): 1–16.

Graburn, Nelson. "Tourism: The Sacred Journey." In *Hosts and Guests: The Anthropology of Tourism*, edited by Valene L. Smith, 21–36. Philadelphia: University of Pennsylvania Press, 1989.

Grimes, Ronald. "Jonathan Z. Smith's Theory of Ritual Space." *Religion* 29, no. 3 (1999): 261–273.

Havini, Marilyn Taleo. "The Role of Bougainville Women in the War and Peace Process." In *Building Peace in Bougainville*, edited by Geoff Harris, Naihuwo Ahai, and Rebecca Spence, 39–43. The Centre for Peace Studies, University of New England, Australia and the National Research Institute, 1999.

Hermkens, Anna-Karina. "The Holy War of Bougainville: The Power of Religion in Times of Crisis and Reconciliation." In *Powers: Religion as a Social and Spiritual Force*, edited by Meerten B. ter Borg and Jan Willem van Henten. New York: Fordham University Press, 2010.

———. "Josephine's Journey: Gender-Based Violence and Marian Devotion in Urban Papua New Guinea." *Oceania* 78, no. 2 (2008): 151–167.

———. "Mary's Journeys through the Warscape of Bougainville." In *Moved by Mary: The Power of Pilgrimage in the Modern World*, edited by Anna-Karina Hermkens, Willy Jansen, and Catrien Notermans, 69–85. Aldershot, UK: Ashgate, 2009.

———. "The Power of Mary in Papua New Guinea." *Anthropology Today* 23, no. 2 (2007): 4–8.

———. "Religion in War and Peace: Unravelling Mary's Intervention in the Bougainville Crisis." *Culture and Religion* 8, no. 3 (2007): 271–289.

Hermkens, Anna-Karina, Willy Jansen, and Catrien Notermans, eds. *Moved by Mary: The Power of Pilgrimage in the Modern World*. Aldershot, UK: Ashgate, 2009.

Herzfeld, Michael. *Cultural Intimacy: Social Poetics in the Nation-State*, 2nd ed. New York: Routledge, 2005.

Howley, Patrick. *Breaking Spears and Mending Hearts: Peacemakers and Restorative Justice in Bougainville*. London: Federation Press, 2002.

Keane, Webb. *Christian Moderns: Freedom and Fetish in the Mission Encounter*. Berkeley: University of California Press, 2007.

Klima, Alan. *The Funeral Casino: Mediation, Massacre and Exchange with the Dead in Thailand*. Princeton: Princeton University Press, 2002.

"Man Throws Bucket of Red Paint in Rome's Trevi Fountain." Yahoo! News, October 19, 2007. http://news.yahoo.com/s/ap_travel/20071019/ap_tr_ge/travel_brief_italy_trevi_fountain (accessed January 20, 2009).

Marcus, George, and Fred Myers. "The Traffic in Art and Culture: Introduction." In *The Traffic in Culture: Refiguring Art and Anthropology*, edited by George Marcus and Fred Myers, 1–51. Berkeley: University of California Press, 1995.

Marinetti, Filippo Tommaso, Emilio Settimelli, and Bruno Corra (trans. Suzanne Cowan). "The Synthetic Futurist Theatre: A Manifesto." *Drama Review* 15, no. 1 (1970): 142–146.

Mazzarella, William. "Culture, Globalization, Mediation." *Annual Review of Anthropology* 33 (2004): 345–367.

"Minister Sees Red at Trevi Prank." BBC News Online, October 20, 2007. http://news.bbc.co.uk/2/hi/europe/7053908.stm.

Mlak, Zdzislaw. *Pilgrim of Peace*. Unreleased film. Port Moresby: Religious Television Association, 1997.

Moore, Malcolm. "'Artist' Dyes Rome's Trevi Fountain Red." *Telegraph*, October 22, 2007. http://www.telegraph.co.uk/news/worldnews/1566893/Artist-dyes-Romes-Trevi-Fountain-red.html (accessed January 20, 2009).

Moran, J., and D. Connel, eds. *The Official Handbook of the Legion of Mary*. Dublin: Concilium Legionis Mariae, 1993.

Morgan, David. "Aura and the Inversion of Marian Pilgrimage: Fatima and Her Statues." In *Moved by Mary: The Power of Pilgrimage in the Modern World*, edited by Anna-Karina Hermkens, Willy Jansen, and Catrien Notermans, 49–65. Aldershot, UK: Ashgate, 2009.

———. *The Sacred Gaze: Religious Visual Culture in Theory and Practice*. Berkeley: University of California Press, 2005.

Neutres, Julien. "Le cinéma fait-il l'histoire? Le cas de 'la dolce vita.'" *Vingtième Siècle. Revue d'histoire* 83 (2004): 53–63.

"Police Name Trevi Fountain Red Dye 'Vandal,'" *The Guardian*, October 23, 2007.

Povoledo, Elisabetta. "Dye in Roman Fountain May Have Been Art." *International Herald Tribune*, October 23, 2007.

———. "Dye in Trevi: Some Romans See Red, but Others Cry 'Art'!" *New York Times*, October 24, 2007.

Regan, Anthony J. *The Bougainville Conflict: Origins and Development, Main "Actors," and Strategies for Its Resolution*. Port Moresby: Faculty of Law, University of Papua New Guinea, 1996.

Ross, Marc Howard. *The Management of Conflict: Interpretations and Interests in Comparative Perspective*. New Haven: Yale University Press, 1993.

Salerno, Nicholas A. "La Dolce Vita or La Vita Nuova?" *College Composition and Communication* 14, no. 4 (1963): 223–228.

Schnapp, Jeffrey T. "The Fabric of Modern Times." *Critical Inquiry* 24, no. 1 (1997): 191–245.

Spretnak, Charlene. *Missing Mary: The Queen of Heaven and Her Re-emergence in the Modern Church*. New York: Palgrave-Macmillan, 2004.

Spyer, Patricia. "Fire without Smoke and Other Phantoms of Ambon's Violence: Media Effects, Agency, and the Work of Imagination." *Indonesia* 74 (2002): 1–16.

Stoller, Paul. *Embodying Colonial Memories*. New York: Routledge, 1995.

Sukhadwala, Ishita. "Man Throws Red Dye into Trevi Fountain in Rome Denouncing Rome Film Festival." AHN (All Headline News), October 20, 2007. http://www.allheadlinenews.com/articles/7008891368 (accessed January 20, 2009).

Taussig, Michael. *Mimesis and Alterity: A Particular History of the Senses*. New York: Routledge, 1993.

Todorov, Tzvetan. "Avant-gardes and Totalitarianism." *Daedalus*, Winter (2007): 51–66.

"Trevi Coins to Fund Food for the Poor." BBC News Online, November 27, 2006. http://news.bbc.co.uk/2/low/europe/6188052.stm.

"Turning the Trevi Fountain Red." The Cranky Professor, October 31, 2007. http://www.crankyprofessor.com/archives/001352.html.

van Dijk, Marc. "Vergelijkend onderzoek / Maria heeft ook militaire talenten." *Trouw*, De Verdieping, September 23, 2006. http://www.trouw.nl/deverdieping/religie_filosofie/article490196.ece/Vergelijkend_onderzoek_Maria_heeft_ook_militaire_talenten.

Vatican Archives. "Lumen Gentium, Dogmatic Constitution on the Church Solemnly Promulgated by His Holiness Pope Paul VI on November 21, 1964." http://www.vatican.va/archive/hist_councils/ii_vatican_council/documents/vat-ii_const_19641121_lumen-gentium_en.html (accessed January 20, 2009).

Venbrux, Eric, and Theo Meder. "The False Teeth in the Cod: A Legend in Context." *Contemporary Legend* 5 (1995): 115–131.

Ware, Helen. "Demography, Migration and Conflict in the Pacific." *Journal of Peace Research* 42, no. 4 (2005): 435–454.

Warner, Marina. *Alone of All Her Sex: The Myth and the Cult of the Virgin Mary*. New York: Vintage, 1983.

"The Waters Run Red." *New York Times*, October 20, 2007.

Webb, Michael. "The City in Film." *Design Quarterly* 136 (1987): 1–32.

Wuthnow, Robert. *Producing the Sacred: An Essay on Public Religion*. Urbana: University of Illinois Press, 1994.

Zucker, Paul. "Space and Movement in High Baroque City Planning." *Journal of the Society of Architectural Historians* 14, no. 1 (1955): 1–13.

4

Ritual as a Source of Conflict

*Robert Langer, Thomas Quartier, Udo Simon,
Jan Snoek, and Gerard Wiegers*

Ritual connects people, but it is also a source of conflict within and between groups, especially those whose practices are made public by way of media. In each of the following four case studies, at least one of the conflicting parties perceives a contested practice as a strategy for redefining social and religious boundaries. In the first instance, that of the Masonic oath, ritual becomes a medium for claiming sovereignty. In the second, the Muslim call to prayer in European countries expands into the space of the majority, where it is often interpreted as an attempt at domination. The third example demonstrates the shifting boundaries of ritual deployed in Alevi identity making. The fourth, that of evangelical education practices, discusses mediatized attempts to gain political influence in American society.

We take conflict to be any situation in which mutually exclusive aspirations, opinions, and views exist, and in which the subordination of one group to another is intended. Such conflicts can arise over any aspect of a ritual, ritual building block, or ritual complex. Is the ritual under consideration performed publicly? Should it be? Is it also possible to perform it privately or secretly? Should the ritual be performed at all? Is it performed correctly, that is, canonically? Is it rightly interpreted by the group itself and by outsiders? Does the ritual use manipulative elements that are capable of threatening civil society?

Internal conflicts, such as controversies over liturgical issues within a religious community, as well as external conflicts, such as those between a religious group practicing ritual slaughter and animal rights activists, may appear in a structured way and be characterized by assemblies, public discussions, and declarations. Established patterns of conflict resolution tend to develop ritualistic features. However, in many cases conflicts go out of control, spilling over boundaries and becoming highly emotional, aggressive, and even violent.

While internal conflicts (within a group) are distinct from external conflicts (between groups), individuals usually participate in more than one group at a time, and thus may be involved on both sides of a conflict. The specific constellation of an individual's involvement can make a great deal of difference. For example, when papal bulls condemned Freemasonry in the nineteenth century, English Freemasonry was not concerned, since it had so few Roman Catholic members. French Freemasonry, on the other hand, had a high number of Catholic adherents and reacted strongly to the condemnation. Eventually, many of its Roman Catholic members gave up church membership rather than relinquish their loyalty to Freemasonry, becoming strong proponents of secularism and creating an anticlerical brand of Freemasonry.

Criticism and quarrels over rituals are usually embedded in broader discourses that reflect social conflicts and challenge political and religious authority. A typical backdrop to conflict is a majority-minority relationship between ethnic and religious groups, especially if they are immigrants. In such instances, the transfer of a ritual can be interpreted by the majority as a kind of occupation.[1] Because a minority's ritual, once it leaves the private sphere, is a highly visible part of religious practice, it is a ready target for allegations that ritual performance is really an attempt to claim territory or cultural space. The minority's reactions to the majority's rejection can range from resignation to ostentatious performances of the controversial ritual.

In cases of hidden conflict, quarrels over ritual are usually symptoms of disputes over power, resources, participation, and hierarchy. Thus, debates about Islamic ritual practices in Europe or Alevi rituals in Turkey are processes of negotiating participation and recognition in society. A multiplicity of institutions, organizations, agents, and social subsystems, each of which has its own special interests and acts according to its own logic, is implicated in arguments about ritual practices. One of the social subsystems most frequently involved is the legal sector, especially if ritual performances affect the public sphere.

The media, too, constitute a subsystem with its own rules. The aim of media is to focus attention and transmit information, but media also tend to overemphasize those aspects of an event that will guarantee a high level of stimulation. A global world, where communities experience their relationships to each other through media, giving small groups, or even individuals, the opportunity to influence public debate, makes media representation a powerful factor in identity making. As a rule, however, mass media direct attention away from the marginalized and toward experts, politicians, and opinion makers.

Our case studies show that transferring rituals from one cultural context to another, transposing them from one medium to another, or shifting them from small scale to large scale requires reinterpretations of participants' original intentions. Consequently, rituals themselves can be employed as discursive elements in the process of negotiating conflicting claims.

Conflicts take different forms: latent and manifest, cold and hot, localized, national, and global, short term and long term, hidden and open. Some conflicts aim at the complete subordination of one party to another; some do not.[2] Some conflicts are between two religious belief systems, others between a secular and a religious frame of reference.

Competition, rivalry, and goal incompatibility do not necessarily result in violence even if tensions rise. Violence is likely when opponents do not share a common normative frame, yet even when they do, attitudes do not necessarily guide actions. Moreover, strategic considerations or lack of power may hide the conflict. As long as parties do not enforce their views by infringing on common ground, boundaries and rules can remain intact, and the conflict proceeds in a controlled, regulated way. The possibility for violence increases when persistent incompatibility of goals and views cannot be mediated by a third party such as a mutually acknowledged authority, tradition, or legal system. When authorities themselves compete, the implications for ritualized practices are strong, especially for religious minorities, even in liberal countries.

A decisive factor in conflict formation is the perceived incompatibility of goals. The question whether these goals are objectively incompatible often cannot be answered, and media—the sphere in which influential images are produced—come to play a crucial role. For most people, their perception of the world is media based; their reality is media fed. As a result, the intensity of conflict is perceived and evaluated by the extent of media coverage.

The Masonic Oath

Prior to today's electronic mass media, including radio, television, or the Internet, "media" meant primarily print documents, and pamphlets were often used to communicate to the public knowledge, both true and feigned. Our first case study shows how conflict between the Roman Catholic Church and Freemasonry over the oath that a candidate must swear on his initiation into Freemasonry was sparked and exacerbated by such documents.

The number of arguments used against Freemasonry is actually quite small, certainly less than ten. One of these—the swearing of an oath during the initiation ritual—was formulated in the oldest known anti-Masonic text, a pamphlet from 1698, and has remained influential in virtually all anti-Masonic publications ever since:

TO ALL GODLY PEOPLE, IN THE CITIE OF LONDON

Having thought it needful to warn you of the Mischiefs and Evils practised in the Sight of God by those called Freed Masons, I say take Care lest their Ceremonies and secret Swearings take hold of you; and be wary that none cause you to err from Godliness. For this devllish Sect of Men are Meeters in secret which swear against all without their Following. They are the Anti Christ which was to come leading Men from Fear of God. For how should Men meet in secret Places and with secret Signs taking Care that none observe them to do the Work of God; are not these Ways of Evil-doers?

Knowing how that God observeth privilly them that sit in Darkness they shall be smitten and the Secrets of their Hearts layed bare. Mingle not among this corrupt People lest you be found so at the World's Conflagration.

Set forth as a Warning to this Christian Generation by *M. Winter*, and Printed by *R. Sare* at Gray's Inn-gate, in *Holbourn*. 1698.[3]

We do not know who M. Winter was, nor where he got his information. There are no earlier publications that mention Freemasons swearing an oath, but there are several older manuscripts that do, including the Edinburgh Resister House Manuscript of 1696, which even includes the text of the oath. Given that only one copy of this pamphlet from 1698 is known, it seems unlikely that it was widely disseminated. Furthermore, the pamphlet sets forth an anti-oath argument before such protest was even warranted, because at this time, what Freemasonry demanded from its members was no more than a serious promise: "These Charges that you haue Received you shall well and truly keepe not discloseing the secresy of our Lodge to man woman nor Child: sticke nor stone: thing moueable nor vnmoveable soe god you helpe and his holy Doome Amen."[4]

Technically, an oath has two parts: the promises and the imprecations. This form only came into use within Freemasonry during its reorganization in London, between 1715 and 1725. From 1723 onward, summary descriptions of the rituals in use were published, probably by Freemasons for Freemasons,[5] in pamphlet form and contained the full text of the oath. The text found in Samuel Prichard's booklet, *Masonry Dissected*, from 1730 serves as an example:

I Hereby solemnly Vow and Swear in the Presence of Almighty God and this Right Worshipful Assembly, that I will Hail and Conceal, and never Reveal the Secrets or Secresy of Masons or Masonry, that shall be Revealed unto me; unless to a True and Lawful Brother, after due Examination, or in a Just and Worshipful Lodge of Brothers and Fellows well met.

I furthermore Promise and Vow, that I will not Write them, Print them, Mark them, Carve them or Engrave them, or cause them to be Written, Printed, Marked, Carved or Engraved on Wood or Stone, so as the Visible Character or Impression of a Letter may appear, whereby it may be unlawfully obtain'd.

All this under no less Penalty than to have my Throat cut, my Tongue taken from the Roof of my Mouth, my Heart pluck'd from under my Left Breast, them to be buried in the Sands of the Sea, the Length of a Cable-rope from Shore, where the Tide ebbs and flows twice in 24 Hours, my Body to be burnt to Ashes, my Ashes to be scatter'd upon the Face of the Earth, so that there shall be no more Remembrance of me among Masons. So help me God.[6]

The first two paragraphs of this text contain the promises; the last one contains the imprecations. From 1735 on, states and churches protested the swearing of such an oath. The reason is not difficult to find, since there are biblical injunctions against oath taking, such as Matthew 5:33–37:

Ye have heard that it hath been said by them of old time, Thou shalt not forswear thyself, but shalt perform unto the Lord thine oaths: But I [Jesus] say unto you, Swear not at all; neither by heaven; for it is God's throne: Nor by the earth; for it is his footstool: neither by Jerusalem; for it is the city of the great King. Neither shalt thou swear by thy head, because thou canst not make one hair white or black. But let your communication be, Yea, yea; Nay, nay: for whatsoever is more than these cometh of evil.

This text is taken from the Sermon on the Mount, in which Jesus revises a number of historic commandments given to the Jews. According to Matthew 5:17, Jesus says, "Think not that I am come to destroy the law, or the prophets: I am not come to destroy, but to fulfil." The text about swearing goes back to several commandments in the Old Testament, for example, Leviticus 19:12 ("ye shall not swear by my name falsely, neither shalt thou profane the name of thy God") and Deuteronomy 5:11 ("Thou shalt not take the name of the Lord thy God in vain: for the Lord will not hold him guiltless that taketh his name in vain"), all of which relate to the third of the Ten Commandments: "Thou shalt not take the name of the Lord thy God in vain; for the Lord will not hold him guiltless that taketh his name in vain" (Exodus 20:7).

"Taking the name of the Lord thy God in vain" meant swearing an oath with imprecations, while calling upon God as a witness. This is the act forbidden by the third commandment and the Gospel of Matthew. Not surprisingly, this interdiction found its way into church law. Less obvious perhaps is that from there it also found its way into state law in countries with an official state religion, such as the Netherlands in the eighteenth century. However, neither the churches nor the states would interdict the swearing of an oath completely. Both allowed it if and only if they, as sovereign powers, demanded someone do so. Conversely, therefore, the fact that Masonic Grand Lodges and lodges demanded their members swear such an oath implied a claim of sovereignty.

That Masonic Grand Lodges and lodges did indeed claim sovereignty cannot be doubted. Not only did, and do, they have their own constitutions, but when the Grand Master entered the Grand Lodge in procession, he was invariably preceded by the Grand Sword-bearer and followed by the Grand Standard-bearer—the latter carrying the banner or standard of the Grand Lodge, while the former carried the Sword of Sovereignty. A clearer expression of claiming sovereignty is hardly possible. And it was precisely this claim that sovereign states and churches could not accept.

On November 30, 1735, the states of Holland and West Friesland, that is, the government, were the first institutions to interdict Freemasonry, and the interdiction was again issued in the form of pamphlets.

Three official reasons were given, although there can be no doubt that none of them applied; they were chosen mainly because they were supposed to be readily accepted by the general public. However, there must have been underlying reasons, or else no interdiction would have taken place, but these must have been other than those formulated officially. Close observation of the events surrounding this interdiction reveal that the claim of sovereignty was likely a major reason, and that the swearing of the oath was a crucial point.[7] Some days before the interdiction was proclaimed, the states demanded that lodges in The Hague turn over certain documents, and there are good reasons to assume that these documents also included the text of the oath.

The interdiction of 1735 was never lifted explicitly, yet from 1744 on the Dutch lodges resumed. Dutch law had precise rules for when something was counted as the swearing of an oath. Apart from the fact that the text had to include imprecations and invoke God, the oath taker must have his right hand on an open Bible and see that it is the Bible. In order to prevent breaking the law, the brethren invented creative alternatives to the usual procedure, for example, having the candidate pronounce the oath blindfolded, after which the blindfold was removed and the candidate asked if he were prepared to repeat his oath now that he had seen the light.

Nevertheless, on June 28, 1761, the Dutch Grand Lodge decided to abolish oath taking with one's hand on the Bible, invoking the Great Architect of the Universe.[8] Shortly afterward, the imprecations were dropped altogether. About nine years later, the Dutch Grand Lodge received a letter from the English one, dated March

2, 1770, stating that the "Sublime Grand Lodge of Freemasonry seated in London, being aware that the Freemasons, more than anyone else, must conform to the laws of their country, has not been able to, and cannot disapprove of the alteration which the before mentioned Grand Lodge [of the Netherlands] has found necessary to make for that purpose in our obligation formula."[9] Other countries would eventually follow the Dutch example.

Meanwhile, Pope Clement XII had followed the example of the Dutch state and interdicted Freemasonry in his bull *In eminenti* (1738), using the argument against the swearing of an oath. It is generally assumed that the pope was well aware of the pamphlets published by the states of Holland and West Friesland. In addition, the text of the bull was published in pamphlet form. Pamphlets of the papal bulls were sent to all the bishops to be read in the cathedrals, an action that made them church law, valid in the bishopric concerned.

The emerging conflict between the Freemasons and the Roman Catholic Church escalated in nineteenth-century France following the nationalist movement in Italy, which was led by two Freemasons, Giuseppe Garibaldi (1807–1882, initiated in 1844) and Camille Benso, Comte de Cavour (1810–1861). This escalation caused successive popes to fight, unsuccessfully, against them and to maintain the church state by using the weapons at hand, namely, papal bulls that repeated the same kind of arguments against Freemasons over and over again. The mainly Roman Catholic French Freemasons who were not aware of the reasons behind these bulls assumed the assault was directed at them, and thus many of them turned increasingly anticlerical. This development culminated in the creation of an explicitly anticlerical form of Freemasonry in France around 1877.

Freemasonry in the United Kingdom was not confronted with anti-Masonic actions from either the state or from any church to which a significant number of the order's members belonged, at least not until the end of the twentieth century when the 1985 report of the Faith and Works Committee of the Methodist Conference was published, addressing the question: "Is membership of Freemasonry and of the Church incompatible?"[10] The answer to the question was a clear yes. The many Methodist Freemasons thereupon founded the Association of Methodist Freemasons, which protested the report, pointing out the large number of factual errors it contained. In 1993, the report was referred back to the Faith and Works Committee for revision, but no revision was ever published, a fact that implies the report was actually withdrawn.

After the publication of the 1985 report, the General Synod of the Church of England appointed a working group to study the Methodist document, and two years later it published a report, *Freemasonry and Christianity. Are They Compatible? A Contribution to Discussion*. This report does not answer the question posed but—not surprisingly—it condemns, among other things, the swearing of an oath.

Twenty years earlier, in 1964, the United Grand Lodge of England had made the oath optional, but in 1986, in response to the report of the Anglican Church, the oath was abandoned.

In that same year, the General Assembly of the United Reformed Church in England discussed the same theme, but came to no negative conclusions about Freemasonry. Compared to the large interest in the condemnations by Methodists and Anglicans, there was remarkably little attention from the media regarding this event.

In sum, this case is an example of a ritual practice revealed to the public by means of pamphlets, a popular contemporary medium, causing an escalating series of conflicts between the performing institution and certain external organizations. Several kinds of documents (pamphlets, bulls, reports) then communicated the attitudes of the offended to the offenders, while the outside world was informed in newspapers and, more recently, other news media such as television. In response, the Freemasons eventually dropped the imprecations from the text of their oath, though at different times in different countries. In the United States the imprecations were not dropped, while in France the conflict culminated in an explicitly anticlerical brand of Freemasonry.

The media, that is, the publications, gave rise to the conflict in the first place. The first ones, such as the 1698 anti-Masonic pamphlet *To all godly people, in the citie of London* by M. Winter, simply mentioned that the Freemasons swore an oath. Later publications gave the text of the oath in full. From 1723 onward, such publications included the recently introduced imprecations, and it was this form that actually triggered substantial opposition from states and churches. As long as the Freemasons succeeded in keeping their rituals completely secret, no conflict over them emerged. Earlier manuscripts and publications that mentioned, or even included, the text of the oath met with no substantial opposition. Real conflict only emerged once the divulged texts showed that, through the recent inclusion of the imprecations, Freemasonry effectively claimed sovereignty, something traditional states and churches regarded as their exclusive prerogative.

The Muslim Call to Prayer in Europe

It is an impressive experience to hear muezzins call the faithful to worship, joining each other one by one, all with different voices and in their own style. This experience is described as impressive and emblematic not only by practicing Muslims but also by cultural Muslims and Christians who have lived in the Middle East. Unfortunately, in some places, such as Amman and probably Cairo in the near future, there is to be only one standardized call, which is simultaneously transmitted to the mosques from a central point. Tradition is contested even in Muslim countries, while in some parts of Europe there is considerable debate about whether the public Muslim call to prayer should be allowed at all. By communicating controversies about the presence of Islam in general and the *adhān* in particular as one of the most conspicuous symbols of Islam in the public sphere, the media play a crucial role in both inciting and moderating these debates and their interplay on both national and local levels.

According to Islamic religious law, the ritual call to prayer (*adhān*) should precede all types of Muslim ritual prayer (*ṣalāt*), not only the obligatory five daily prayers (including the *ṣalāt al-jumʿa*, or Friday prayer held in the mosque, the performance of which is obligatory for male adult Muslims) but also prayers at the two canonical festivals and supererogatory prayers. *Adhān* is an Arabic word meaning "announcement," and it is not restricted to public collective settings but may also be found in private, individual settings, as, for example, when it is pronounced in the right ear of a newborn child.[11] The call was instituted only after the emigration of the first Muslims from Mecca to Medina in 622 C.E., when the Prophet Muhammad was consulted about the best way to call the faithful to prayer. When asked whether the *adhān* could be performed by flags, fires, *nāqūs* (a kind of wooden plank), drums, or horns, the Prophet replied, "The human voice could best communicate the religious inspirations, and feelings and the solemnity of the occasion."[12] He also rejected the use of bells, the medium used by Christians. Muslims are supposed to be different from, not like, adherents of other religions. Thus since the seventh century, in most places where its performance has been allowed, the *adhān* is pronounced by human voices in Arabic.[13] If the muezzin (*muʾadhdhin*) or the community does not know Arabic, the call, according to all schools of law except the Hanbalite School, can be pronounced in another language.

Muslim scholars have discussed the question whether the *adhān* should be amplified. The Saudi scholar Ibn Jibrīn gave it as his expert opinion in a *fatwā* that Muslims who are not allowed to make the call public by amplification need not migrate to a Muslim country, that is, perform the *hijra*, since the use of amplifiers and loudspeakers is an innovation (*bidʿa*) and thus may be omitted.[14]

There are minor differences among the law schools, including the Shiites, but for the most part, the formula of the call is more or less fixed, its wording repeated twice: "God is the greatest. I bear witness that there is no god but Allah. I bear witness that Muhammad is the messenger of Allah. Come to Prayer. Come to the Success. God is the greatest. I bear witness that there is no god but Allah."[15] There is a second call to prayer inside the mosque (*iqāma*) indicating the commencement of the *ṣalāt*. The formulas are the same except that the words "now begins the *ṣalāt*" are added. The *adhān* is to be performed from a high place in the mosque or from the minaret, and believers who hear it are supposed to answer its call by uttering a number of affirmative sentences and then starting the prayer. The *adhān* is not performed outside a religious setting and, in this respect, it differs from church bells, which are tolled in times of danger and during secular festivities.

The status of the *adhān* is, according to most Islamic schools of law, either a constant practice, which is strongly recommended (*sunna muʾakkada*), or a collective duty (*farḍ kifāya*), meaning that it suffices if one person from a group performs it. According to Malik Ibn Anas, founder of one of the schools of law, the performance of the *adhān* is an obligation for congregational mosques, not small ones.[16] Obligatory or not, most Muslims regard the *adhān* as one of the characteristic religious practices of Islam (*shaʿāʾir*).

According to the Moroccan imam al-Khamlīshī, who served for a time as an imam in Rotterdam, the *adhān* is one of the most important rites in Islam. When Muslims cannot perform the ritual fully and publicly, and are subject to fanaticism, they should migrate to an Islamic country.[17] Of course, al-Khamlīshī admitted, the *adhān* can be performed inside mosques, rather than publicly, but then it does not serve the goal of informing people about the time of prayer. He considers the prohibition against performing the public call an infringement of basic religious freedom. Indeed, in non-Muslim countries, the call is done apart from the mosque and its minaret, demonstrating that it is a paradigmatic element in the public manifestation of Islam. However, even in countries with a Muslim majority, such as Turkey, the public manifestation of the *adhān* may become a source of conflict.[18]

The public performance of the *adhān* in Europe is not a recent phenomenon. John Boswell describes the singing of the *ṣalāt*, or "the crying of the name of Muhammad," as it was called by the Christian authorities, "as a focal point of the whole controversy of Mudéjar [Muslims in medieval Christian Spain] religious liberties."[19] Nonetheless, as comparative studies on Islam in European countries indicate, there are specific differences between contemporary national discourses on the *adhān* problem.[20] These media-driven controversies seem to be connected with different national and local policies toward multiculturalism and Islam, claims of institutions and organizations, including those of migrants, and the socioeconomic conditions in which they are embedded.

Here, we argue that the public display of the rite initially incites controversies on a local level in places where no juridical arrangements about its performance exist on a national level. We also argue that in order to prevent conflicts, Muslims often limit the practice of *adhān* to its performance inside the mosque.

Recent history of the *adhān* in Europe begins with the Dutch city of Oss, where the call to prayer was publicly performed, beginning in September 1985. Permitting its Muslim citizens to perform the *adhān* for a few minutes before the Friday prayer, Oss became the first European city to allow its public performance. At the end of 1985, another Dutch city, Leiden, followed, allowing two Islamic communities to perform an amplified *adhān* on Fridays, at least as an experiment for a brief period of time. The amplified performance was to take no longer than three minutes, and since no official protests reached the community council, permission was granted for an indeterminate length of time.

At the end of the 1980s, an increasing number of Muslim communities in the Netherlands began to practice the *adhān* publicly, sometimes without duly consulting local authorities, hence the need to find a solution for conflicts that might surface nationally. When the issue was discussed in parliament, it appeared that the majority of parliamentarians saw the ritual as equal to the tolling of church bells, so, on the basis of the principles of the freedom of religion and the equality of all religions and philosophies of life before the law, parliament deemed the practice allowable in the Netherlands. A minority of Christian parties voted against this decision. As a result, the issue was included in the 1988 "Bill of Public Manifestations," in which article 10 states that each municipality has the right to make precise regulations. Thus, the bill delegated the issue to local authorities to decide on the basis of local regulations about limiting noise in public.

Some years ago, Nico Landman, in a thesis about the institutionalization of Islam in the Netherlands, predicted that the public performance of the *adhān* would become increasingly frequent.[21] This prediction has not come true. Many mosques do not perform the public call, and many perform it only indoors. While we know of no empirical data that explain this development, it seems likely that the increasingly mediatized conflicts about Muslim presence in Europe and the Netherlands, in particular, are the main factor behind refraining from performing the ritual publicly. On the basis of the Dutch case, it seems reasonable to assume that a process of conflict prevention took place. Instead of exercising their right to perform the mediated, amplified ritual openly, Muslims in the Netherlands have tried to avoid conflict by refraining from doing so.

In the United Kingdom, where Muslim minorities do not have the same legal status as Christians, the matter of the *adhān* is decided strictly at the local level.[22] In fact, in areas where few Muslims live and antagonisms exist, either latently or openly, even establishing a mosque may lead to problems. In April 2008, members of the Central Oxford Mosque wished to start transmitting the public *adhān* three times a day using loudspeakers. The issue was hotly debated in the media, and Dr. Allan Chapman of Oxford University was quoted as saying that the *adhān* is a torment to non-Muslims.[23] "It's not a matter of people's right to religious freedom, it's about making Islam the religion of public space—getting into people's houses and work places," Chapman said. Attempts at mediation were undertaken by the imams, who declared, "We will perform the public call to prayer on Fridays only," and one of the bishops, who said, "We should be happy with this diversity, and the presence of Muslims. A public expression of that faith is both natural and reasonable." Others proposed using Birmingham, where local radio stations transmit the call to Muslim listeners, as an example.[24] Seán McLaughlin found that, even though conflicts about mosques in general and the call to prayer in particular have occurred in many places, they were absent in the city of Bradford. There some mosques perform the public call two or three times a day, depending on local demographic and political factors such as the percentage of Muslims in areas where mosques were established, the presence of Muslim councilors, and their influence in maintaining good relations with non-Muslim populations.[25] However, in general the call to prayer is rarely heard in public in the United Kingdom.

In France, the law that regulates the call to prayer is in theory the same as that regulating church bells. The mayor, as the representative of local authorities, is entitled to make the decision, while the representative of the religious association is restricted to a consultative role. According to van Koningsveld and Shadid, Muslims in France have until now refrained from performing the call to prayer from the minaret and do so only inside the mosque.[26] Their doing so, they say, is discretionary but also based on their perception that there is little chance that the call to prayer would be accepted since it does not belong to French tradition. Muslims did not even apply for permission to perform the call for the Friday prayer, preferring to concentrate on issues essential to overall well-being, such as improving the social and economic position of the communities in question.

Unlike Great Britain and France, where immigrants from North Africa and the Indian subcontinent form the majority of Muslims, Germany's Turkish immigrants have become the dominant Muslim group.[27] For a long time, Germany refused to recognize itself as a country of immigration. Now, however, immigration has become accepted as a matter of course, but it has taken time to accept the fact that immigrants also bring their religion with them. Conflicts over the representation of Islam in public space focus on a limited number of Muslim symbols, such as the headscarf, ritual slaughter, the building of mosques, minarets, and the *adhān*.

In Germany, Muslims are not organized as corporations under public law, so Muslim organizations are in a different position than Christian ones, which have certain privileges when it comes to urban planning. This disparity means that building mosques, including minarets, and publicly performing the *adhān* is a matter of negotiations between different local parties. On the non-Muslim side, these may include municipal administrations, representatives of political parties, spokespersons for citizens' initiatives, and Christian churches.[28] On the Muslim side, national or even transnational organizations such as the Turkish-Islamic Union for Religious Affairs (DITIB), the Islamrat (dominated by the Milli Görüş movement),[29] the Zentralrat der Muslime (Central Council of Muslims in Germany, often Muslims of Arabic origin and converts), and the VIKZ (the Turkish-dominated

Association of Islamic Cultural Centers) play a decisive role. While each of these umbrella organizations pursues strategic goals of its own—for example, the DITIB aims at maintaining Turkish state influence on Muslims in Germany—all the organizations strive to represent the whole Muslim community in Germany. All Islamic groups refer to the *adhān* as an obligation, or at least as part of the prophetic tradition, although some keep a low public profile.[30]

Beginning in 1987 and proceeding on a strictly local basis, the conditions for performing *adhān* were negotiated in a number of German cities, including Düren (1987, *adhān* five times a day), Bochum (once a day), Bergkamen (once a week), Dortmund (1993, once a week, now up to three times a day), and Siegen. The most conspicuous conflict over *adhān* took place in the city of Duisburg, which has a high ratio of immigrants. Starting in 1995, and with delaying tactics exercised by the municipal administration, the conflict eventually ended after heated debates that attracted international attention. The compromise allowed the public transmission of *adhān* without amplification.[31]

In German legal reasoning, neither an unconditional allowance of *adhān* and its amplification nor a principled prohibition is possible. Unlike bell ringing, the call for prayer's wording has religious implications. On the other hand, as distinguished from church bells, amplifiers do not fall under the category of *res sacra* (sacred things). In both cases, protection against excessive noise must be taken into account.[32]

In Germany, potential conflict was fed by ideas centering on ethnicity, culture, religion, and space. The main motive for rejecting *adhān* seems to be fear of foreign domination.[33] As in many other places in Europe, the *adhān* in Germany is seen by many non-Muslims as a step toward Islam's conquest of Europe.[34] Almost half of non-Muslim Germans say they would experience the call to prayer in their residential area as a source of annoyance. Twenty-seven percent feel disturbed by mosques and 20 percent by a minaret in their neighborhood. The *adhān* issue then is more emotionally charged than debates about other symbols of Muslim presence in the public sphere.

The most frequent representations of Islam in the media concern Allah, jihad, the Koran, minarets, mosques, and muezzins. Minarets, mosques, and muezzins appear in contexts where the expansion of Islam is an issue, often with the call of the muezzin displayed in polemical ways.[35] Where immigrants form a substantial ratio of citizens, many of the longer-established citizens consider permission to transmit *adhān* publicly as the ritual equivalent of handing over the keys to the city.[36]

However, when it comes to demonstrating against mosques or the *adhān*, few non-Muslims actually attend public protests. One reason may be simply to escape blame for xenophobia, or to avoid being lumped together with members of right-wing organizations. Nevertheless, catchwords, often originating from the relatively small rightist camp, are picked up from the media by individuals and then used to express their own attitudes, while concrete action confirming personal commitment is avoided. The same pattern is true among Muslims; they too avoid public demonstrations. The first unamplified pronouncement of the *adhān* in Duisburg in January 1997 was a media event that more journalists than worshippers attended.[37]

Case studies of conflicts over Muslim religious symbols show a remarkable parallelism in argumentative strategies, on the side of proponents as well as opponents. Both parties seem to be heavily influenced by national discourses, applying arguments selectively garnered from the local media.[38] During the Duisburg debate over *adhān*, local players picked up and reproduced selective anti-Islamic statements that were also in the national debate, statements portraying Islam as a totalitarian politico-religious movement aimed at expanding its territory into Germany.[39]

The symbolic impact of conflicts over Muslim rituals can only be understood if one takes into account the fact that half of the Muslims in Germany report feeling excluded from German society or discriminated against. Moreover, empirical research shows an increasing gap between Turkish immigrants and the majority of the German population as a consequence of 9/11.[40] Recent data also show that Muslims feel that Islamophobia is fueled by the media.[41]

Most researchers today view the wish of immigrants to establish mosques, including minarets, as a sign of commitment to the societies in which they live. In other words, those who build houses make themselves at home. From this perspective, to claim the right publicly to perform *adhān* once a week is to claim participation in society. The action is a sign of normalization and integration, a ritual display of the permanent and public presence of Islam. In this view, debates about Islamic symbols and practices are a catalyst not only for conflict but also for cooperation and conflict resolution. What could be described as conflict is actually a process of negotiating participation and agency in a multicultural society. In Germany, negotiations often result in compromises that link the waiver of *adhān* to some other form of compensation. For instance, instead of allowing the *adhān*, some other symbolic representation of Islam is permitted, for example, the building of a higher minaret.

Public discourse also triggers debates within the Muslim community. For instance, some voices argue against the amplification of *adhān* because it lacks warmth and weakens the emotional appeal of the call.[42] In the beginning of the Duisburg controversy, some Turkish groups warned against a worsening of relations with the German majority. Conflicting lines between groups of different political (secular, left-wing, nationalistic) and religious (Sunni, Alevi) orientations are not always adequately reflected in media coverage. Tellingly, in the course of the debate, solidarity between these groups grew under pressure from outside.[43] For most Muslims, the *adhān* issue is not so much a theological issue as a matter of equal rights for all citizens of the country.

Non-Muslims often reject petitions for public *adhān*, viewing them as an attempt at Islamizing public space and dominating it by infringing on established territorial rights. Arguing that it is more difficult to escape sounds than sights, critics experience the call to prayer as a threat. Moreover, while the architecture of a mosque is often adapted to its environment, the *adhān* has a fixed form and content whose only variables are volume, timing, and geographical placement. The options then are public performance amplified, not amplified, or done strictly inside the mosque.

Protest against Islamic symbols is often intermingled with protest against serious deficits in deprived areas, such as poor urban planning. Inhabitants of areas in decline often experience publicly performed Islamic practices as the last straw, the one that breaks the camel's back.[44] It is not only deprived and uneducated non-Muslims who reject *adhān* but also middle-class and wealthy intellectuals. Moreover, rejection of *adhān* occurs in areas other than those characterized by social tension and disinegration.[45]

The fracture lines of conflict can be drawn in varying ways. The opposition is not always or only Muslims versus Christian Europeans, or the majority versus the minority. Sometimes moderate Muslims and Christians stand on one side and noncompromising Christians and Muslims on the other.

The media help transform local debates into national ones. This process is characterized by progressive delocalization, during which information becomes increasingly imaginative. In the Duisburg conflict, a local cleric arguing against *adhān* was made a figurehead of resistance by the media. Indeed, sound bites—tersely worded pronouncements—have the best chance of being highlighted in media coverage. Not surprisingly then, a single protagonist can quickly become a symbol of rigid attitudes on behalf of an otherwise silent segment of the population that shares his attitudes but not his experience. In this way, media underscore or even help establish communities with shared values and ways of imagining the world.

Although media often generalize, with a pointed emphasis on conflict,[46] oversimplified views of media as purveyors of stereotypes are misleading.[47] In fact, the role of media is ambiguous; they provide opportunities for dialogue, and detailed and balanced information, as well as stereotypes for media consumers to integrate into already existing attitudes.

The media relate local conflicts to other incidents and debates of a similar kind. With respect to Islam, people get their information in a mediatized form.

Even in neighborhoods where conflicts originate, people get their information about them through the media. During the debate over *adhān* in the city of Lünen, the local mosque association was informed about the harsh reaction of residents only through the media. Members of the mosque were even more startled, since they had believed they were understood by the neighborhood.[48] The flow of information usually circulates within one party's network. Mosque associations get their information from other mosques; municipal administrations from other administrations, and so on. Information provided by "the others," or by the media of "the others," is perceived in a highly selective way, if at all.[49] Only during the course of the conflict do the parties become part of a greater network of public participation and debate.

Alevi Rituals and Their Mediatization

The Alevis are a non-Sunni, nonorthodox Muslim ethnoreligious group settled mainly within modern Turkey with subgroups in northern Iraq, Syria, and the former Ottoman territories in the Balkans.[50] Alevis form a large proportion of the Western European migrant population originating in Turkey. In Germany, for instance, there are around 550,000 Alevis.[51] In Turkey, the estimation is that Alevis form between 10 and 20 percent of the total population.[52] The majority of Alevis speak Turkish, some speaking Kurmâncî-Kurdish or Zâzâkî as their mother tongue; both are Iranian, that is, Indo-European, not Turkic, languages.

The ethnogenesis of the Alevis is connected to several socioreligious movements constituted as rebellions against the Sunni states and dynasties created in Anatolia by the Seljūqs and later the Ottomans. These movements culminated in a conflict over eastern Anatolia between the Ottomans and the Safavids in the fifteenth and sixteenth centuries. This uprising led to persecution of such nonconformists as the Anatolian Kızılbaş (proto-Alevis), which were composed of the Turkmen and Kurdish tribes—commonly referred to as "heterodox" in Orientalist literature—that supported the Safavi dervish order that had reigned as a dynasty in Iran since Shah Ismail (1501). Parallel to the persecutions, the Ottomans developed a distinct Sunni Muslim identity in contrast to the Safavids, who had become supporters of orthodox Shiism since the reign of Shah Ismail. In turn, the Ottomans supported the mildly heterodox Bektashi dervish order, which absorbed several heterodox Muslim movements and groups, such as parts of the Kızılbaş, into the Ottoman social system. Because of these developments, the Ottoman Kızılbaş lost contact with the Safavi order, which became restricted to Iran.

In contrast to this historical view of formative events from the eleventh to sixteenth centuries, the Alevis' own narrative emphasizes their descent from the immediate family of the Prophet Muhammad and their supporters. Consequently, the Alevis consider their religious leaders and holy lineages as direct or indirect offspring of the Twelve Imams (*oniki imam*) of the Twelver-Shia, with Ali and his son Hüseyin (Arabic: al-Husayn) as the most prominent holy figures—Ali being a cousin as well as son-in-law, and Hüseyin the grandson, of Muhammad.

Along with this history of mutual estrangement, a major source of conflict in Alevi-Sunni relations in contemporary Turkey is mediatized and publicized ritual performances. The most important of these to Alevi identity is the so-called *âyîn-i cem*, or congregation ritual, (hereafter, the short form *cem* is used).[53] It is a collective service led by ritual specialists and religious leaders.[54] Traditionally a major event observed once or twice a year in Alevi village communities, this ritual developed into a standardized weekly communal service with a canonized repertoire of songs and ritual dances. This shift happened partly as a reaction to Sunni Muslim groups, political Islamists, in the 1980s, who emphasized the Sunni Friday mosque prayer as their central ritual, which the Alevis in turn do not practice. This ritual became an occasion for political protest against the secular Turkish Republic and a starting point of physical violence against Alevis by radical Sunni Islamists.

A *cem* begins with a congregation of Alevis—traditionally from one village community, but in modern, urban contexts, originating from different regions—assembling on a Thursday evening, called Friday evening (*cuma akşamı*), since the start of the day in traditional Oriental reckoning is sunset before the actual day, not midnight as in Western calendar systems.[55] Before the service, sheep are sacrificed and other foodstuff brought to the kitchen of the house for the *cem*, where it is prepared and packed in portions (*lokma*) for distribution. The congregation sits in front of the ritual specialists (*dede*), usually in a semicircle. After a speech by the *dede* (*sohbet*) and, among other prayers, the ritual invocation of "agreement" (*râzîlik*) of all community members, including the *dede* himself, to commence the ritual in a state of mutual peace and brotherhood, a musician, either the *dede* or a so-called *zâkir*, begins singing hymns accompanied by a lute (*saz*). One of these hymns calls the "servants" (*hizmetçi*, recruited from both sexes) to the ritual square (*meydân*) in the middle of the room, where they are sworn in by the *dede* before carrying out their duties: preparing the *dede*'s seat (*post*), symbolic handwashing, lighting candles, and symbolic sweeping of the ritual square. Those who carry out their duties outside the actual ritual space are door guards, slaughterers, cooks, and kitchen helpers.

Next, religious hymns describing the suffering of the Twelve Imams are sung by the *zâkir*, and the congregation, which grows increasingly ecstatic, sing and move to the melodies, sometimes rhythmically flogging themselves, hands on thighs, especially during hymns confessing their faith in "oneness" (*tevhîd*, "oneness [of and with God]"). Interrupted by prayers, prostrations, and collective verbal repentance for sins, the musical service finally culminates in a ritual dance (*semâh*), which also counts as one of the services. Laments are sung for the martyrs, especially those who died with Hüseyin during the massacre at Kerbelâ, Iraq, in 680 C.E. Water is distributed or sprayed to quench Kerbelâ's desert thirst, the ritual square is swept once again, the candles are extinguished, and, after prayers, food is distributed evenly to the exhausted congregation.

These weekly services, however consolatory to an Alevi, can seem offensive to a Sunni Muslim, especially since the Alevi designation for the service is *ibâdet*, the same term used in orthodox Islamic law to include the ritual prayers used in a mosque. For Sunni Muslims, *ibâdet* excludes music and dance, both generally considered rather immoral by Muslim orthodoxy.

Public Alevi *cem* was established in the 1990s at several Alevi "cultural centers," mainly in Istanbul and Ankara, which were also attacked in the beginning by radical Sunnis. Now the conflict between Alevis and the state continues over the question of whether these *cemevi* (houses for the *cem*) should be officially recognized as places of worship (*ibâdethâne, mabed*), the same as Sunni mosques. An official recognition would result in economic advantages for Alevi communities, because official Muslim places of worship such as mosques are financed by the Turkish Directorate of Religious Affairs.[56]

Discourse on Alevi rituals is heavily mediatized in the form of films and broadcasts of religious activities such as *cem*, commemoration ceremonies for Alevi martyrs, and *semâh* dances. On television and the Internet, pictures and plans of *cemevi* also appear. Among media that are mainly Alevi owned or run are books, magazines, several radio and television stations, and a mass of institutional as well as private Internet sites.[57] As Alevis began leaving their villages in the 1950s, becoming a transregional and transnational community, these representations of performances and places emerged as one of the most important means of establishing, enforcing, reproducing, and differentiating Alevi identity. Another important part of the discourse on Alevi-Sunni relations is the representation of orthodox Islamic rituals in Alevi religious discourse. Such Sunni rituals as daily ritual prayer (*salât/namâz*) or the pilgrimage to Mecca (*hacc*) figure in Alevi theology as "rituals of the şerîat [regulations of the Islamic law] level of human religiosity," a state that Alevis claim to have overcome collectively. They place themselves on the level of *tarîkat* (path), which means that such "orthodox" Muslim rituals are potentially obsolete, though not forbidden. This designation is considered an offense to "true Islam" by the Sunni majority.

The Alevi *cem* is the most prominent example of Alevi ritual practice. It was classified as a Sufi *zikir* (collective, ecstatic prayer ritual, including song, music, and dance) by Oriental as well as Western outsiders, and historical data on rituals in Anatolia make it clear that the *cem* has many links to such dervish practices. Direct influences from the Safavi and Bektashi orders are also known from historical sources. In modern times, the strong link of many Alevi groups to the Bektashi order of dervishes, which tried to establish leadership over the rural Alevi, influenced the form and content of the *cem*. The ritual was performed traditionally within closed village communities, where women and men both participated. Although religious specialists were male, the fact that both sexes took part in the service was and still is suspect to outsiders, since majority Islamic practices usually segregate the sexes, especially in ritual contexts such as communal prayer. Moreover, a final initiation ritual after marriage, the *musâhiblik*, in which two married couples (i.e., four persons) are bound together in a form of pseudo-kinship (their children are not allowed to marry each other)—a prerequisite for full religious socialization and full participation in the ritual—aggravated outsiders' accusations that the Alevis practice immoral behavior such as promiscuity and even incest. Accusations about promiscuity in certain Sufi orders are long-standing in Muslim religious discourses, the first sources dating back to the ninth century.[58]

From the founding of the modern Turkish Republic in the 1920s, Sufi rituals were prohibited, a move achieved legally by the so-called *Tekke ve Zaviye Kanunu* (Law on Dervish Lodges), by which all dervish lodges were officially closed and dervish titles, including that of *dede*, costumes, rituals such as *zikir*, and teachings were either explicitly forbidden or forced into strict privacy. At first, this suppression did not affect the village communities, who continued to conduct their secret rituals. As oral sources suggest, the persecution finally hit the villages in the early 1960s as an indirect result of the re-Islamization policy of the Democratic Party regime of the 1950s.[59] At that time, young Alevis had already begun incorporating leftist liberation ideologies into their worldview. The antiheterodox persecution at that time was achieved by police raids of Alevi villages. The raids disturbed religious ceremonies and later on went hand-in-hand with antileftist actions by the state.

With regional exceptions, beginning in the 1960s, Alevi rituals ceased to be conducted in their traditional form, with hereditary religious leaders (*dede*) presiding over the services and holding legal courts in the congregation. Nevertheless, Alevi youth who migrated into city centers began using ritual symbols, texts, and music in political activities. The symbolism of Alevi ritual was easy to adapt to discourses on class struggle, especially since its narrative portions, paralleled by performances during the *cem*, tell the story of the oppression of the Alid family (the *ehl-i beyt* and the Twelve Imams) by the "evil" Sunni rulers, especially the Umayyad caliph, Yazīd Ibn Muʿāwiya; such oppression first peaked in the massacre at Kerbela under the rule of Yazīd (Turkish: Yezid).

The activists' exploitation of Alevi symbolism and the Kerbelâ story as a motive for political struggle made the *cem*'s texts and songs public before the ritual's actual revival in the late 1980s. This instrumentalization of cultural resources ensured the transmission of ritual content and knowledge throughout this transfer phase from premodern to modern, a shift that, until recently, was perceived by scholars as a major disruption, rather than a continuation, of the ritual tradition.[60]

Two developments preceded the *cem*'s publicization. First, in the early 1970s, Alevi intellectuals of a more religious background than their leftist counterparts started publishing Alevi magazines. Second, Alevis in Istanbul and Ankara, who had migrated there en masse during the 1960s and 1970s, started seeking places to meet for holidays and other ritual services such as animal sacrifices and sacrificial communal meals. Places formerly held by the Bektashi order were considered appropriate because they shared the same religious symbolism and had a long history of mutual influence. Additionally, tombs of local saints with folk religious legends were informally appropriated. In the 1980s, the first *cemevi*, or cultural centers, emerged around such places.[61] In an urban context, the rituals could no longer be conducted in total secrecy except in private apartments, where only the closest family members could gather around their village *dede*. It was in the *cemevi* that the *cem* was made public, first by print media such as magazines and books,[62] then, as the Turkish broadcasting market liberalized in the 1980s, also by Alevi-run radio and television. Publicity about heterodox rituals in Turkish megacities provoked resentment among the Sunni masses and was politicized by Islamists who absorbed a large part of the followers of the formerly more influential anticommunist (and therefore generally anti-Alevi) Turkish ultranationalists. Conflicts arose in Istanbul, for example, around the *cemevi*, which were attacked and threatened with destruction, even by town officials, during the mayorship of the populist, moderate Islamist Recep Tayyip Erdoğan, present prime minister of Turkey.

Another means of Alevi mediatization is the recently established set of festivals and conferences that include ritual dance and music, the largest being the pilgrimage to Hacıbektaş, the burial site of the saint Hacı Bektaş Velî, patron of the Bektashi order. Such a conference-festival was held in 1993 in the town of Sivas to commemorate the sixteenth-century anti-Ottoman poet-rebel and Alevi saint, Pir Sultan Abdal. When this event came under attack by a radicalized Sunni mob, the conference hotel was set on fire. State officials, police, and rescue units withheld help, and thirty-seven persons (thirty-four of Alevi background) lost their lives in the fire. This tragic incident was integrated into the Alevi symbolic repertoire of refrains about perpetual sacrifice to a cruel, tyrannical regime. The event was incorporated into a movement that both defended and strategically used the community's central congregational ritual, symbols, and practices. This instrumentalization of the *cem* and its elements, especially its music and ritual dance, *semah*, perturbed the prevailing Alevi religious authorities (*dede* and their "holy lineages," *ocak*), who had lost their grip on Alevis as village communities dissolved into urban networks.

The commemoration of these recent Alevi martyrs (*şehîd*), parallel to the Shia's commemorated martyrs, finally emerged in commemoration rituals, first in the diaspora, then in Turkey, where they took the form of protest marches and ceremonies at the martyrs' graves. In Germany, they were first staged at stadium events organized by the German Alevi Federation, then later, within local ceremonies held by diaspora communities. These rituals derived their standardized elements and general layout largely from mediatized sources, including magazine reports, radio and television broadcasts, Internet home pages, and YouTube representations of the commemoration ceremonies. Media representations of large commemoration festivals organized by the German and European Alevi federations served as a resource for designing commemoration rituals in the local European communities and back in Turkey (see figure 4.1).

Prior to the communal elections of 2009, in which the ruling Islamist Party lost many voters, the state-run Turkish television, TRT, established a Kurdish program and broadcast parts of the Alevi ritual mourning ceremonies for the 2009 feast of Âşûrâ. On this annual feast, Shiites all over the world commemorate the massacre at Kerbela, the central "mythological" narrative in Alevi ritual.[63] This step was a sign that the majority institutions, dominated by Sunni Muslims and secularists, were willing to use the mediatization of ritual to solve conflicts with the Alevi ethnoreligious minority. With the move to incorporate Alevi ceremonies into official

FIGURE 4.1. Sivas commemoration during a protest meeting, Mannheim, Germany, 2005. Photo courtesy Hasan Gazi Öğütcü.

state television programs, a new round of mediatization began. Now Alevi ritual could become more widely accepted as normal or even official. Another scenario, however, would be a revival of the interdenominational conflicts of the 1980s and 1990s, because cultural and economic resources, such as tax revenues for recognized religious communities, would have to be redistributed. It remains to be seen whether this publicizing of Alevi rituals—itself a process of selection and standardization—will lead to the normalization of Sunni-Alevi relations.

Ritualized Evangelical Education in the Film *Jesus Camp*

In the eighteenth and nineteenth centuries, the evangelical Christian movement emerged out of American and English Protestantism and spread in the twentieth century to other countries around the world.[64] Today, American evangelicalism looms large in public debate because of its prominent representation in mass media and its controversial engagement in political struggles about socially divisive issues such as abortion. On the one hand, America is one of the most modernized societies in the world. On the other, it is especially conservative, and its evangelicalism has grown in numbers and influence.[65] The position of evangelicals in society has changed significantly during the last decades. In the 1960s, evangelicals were characterized by "principled disengagement" in society, whereas in the 1980s and 1990s, the emergence of evangelicals in the political arena could be observed.[66] With the election of president George W. Bush, this development reached its climax.

Today, evangelicals, as a religious minority with a strong missionary emphasis, aim to change society and establish conservative Christian values. According to the American anthropologist Susan Rose, who did research on American evangelicalism and the Christian school movement, the motivation for their religious engagement is "the search for coherence, the struggle for control, and the building of community."[67] Evangelical Christians want to "change the world in this generation,"[68] a goal implying that every member of an evangelical community must contribute to the effort. Since one of the main characteristics of evangelicalism is personal experience of one's redemption by Jesus Christ, the education of young children is an especially important medium for establishing the evangelical worldview. Children need to experience being part of the body of Christ, that is, the Christian community, in order to guarantee their religious and social position.[69] The educational practices used by evangelicals to realize this kind of experience-based religious engagement are ritualized, if by this term we mean what Dutch ritual studies scholar Goedroen Juchtmans means: multisensory, symbolic practices that are stylized and thus made special.[70]

Recently, such educational practices have become better known to the general public because of the growing influence of mass media. Evangelicals publicize their own educational practices. Religious education is transmitted not only through written publications and church services but also via television broadcasts. Televangelism, for instance, uses mass media almost exclusively, thereby making evangelical practices visible to the viewing public.[71]

Another kind of mediatization is representations by nonevangelicals, for example, journalists who document and comment on home schooling, the practice of teaching children at home rather than sending them to secular public schools, to guarantee religious socialization.[72] This kind of media representation, like that of televangelism, is well known in the United States. Already in the first decades of the twentieth century, evangelicals were aware of the possibilities mass media could offer. Believers could make their practices better known to a broader audience, gaining fuller acceptance in society.[73] In the 1980s and 1990s, leaders of evangelical churches took the media seriously as a way of entering the public sphere. The election of 2004 made clear that representation of religion in the media was important for Christianity's political impact. The representation of conservative Christian candidates contributed to the result of the election in a strong way.[74]

Along with the influence that religious groups gained through media representation came media-disseminated stereotypes. All religious groups represented in the media run this risk. For example, the perception of Islam in North America is saturated with mediatized stereotypes. Rubina Ramji, who conducts research on the portrayal of religion in mass media, shows that the medium of film "reproduces and recycles" stereotypes. "The commercial film industry creates cultural products that often reflect societal norms," she says.[75]

A striking example of a film that portrays the educational practices of evangelicals, the topic of this case study, is *Jesus Camp*, directed by Rachel Grady and Heidi Ewing and released in 2006. The filmmakers document an evangelical summer camp for children. The moviemakers, both journalists, wanted to show the educational practices of evangelicals without prejudice. The educators themselves, such as the camp founder, Pastor Becky Fisher, collaborated with the filmmakers to make their own aims visible to a broader audience. But is the film really an arena for evangelicals to display their practices to a broader public? Is it really neutral, without prejudice, as the filmmakers suggest? Or is it a recycling of stereotypes? Is the conflict about stereotypes due to the film, or does the stereotyping arise only in the perception of the film?

For the purposes of our analysis, we will focus on the ritualized educational practices that sparked controversy after the film's release. The movie caused considerable conflict in the United States. Some evangelical groups found the film's representation less than neutral, while liberal groups found the practices shown to be entirely unacceptable.

The ritualized character of the educational practices is troublesome, because it goes beyond purely cognitive modes of learning, leading viewers to worry about indoctrination. If children are educated in a ritualized way as the "army of God," as the film shows, liberal viewers will question the ritual's role in preparing children to live in civil society.[76] Education is generally a public task, but through the practice of a kind of home schooling that rejects Darwin's theory of evolution in favor of creationism, evangelicals might gain undue influence over the formation of their children's social attitudes.[77] As soon as education departs from standard cognitive approaches in favor of symbolic, stylized, and special practices, that is, ritual, a pedagogical and political debate about the nature of the whole educational experience starts to foment. These conflicts are profoundly interrelated, which is why this case study addresses the question: in what sense are ritualized and educational practices as mediatized in the film *Jesus Camp* a source of a pedagogical and political conflict?

When directors Rachel Grady and Heidi Ewing said that they were prepared to take an "honest approach to a delicate subject matter," they were granted "unprecedented access into hidden worlds."[78] That world was an evangelical summer camp for young children, organized once a year by Pastor Becky Fisher and her ministry, Kids on Fire School of Ministry, in Devils Lake, North Dakota.

The camp is an example of evangelical education aimed at enabling young people to convert into "real Christians" by having a new birth, one of the major themes of evangelicalism.[79] Fisher's intention is that children "learn and practice their prophetic gifts to take back America for Christ." The children come together for a week, to be taught evangelical beliefs, but there is also a strong experiential dimension to the camp. For example, the children handle small embryo models that help form their attitude toward abortion and, by association, all unborn children. In addition, media are sacralized. During the training process, PowerPoint presentations are prayed for, as they help spread the message of redemption. The fact that Pastor Fisher and her colleagues allowed Grady and Ewing access to make the film indicates not only the organizers' appreciation of the media but also their explicit interest in having their work mediatized.[80]

The film's release in the United States in 2006 and subsequent Oscar nomination the following January triggered a huge debate, largely dominated by questions about the camp's educational practices and their representation in the film. While the aim of the camp is to create special experiences for participating children,[81] liberal groups expressed concern about whether the camp's practices really constituted a means of religious education or were a form of indoctrination. Evangelicals, however, asked about the role of the documentary film in stirring up public debate about what, for them, are commonly used educational practices. The film's presentation of these practices is important to understanding both sides of the conflict, since for both liberal and evangelical groups, the education of small children is a potentially explosive topic.

Three types of ritualized educational practices, all coupled with corresponding political motivations, can be distinguished in the film: small-scale private practices, semipublic practices, and public practices. Small-scale private practices are conducted with small groups of children, comparable to classroom rituals.[82] An example is the use of symbols that help children learn about or identify with a particular topic. At Jesus Camp, an important way of stylizing symbols is dancing, and the movie shows the children in a martial arts–type dance. Small kids in war paint and uniformlike clothing dance to Christian hard-rock music. Becky Fisher explains that this practice enables children to purify themselves, thereby becoming part of the army of God. The children, in other words, express their belonging by dancing and shouting. Fisher is convinced that "children need to be in the forefront of turning America toward conservative Christian values." These activities are similar to Islamic educational practices in which Muslim children too are educated to be part of the army of God. Fisher is aware of this fact and says, "Christians need to focus on training kids, since the enemies are focused on training theirs."

Other practices help the children channel their emotions for Christ. For instance, at one point when children grow upset about liberal tendencies in American religious culture, they are asked to break cups while repeatedly shouting the refrain, "Break this cup in the name of Jesus." In such acts, aggression is ritualized. Children learn to channel strong, even violent, emotions toward liberal society. Political messages are also explicit in these training practices. When a woman brings a life-sized cutout of President George W. Bush to the front of the classroom, she has the children stretch their hands out toward it. While outstretched hands are symbolic of prayer and the laying on of hands, common practices in evangelical churches, this particular gesture led some commentators to see it as a way of worshipping President Bush. According to the woman with the cutout, this was not the case at all. Rather, she responded to critics, the children "pray over Bush," not to him.

In addition to small-scale practices, the children take part in semipublic practices such as church services, a ritual activity in which preaching is central. As "a new form of public teaching," preaching is important in all evangelical churches.[83] In the movie, such preaching becomes a source of conflict because of its explicit political and moral messages. A major topic of the preaching is the evil of abortion, and preacher Lou Engle uses small embryo models again to illustrate his point. Using symbolic objects enriches the effects of the preaching. As Becky Fisher points out, "All visible things say more than words." Engle and Fisher want the children to join the antiabortion movement.

Not surprisingly, campers also preach. Levi, a young boy, for instance, preaches to the other children and their parents: "Our generation is the key to Jesus' return." The children are actively socialized to preach and to fight politically against social tendencies that conflict with the espoused stance of evangelical churches. In the film, this training culminates in a large service featuring the renowned preacher Ted Haggard. Haggard is depicted as both an entertainer and political speaker railing against homosexuality. Such megachurch events are popular but also a continuing source of conflict because of their large-scale, manifest aggression toward other groups.[84]

The service led by Haggard points to the third kind of practice—public practice—captured in the film. His statements against abortion are stylized symbolically and rendered special by virtue of their utterance in a set-aside place. The protesting kid campers wear red stickers on their mouths with the word *Life* written on them. In this way, the small-scale educational practices and preaching are thrust by way of a film into a public setting. While the relationship between evangelical practices and politics is sometimes implicit, in this instance, it is both explicit and overt.[85]

All three levels of practice have become sources of conflict among those who disagree with their use in socializing and motivating children to fight for a better world. Despite the filmmakers' intention not "to make controversy but to explore faith through the eyes of a child,"[86] mediatization is never neutral. How rituals are depicted in or conveyed by mass media has a strong impact on how rituals are perceived by the public.[87] In this movie, the representation of the camp is handled in ways that lead viewers to raise questions about all three levels of ritualized practice. Several elements are worth examining: the use of music, camera shots, scene arrangement, and editing.[88] Music backgrounds the small-scale rituals. In some parts of the film, gloomy music is laid under the original sound track, creating the impression of a horror movie. Intentional or not, the emotions evoked by such music color the viewers' perception of evangelical practices.

Ted Haggard's sermon, a semipublic ritual, is shot with close-ups that leave the impression Haggard is demonic, busy mobilizing children for a war against society. Whether this is in fact his or the filmmakers' intention is beside the point. The camera angles are not neutral, nor do they represent an impartial representation of his performance.

In one scene Becky Fisher is a phone-in guest on a radio talk show, *Ring of Fire*, with host Mike Papantonio. The viewer sees only Papantonio while hearing the distant voice of Fisher on the phone. As Papantonio grows more and more frustrated with Fisher's answers to his questions, the spectator is drawn to the host, who is presented as a reasonable discussant confronted with an unreasonable conversation partner. The scene is shot and edited in such a way as to question Fisher's message.

Of course, media representation can and in some cases should be critical. However, this agenda should be made explicit. The filmmakers report that it was not until they began working with the film footage after the camp that they realized what they had seen. The documentary then reflects their editing, thus editorializing, as much as it reflects the original camp experience. In this way, mediatization can and does become a significant source of conflict, especially if the group being documented is under the impression that the film will be an unbiased view of their world.

Both the religious practices and their representation in the documentary instigated conflicting responses. People reacted privately and publicly to the movie, raising doubts about whether such ritualized educational practices could be tolerated in modern societies. Internet forums, for instance, often used the term *brainwashing*.[89]

Conflict did not begin and end with words. Becky Fisher reports that "due to some vandalism, which could be directly linked to negative reaction to the movie, the camp owners have understandably asked us not to return for a while." Negative reactions toward the camp and its practices are listed, along with Pastor Fisher's comments, on the Kids in Ministry Web site.[90] Meanwhile, in the same forum, people ask, "Why did you let them film you?" Becky Fisher responds on a positive note, "The news media has made it sound like this is shutting down our whole ministry. Nothing could be further from the truth."

Another indication of controversy is the film's rating for "mature subject matter." Becky Fisher cannot understand this choice. She responds, "There is no inappropriate language, sexual content, violence, or any of the other things you normally think of.... What we say about abortion and martyrdom is totally appropriate for children to hear."[91]

Apparently, all participants in the film except for Ted Haggard were pleased with how they were represented. Becky Fisher sees the film's trailer as the reason for initial negative reactions: "Very few people have actually seen the movie and are only reacting to the trailer that has been released. That trailer is painting us out to be cult like and warlike when nothing could be further from the truth." Other evangelicals go further, pointing to the consequences of public screenings at, for example, Michael Moore's Traverse City Film Festival, against the wishes of the distribution company, Magnolia Pictures. Magnolia president Eamonn Bowles said, "I don't want the perception out in the public that this is an agenda-laden film." Regardless, public acts of vandalism at the camp and at film festival screenings show that the conflict raised by the film once again functions as a catalyst for both sides. Even if evangelicals were to argue that there are no stereotypes in the film, those who view it may bring their own. As Stewart Hoover points out, cultural processes surrounding or suffusing media can themselves be occasions for or sources of conflict.[92]

These conflicts between evangelicals and those who react negatively to their practices can be interpreted as expressions of persistent tensions between liberal and fundamentalist religious perspectives on ritualized educational practices. While such practices can have a unifying effect on the in-group,[93] they can be a source of conflict once they become public in a liberal society that is ambivalent about a minority religious group's aims and its techniques for achieving those aims with young children. On the one hand, a basic tenet of liberal society is the assumption that all groups should be able to educate their children religiously in whatever ways they deem appropriate. On the other hand, there are real risks to this freedom once a group's educational practices are perceived as incompatible with the greater social good.

The usual conflict between liberalism and religious fundamentalist education becomes heightened with the film's publicizing of the latter's ritualized educational practices. While the occasion for the conflict is mediatization, the reason for the conflict lies in differing views of appropriate ways to educate children. Ritualized practices that are especially problematic are those infused with political messages that do not fit with the overall drift of society. As evangelicals constitute a religious minority with explicit standpoints on controversial issues—abortion, stem cell research, evolution, homosexuality, and so on—their case is a poignant example of how mediatized and ritualized practices become flash points once they are made public.

Contesting Rituals

The contexts in which conflicts are embedded are often marked by tensions between majority and minority groups or state authorities and social subgroups. Controversies about rituals reflect such tensions and are therefore symptomatic of attempts at social change, for instance, striving for the emancipation of ethnoreligious minorities. If rituals are offensively publicized in the media, thus interpreted in ways that diverge from indigenous meanings ascribed to the rituals by believers, conflict not only arises, it becomes instrumental in social struggle and identity politics. Such is the case with Muslims in Western Europe, where the public call to prayer is often interpreted as an expression of the desire to dominate Western societies.

As the Alevi case demonstrates, rituals can stir conflict, and conflict can attract mediatization. Here, in a classic case of modern identity politics, the *cem*, formerly only accessible to insiders, is publicized to achieve official recognition from state authorities. The ritual, normally used to reproduce the group's inner structures and values, is mediatized in order to achieve acceptance by the dominant majority.

The mediatization of ritualized practices, however, can also offend practitioners, as the evangelical reception of *Jesus Camp* illustrates. This film trains the spotlight on practitioners and their role in civil society, while showing how the group's ritualized practices are used to gain political and moral ascendancy. Once this agenda becomes public, it becomes the focus of controversy.

Contesting a ritual, as well as using a ritual to contest something else, are means of challenging authority, establishing agency, and negotiating power. Whoever attacks accepted ritual practices instigates intense debate, making attacks of this kind potentially or profoundly efficacious. Ritual practices, ritual places, and media representations of ritual are regular targets of aggression. Ritual becomes the source of conflict precisely because it is ritual, an identity-forming activity and means of reproducing a group's values, social structures, and habitual properties. Thus, from a perspective outside the group, a ritual is perceived as a collective symbol. Therefore, attacks on a group's rituals challenge that community where it is most sensitive. The formal, stylized, and structured character of a ritual makes it appear almost official to others. Recognizing a community's rituals is thus a significant step toward that group's inclusion in the prevailing social network.

Conflicts over rituals show remarkable constancy as well as variability. Rituals may become the occasion for conflict because they penetrate the public sphere, for example, the politically suffused practices at Jesus Camp, the Muslim call to prayer, and the publicly performed or broadcast Alevi *cem*. However, rituals may also exclude the public, for example, Masonic oath taking or the Alevi *cem* in premodern contexts. It is, however, at the public end of this spectrum that conflict is most likely to arise. When rituals penetrate the public sphere to the extent that the general public cannot avoid confronting them, the practices may provoke those who do not want to be implicated or involved. On the other hand, if rituals explicitly exclude the general public, at least some of those excluded may feel offended as well, because they cannot verify that the ritual is harmless. This kind of threat may result in outsiders assuming that the ritual is dubious or immoral.

Rituals with the potential to cause conflict originate more frequently in minority status groups regarded as out of step with accepted mainstream codes of behavior. For example, in the United States extremely conservative evangelicals are sometimes regarded as fundamentally in conflict with basic American values. So, too, anti-Masonic propaganda developed in the context of conspiracy theories. It had, and still has, more to do with scapegoating than with Freemasonry. This dynamic applies also to Alevi and similar Sufi rituals, such as those of the Bektashis, which are depicted as flouting the social order prescribed in orthodox Muslim law and thus as immoral, abusive, exploitative, and reactionary. Guardians of the established order typically fight against perceived deviance and the loss of integrity, and this situation is invariably troublesome for minorities who must find productive ways to respond. For example, Muslims in Europe often make what one might call "a ritual sacrifice of ritual itself." They refrain from making the call to prayer public, thus accepting their inequality vis-à-vis established religious groups. They are instead offered other symbolic forms of participation in the public space as compensation. In any case, when a general "right to ritual" is granted to a religious denomination, argumentation against that particular ritual must then refer to specific, intolerable qualities of the ritual. If this quality is regarded by practitioners as an indispensable part of the ritual, performing or not performing it becomes a crisis.

Rituals may be contested by different groups for a multiplicity of reasons or on the basis of multiple characteristics. For example, evangelical educational rituals have become a source of conflict because of their mediatization, political messages, and aggressiveness. Moreover, conflict can emerge on different levels at the same time, as both an overt conflict and an underlying conflict. In the case of *adhān* for instance, the overt conflict centers on neighborhood noise reduction, yet opposed parties read the call to prayer in terms of an underlying conflict. Paradoxically, in this view the overt conflict is actually symbolic. In the case of *adhān*, the underlying conflict as perceived by the parties is marked by the opposing positions of "Muslim conquest of Europe" versus "Islamophobia of the West." Here the imagined conflict is seen as the "real" one.

In the process of relating one layer of conflict to another, the media play a crucial role, especially since they exercise both a selective and a generalizing force at the same time. For instance, differences of opinion within the Muslim community on the question whether the *adhān* should be performed are typically minimized in media coverage. When the media do provide differentiated information, the effects of it on recipients tend to correlate with factors such as interest and education. However, as the *adhān* case demonstrates, social status is not a reliable indicator of a specific attitude toward the inflow of new cultural elements when it comes to negotiating cultural space. In other words, a higher status does not necessarily correlate with a higher degree of tolerance and vice versa.

In sum, media not only present, they also define, elaborate, and evaluate conflicts. They generate headlines, catchphrases, and keywords that qualify, mediate, or incite conflict. Unfavorable accounts of minority groups abound, as do examples of compassionate journalism. As a rule, however, conflict sells, and so the media accentuate it. Even if the intention of journalists is not to incite conflict, their representations invariably color depictions of ritual practices, thereby making an implicit conflict explicit.

Groups, of course, can sometimes take charge of media. Alevis use television and the Internet to their own advantage to publicize their ritual. This move has led to standardization of the *cem* and to the dissemination of ritual forms such as martyr commemoration rituals. In addition, representations of divergent performances have disseminated information about inner Alevi quarrels over the appropriate way to enact the *cem* or over its acceptability in secular, political contexts. Unwittingly, such mediatization has generated conflict.

Nonetheless, ritual-and-media conflicts sometimes provide common ground for disparate groups, thus facilitating the integration of society. *Adhān* conflicts, for example, have often led to increased involvement of Muslim organizations in municipal decision making, thus making them part of the local network. The step to include Alevi rituals in state-run broadcasts in Turkey is another example of de-escalating conflict by integrating a minority into public discourse. In an important sense, then, conflict is also a medium of transformation that helps develop a society's capacity for real integration.

NOTES

1. Ritual transfer occurs in processes of migration and when a ritual is adopted by one group from another. See Robert Langer, Dorothea Lüddeckens, Kerstin Radde[-Antweiler], and Jan Snoek, "Transfer of Ritual," *Journal of Ritual Studies* 20 (2006): 1–10.

2. For a typology of conflict formations see Johan Galtung, *Peace by Peaceful Means: Peace and Conflict, Development and Civilization* (London: Sage, 1996), 70.

3. Douglas Knoop, Gwilym Peredur Jones, and Douglas Hamer, *Early Masonic Pamphlets* (Manchester: Manchester University Press, 1945), 35; (London: Q. C. Correspondence Circle, 1978), 35.

4. Douglas Knoop, Gwilym Peredur Jones, and Douglas Hamer, "Buchanan Manuscript, c. 1670," in *The Early Masonic Catechisms* (Manchester: Manchester University Press, 1963), 8.

5. Joannes A. M. Snoek, "Printing Masonic Secrets—Oral and Written Transmission of the Masonic Tradition," in *Alströmersymposiet 2003: Fördragsdokumentation*, ed. Henrik Bogdan (Göteborg: Frimureriska Forskningsgruppen i Göteborg, 2003), 39–56.

6. Samuel Prichard, *Masonry Dissected* (London: 1730), 11–12.

7. Joannes A. M. Snoek, "Recensie van 'De Uitvaert van het Vryje Metzelaersgilde; een anti-maçonnieke klucht uit 1735' door Machteld Bouman" (Review of "The Obsequies of the Guild of Freemasons; An Anti-Masonic Farce of 1735" by Machteld Bouman), *Mededelingen van de Stichting Jacob Campo Weyerman* 17, no. 1 (1994): 28–31.

8. Egbert Adriaan Boerenbeker, "De betrekkingen tussen de Nederlandse en de Engelse vrijmetselarij in de jaren 1734 tot 1771," *Thoth* 18, no. 3–4 (1967): 97–141, here 110–111.

9. "[L]a Sublime Grande-Loge de la Maçonnerie séant à Londres . . . sachant que les Maçons, plus que les autres hommes, doivent se conformer aux loi de leur pays n'a pu et ne peut désapprouver l'altération qu'à cet effet la dite Grand-Loge Nationale [des Pays Bas]

a cru devoir adopter dans notre formule d'obligation," quoted in Petrus Jacobus van Loo, *Geschiedenis van de Orde van Vrijmetselaren onder het Grootoosten der Nederlanden* (Den Haag: Ritus an Tempelbouw, 1967), 25–26.

10. John Hamill, *The Craft: A History of English Freemasonry* (Wellingborough: Crucible, 1986), chapter 10: "Attacks on the Craft," and especially the updated version in the second edition, under the title *The History of English Freemasonry* (Wellingborough: Crucible, 1994).

11. Theodor W. Juynboll, "Adhān," in *The Enyclopaedia of Islam*, 2nd ed., vol. I (Leiden: Brill, 1960), 187b–188a.

12. Umar Ryad, *The Call of Adhān and Religious Freedom in the Netherlands: A Case Study in Leiden* (unpublished MA thesis, Leiden University, Leiden 2000), 3.

13. See also ʿAbdarraḥmān al-Jazāʾirī, *Kitāb al-Fiqh ʿalā l-madhāhib al-arbaʿa*, 3rd ed., vol. I (Beirut: Dār al-iḥyāʾ at-turāth al-ʿarabī, s.a.), 313–314.

14. Sheikh Muhammed Salih Al-Munajjid. *Islam QA*. http://www.islam-qa.com/fr/ref/3309 (accessed July 20, 2010).

15. The major Shiite law schools maintain that there is another clause between the fifth and sixth: "Come to the best of acts."

16. See al-Jazāʾirī, *Kitāb al-Fiqh ʿalā l-madhāhib al-arbaʿa*, 313–314; "ḥukm al-adhān"; and Abu l-Walīd Muḥammad Ibn Aḥmad Ibn Rushd, *Bidāyat al-mujtahid wa-nihāyat al-muqtaṣid*, vol. I, ed. Mājid al-Ḥamawī (Beirut: Dār Ibn Ḥazm, 1995), 205–214, for discussion of the differences between the Sunni schools of law.

17. Ryad, *The Call of Adhān*, 16; ʿAbdallah al-Khamlīshī, *al-Janna wa-ṭarīquhā al-mustaqīm wa-n-nār wa-ṭarīquhā adh-dhamīm* (Rotterdam: s.n., 1995 = 1415), 474–477.

18. See the YouTube film, "Adhan al-Muhammadi," in which Naqshbandi sheikh Nazim Haqqani protested against the official state policies of performing the *ṣalāt* in Turkish by performing the *adhān*. Here, the ritual act itself is used as protest: http://nl.youtube.com/watch?v=bNi5YL5kM_8.

19. See John Boswell, *The Royal Treasure: Muslim Communities under the Crown of Aragon in the Fourteenth Century* (New Haven: Yale University Press, 1977), 261–267.

20. See for example Ruud Koopmans, Paul Statham, Marco Giugni, and Florence Passy, *Contested Citizenship: Immigration and Cultural Diversity in Europe* (Minneapolis: University of Minneapolis Press, 2005), 55ff. For case studies on mosque conflicts in European cities, including the *adhān* problem, see *Journal of Ethnic and Migration Studies* 31, no. 6 (2005), especially Richard Gale, "Representing the City: Mosques and the Planning Process in Birmingham," 1161–1179, 1163 et seq. On Islam in Europe, see also Brigitte Maréchal, Stefano Allievi, Felice Dassetto, and Jørgen Nielsen, eds., *Muslims in the Enlarged Europe* (Leiden: Brill, 2003); Sigrid Nökel and Levent Tezcan, eds., *Islam and the New Europe: Continuities, Changes, Confrontations* (Bielefeld: Transaction, 2006).

21. Nico Landman, *Van Mat tot Minaret: De institutionalisering van de Islam in Nederland* (Amsterdam: VU Uitgeverij, 1982), 309.

22. Urfan Khaliq, "Islam and the European Union: Report on the United Kingdom," in *Islam and the European Union*, ed. Richard Potz and Wolfgang Wieshaider (Leuven: Peeters, 2004), 219–262, 328–329 on the *adhān*.

23. Zaynab Hemani in the *Muslim News* 228 (April 25, 2008), see http://www.muslimnews.co.uk/paper/index.php?article=3489 (accessed November 25, 2008).

24. "East Oxford Mosque Call to Prayer," February 4, 2008, http://www.distinctlywelcoming.com/call_to_prayer/.

25. Seán McLaughlin, "Muslims and Public Space in Bradford: Conflict, Cooperation and Islam as a Resource for Integration?" *Journal of Ethnic and Migration Studies* 31, no. 6 (2005): 1045–1066, 1054.

26. See Pieter Sjoerd van Koningsveld and Wasif Shadid, *Religious Freedom and the Position of Islam in Europe*, 2nd ed. (in press).

27. For an overview, see Ala Al-Hamarneh and Jörn Thielmann, eds., *Islam and Muslims in Germany* (Leiden: Brill, 2008); on conflicts see also Jörg Hüttermann, "Konflikte um islamische Symbole in Deutschland: Asymmetrien der Konfliktkommunikation," in *Konfliktfeld Islam in Europa*, ed. Monika Wohlrab-Sahr and Levent Tezcan (Baden-Baden: Nomos, 2007), 201–220. According to a recent survey, between 3.8 and 4.3 million Muslims (between 4.6 and 5.2 percent of the population) live in Germany; 2.5 to 2.7 million of them have their roots in Turkey. Also, 55 percent still have a foreign nationality, and 86 percent regard themselves as believers. See Sonja Haug, Stephanie Müssig, and Anja Stichs, *Muslimisches Leben in Deutschland* (Nürnberg: Deutsche Islam-Konferenz, Bundesamt für Migration und Flüchtlinge, 2009).

28. An example of conflicting opinions on a national scale was the debate over the 2006 position paper, "Clarity and Good Neighborly Relations: Christians and Muslims in Germany," http://www.ekd.de/english/1716.html (accessed July 19, 2010). The paper argued against *adhān* and was heavily criticized by Muslim representatives. See also "Christians and Muslims Hold High-Level Meeting in Berlin: Participants Commit Themselves to Constructive Debate," October 22, 2008, http://www.ekd.de/english/4250-4307.html.

29. Milli Görüş (National Worldview) is a religious and political movement inspired by the ideas of former Turkish Prime Minister Necmettin Erbakan, who aimed at the re-Islamization of Turkey. In Germany, this movement controls more than 300 mosques.

30. See Thomas Lemmen and Melanie Miehl, *Islamisches Alltagsleben in Deutschland* (Bonn: Friedrich-Ebert-Stiftung, 2001), 29; Thomas Schmitt, *Moscheen in Deutschland: Konflikte um ihre Errichtung und Nutzung* (Flensburg: Deutsche Akademie für Landeskunde, 2003), 332.

31. For a detailed study of the conflict history, see Schmitt, *Moscheen in Deutschland*, 274–345.

32. See Stefan Muckel, ed., *Der Islam im öffentlichen Recht des säkularen Verfassungsstaates* (Berlin: Duncker and Humblot, 2008), 257–260.

33. Schmitt, *Moscheen in Deutschland*, 352.

34. Similar reactions are reported from Switzerland where more than 300,000 Muslims live, mainly immigrants from the Balkans. In the Swiss village of Wangen, for example, dispute over a planned mosque and a minaret led to a struggle between fundamentalists on both sides. Typical statements of the old, established Swiss residents include, "It's a symbol of political power" and "Islam is not only a religion, it's an ideology." The common ground among negative attitudes appeared to be fear of foreign domination, as expressed in the following comments: "First it was a cultural center, then a prayer room, and now a minaret. It's salami tactics. The next thing it will be loudspeakers and the calls to prayer will be echoing up and down the valley. Our children will ask 'what did our fathers do,' and their answer will be—they did nothing." Ian Traynor, "The Rise of

Mosques Becomes Catalyst for Conflict across Europe," *The Guardian*, October 11, 2007, http://www.guardian.co.uk/world/2007/oct/11/thefarright.religion.

35. See Sabine Schiffer, "Die Darstellung des Islams in der Presse: Sprache, Bilder, Suggestionen" (PhD diss., University of Erlangen/Nürnberg, 2004), 123–127.

36. Schmitt, *Moscheen in Deutschland*, 342–343.

37. See Schmitt, *Moscheen in Deutschland*, 300–301.

38. Schmitt, *Moscheen in Deutschland*, 352.

39. See Schmitt, *Moscheen in Deutschland*, 343.

40. Faruk Şen and Martina Sauer, *Islam in Deutschland: Einstellungen der türkischstämmigen Muslime* (Essen: Zentrum für Türkeistudien, 2006), 20.

41. Katrin Brettfeld and Peter Wetzels, *Muslime in Deutschland: Integration, Integrationsbarrieren, Religion sowie Einstellungen zu Demokratie, Rechtsstaat und politisch-religiös motivierter Gewalt* (Berlin: BMI, 2007), 194–195. Correspondingly, some scholars expect an increasing tendency toward what they call "Islamophobia" among the German population. They interpret their survey data as evidence for Islamophobia as an emerging form of out-group rejection. See Steffen Kühnel and Jürgen Leibold, "Islamophobie in der deutschen Bevölkerung: Ein neues Phänomen oder nur ein neuer Name?," in *Konfliktfeld Islam in Europa*, ed. Monika Wohlrab-Sahr and Levent Tezcan (Baden-Baden: Nomos, 2007), 153.

42. Schmitt, *Moscheen in Deutschland*, 305.

43. See Schmitt, *Moscheen in Deutschland*, 313, 344.

44. Heiner Bielefeldt, and Wilhelm Heitmeyer, "Konflikte um religiöse Symbole. Moscheebau und Muezzinruf in deutschen Städten," *Journal für Konflikt- und Gewaltforschung* 2 (2000): 150ff.

45. Schmitt, *Moscheen in Deutschland*, 333ff.

46. For instance, the German weekly magazine *Der Spiegel* implicitly counted all Muslims who advocated the public *adhān* as fundamentalists: "In Duisburg tragen Fundamentalisten einen bizarren Konflikt aus: Moslems und Protestanten streiten sich darüber, ob der Muezzin per Lautsprecher zum Gebet rufen darf." *Der Spiegel* 46 (1997): 72.

47. See Simon Cottle, *Mediatized Conflict: Developments in Media and Conflict Studies* (Berkshire: Open University Press, 2006), 192.

48. Schmitt, *Moscheen in Deutschland*, 239.

49. Schmitt, *Moscheen in Deutschland*, 357.

50. For a general overview, see Markus Dressler, "Alevīs," in *The Encyclopaedia of Islam*, 3rd ed. (Leiden: Brill, 2007), 93a–121b.

51. For Germany, see Martin Sökefeld, *Struggling for Recognition: The Alevi Movement in Germany and in Transnational Space* (New York: Berghahn Books, 2008).

52. For Turkey, see David Shankland, *The Alevis in Turkey: The Emergence of a Secular Islamic Tradition* (London: Routledge, 2003).

53. *Ayin-i cem*. *Ayin* means "ritual" and *cem*, "congregating." Thus, "congregation ritual."

54. See Janina Karolewski, "*Ayin-i Cem*—das alevitische Kongregationsritual: Idealtypische Beschreibung des *İbadet ve Öğreti Cemi*," in *Migration und Ritualtransfer: Religiöse Praxis der Aleviten, Jesiden und Nusairier zwischen Vorderem Orient und Westeuropa*, ed. Robert Langer, Raoul Motika, and Michael Ursinus, Heidelberger Studien zur

Geschichte und Kultur des modernen Vorderen Orients, 33 (Frankfurt am Main: Peter Lang, 2005), 109–131.

55. Similarly, the Jewish Sabbath begins on Friday evening.

56. *Diyanet İşleri Başkanlığı*. For recent developments in connections with the *cem*, see Raoul Motika and Robert Langer, "Alevitische Kongregationsrituale: Transfer und Re-Invention im transnationalen Kontext," in *Migration und Ritualtransfer: Religiöse Praxis der Aleviten, Jesiden und Nusairier zwischen Vorderem Orient und Westeuropa*, ed. Robert Langer, Raoul Motika, and Michael Ursinus, Heidelberger Studien zur Geschichte und Kultur des modernen Vorderen Orients, 33 (Frankfurt am Main: Peter Lang, 2005), 73–107.

57. For an initial study of Alevi Internet representations, see Martin Sökefeld, "Alevism Online: Re-imagining a Community in Virtual Space," *Diaspora* 11, no. 1 (2002): 85–123.

58. Ahmet T. Karamustafa, *Sufism: The Formative Period*, ed. Carole Hillenbrand, The New Edinburgh Islamic Surveys (Edinburgh: Edinburgh University Press, 2007), 35.

59. See Robert Langer, "Alevi Ritual Practice in an Alevi Village: Oral History Sources," in *Reception Processes of Alevi Ritual Practice between Innovation and Reconstruction*, ed. Janina Karolewski, Robert Langer, and Michael Ursinus, Heidelberger Studien zur Geschichte und Kultur des modernen Vorderen Orients (Frankfurt am Main: Peter Lang, in press).

60. As recent research has shown, the ritual *semah* dance was already publicized before the 1980s through state-sponsored folklore clubs. See Kabir Tambar, "Paradoxes of Pluralism: Ritual Aesthetics and the Alevi Revival in Turkey" (unpublished paper, University of Chicago, Department of Anthropology), 14.

61. For the example of the *türbe* and complex of Karacaahmet Sultan Dergahı, see Robert Langer, "Das Re-Framing alevitischer Gemeinderituale im Kontext von Ritualtransfer und Migration," in *Rituale in Bewegung: Rahmungs- und Reflexivitätsprozesse in Kulturen der Gegenwart*, ed. Henrik Jungaberle and Jan Weinhold, Performanzen: Interkulturelle Studien zur Ritual, Spiel und Theater 11 (Berlin: LIT Verlag, 2007), 129–144.

62. See Ina Paul and Johannes Zimmermann, "Zur Funktionalität des *Cem*-Rituals als Instrument alevitischer Identitätsstiftung in der *Cem Dergisi*," in *Migration und Ritualtransfer: Religiöse Praxis der Aleviten, Jesiden und Nusairier zwischen Vorderem Orient und Westeuropa*, ed. Robert Langer, Raoul Motika, and Michael Ursinus, Heidelberger Studien zur Geschichte und Kultur des modernen Vorderen Orients, 33 (Frankfurt am Main: Peter Lang, 2005), 175–202.

63. "TRT'den Aleviler İçin Özel Yayın; CNN TÜRK Video," CNN Türk: Haber, January 8, 2009, http://www.cnnturk.com/2009/turkiye/01/07/trtden.aleviler.icin.ozel.yayin/507811.2/index.html. Also see "Muharrem Ayında TRT'den Alevi Açılımı; CNN Türk Video," CNN Türk: Haber, December 29, 2008, http://www.cnnturk.com/2008/turkiye/12/29/muharrem.ayinda.trtden.alevi.acilimi/506795.2/index.html.

64. Alister McGarth, *Evangelicalism and the Future of Christianity* (Westmont: InterVarsity Press, 1995).

65. James D. Hunter, *American Evangelicalism: Conservative Religion and the Quandary of Modernity* (New Brunswick, NJ: Rutgers University Press, 1983), 4.

66. Jeffery L. Sheler, *Believers: A Journey into Evangelical America* (London: Penguin, 2006), 14.

67. Susan D. Rose, *Keeping Them out of the Hands of Satan: Evangelical Schooling in America* (New York: Routledge, 1988), 3.

68. Denton Lotz, "The Evangelization of the World in This Generation": The Resurgence of a Missionary Idea among the Conservative Evangelicals (Hamburg: University of Hamburg, 1970).

69. Hans-Georg Wünsch, *Autorität in der christlichen Schule: Eine Untersuchung zur Autoritätsdiskussion an evangelikalen Bekenntnisschulen in Deutschland* (Bonn: Culture and Science, 1995).

70. Goedroen Juchtmans, *Rituelen thuis. Van christelijk tot basaal sacraal* (Tilburg: Liturgisch Instituut, 2008), 45.

71. Steve Bruce, *Pray TV: Televangelism in America* (London: Routledge, 1990).

72. Lynn Schofield Clark, "The 'Protestanization' of Research into Media, Religion, and Culture," in *Practicing Religion in the Age of the Media*, ed. Stewart M. Hoover and Lynn Schofield Clark (New York: Columbia University Press, 2002), 17.

73. Stewart M. Hoover, *Religion in the Media Age* (Abingdon, UK: Routledge, 2006), 33.

74. Hoover, *Religion in the Media Age*, 58–59.

75. Rubina Ramji, "Representations of Islam in American News and Film: Becoming the 'Other,'" in *Mediating Religion: Conversations in Media, Religion and Culture*, ed. Jolyon Mitchell and Sophia Marriaga (London: Continuum, 2003): 65–72, 68. See also Hunter, *American Evangelicalism*, 3.

76. Chris Hermans, *Participatory Learning: Religious Education in a Globalizing Society* (Leiden: Brill, 2003).

77. Simon Coleman and Leslie Carlin, ed., *The Cultures of Creationism: Anti-Evolutionism in English-Speaking Countries* (Hampshire: Ashgate, 2004).

78. Cf. the Web site of their production company, www.lokifilms.com.

79. Edward Dutton, *Meeting Jesus at University: Rites of Passage and Student Evangelicals* (Hampshire: Ashgate, 2008).

80. Wünsch, *Autorität in der christlichen Schule*.

81. Mathew Guest, *Evangelical Identity and Contemporary Culture* (Colorado Springs, CO: Paternoster, 2007).

82. Amy Florian, *Sign, Symbol, Word and Song: Creating and Celebrating Classroom Rituals* (Notre Dame: Ave Maria Press, 2001); Catherine Bell, *Teaching Ritual* (Oxford: Oxford University Press, 2007).

83. Guest, *Evangelical Identity and Contemporary Culture*, 98ff.

84. Lotz, "The Evangelization of the World in This Generation", 77.

85. Bruce, *Pray TV*, 179.

86. "Innovators—Documentary Film Makers," *Time*, November 6, 2006. *Jesus Camp* Web site: www.jesuscampthemovie.com.

87. Ronald L. Grimes, *Rite out of Place: Ritual, Media, and the Arts* (Oxford: Oxford University Press, 2006), 16.

88. Werner Faulstich, *Einführung in die Filmanalyse*. 4. unveränd. Aufl. (Tübingen: G. Narr-Verlag, 2004).

89. "Thoughts upon Watching Jesus Camp: The Art of Brainwashing Children," http://blogcritics.org/culture/article/thoughts-upon-watching-jesus-camp-the/.

RITUAL AS A SOURCE OF CONFLICT   129

90. "A message from Becky," www.kidsinministry.org.
91. Viewers' comments, www.kidsinministry.org.
92. Hoover, *Religion in the Media Age*, 32.
93. Guest, *Evangelical Identity and Contemporary Culture*, 102ff.

REFERENCES

Bell, Catherine. *Teaching Ritual*. Oxford: Oxford University Press, 2007.
Bielefeldt, Heiner, and Wilhelm Heitmeyer. "Konflikte um religiöse Symbole: Moscheebau und Muezzinruf in deutschen Städten." *Journal für Konflikt- und Gewaltforschung* 2 (2000): 150–165.
Boerenbeker, Egbert Adriaan. "De betrekkingen tussen de Nederlandse en de Engelse vrijmetselarij in de jaren 1734 tot 1771." *Thoth* 18, no. 3–4 (1967): 97–141.
Boswell, John. *The Royal Treasure: Muslim Communities under the Crown of Aragon in the Fourteenth Century*. New Haven: Yale University Press, 1977.
Brettfeld, Katrin, and Peter Wetzels. *Muslime in Deutschland: Integration, Integrationsbarrieren, Religion sowie Einstellungen zu Demokratie, Rechtsstaat und politisch-religiös motivierter Gewalt*. Berlin: BMI, 2007.
Bruce, Steve. *Pray TV: Televangelism in America*. London: Routledge, 1990.
Coleman, Simon, and Leslie Carlin, eds. *The Cultures of Creationism: Anti-Evolutionism in English-Speaking Countries*. Hampshire: Ashgate, 2004.
Cottle, Simon. *Mediatized Conflict: Developments in Media and Conflict Studies*. Berkshire: Open University Press, 2006.
Dressler, Markus. "Alevīs." In *The Encyclopaedia of Islam*, 3rd ed. Leiden: Brill, 2007, 93a–121b.
Dutton, Edward. *Meeting Jesus at University: Rites of Passage and Student Evangelicals*. Hampshire: Ashgate, 2008.
Faulstich, Werner. *Einführung in die Filmanalyse*. 4. unveränd. Aufl. Tübingen: G. Narr-Verlag, 2004.
Florian, Amy. *Sign, Symbol, Word and Song: Creating and Celebrating Classroom Rituals*. Notre Dame: Ave Maria Press, 2001.
Galtung, Johan. *Peace by Peaceful Means: Peace and Conflict, Development and Civilization*. London: Sage, 1996.
Grimes, Ronald. *Rite out of Place: Ritual, Media, and the Arts*. Oxford: Oxford University Press, 2006.
Guest, Mathew. *Evangelical Identity and Contemporary Culture*. Colorado Springs, CO: Paternoster, 2007.
Hamarneh, Ala Al-, and Jörn Thielmann, eds. *Islam and Muslims in Germany*. Leiden: Brill, 2008.
Hamill, John. *The Craft: A History of English Freemasonry*. Wellingborough: Crucible, 1986. Second edition: *The History of English Freemasonry*. Wellingborough: Crucible, 1994.
Haug, Sonja, Stephanie Müssig, and Anja Stichs. *Muslimisches Leben in Deutschland*. Nürnberg: Deutsche Islam-Konferenz, Bundesamt für Migration und Flüchtlinge, 2009.
Hermans, Chris. *Participatory Learning: Religious Education in a Globalizing Society*. Leiden: Brill, 2003.

Hoover, Stewart M. *Religion in the Media Age*. Abingdon, UK: Routledge, 2006.
Hunter, James D. *American Evangelicalism: Conservative Religion and the Quandary of Modernity*. New Brunswick, NJ: Rutgers University Press, 1983.
Hüttermann, Jörg. "Konflikte um islamische Symbole in Deutschland: Asymmetrien der Konfliktkommunikation." In *Konfliktfeld Islam in Europa*, edited by Monika Wohlrab-Sahr and Levent Tezcan, 201–220. Baden-Baden: Nomos, 2007.
Ibn Rushd, Abu l-Walīd Muḥammad Ibn Aḥmad. *Bidāyat al-mujtahid wa-nihāyat al-muqtaṣid*, vol. I, edited by Mājid al-Ḥamawī. Beirut: Dār Ibn Ḥazm, 1995.
Jazāʾirī, ʿAbdarraḥmān Al-. *Kitāb al-Fiqh ʿalā l-madhāhib al-arbaʿa*, 3rd ed., vol. 1. Beirut: Dār al-iḥyāʾ at-turāth al-ʿarabī, s.a.
Juchtmans, Goedroen. *Rituelen thuis: Van christelijk tot basaal sacraal*. Netherlands Studies in Ritual and Liturgy, 8. Tilburg: Liturgisch Instituut, 2008.
Juynboll, Theodor W. "Adhān." In *Enyclopaedia of Islam*, 2nd ed., vol. 1, 187b–188a. Leiden: Brill, 1960.
Karamustafa, Ahmet T. *Sufism: The Formative Period*, edited by Carole Hillenbrand. The New Edinburgh Islamic Surveys. Edinburgh: Edinburgh University Press, 2007.
Karolewski, Janina. "*Ayin-i Cem*—das alevitische Kongregationsritual: Idealtypische Beschreibung des *İbadet ve Öğreti Cemi*." In *Migration und Ritualtransfer: Religiöse Praxis der Aleviten, Jesiden und Nusairier zwischen Vorderem Orient und Westeuropa*, edited by Robert Langer, Raoul Motika, and Michael Ursinus, 109–131. Heidelberger Studien zur Geschichte und Kultur des modernen Vorderen Orients, 33. Frankfurt am Main: Peter Lang, 2005.
Khaliq, Urfan. "Islam and the European Union: Report on the United Kingdom." In *Islam and the European Union*, edited by Richard Potz and Wolfgang Wieshaider, 219–262. Leuven: Peeters, 2004.
Khamlīshī, ʿAbdallah Al-. *Al-Janna wa-ṭarīquhā al-mustaqīm wa-'n-nār wa-ṭarīquhā adh-dhamīm*. Rotterdam: s. n., 1995.
Knoop, Douglas, Gwilym Peredur Jones, and Douglas Hamer. *The Early Masonic Catechisms*. Manchester: Manchester University Press, 1945; 1963.
———. *Early Masonic Pamphlets*. Manchester: Manchester University Press, 1945; London: Q. C. Correspondence Circle, 1978.
Koningsveld, Pieter Sjoerd van, and Wasif Shadid. *Religious Freedom and the Position of Islam in Europe*, 2nd ed. In press.
Koopmans, Ruud, Paul Statham, Marco Giugni, and Florence Passy. *Contested Citizenship: Immigration and Cultural Diversity in Europe*. Minneapolis: University of Minneapolis Press, 2005.
Kühnel, Steffen, and Jürgen Leibold. "Islamophobie in der deutschen Bevölkerung: Ein neues Phänomen oder nur ein neuer Name?" In *Konfliktfeld Islam in Europa*, edited by Monika Wohlrab-Sahr and Levent Tezcan, 135–154. Baden-Baden: Nomos, 2007.
Landman, Nico. *Van Mat tot Minaret: De institutionalisering van de Islam in Nederland*. Amsterdam: VU Uitgeverij, 1982.
Langer, Robert. "Alevi Ritual Practice in an Alevi Village: Oral History Sources." In *Reception Processes of Alevi Ritual Practice between Innovation and Reconstruction*, edited by Janina Karolewski, Robert Langer, and Michael Ursinus. Heidelberger

Studien zur Geschichte und Kultur des modernen Vorderen Orients. Frankfurt am Main: Peter Lang, in press.

———. "Das Re-Framing alevitischer Gemeinderituale im Kontext von Ritualtransfer und Migration." In *Rituale in Bewegung: Rahmungs- und Reflexivitätsprozesse in Kulturen der Gegenwart*, edited by Henrik Jungaberle and Jan Weinhold, 129–144. Performanzen: Interkulturelle Studien zur Ritual, Spiel und Theater, 11. Berlin: LIT Verlag, 2007.

Langer, Robert, Dorothea Lüddeckens, Kerstin Radde[-Antweiler], and Jan Snoek. "Transfer of Ritual." *Journal of Ritual Studies* 20, no. 1 (2006): 1–10.

Lemmen, Thomas, and Melanie Miehl. *Islamisches Alltagsleben in Deutschland*. Bonn: Friedrich-Ebert-Stiftung, 2001.

Lotz, Denton. *"The Evangelization of the World in This Generation": The Resurgence of a Missionary Idea among the Conservative Evangelicals*. Hamburg: University of Hamburg, 1970.

Maréchal, Brigitte, Stefano Allievi, Felice Dassetto, and Jørgen Nielsen, eds. *Muslims in the Enlarged Europe*. Leiden: Brill, 2003.

McGarth, Alistair. *Evangelicalism and the Future of Christianity*. Westmont: InterVarsity Press, 1995.

McLaughlin, Seán. "Muslims and Public Space in Bradford: Conflict, Cooperation and Islam as a Resource for Integration?" *Journal of Ethnic and Migration Studies* 31, no. 6 (2005): 1045–1066.

Motika, Raoul, and Robert Langer. "Alevitische Kongregationsrituale: Transfer und Re-Invention im transnationalen Kontext." In *Migration und Ritualtransfer: Religiöse Praxis der Aleviten, Jesiden und Nusairier zwischen Vorderem Orient und Westeuropa*, edited by Robert Langer, Raoul Motika, and Michael Ursinus, 73–107. Heidelberger Studien zur Geschichte und Kultur des modernen Vorderen Orients, 33. Frankfurt am Main: Peter Lang, 2005.

Muckel, Stefan, ed. *Der Islam im öffentlichen Recht des säkularen Verfassungsstaates*. Berlin: Duncker and Humboldt, 2008.

———. "Islam in Germany." In *Islam and the European Union*, edited by Richard Potz and Wolfgang Wieshaider, 41–78. Leuven: Peeters, 2004.

Nökel, Sigrid, and Levent Tezcan, eds. *Islam and the New Europe: Continuities, Changes, Confrontations*. Bielefeld: Transaction, 2006.

Paul, Ina, and Johannes Zimmermann. "Zur Funktionalität des *Cem*-Rituals als Instrument alevitischer Identitätsstiftung in der *Cem Dergisi*." In *Migration und Ritualtransfer: Religiöse Praxis der Aleviten, Jesiden und Nusairier zwischen Vorderem Orient und Westeuropa*, edited by Robert Langer, Raoul Motika, and Michael Ursinus, 175–202. Heidelberger Studien zur Geschichte und Kultur des modernen Vorderen Orients, 33. Frankfurt am Main: Peter Lang, 2005.

Prichard, Samuel. *Masonry Dissected*. London: s.n., 1730.

Ramji, Rubina. "Representations of Islam in American News and Film: Becoming the 'Other.'" In *Mediating Religion: Conversations in Media, Religion and Culture*, edited by Jolyon Mitchell and Sophia Marriaga. London: Continuum, 2003.

Rath, Jan, Rinus Penninx, Kees Groenendijk, and Astrid Meyer, eds. *Western Europe and Its Islam*. Leiden: Brill, 2001.

Rose, Susan D. *Keeping Them out of the Hands of Satan: Evangelical Schooling in America.* New York: Routledge, 1988.

Ryad, Umar. *The Call of Adhān and Religious Freedom in the Netherlands: A Case Study in Leiden.* MA thesis, Leiden University, 2000.

Sax, William. "Agency." In *Theorizing Rituals: Issues, Topics, Approaches, Concepts,* edited by Jens Kreinath, Jan Snoek, and Michael Stausberg, 473–481. Leiden: Brill, 2006.

Schiffer, Sabine. "Die Darstellung des Islams in der Presse: Sprache, Bilder, Suggestionen." PhD diss., University of Erlangen/Nürnberg, 2004. Published as *Die Darstellung des Islams in der Presse: Sprache, Bilder, Suggestionen. Eine Auswahl von Techniken und Beispielen.* Bibliotheca academica. Reihe Orientalistik, 10. Würzburg: Ergon, 2005.

Schmitt, Thomas. *Moscheen in Deutschland: Konflikte um ihre Errichtung und Nutzung.* Flensburg: Deutsche Akademie für Landeskunde, 2003.

Schofield Clark, Lynn. "The 'Protestanization' of Research into Media, Religion, and Culture." In *Practicing Religion in the Age of the Media,* edited by Stewart M. Hoover and Lynn Schofield Clark, 7–34. New York: Columbia University Press, 2002.

Şen, Faruk, and Martina Sauer. *Islam in Deutschland: Einstellungen der türkischstämmigen Muslime.* Essen: Zentrum für Türkeistudien, 2006.

Shankland, David. *The Alevis in Turkey: The Emergence of a Secular Islamic Tradition.* London: Routledge, 2003.

Sheler, Jeffery L. *Believers: A Journey into Evangelical America.* London: Penguin, 2006.

Snoek, Joannes A. M. "Printing Masonic Secrets—Oral and Written Transmission of the Masonic Tradition." In *Alströmersymposiet 2003. Fördragsdokumentation,* edited by Henrik Bogdan, 39–56. Göteborg: Frimureriska Forskningsgruppen i Göteborg, 2003.

———. "Recensie van 'De Uitvaert van het Vryje Metzelaersgilde; een anti-maçonnieke klucht uit 1735' door Machteld Bouman" [Review of "The Obsequies of the Guild of Freemasons: An Anti-Masonic Farce of 1735" by Machteld Bouman]. *Mededelingen van de Stichting Jacob Campo Weyerman* 17, no. 1 (1994): 28–31.

Sökefeld, Martin. "Alevism Online: Re-imagining a Community in Virtual Space." *Diaspora* 11, no. 1 (2002): 85–123.

———. *Struggling for Recognition: The Alevi Movement in Germany and in Transnational Space.* New York: Berghahn Books, 2008.

Tambar, Kabir. "Paradoxes of Pluralism: Ritual Aesthetics and the Alevi Revival in Turkey." Unpublished paper, University of Chicago, Department of Anthropology, 2009.

van Loo, Petrus Jacobus. *Geschiedenis van de Orde van Vrijmetselaren onder het Grootoosten der Nederlanden.* Den Haag: Ritus en Tempelbouw, 1967.

Wünsch, Hans-Georg. *Autorität in der christlichen Schule: Eine Untersuchung zur Autoritätsdiskussion an evangelikalen Bekenntnisschulen in Deutschland.* Bonn: Culture and Science, 1995.

5

Place, Action, and Community in Internet Rituals

Marga Altena, Catrien Notermans, and Thomas Widlok

The Internet seems an improbable medium for investigating rituals, which appear to belong to a different, even conflicting, world. For some, rituals are old, traditional, and constant, while the Internet is contemporary and dynamic. For others, the isolated user of the Internet, cut off from direct interaction with fellow humans, is far removed from the smells, sounds, and sights of rituals experienced in socially shared, bodily experience.[1] From either point of view, the contrast between rituals and the Internet is marked. However, Internet representations of rituals abound in a great number of diverse Web sites, as sites of instruction, points of information, and means of expression, as well as combinations of all these. The medium is used to inform about existing rituals and to instruct practitioners how to perform them. People search for inspiration on the Internet about how to give shape to a wedding, a funeral, or a prayer. Web sites are places for the expression of personal, spiritual feelings on individual Weblogs as well as for collective, institutionalized religious beliefs. Exploring new spiritual movements or religions on the Internet, ritual practitioners, pilgrims, and like-minded people can contact one another and even build lasting relationships. Through Web sites, distant friends and family can join in kinship rituals online. Recorded rituals are displayed on Web sites, making private memories public. People create digital rituals, leaving messages, condolences, prayers, and even burning candles at virtual sites representing shrines, memorials, or pilgrimage sites.

Notwithstanding their abundance and variety, Internet rituals are typically connected to a shared history that originated in the nondigital world and are all subject to specific conditions that make them more or less effective. Despite the alleged modernity of the medium, the Internet, including its rituals, draws on existing traditions and cultural conventions. This genealogy seems to confirm anthropologist Roy Rappaport's claim that the possibilities for inventing new rituals are limited.[2] Rituals composed entirely of new elements, he states, are likely to fail to become established. Especially in the case of Web pages related to religious rituals, the Internet does not seem to offer something completely new. However, by opening up a familiar ritual to a large and unknown community of site visitors, the supposed attachment of a ritual to a specific physical location appears to have been broken or supplanted by the apparent placelessness of Internet sites that transcend geographical distance.

Thomas Widlok studied Australian Aboriginal smoking ceremonies; Catrien Notermans, Marian pilgrimage in Lourdes, France; and Marga Altena, rituals of mourning and dying in the Netherlands. We are struck by the variety of content and use of Internet rituals in our disparate cases and intrigued by the ways Web sites work. We realize there are contradictory qualities in a medium that, paradoxically, is considered to be the same the world over. Internet Web sites are sometimes marginal and sometimes central to people's ritual performances. Web sites may be traditional or revolutionary with respect to the creation of rituals. Internet ritual may be incapable of replacing people's embodied ritual experience or, to the contrary, crucial to people's participating in collective ritual performances. We felt challenged to explore the Web sites connected to our own research projects in order to better appreciate what the Internet adds to ritual practices in general, how it changes them, and what conflicts arise when existing rituals are transferred from physical space to cyberspace.

Our theoretical position in this essay is inspired by two religious studies scholars, Jonathan Z. Smith and Ronald L. Grimes, whose views on the importance of place in ritual diverge. In *To Take Place: Towards Theory in Ritual*, Smith seems to suggest that location is the crucial element in the creation of sacrality in a ritual: "The specificity of place is what is remembered, is what gives rise to and is perpetuated in memorial."[3] Smith regards the creation of new ritual sites as a potential risk and as a threat to the ideological quality of a ritual.[4] Grimes, on the contrary, seems to espouse an action- rather than space-oriented theory of ritual. In his article "Jonathan Z. Smith's Theory of Ritual Space," he argues that what determines ritual is not only place but also bodily action, how particular objects are handled, and how specific gestures are made. Human action and interaction with sacred objects can take place at more than one specific place.[5] In contrast to Smith, who considers displacement a risk to the power and meaning of ritual, Grimes considers innovation and creativity essential for the persistence of ritual. Although we realize that Smith and Grimes published their texts before the heyday of the Internet and did not take virtual media into account, we feel that their views on place in ritual might provide a useful point of departure when studying Internet ritual.

Our focus here is on investigating whether existing religious rituals can be successfully removed from their physical domain and transferred to cyberspace. We want to know the ritual consequences of such displacement. Following Smith's space-oriented perspective, one might expect that rituals lose power and sense when lifted from their original physical site; following Grimes's action-oriented perspective, one might expect that rituals can readily be reenacted and reinvented if they are transferred from place to place or from place to virtual space. Analyzing Web sites related to smoking rituals in Australia, the official Web site of the Lourdes shrine in France, and Weblogs on dying and mourning in the Netherlands, we ask what happens when rituals based in geographical places are relocated or transmitted to cyberspace. How do Internet sites change or affect people's ritual experiences, and what conflicts does this transference provoke?

Australian Aboriginal Smoking Ceremonies on the Internet

In contemporary Australia, smoking rituals are the most visible form of Aboriginal ceremonies, in large part because they are performed at places and events that attract public and media attention. Reports and images of smoking rituals are abundantly featured in conventional media and the Internet. Newspaper and television coverage of public events such as formal openings of new public buildings, for instance, the new National Museum in Canberra in 2001, usually include the smoking ceremony with which procedures and festivities begin. Although Aboriginal Australians themselves now also make use of the Internet to display ceremonies, most Web sites that feature smoking rituals are produced either by non-Aboriginal Australians or in close cooperation with them. Aboriginal corporations, in themselves created in the interplay between Aboriginal groups and government institutions, now make use of not only newsletters and radio stations to distribute information—including information about rituals—but also the Internet, as, for instance, the Web site of the Pitjantjatjara Yankunytjatjara Media (PY Media) Aboriginal Corporation.[6]

Today's smoking ceremonies usually consist of a fairly small set of ritual actions. Practitioners hold leafy branches over a smoking fire and then over places, objects, and people, which are thereby smoked. Sometimes this ritual action is accompanied by words from indigenous languages, by songs, or by commentary. Ritualized smoking of this sort is also part of other Aboriginal rituals such as funerals or "payback" ceremonies.[7] In such cases, the smoke and smoking branches are used to clean objects left by a deceased person, to make personal belongings and other things associated with that person fit for use again. Smoke is also used in the ritual treatment of a deceased person's relatives, who are frequently painted in white and ushered into a largely passive group during the ritual proceedings.

In contemporary Australia, however, the smoking ceremony has gained widespread acceptance as an important public act. It is almost inconceivable, for instance, that a major public building would be opened without a smoking ceremony. Typical smoking ceremony events include the inauguration of a construction site by the New South Wales Health Department and the opening of public buildings and structures such as museums and bridges.[8] Even abroad, as in Edinburgh, Scotland, in 2008, when the remains of an Aboriginal woman in the university's collection were returned to Aboriginal Australians, a smoking ceremony was carried out.[9] Along with Web sites that report on smoking ceremonies as news are sites that elaborate on smoking rituals produced by companies and organizations that define their identity in relation to Indigenous Australian culture, while promoting the authentic quality of their products and their association with "the Aboriginal heritage." Thus the smoking of a bridge, presented on the Web site of a small West Australian business, becomes part of an economic enterprise, or, in the case of the Tasmanian Aboriginal Organization of the Lia Pootah, part of a political stance toward the Australian public and other Aboriginal groups.[10]

Since Aboriginal communities in Australia are formally registered as corporations, the spectrum of sites seamlessly includes government-funded, nonprofit organizations (often selling media related to Aboriginal culture) as well as profit-oriented corporations with Aboriginal connections, all of them with more or less direct government support. To the Internet user, subtle differences between the organizations that run sites are not easy to discern. References to smoking rituals are found across the whole spectrum. For instance, the Wandoo Didgeridoo Web site (www.wadidge.com.au) is produced by a company selling didgeridoos by stressing its logistical support for Aboriginal artists and promotion of their art. The company underlines its connection to Aboriginal culture by explicitly thanking local Aborigines for "accept[ing] us in their land and culture." Aboriginal names are used, and links to the Aboriginal heritage are underlined. However, as with most corporations of this sort, such a link may be contested. The Web page itself includes a quotation from an Aboriginal artist who objects to translating her "oral tradition into a medium such as the cyber world," a statement that reveals doubts about the Internet but also about the company's self-identification. Apart from an address list referring to other sites concerning Aboriginal culture, the Web site also displays an ethical statement concerning the company's code of behavior: "If

Wandoo Didgeridoo feels that its activity is clashing with the environment or the Australian Aboriginal culture, we will adjust our business accordingly."

The Wadidge Web site does not pretend to be the Web site of a representative Aboriginal body, but it shares many features with sites presenting Aboriginal art and culture that identify as "100 percent Aboriginal owned and operated," being run by registered Aboriginal corporations from specific localities.[11] Although the Wadidge Web site does not claim to stand for the Aboriginal community as a whole, the site is representative of ways in which Australian Aborigines are connected to the wider public through the Internet, namely, by means of hybrid entities consisting of corporations and individuals with links to both Aboriginal culture and to a non-Aboriginal audience interested in this culture. For instance, Wandoo's emphasis on art and playing the didgeridoo are both directed at a worldwide audience targeted through the Internet.[12] Moreover, the polarity, "Aboriginal culture versus Western culture," in effect, legitimizes organizational entities that see themselves as mediating bodies. With Aboriginal arts and music so deeply embedded in religious practices, we may assume that rituals, too, are subject to the interest of individuals and groups that are self-proclaimed mediators who, using modern media, continue the work of those gatekeepers and culture brokers of the past who negotiated access between Aboriginal and non-Aboriginal lifeways.[13]

The smoking ceremony featured on the Wadidge Web site was performed on the occasion of a bridge completion on the Canning River, near Perth, in Western Australia. The ritual, conveyed by photos and texts, symbolizes the double function attributed to smoking ceremonies in present-day Australia: cleansing a place for new purposes and reconciling non-Aboriginal Australians with Aboriginal Australians.

Smoking ceremonies in precolonial settings had a cleansing aspect and dealt with negative apprehensions, memories, and conflicts.[14] Smoking ceremonies today, implicitly or explicitly, also deal with the colonial confrontation between immigrants (or invaders) and indigenous people, as well as with past and present conflicts between groups of indigenous people. The smoking ritual at the Canning Bridge is no exception. The text on the Web page makes explicit reference to all these meanings and associations, stressing the historic encounter between Indigenous Australians and European colonizers:

> We were invited to the smoking ceremony of the completion of the Canning River Bridge representing a link between two traditionals [sic] tribes, (the Beeliar people and the Beeloo people).... The area is a significant Aboriginal site where a complex ecosystem provided livelihood and cultural meaning to the original Nyoongar people. It borders the boundaries of the Beeloo and Beeliar clan which looks after

the land north and south of the river respectively. It is also where Europeans chose to settle in 1829.[15]

The motive for holding a smoking ceremony for the Canning River Bridge springs directly from its relevance as a public act that unifies Aboriginal and European Australians: "Naming the bridge Djarlgarra acknowledges the great importance of the river and its surrounds to the Nyoongar people and the Aboriginal community as a whole. This process has successfully brought together Aboriginal and European culture."

Important to note is that the smoking ritual itself is declared authentic. In doing so, the Web site underlines the importance of making space for Aboriginal culture in modern-day Australia: "The smoking ceremony, celebrated by Patrick Hume from the Metropolitan Council of Nyoongar Elders, is part of the Nyoongar tradition and culture. Smoke from Balga (grass tree), Wattle and other native plants takes away the bad spirits. It cleanses and heals when you walk through it." Such comments show how the traditional use and meaning of smoking rituals have been adapted to new situations. The conventional meaning of smoking ceremonies as an instrument of cleansing has taken on new meaning, and both European and Aboriginal Australians now take part in active ways. Although the introduction of the Internet signaled an important change in modern communications, among Aborigines, a radical change in the smoking ritual and its functions took place much earlier, namely when those affected by indigenous rituals included outsiders. The "silent revolution" in the second half of the twentieth century opened up ritual performances beyond the circle of initiated practitioners.[16] The coming of the Internet enhanced the already public presence of smoking rituals, making them available to a global as well as local audience.

Even before the emergence of the Internet, smoking ceremonies were reported extensively in local print media, radio, and television, all of which have been produced and consumed by Aboriginal Australians for several decades. The Internet, though, enhanced the capacity to include people the world over. New, too, is the possibility of immediately connecting message senders with receivers beyond the more limited precursors such as call-in programs on Aboriginal radio. These differences from earlier media enable individual agents to gain access to a means of mass distribution, though not necessarily mass attention, while allowing for feedback from a large, diversified audience. Today, however, these options are limited by the power of governing political and dominant commercial bodies. It remains to be seen to what extent the potential of the Internet will be tapped by Aboriginal Australians.

What is noteworthy is that the Aboriginal conception of ritual recognizes that the effects of a ritual go well beyond the circle of those present. Rituals are considered essential for the maintenance of the world at large, affecting everyone.[17] Even so, physical presence continues to be considered to be critical. For instance, in present-day funerals, the physical presence of the mourners still matters to Aboriginal participants. Participants make substantial efforts, including traveling long distances at great expense, to witness these events. Even distant kin of the deceased attach great value to being present at the event, and they are reluctant to leave the ritual ground before the smoking has taken place.[18]

The Internet's facility to allow virtual participation in a ritual potentially offers an alternative to those who face difficulty being physically present. But while the opportunity for interactive communication during a ritual performance and the chance to take part in commentaries or prayers could in principle make the medium an instrument for connecting ritual practitioners who are distant or dispersed, this kind of virtual linking has not yet taken place in Australia. So far, it seems, virtual presence is no substitute for actual presence. If and when such a practice does emerge, it may be because Australian Aborigines adopt a Westernized notion of virtual presence that equates it with bodily presence.

The smoking ceremony as it is depicted on the Wadidge Web site is representative not only of smoking ceremonies across the country but of the current place of Aboriginal rituals in Australia. The double function of smoking rituals as marking an important event and facilitating reconciliation is widespread. When the National Museum of Australia was opened in Canberra in 2001, the day's festivities and speeches began with a smoking ceremony by Aborigines considered descendants of the local owners of the peninsula where the museum is situated. Even in a place that has long been colonized and that today has more of a non-Aboriginal than Aboriginal presence, and even at an event under the auspices of the Australian head of state, who strongly opposes special rights for Aboriginals, there was no question that a smoking ceremony by local Aborigines should be included in the event. There are also examples of individual non-Aboriginal artists inviting Aborigines, including those not directly related to local descendents of Aboriginal land owners, to perform smoking rituals as a blessing. In at least one case, the ceremony was accompanied by Hebrew chants and conducted before proceeding with an art installation.[19]

On such occasions, including a smoking ceremony is critical for European Australians who want to ensure the correctness of their behavior regarding Aborigines and, by implication, justify their own presence and place on the continent. The inclusion of smoking ceremonies in such events is also important for Aboriginal Australians who strive for recognition of their status as first owners of the land. For these reasons, smoking rituals on Web sites contain several layers; their messages serve different agents and are aimed at varied goals. Web site representations of smoking rituals serve the European Australian sense of belonging and reconciliation, while also serving Aboriginal Australian promotion of their public presence and legal rights. Such representations serve a bundle of interests including postcolonial reconciliation in general and the more particular interests of corporations that want to construct politically correct corporate profiles, as well as the interests of politicians, artists, and other parties.

The history of the ritual tradition shows that smoke was used for many and varied purposes. It was a communication tool to signal presence over long distances, and it was also one of the main Aboriginal ways of "looking after one's country." Fire and smoke were an integral part of a mobile way of life.[20] The smoking of the country, a kind of ritual looking-after-the-country, was not merely a matter of revisiting geographical places but part of "making places" as the result of movement. To what extent, then, is there a parallel between place making through rituals and the creation of Internet sites?

The localized character of Aboriginal ritual has been highlighted as a key element by ethnographers.[21] In Australia, ritual action and mythology are said to be tied intimately to the land, a worldview "not based on time and history but, at an absolute level, on sites and places."[22] The fact that many Indigenous Australians were pushed off their land may have even increased the tie between land and ritual insofar as ritual sites have now become a major element in Aboriginal land rights struggles and more recently in native title claims.[23] According to Aboriginal notions, the problem of access to land and ritual sites, which is due to colonial depopulation and displacement, affects specific sites as well as the whole country. Moreover, ritual negligence will lead to infertility of the land and the people at specific places.[24]

The established view of Aboriginal religion and ritual seems to support Jonathan Z. Smith's theorizing about ritual space. Certainly there is a strong connection in "totemic" rites between the landscape and religion; the two are inseparable. However, it is important to note that there is also an Aboriginal tradition of rituals that are not so intimately tied to specific sites.[25] Known as "traveling rituals" in the literature,[26] these ceremonies are either not tied to particular sites or are in principle transportable and can be performed at various places. In this respect, smoking ceremonies are similar to traveling rituals, since they can transpire in new places and acquire new meanings. At the same time, physical place remains critical in two ways. First, the Aboriginal perspective reflected in the ethnography of traveling and of smoking rituals is not so much that each ritual demands a specific place but that place requires ritual treatment and that social relations require both places and rituals. In other words, a ritual not only constitutes a place, but the fact that humans affiliate themselves constantly with places—places of memory and places of expected new interactions—calls for a ritual action such as cleansing.[27] Insofar as making places and creating sites is universal, the link between place and action is not erased even when a change of place is involved. Second, insofar as human agency is always embodied—that is, tied to the human body in place and space—a theoretically posited opposition between place and action seems flawed to begin with. In Aboriginal Australia today, ritual on the Internet remains limited. It opens new forms of public action, in particular those of conflict resolution and reconciliation, but not in radically different ways from other media. With regard to smoking rituals, Indigenous Australians have not yet taken to the late-modern "illusion" that shifting between Web sites will release one from the limitations of the body and allow for a new mode of ritual activity. With increasing use of the Internet among Aboriginal Australians, these attitudes and practices may, of course, change in the future.

One may speak of reappropriating a place through ritual when a smoking ceremony is carried out today by Indigenous Australians, including urbanized Australians of mixed descent who use the ceremony to celebrate and express their Aboriginal identity. This reappropriation is also the case in the state of Tasmania, which, according to the general perception of the Australian public, has no surviving original indigenous population but where reports of rituals are prominent in the self-definition of Indigenous Australian persons and groups.[28]

Aboriginal smoking rituals mediated through the Internet can, therefore, also connect to ritual practices with a long tradition on the continent. That said, it is still valid to argue that the step from documenting or referring to a ritual to conducting one on the Internet is still a major move. The notion that by going to a Web site one can participate in a rite is only possible if one embraces the late-modern assumption that one can hop from one ritual event to another in virtual space as if the physical movement has no effect on oneself and the way in which one understands the world. This assumption is challenged by anthropologists who regard the notion as a recent culmination of a strong underlying Western illusion ultimately based on the separation of body and mind.[29] The difficulty of not being able to be physically present at a ritual that is documented on the Internet can only be resolved, it seems, by ignoring the inevitable problem that all mental and emotional states are invariably tied to bodily existence. It remains to be seen whether Indigenous Australians, with their own tradition of spiritual journeys and their own conventions of interpreting dreams, consider this problem unsolvable.

The Web Site of the Sanctuary of Our Lady of Lourdes

The Marian shrine of Lourdes in southern France is a site of global renown visited by 6 million pilgrims yearly. From the time of Bernadette's visions of Mary in 1858, Lourdes rapidly developed a national and international reputation.[30] With the Catholic Church's official recognition of the site in 1862, the town developed into one of the best-known Marian pilgrimage sites in the Christian world.

From the beginning, church representatives deployed the tools available in a modernizing, capitalist economy to promote the Lourdes shrine. Nineteenth-century technological innovations such as mass production, railways, photography, the illustrated press, and picture postcards, as well as tourist guidebooks and religious objects, became instrumental in attracting and facilitating the ever-growing flow of pilgrims.[31] Having arrived in Lourdes, pilgrims were effectively accommodated by newly built streets, shops, and hotels. Considering these historic developments, it is no surprise that the first religious Web site in France was the official Web site of the Lourdes sanctuary, constructed in 1996. Again, the coordinators' adaptability to modern media proved rewarding. By 2004, the site was visited by 10,000 people daily.

The Internet site of the Sanctuary of Our Lady of Lourdes is intended for sick, immobile, or poor people who are not able to visit the physical site. It also prepares pilgrims who want to come to the site and helps those who want to have a look back at the site after their visit. Moreover, the Internet site helps in distributing the message of Lourdes on a larger scale. It welcomes visitors in six different languages (French, English, Italian, Spanish, Dutch, and German), although not every page of the site is multilingual.[32] On the home page, visitors are given a direct view of the grotto and are invited to make a virtual tour to the shrine and the town of Lourdes; to send a personal prayer to the grotto; to experience what is transpiring at the holy site by viewing images captured by several Webcams; or to view the Lourdes Web TV. There are links to information about the history and messages of the shrine and directions for how to make a pilgrimage. There is also an overview of useful addresses, ranging from the Information Centre, *Lourdes Magazine*, Medical Bureau, and Bookshop to names and phone numbers of chaplain coordinators who offer their services in French, German, Spanish, Italian, and Dutch. Next to these is a window that displays the latest news items related to the shrine, such as the visits of Ingrid Bétancourt and Pope Benedict XVI in 2008. The visitor is then able to choose from five chapters: "Contact," "Your Petition," "Frequently Asked Questions," "Forum," and "The Word of God," a chapter quoting biblical texts. The "Frequently Asked Questions" option provides extensive information about the shrine's itinerary and accessibility as well as about pilgrim etiquette. As virtual pilgrims, Web visitors can become informed about ritual matters such as how to have a Mass said, how to have a candle burned, and how to offer an ex-voto.[33] Web visitors can also learn the meaning of key religious terms such as *immaculate conception* and *rosary*.

At the predominantly one-way Web site, only official representatives of the shrine are allowed to lead the ritual. In other words, Lourdes hosts a directive Web site in which the possibilities for expressing personal devotion to Mary are limited. Alternative Web sites, blogs, and forums where devotees can perform or discuss their own rituals are lacking. Web pilgrims are almost immediately directed toward the officially recognized Web site of the Lourdes sanctuary, and there is no mistaking the official character of the site, which is also emphasized by its Google listing.

Although the Web site offers predominantly one-way communication, at least one interactive possibility is offered: the option of sending prayers to a prayer box next to the grotto. The Web master offers instructions about how such digital petitions are processed (see figure 5.1).[34]

A specific Web page, "Intentions de prières," diagrammatically depicts the process and informs the visitor that prayers sent by e-mail are collected by the multimedia service in Lourdes where they are burned onto a CD that is then put into Mary's mailbox in the grotto. Each day, a priest celebrating Mass in the grotto will read some of the e-mails that were sent. The Forum, too, is presented as a place where pilgrims can leave personal messages for Mary and for fellow pilgrims. Next to calls for collective prayers are visitors' reports of happy or sad moments in life, as well as reflections on them. Web site visitors can then respond to these messages, leaving words of comfort and support. There are mothers' accounts about their newborn babies, stories about their pregnancies, and congratulations to the mothers and babies who are celebrated and prayed for: "A real little miracle. We all pray that Mary will watch over the child."[35] Inspired by this call, an anonymous

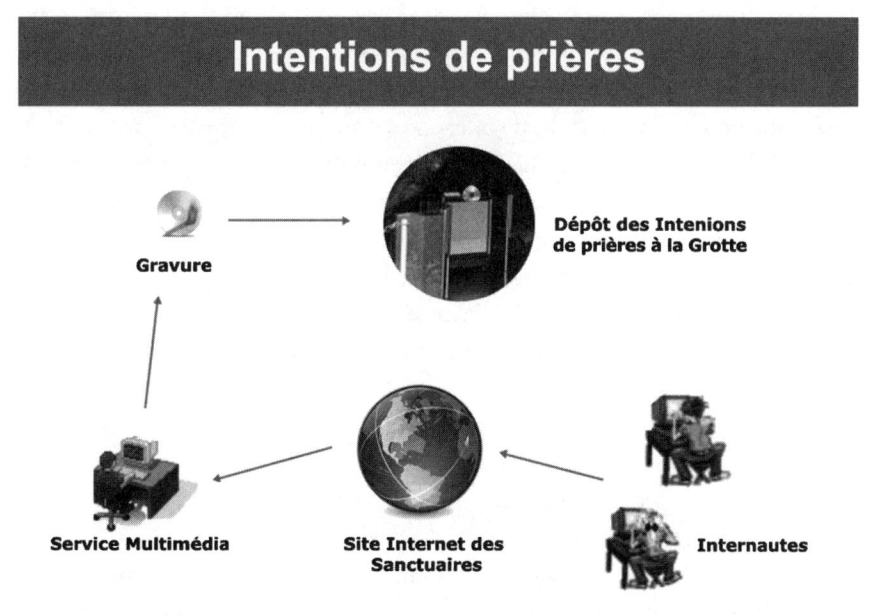

FIGURE 5.1. Lourdes Internet site, sending prayers by e-mail.

visitor encourages fellow visitors to pray for "deserted women, chaste or not, who are alone in raising their children,"[36] as well as for women hoping to become mothers. The gendered nature of this virtual practice corresponds to the practice of physical pilgrimage, in which women are similarly overrepresented.

The presence and use of Web cameras is also explained by the Web site editor. Web cams "record the surrounds of the Grotto every 15 minutes throughout the day," as well as covering events such as the three daily Masses, the praying of the rosary as it is broadcast daily, the Blessed Sacrament Procession, the Torchlight Marian Procession, and the grotto at night. Another camera offers a view of three main sites: the Rosary Basilica, the Crowned Statue, and the Rosary Square. Just as with a proper tour guide, the Web pilgrim is informed about what to see, when, and where. In addition, the display of events and timetables catalogs the must-sees of Lourdes, compelling the devout pilgrim not to miss a thing.

Although subject to a Webmaster and the site's information desk editing all incoming messages, the Forum gives the impression of being a free and open forum for virtual pilgrims. It provides them with an opportunity to connect with fellow pilgrims and to respond to each other's prayers. In this respect, the Web site offers the possibility of leaving personal messages and connecting with other people while guaranteeing anonymity and privacy. Still, although the forum looks like the prayer books that used to be situated next to the main statues of Mary at the shrine (see figure 5.2), it falls short of offering the same religious experience.

Previously, when pilgrims wrote down their wishes and prayers next to the statue, they could look directly into Mary's eyes, touch her face or feet, kiss her, and silently talk with her, and they often left small notes and photographs behind. For these intimate actions, the Web site offers no substitute. The ritual of private communication with Mary, of leaving handwritten notes for her in the prayer books, was banned by officials in 2000. Instead, for efficiency's sake, they offered the option of sending prayers by e-mail. Prayer books were then removed from the basilicas, because the Web sites were expected to fulfill pilgrims' needs. However, as liberating as the Internet may be, its mediated mode of contact cannot replace the personal communication with Mary and fellow pilgrims at the actual Lourdes shrine.

"Virtual pilgrimage" is an Internet neologism for a Web site through which people can simulate a sacred journey.[37] The presence of many well-documented Marian shrines on the Internet illustrates that Marian pilgrimages are part of the modern world. Like Lourdes, old and established Marian shrines such as Our Lady of Guadalupe in Mexico (www.sancta.org) and the shrine of Our Lady of Glastonbury in the United Kingdom (www.glastonburyshrine.co.uk) use the Internet to distribute information, while offering interactive instruments so visitors can pray or leave messages with lit candles, make petitions, or send flowers to the Lady.

FIGURE 5.2. Handwritten prayers, names, and personal souvenirs left by pilgrims at the Lourdes shrine.

Although virtual pilgrimages are an important religious phenomenon for understanding new modes of spirituality, little research has been done on the relation between virtual and physical pilgrimage.[38] It does seem reasonable, however, to assume that virtual pilgrimage is attractive to people because it offers the possibility of taking part in rituals from which they would otherwise be excluded for financial, geographical, age-related, or health reasons.

Concerning the Lourdes site in particular, one would expect the power of the virtual site not to differ much from the power of the physical site, given the numerous reproductions of the shrine at many other places. "Catholic pilgrims around the world," states religious studies scholar Robert Orsi, "journey to replicas of the Lourdes grotto far from the European site to drink and bathe in the waters flowing from plumbing hidden in artfully arranged rocks and insist these waters have healing powers though they almost always know that the waters flow from local reservoirs."[39] Because of their similarity to the original grotto, reconstructed grottos appear to have the same power and appeal to pilgrims as the official site in Lourdes. There is no dualistic spilt between action and place here. This phenomenon seems to contrast with Smith's argument about place as the crucial element in ritual.[40] The ritual is not place-bound in a geographical sense, because similarity of form, not continuity of location, makes the replicas efficacious. Because the reproductions look like the original, they invoke that place and make human action at the replicas meaningful. The Lourdes site has become transportable then in much the same way as Australian smoking rituals—that is, Lourdes devotion is not fixed in space but rather moves through it.

Also, at least with respect to the original Lourdes site in France, one would expect little difference between the power of the virtual and that of the physical site, since both are arenas of mass consumption through which visitors quickly pass. Due to its global popularity, Lourdes has grown into a cosmopolitan destination filled with a continuous stream of pilgrims and tourists. The modest town of Lourdes, with only 15,000 inhabitants, is second only to Paris with respect to the number of hotels it offers. In fact, the Lourdes sanctuary is crowded with thousands of individuals whose itineraries briefly connect and overlap. From a place defined by anthropologist Marc Augé as "relational, historical and concerned with identity," Lourdes has been transformed into a "non-place," a place of transit where travelers pass in anonymity just as in airports, museums, and supermarkets.[41] From the perspective of the shrine's management, pilgrims are temporary passengers guided by the shrine's Web site, timetables, and instruction guides. Pilgrims are expected not to bond with the space and to leave no trace—both of which severely conflict with the interests of pilgrims whose aim it is to leave personal traces at the site (see figure 5.2). Efficient control and powerful management deliberately redirect, even thwart, such plans by preventing pilgrims from creating their own ritual space. To retain a relevant religious tradition in a modern, secular world, officials must distance themselves from popular expressions of Marian devotion and keep the place "clean." In this respect, the official Internet site of Lourdes does not differ much from the official physical site, where the same powerful groups construct a dominant, church-supported image of the shrine.

Despite the similarities between the geographical site of Lourdes in southern France and its virtual presence on the Internet, we think there are important differences. Although both the Internet and the physical site offer limited interactive possibilities, pilgrims are in a better position to solve conflicts on site, rather than through the shrine's Web site. Pilgrims may circumvent dominant power structures at the physical site by hiding their personal notes or offerings to Mary beneath the cloth of the altar in the grotto or amid the flowers offered to the crowned statue of Mary in front of the Basilica of the Rosary. Pilgrims may temporarily leave ex-votos next to the statues of Mary or Bernadette, where they may be seen by other pilgrims, at least before officials remove them. In contrast, at the official Internet site, these secret or subdominant expressions of Marian devotion cannot take place.

There are additional reasons to accept the argument that visiting the Internet site cannot replace traveling to the physical Lourdes site in France. The virtual pilgrimage lacks the emotional bonding between pilgrims, who mourn their dead loves ones, cry for lost children, or struggle with kinship trouble and shameful secrets in the family.[42] The feeling of communitas, of "being one big family," as the pilgrims often say, is lacking in virtual pilgrimage.[43] Even though proponents of new media sometimes argue that the new options enhance rather than restrict pilgrims' abilities to connect with one another, Notermans argues the opposite. Traveling in organized pilgrimage groups, people can listen to each other's stories of pain and suffering and offer each other a shoulder to cry on. This performance of pain and mourning is essential to the healing process during pilgrimage. The meaningful sequence of ritual activities that brings about emotional healing during the pilgrimage process, as well as sensory experiences such as smelling incense, witnessing each other's physical suffering, experiencing bodily exhaustion, hearing pilgrims' stories and the familiar chants in church, and touching or embracing the grotto all contribute to the profound physical and emotional experience of an actual pilgrimage to Lourdes that virtual pilgrimage cannot offer. The performative and material aspects of Marian devotion that are of central importance in the experience of pilgrimage can hardly be carried out via the Internet.[44]

Returning to Smith's and Grimes's diverging views on ritual and place, we conclude that in the case of the official Web site of Lourdes it appears, again, that place and action are not an either-or issue. Considering the many reproductions of the Lourdes site the world over, the form of the original spatial setting, but not its geographical location, may appear to be of primary importance for the power of the site. In addition, the Lourdes case shows that the reproduction of place also constitutes a problem in cyberspace, since power relations are imbalanced and limitations are imposed on visitors. At both the physical and the Internet site, dominant and subdominant groups have conflicting interests. For the pilgrims, these conflicts are more severely felt at the Internet site, because the physical site, whether original or copied, allows them more room to maneuver and to find possibilities for creative action in the face of official restrictions. At this point, Grimes's argument for the power of human action becomes decisive: because human action and interaction with religious materiality is so restricted at the Lourdes Internet site, virtual ritual effectively loses meaning and power.

Dutch Weblogs on Death and Mourning

In the last few decades, the religious landscape of the Netherlands generally and Dutch funerary culture in particular have gone through major transformations fueled by immigration, secularization, and individualization.[45] The two main church communities of the Netherlands, the Catholic Church and the churches of the Reformation, have been challenged by religions introduced by immigrants from former colonies and North Africa, as well as by alternative, or New Age, forms of spirituality.

These changes began opening up established Dutch funerary culture as people rethought ceremonies relating to death and mourning. About 72 percent of Dutch people define themselves as nonreligious or as not religiously affiliated.[46] However, many are unable to do without rituals during major transitions.[47] As secularization reduces the influence of institutional religion in matters of life and death, people want to determine for themselves the form of their exit from life, resulting in great funerary creativity. The desire for more openness and public visibility of death has resulted in increased use of the Internet.[48] For example, dying and bereaved individuals now create and employ Weblogs. These are being studied as part of a research project on biographies of the dying and the dead in films, television, and the Internet as ways of accessing ritual innovation in Dutch funerary culture.[49]

Research on the Internet and its impact on social life is still new;[50] so is the study of religious and funerary ritual on the Internet.[51] Inspired by the work of Andreas Kitzmann, who regards digital media as engendering new social and cultural practices,[52] this case investigates the desires of dying and bereaved individuals to express themselves through Weblogs that include digital biographies and memorials.[53]

In the Netherlands, people suffering from a terminal disease and those mourning the death of a loved one express themselves quite openly through virtual diaries, or Weblogs. The Weblogs made by those who are gravely ill usually consist of images and texts, sometimes also of movies and music, presenting life stories and focusing on the experience of coping with a deadly illness as well as the prospect of imminent death. Those facing bereavement also keep digital records that express their feelings about dealing with the loss of a spouse, family member, or friend.

Internet sites offer people not only the means to express themselves but also an instrument to contact like-minded people. Thus, patients who have little time or energy to communicate with family and friends can do so online.[54] As a Weblog author afflicted by cancer writes, "I have got no energy to keep everyone posted, to tell fifteen times a day about how I am doing."[55] Equally important is that Weblogs allow fellow sufferers to connect, exchange information, and reflect on being terminally ill. Spouses, parents, and friends also find relief through Weblogs by relating online with like-minded people. Parents of deceased children have the possibility of expressing themselves, sometimes after many years of silence. Since many of these parents feel a continuing need for public recognition of their dead children, they not only appreciate family, friends, and colleagues talking about their children, but also explore the available media to create memorial sites using drawings, photos, jewelry, and such to keep their memories alive. In addition to individual Web sites, collective Weblogs have also appeared, some of which are closely intertwined with television shows such as *Over My Dead Body* (in Dutch, *Over Mijn Lijk*).[56]

Unlike commercial sites linked to Aboriginal smoking rituals or the heavily managed official Lourdes site, Dutch Weblogs on death and mourning are directed by individual practitioners themselves. Altena's argument is that the freedom these Weblogs provide for communicating thoughts, beliefs, and emotions about death make the logs a uniquely innovative funerary medium. Because of their repetitive and symbolic qualities, these sites are ritualized. This is not merely the view of scholars; Weblog authors themselves describe their maintenance of Weblogs as ritual.[57] The question then is not so much whether digital rituals can replace real-life actions, but rather in what ways Internet rituals meet people's needs for ritual experience.

A frequently asked question is why people feel the need to convey such messages to an unknown audience and what they hope to achieve by doing so. It is important to recall that people have always needed images to remember loved ones. Portraits and objects of the dead not only help people left behind to keep memories alive, they also redefine the relations between the deceased and the bereaved. Images and objects reflect and help construct lost and new identities, serving as tangible proof of the ties between the living and dead loved ones. Historical objects show both the diversity and continuous changes in funerary imagery. In the Netherlands in 1998, only some 150 drawings, prints, and paintings of dead persons were counted in museum collections dating from 1500 to the present.[58] These portraits represent a small part of the total number of portraits made of dead friends and family, as most of them were usually destroyed after time passed. Then, at the dawn of the twenty-first century, new funerary rituals emerged that made prominent use of popular media, such as television and the Internet. Now television and the Internet have become broadly accepted means of communication about dying and death.[59] In Web sites and Weblogs, people have found platforms to address delicate issues concerning dying and death, turning both into an appreciated means of communication.

This case study is based on a selection of ten Weblogs about people suffering from cancer. The logs were created by patients themselves, by their loved ones, or by their bereaved. Because of their continual high ranking in Google search results, these Weblogs are among the most frequently visited Weblogs about cancer patients. The Weblogs, studied in 2008 and 2009, usually consist of several parts: an introduction of the protagonist, a diagnosis and prognosis, a diary (the most prominent feature), a postal facility for visitors to leave comments and messages, a description of the funeral, and an overview of memorial activities. Often, the diary contributions were laced with inspiring quotations, photographs, or films. The Weblogs lasted from a few years to more than a decade. The research method made use of a qualitative approach consisting of a close reading of the Weblogs, as well as relating their shape and content to the attributed meanings of the Weblogs and the way they are used in people's lives. For reasons of privacy, illustrations are left out, and the names of the Weblogs and their authors are anonymous.

Weblogs build on actual funeral and mourning traditions such as conventional handwritten diaries, extending their function by addressing an Internet audience that, in turn, comments and reflects on the entries. This innovation usually results in the log's author redirecting his or her writing so it can be understood by an anonymous public. Since it is no longer intended for private use only, the entries of a digital diary require explicit explanation. When Weblogs contain references or symbols that are not generally known, they are often explained by author's notes that elaborate on the private meaning of the displayed poem, song, or picture. Despite the extra effort required for the construction of digital diaries, the chance to gain public access and feedback makes the effort worthwhile. Access to a public platform and the chance for mutual exchange are key to how these Weblogs function. Their possibility for receiving and discussing comments increases their attractiveness.

A woman suffering from breast cancer describes her Weblog as "a fantastic way to deal with my period of illness. Friends, acquaintances, colleagues and such can be informed."[60] The digital guest book collects messages from friends and family as well as anonymous visitors, among whom are fellow sufferers. The condolences, informed advice, and consolation by unprejudiced visitors to the site represent a priceless point of contact for many patients. The parents of a dead child state, "The great numbers of visitors of this website does us good."[61] Another couple writes, "When we receive a visitor's message, it makes our day."[62] Unlike family and friends who sometimes act overly worried, sympathetic strangers provide recognition and advice based on practice. Therefore, supportive Weblog comments constitute social and emotional recognition that people respond to with gratitude. As a bereaved mother put it, "So many sweet people who have taken the trouble to write us, it's really great!"[63]

A striking characteristic of Weblogs is the degree of agency displayed by the protagonists. It is their story, their focus, and their choice of method for memorializing; they act independently of ritual or media specialists. In Internet diaries, the authors' choices dominate the shape and content, demonstrating a unique degree of autonomy and control compared to nonprofessionals appearing in mass media such as newspapers, film, radio, or television. The protagonists define the range of topics and what can be shared with their audience. Their personal reflections are central in a way that circumvents today's sound-bite culture. Discussing the topic of death offers ordinary people media power to constitute monuments for the dying that would not otherwise exist. By employing the Internet, authors can use whatever creative input they choose to create unique, personal memorials for family and friends.

A Weblog functions to organize an author's personal life as well as to construct a public digital community. As in traditional diary keeping, people report that writing about their daily lives is an opportunity to organize their feelings. A sick man, happy to be able to make a Weblog contribution for his friends, writes, "Now I am writing this, things become clear to me."[64] A woman reflects on her losses: "I have got cancer and I feel lonely. . . . I need to give up my beautiful hair, my health, my physical strength, my youthful appearance, my self-assurance. . . . What will remain of me?"[65] The act of keeping a diary blog works as a strategy to give meaning to experience. In sum, routine, steady diary keeping can become a comforting ritual act.

Weblogs provide those who are dying or mourning the possibility of achieving almost complete control over the conveyance of their story. They can design and compose their Web content, as well as take the liberty of editing contributions by themselves and others, or they can even delete a contribution. By taking control of Web sites, authors often realize they can direct their lives too. Web sites are used as instruments to instruct others: "No more than three visitors. . . . Preferably not too many flowers."[66]

For bereaved parents, texts and photos document events in the life of their deceased child. Once on the Web site, each photo can become an object of pride. Visitors are invited to confirm the beauty or the courage of the child. The mother of a child diagnosed with a brain tumor claimed, "She sure is a tough little lady."[67] Anyone looking at the Web photos is addressed in the same way he or she would be addressed on a personal visit.

Those who are using such Web sites say that preserving the memory of their loved ones in this way meets an urgent need. For parents of young dead children, such sites are an ongoing confirmation that the dead really existed. A parent of a deceased child wrote, "Our own website, that feels great!"[68] A mother stated, "Our child will not be forgotten."[69] Weblog visitors are welcomed and told what their attention means to the authors. The number of guests, their comments, and even the various times of day or night the site is frequented are experienced as proofs of acknowledgment. To the authors who may have experienced rejection, the visibility of the deceased person is a welcome source of consolation and inspiration.

The presumed deficiency of the Internet and its supposed inability to connect people as in real life—an argument implied by the cases of the Aboriginal smoking rituals and the Lourdes site—is relativized by entries in Weblogs about death and mourning. In the perception of those who create the death and mourning sites, they are open spaces where people can share deeply felt emotions, leave traces, and create relations lasting many years.[70]

In theories of ritual, the Internet is generally treated as a medium independent of place. If we were to base our reasoning strictly on Jonathan Z. Smith's perspective, we might conclude that digital media lack the spatial dimension needed to provide sacrality for ritual.[71] However, if we follow Grimes in concentrating on the importance of action and creativity in ritual, the death and mourning Web sites appear to be expressions of ritual creativity that are less time- and space-bound than nondigital rituals. Transcending the limits of time and space is a concern when, for example, Web authors declare that, in the afterlife, they will "still be there" through their Weblog. One wrote, "I think it is important that something will remain of me, something positive."[72]

Weblogs on dying and mourning function on different levels as a means of communication between the dying protagonist and his or her family and friends, the bereaved, and, in some cases, the bereaved and the deceased. The awareness that someone's Weblog represents his or her last thoughts and actions makes the deceased's site a revered memorial, a sacred "place." So, bereaved people leave messages in the Weblog's guest book, addressing the deceased as an intermediary between the living and the dead. One parent imagines her dead daughter to be her little guardian angel whom she asks to provide her and her husband with a new baby brother and sister.[73] A mother addresses her deceased child, asking it to support its parents from heaven.[74] Visitors' messages turn into prayers and requests for intervention in real life. Because of the alleged eternal quality of the Internet, the deceased not only remains alive on the Internet forever but is thought to acquire supernatural power to intervene in the world of the living.

The Internet's perceived independence from place and time makes the medium particularly attractive to ritual practitioners. Compared to conventional media, the Internet offers relative geographical, temporal, and social freedom. Everyone is provided with freedom of expression despite the Internet's national, cultural, economic, gender, and age limitations. Gender is a key consideration, since technical maintenance is often provided by men, whereas Weblog authors are mostly women. The division of labor seems to have important bearing on the choice of topics as well as on ways they are expressed. In the Weblogs investigated in this case, male authors were highly underrepresented; only two out of ten Weblogs were written by men, and they addressed different topics. Their blogs tend toward descriptions of physical processes, medical treatments, techniques, and medications instead of emotions and relationships. Women in particular have also discovered that Weblogs can be effective instruments for providing caregiver directories and calendars, thus optimizing patients' health and privacy, while facilitating real-life visits, or preventing unnecessary disturbances.

Because Weblog authors make use of the Internet in the privacy of their own homes, comfortably seated at their own computers, working on their own familiar

Weblogs, some of them have trouble understanding that they are indeed connected to a worldwide community. The deceptive intimacy of Web sites and the inconceivability of their global range make it easy to forget that they are public. It remains to be seen whether family and friends of Weblog authors will begin objecting to the public display of their private problems on these sites. Certainly this is a question that needs further exploration, since intimate experiences and emotions are shared with complete strangers. Boundary issues can take various forms. Sometimes, authors act surprised when they find unexpected visitor comments; some prevent these altogether by screening their site. In most cases, however, digital contact between Web site authors and an anonymous mass audience remains a conscious choice. While it may seem contradictory, surrendering intimate stories on a public platform can actually protect someone's privacy, helping create much-needed distance by, for example, limiting intrusive phone conversations or visitors.

Because a Weblog may be constructed over a long period of time, in some cases over a decade, often starting with the report of the discovery of a disease and leading to postmortem memorial celebrations, the shape and function of the site evolve through time. Initiated originally as a point of reflection and contact, the addition of messages and advice by visitors, sometimes even after the death of the author, turn these sites into information centers. Some authors are conscious of this aspect from the start, as is shown by links to informative addresses such as those of hospitals or self-help groups. Others, becoming aware of this function, sometimes present themselves as advisors, drawing on their own experience.

After some time, a Weblog's function as a daily point of reference is replaced by that of being an ongoing memorial. Additional sections may be added that announce new phases in the lives of the bereaved, referring to the birth of a new baby, a new love, or a new job. It may also happen that contributors eventually decide to stop updating the Web site. Having benefited from the maintenance of the Weblog, they may relay the message that their needs have changed: "It doesn't feel good that people expect you to be devastated."[75] After expressing their gratitude to supporting visitors, they stop contributing to the Website. This does not necessarily mean that the site is discontinued; it may still exist as a static, unchangeable entity. In effect, the site itself devolves into a memorial monument.

Weblogs about death and mourning in the Netherlands have opened up funerary culture by providing individuals with the opportunity to make a digital memorial of themselves, that is, a mediatized self-portrait. Instead of the traditional solemn portraits such as one finds on obituary cards or headstones,[76] celebrating life and constructing a memorial have now become central. Compared with contemporary media culture, the agency offered by Weblogs gives Internet authors a wide range of freedom, options, and control. Weblogs made by dying and bereaved people represent innovative platforms for the terminally ill and their loved ones to express themselves and to reach out and contact others. Although this medium does not address the senses in the way that traditional ritual performances do, Weblogs about death and mourning make ritual innovation possible, convey feelings of belonging, connect practitioners, and create virtual places less inhibiting than those outside the Internet.

The Functions of Internet Rituals

The Internet rituals discussed in this chapter operate in various ways. Web sites document ritual performances, provide ritual instruments, and instruct practitioners on how to perform rituals. Furthermore, Web sites function as ritual sites themselves, becoming vehicles for participating in digital rituals, for instance, by mediating petitions and prayers at Lourdes and facilitating mourning and memorializing on Weblogs.

The central question of the chapter—what happens when rituals are constructed and enacted in cyberspace rather than in geographical space—cannot be answered without taking into account the power relations involved. As is the case with all media, the Internet is directed by different parties toward different goals. The Web sites of the three case studies vary highly in practitioners' access to and control of their respective sites. Consequently, an analysis of the form, meaning, and function of these sites must necessarily be related to the way people are able to direct or change these. How do the sites relate to life experience outside the Internet?

Widlok's analysis of Web sites for Aboriginal smoking rituals shows that these sites are also vehicles for non-Aboriginal agents to justify their presence on the Australian continent by readily accepting the reconciliatory and conflict-resolution qualities of smoking ceremonies. Widlok finds that, although Aboriginal people are involved in the performance of smoking rituals, and although they value recognition as first owners of the land, their participation in Internet smoking rituals is still limited.

By contrast, the official Lourdes Web site is an unapologetically instructive and informative tour guide that directs proper pilgrims on how to behave. Although visitors to the Web site are offered a forum where they may leave messages, virtual pilgrims, Notermans writes, are confined to a one-way portal that leaves no space for religious action and interaction with Mary, the central figure of the Lourdes experience.

Altena's study of Weblogs on dying and mourning in the Netherlands shows that these sites offer new means of expression and function as a medium for communication and new ways of participating in funerary rituals.

The analyses of these three cases show that rituals on Web sites vary greatly in agency, interactivity, and creative expression. As a result, the question of how digital representation replaces the conventional experience of rituals is met with divergent answers. Widlok suggests that the value Aboriginal people attach to place is matched by the value they attach to ritual as a means for creating meaningful places. The presence of these rituals on the Internet does not create independence from place. Nevertheless, making sites relevant through publicizing rituals on Web sites and other media connects the Internet with an existing Aboriginal tradition of transferring rituals between communities and places. Insofar as these ritually significant sites continue to be tied to the human body and to geographical space, ritual action and ritual place cannot be considered to be mutually exclusive bases for ritual. So far, Aboriginal rituals on the Internet rely on ritual actions and places outside the Internet. The new medium amplifies some of the purposes to which rituals are put, above all those of reconciliation and of asserting ownership, legitimacy, and identity at a national and international level.

In the Lourdes case, virtual pilgrims are more limited in expressing their personal devotion to Mary at the official Internet site than at the physical site. Although at the physical site, popular devotions are also prohibited, pilgrims can more easily get around obstructions, creating their own ritual space, than is possible by visiting the Web site. Lourdes officials use the Web site as a powerful instrument to create standardized worship accepted by the church. By contrast, Dutch Weblogs on death and mourning are highly individualized media, offering almost total control to their creators, thereby creating ample opportunity to exercise individual agency. The result is that these Weblogs offer a powerful means of expression and a way of circumventing traditional funerary taboos.

With regard to change or innovation in rituals, Widlok argues that sites only document or invoke smoking rites that are ultimately tied to the bodily experience of ritual. The rituals themselves remain inseparable from the bodily presence of the practitioners and the actual place where a ritual is performed. Notermans too shows ritual experience cannot be replaced by Internet rituals; the Lourdes Website fails to substitute for people's personal, tactile communication with the Marian shrine and with fellow pilgrims. On the other hand, Altena argues that Weblogs of dying and bereaved people provide recognition, refuge, and appreciation that people do not find elsewhere in conventional funerary culture. These innovations not only contribute by opening up professional funerary culture in the Netherlands, they also point to new spiritual practices.[77]

Regarding the place-boundedness of ritual, the established view of Aboriginal religion and ritual seems to support Jonathan Z. Smith, because in totemic rituals there is a strong connection between the landscape and religion; in fact, the two are considered inseparable. However, there are also traditional Aboriginal rituals not so intimately tied to individual sites,[78] and such rituals can become transportable.[79] Smoking ceremonies can be carried out in new places and acquire new meaning. However, Widlok stresses that, insofar as making places and creating sites is a human universal, the link between place and action is not erased even when change of place is involved. Human agency is always tied to the human body, inherently situated and placed in space. Since there are no places without human action, and no human actions outside of actual places, the notion that one is more central than the other is problematic.

Notermans's analysis of the official Lourdes site seems to support Smith's argument about the importance of place as ritual's crucial element. Still, she hesitates to privilege space over action. Given the many reconstructions of the Lourdes site all over the world—in effect, making the site transportable, not unlike Australian smoking rituals—one could argue that the original place does appear to be of primary importance. However, Notermans's analysis of the Lourdes Web site shows that the reproduction of place becomes problematic in cyberspace because of power relations, in particular, the church's regulatory restrictions of visitors' access to the shrine via its Internet portal. At this point, Grimes's argument on behalf of the power of human action becomes decisive. Because human interference with religious materiality is restricted at the Lourdes Internet site, the result is loss of meaning and power.

Altena finds that Smith's argument fails to anticipate the kind of ritual power that is available via new media. Alternatively, Grimes's view of the importance of creativity in ritual is more in line with Weblog practices. Although it can be useful to distinguish ritual space from ritual action, Altena resists making one more central than the other. She also questions the presumed inability of the Internet to replace conventional real-life experience by showing how Dutch Weblogs about death and mourning function as open spaces where practitioners share deeply felt emotions and create lasting communities comparable to those outside the Internet.

Rappaport's view on the limits of ritual innovation is supported by the analysis of Web sites for Aboriginal smoking rituals and Lourdes.[80] In the latter case invention is restricted because the site follows strict conventions that safeguard the church's power while limiting visitors' options, making ritual creativity subject to the Webmaster's censorship. Widlok also notes the limitation of Web sites connected with conventional rituals. While such sites may foster the use of smoking rituals for conciliatory purposes, that effect seems to be only strengthened, not created, by the Internet. Altena, on the other hand, finds that Dutch funerary Weblogs do foster the construction of communities. This finding is in line with earlier research about the Internet that recognized the medium's potential to promote human relationships, particularly among people with serious illnesses who gain the anonymity and objectivity they desire yet cannot receive from family and friends.[81] As both an innovation and continuation of real-life practices, Weblogs are evidence of an ongoing process of ritual reinvention.[82] The opportunity that these Weblogs provide with respect to individual access to a mass audience, new ritual expressions, and innovation beyond existing funerary culture also supports media scholar Stewart Hoover's suggestion that practitioners become increasingly active agents in using mass media rather than merely being subject to them.[83]

Potential visibility on a global scale and the possibility for immediate and interactive contact with one's audience contribute decisively to a general appreciation of the Internet. Our diverse case studies help to establish whether and in what ways these potentials are in fact realized in practice. In the case of Aboriginal smoking rituals, the traditional meaning of cleansing practices is being appropriated as an instrument to construct postcolonial relationships that cater to commercial or political interests. For Indigenous Australians, smoking rituals have acquired meaning as a powerful medium for raising cultural and political awareness as well as facilitating cultural reconciliation and conflict resolution. While the Lourdes Web site offers limited public access to a digital shrine, making space for virtual pilgrims, the site ultimately reinforces the hierarchical, directive character of the institutional church. However, for individual authors, such as those creating or using Weblogs to reflect on mortality, the Internet provides an alternative to traditional modes of conducting, expressing, and participating in ritual.

NOTES

1. About prejudices regarding the Internet, both dystopian and utopian views, see James Katz and Ronald Rice, *Social Consequences of Internet Use* (Cambridge, MA: MIT Press: 2002), 3.

2. Roy Rappaport, *Ritual and Religion in the Making of Humanity* (Cambridge, MA: Cambridge University Press, 1999), 32.

3. Jonathan Z. Smith, *To Take Place: Towards Theory in Ritual* (Chicago: University of Chicago Press, 1987), 22.

4. Smith, *To Take Place*, 75.

5. Ronald L. Grimes, "Jonathan Z. Smith's Theory of Ritual Space," *Religion* 29 (1999): 261–273.

6. See PY Media Web site, www.waru.org.

7. Thomas Widlok, "Time, Death and Property in Australia," *Journal de la Société des Océanistes* 124, no. 1 (2007): 157–165.

8. See New South Wales Government, NSW Health Department, www.nscchealth.nsw.gov.au; the museum ceremony is at http://museumvictoria.com.au/bunjilaka/about-us/smoking-ceremony/; Wandoo Didgeridoo, www.wadidge.com.au.

9. The Edinburgh ceremony is at http://www.ed.ac.uk/news/all-news/aboriginal-smoking.

10. "The First Initiation in 150 Years," Tasmanian Aboriginal Historical Services, www.tasmanianaboriginal.com.au/initiation.

11. For instance, www.Aboriginalart.com.au, from where the quote is taken, is run by the Pwerte Marute Marute Aboriginal Corporation in Alice Springs.

12. Similarly, the main page of www.Aboriginalart.com.au is available in five European languages, the same set of languages (with the exception of Dutch) as on the Lourdes site.

13. With regard to the intricate politics of Aboriginal identity and ethnic power relations in Australia in the past and present, see Michael Howard, ed., *Aboriginal Power in Australian Society* (St. Lucia: University of Queensland Press, 1982); and Nicolas Peterson and Will Sanders, eds., *Citizenship and Indigenous Australians* (Cambridge: Cambridge University Press, 1998).

14. This aspect is exhibited in funeral rituals; see Widlok, "Time, Death and Property in Australia."

15. Traditional Nyoongar Smoking Ceremony: "Where the Youran (Bobtail Lizard) Meets the Nyingarn (Echidna)," http://www.wadidge.com.au/didgeridoo-news/smoking-ceremony.html.

16. Erich Kolig, *The Silent Revolution: The Effects of Modernization on Australian Aboriginal Religion* (Philadelphia: Institute for the Study of Human Issues, 1981); Ronald Berndt, *An Adjustment Movement in Arnhem Land: Northern Territory of Australia* (Paris: Mouton, 1962).

17. Tony Swain, "Australia," in *The Religions of Oceania*, ed. Tony Swain and Garry Trompf, 9–118 (London: Routledge, 1995).

18. Widlok, "Time, Death and Property in Australia."

19. "Current Research: The Hearth of the Matter," Daphna Yalon: Earth Based Artist, http://patia.com/daphna/outline3.html.

20. Thomas Widlok, "Local Experts—Expert Locals: A Comparative Perspective on Biodiversity and Environmental Knowledge Systems in Australia and Namibia," in *Culture and the Changing Environment*, ed. Michael Casimir, 351–381 (Oxford: Berghahn, 2008).

21. Swain, "Australia," 21.

22. Swain, "Australia," 21.

23. Frank Brennan, "Land Rights: The Religious Factor," in *Aboriginal Religions in Australia: An Anthology of Recent Writings*, ed. Max Charlesworth, Francoise Dussart, and Howard Morphy, 227–275 (Aldershot: Ashgate, 2005).

24. Swain, "Australia," 26.

25. Robert Tonkinson, *The Mardu Aborigines: Living the Dream in Australia's Desert* (Fort Worth: Holt, Rinehart and Winston, 1991).

26. Thomas Widlok, "Practice, Politics and Ideology of the 'Travelling Business' in Aboriginal Religion," *Oceania* 63 (1992): 114–136.

27. See Marcia Langton, "Sacred Geography," in *Aboriginal Religions in Australia: An Anthology of Recent Writings*, ed. Max Charlesworth, Francoise Dussart, and Howard Morphy, 131–139 (Aldershot: Ashgate, 2005). Further, Francesca Merlan, "Do Places Appear?," in *Aboriginal Religions in Australia*, 115–129.

28. See Tasmanian Aboriginal Historical Services, www.tasmanianaboriginal.com.au.

29. Tim Ingold, *A Brief History* (New York: Routledge, 2007).

30. In 1858, a fourteen-year-old peasant girl named Bernadette Soubirous reported appearances of a young woman who, through a series of eighteen encounters, came to be regarded as the Virgin Mary. Mary appeared to Bernadette in a grotto that is now the ritual center of the Lourdes shrine. See for more information on Bernadette's apparitions, see Ruth Harris, *Lourdes: Body and Spirit in the Secular Age* (London: Penguin, 2000).

31. Suzanne Kaufman, *Consuming Visions: Mass Culture and the Lourdes Shrine* (Ithaca, NY: Cornell University Press, 2005).

32. See Sanctuaires Notre-Dame de Lourdes, www.Lourdes-france.org.

33. Ex-votos, a vital part of the material culture of pilgrimage, are expressions of thanks for a miraculous healing or rescue. Pilgrims carry their ex-votos to the shrine, where they offer them to a particular saint before leaving them behind in the holy place.

34. From "Intentions de prières," Sanctuaires Notre-Dame de Lourdes, www.lourdes-france.org/multimedia/images/intentions.jpg.

35. Anonymous visitor contribution on the Lourdes Web site, February 9, 2006.

36. Anonymous visitor contribution on the Lourdes Web site, February 9, 2006.

37. Mark McWilliams, "Virtual Pilgrimages on the Internet," *Religion* 32 (2002): 316.

38. McWilliams, "Virtual Pilgrimages on the Internet," 320.

39. Robert Orsi, "Abundant History: Marian Apparitions as Alternative Modernity," in *Moved by Mary: The Power of Pilgrimage in the Modern World*, ed. Anna Karina Hermkens, Willy Jansen, and Catrien Notermans, 215 (Aldershot: Ashgate, 2009).

40. Smith, *To Take Place*.

41. Marc Augé, *Non-Places: Introduction to an Anthropology of Supermodernity* (London: Verso, 1995), 77–78.

42. Catrien Notermans, "Loss and Healing: A Marian Pilgrimage in Secular Dutch Society," *Ethnology* 46, no. 3 (2007): 217–233.

43. Victor Turner and Edith Turner, *Image and Pilgrimage in Christian Culture: Anthropological Perspectives* (Oxford: Blackwell, 1978).

44. Anna-Karina Hermkens, Willy Jansen, and Catrien Notermans, eds., *Moved by Mary: The Power of Pilgrimage in the Modern World* (Aldershot: Ashgate, 2009).

45. W. B. H. J. van de Donk, A. P. Jonkers, G. J. Kronjee, and R. J. J. M. Plum, eds., *Geloven in het publieke domein: verkenningen van een dubbele transformatie* (Amsterdam: Amsterdam University Press/Wetenschappelijke Raad voor het Regeringsbeleid, 2006).

46. van de Donk et al., *Geloven in het publieke domein*, 176.

47. T. Bernts, G. Dekker, and J. de Hart, eds., *God in Nederland 1966–2006.* (Kampen: Uitgeverij Ten Have, 2007).

48. Janneke Peelen and Marga Altena, "Voor altijd een stralende ster op het web. Digitale herinneringen aan vroeg gestorven kinderen," in *Rituele Creativiteit: Actuele Veranderingen in de Uitvaart en Rouw-cultuur* (Zoetermeer: Meinema, 2008).

49. For project information see: Refiguring Death Rites, Radboud Universiteit Nijmegen, www.ru.nl/rdr.

50. Andrew Herman and Thomas Swiss, eds., *The World Wide Web and Contemporary Cultural Theory* (New York: Routledge, 2000). See also Katz and Rice, *Social Consequences of Internet Use.*

51. For religious ritual, see Simone Heidbrink and Nadja Miczek, "Cyberspace-Ritual Space? Einblicke in die aktuelle Religionswissenschaftliche Erforschung christlicher Ritual im Internet," *Arbeitsstelle Gottesdienst* 21 (2007): 47–52; see also Karin Radde-Antweiler, ed., "Virtual Worlds: Research Perspectives from Cultural Studies," *Online-Heidelberg Journal of Religions and the Internet* 3 (2008), http://www.online.uni-hd.de. For funerary ritual, see Brian de Vries and Judy Rutherford, "Memorializing Loved Ones on the World Wide Web," *Omega* 49, no. 1 (2004): 5–26.

52. Andreas Kitzmann, *Saved from Oblivion: Documenting the Daily from Diaries to Web Cams* (New York: Lang, 2004).

53. See Marga Altena and Nothando Ngwenya, "Sites That Cope, Cure and Commemorate: Weblogs of Terminally Ill," in *Dying and Death*, ed. Asa Kasher and Julia Glahn, in press.

54. Janneke Peelen and Marga Altena, "Voor altijd een stralende ster op het web. Digitale herinneringen aan vroeg gestorven kinderen," in *Rituele Creativiteit: Actuele Veranderingen in de Uitvaart en Rouw-cultuur* (Zoetermeer: Meinema, 2008).

55. Weblog of van R.S.

56. Marga Altena and Eric Venbrux, "Television Shows and Weblogs as New Rituals of Death," in *Die Realität des Todes: Zur gegenwärtigen Wandel von Totenbildern und Erinnerungskulturen*, ed. Dominik Gross and Christoph Schweikardt, 129–140 (Frankfurt am Main: Campus Verlag, 2010).

57. Weblog of van S.v.E.

58. Bert Sliggers, ed., *Naar het Lijk: Het Nederlandse Doodsportret 1500–heden* (Zutphen: Walburg Pers, 1998).

59. Jasper Enklaar, *Onder de Groene Zoden: De Persoonlijke Uitvaart. Nieuwe Rituelen in Rouwen, Begraven en Cremeren* (Zutphen: Alpha, 1995); Marrie Bot, *Een Laatste Groet: Uitvaart—en rouwrituelen in multicultureel Nederland* (Rotterdam: Marrie Bot, 1998); Piet van den Akker, *De Dode Nabij: Nieuwe Rituelen na Overlijden* (Tilburg: Dela, 2006).

60. Weblog of M.

61. Weblog of S.v.E.

62. Weblog of F.d.R.

63. Weblog of L.V.

64. Weblog of C.

65. Weblog of M.

66. Weblog of C.

67. Weblog of J.d.K.

68. Weblog of F.d.R.

69. Weblog of S.v.E.

70. Weblog of terminally ill, report about people getting connected through the Weblog and becoming friends who sometimes stay in touch for years. See Altena and Venbrux, "Television Shows."

71. Smith, *To Take Place*, 22.

72. Weblog of R.S.

73. Weblog of F.d.R.

74. Weblog of S.v.E.

75. Weblog of S.v.E.

76. Sliggers, *Naar het Lijk*.

77. Eric Venbrux, Meike Heessels, and Sophie Bolt, eds., *Rituele Creativiteit: Actuele veranderingen in de uitvaart—en rouwcultuur in Nederland* (Zoetermeer: Meinema, 2008). See also Marga Altena, Sophie Bolt, and Eric Venbrux, "Doing the Right Thing? Public Debate on Human Remains in Dutch Museum Collections," in *Abstrakter Tod-Konkrete Leiche*, ed. Dominik Gross, Julia Glahn, and Brigitte Tag (Hrsg.), 187–201 (Frankfurt am Main: Campus Verlag, 2010).

78. Tonkinson, *The Mardu Aborigines*.

79. Widlok, "Practice, Politics and Ideology of the 'Traveling Business.'"

80. Rappaport, *Ritual and Religion in the Making of Humanity*.

81. Katz and Rice, *Social Consequences of Internet Use*, 116, 121.

82. Ronald Grimes, *Deeply into the Bone: Re-inventing Rites of Passage* (Berkeley: University of California Press, 2000).

83. Stewart Hoover, *Religion in the Media Age* (London and New York: Routledge, 2006).

REFERENCES

Akker, Piet van den. *De Dode Nabij: Nieuwe Rituelen na Overlijden*. Tilburg: Dela, 2006.

Altena, Marga, Sophie Bolt, and Eric Venbrux. "Doing the Right Thing? Public Debate on Human Remains in Dutch Museum Collections." In *Abstrakter Tod-Konkrete Leiche*, edited by Dominik Gross, Julia Glahn, and Brigitte Tag (Hrsg.), 187–201. Frankfurt am Main: Campus Verlag, 2010.

Altena, Marga, and Nothando Ngwenya. "Sites That Cope, Cure and Commemorate: Weblogs of Terminally Ill." In *Dying and Death*, edited by Asa Kasher and Julia Glahn. In press.

Altena, Marga, and Eric Venbrux. "Television Shows and Weblogs as New Rituals of Death." In *Die Realität des Todes: Zur gegenwärtigen Wandel von Totenbildern und Erinnerungskulturen*, edited by Dominik Gross and Christoph Schweikardt, 129–140. Frankfurt am Main: Campus Verlag, 2010.

Augé, Marc. *Non-Places: Introduction to an Anthropology of Supermodernity*. London: Verso, 1995.

Berndt, Ronald. *An Adjustment Movement in Arnhem Land. Northern Territory of Australia*. Paris: Mouton, 1962.

Bernts, T. G. Dekker, and J. de Hart. *God in Nederland, 1966–2006*. Kampen: Uitgeverij Ten Have, 2007.

Brennan, Frank. "Land Rights: The Religious Factor." In *Aboriginal Religions in Australia: An Anthology of Recent Writings*, edited by Max Charlesworth, Francoise Dussart, and Howard Morphy, 227–275. Aldershot: Ashgate, 2005.

Bot, Marrie. *Een Laatste Groet: Uitvaart—en rouwrituelen in multicultureel Nederland*. Rotterdam: Marrie Bot, 1998.

Donk, W. B. H. J. van de, A. P. Jonkers, G. J. Kronjee, and R. J. J. M. Plum, eds. *Geloven in het publieke domein: verkenningen van een dubbele transformatie*. Amsterdam: Amsterdam University Press/Wetenschappelijke Raad voor het Regeringsbeleid, 2006.

Enklaar, Jasper. *Onder de Groene Zoden: De Persoonlijke Uitvaart. Nieuwe Rituelen in Rouwen, Begraven en Cremeren*. Zutphen: Alpha, 1995.

Grimes, Ronald. *Deeply into the Bone: Re-inventing Rites of Passage*. Berkeley: University of California Press, 2000.

———. "Jonathan Z. Smith's Theory of Ritual Space." *Religion* 29 (1999): 261–273.

———. *Rite out of Place: Ritual, Media, and the Arts*. New York: Oxford University Press, 2006.

Harris, Ruth. *Lourdes: Body and Spirit in the Secular Age*. London: Penguin, 2000.

Heidbrink, Simone, and Nadja Miczek. "Cyberspace-Ritual Space? Einblicke in die aktuelle Religionswissenschaftliche Erforschung christlicher Ritual im Internet." *Arbeitsstelle Gottesdienst*: 47–52.

Herman, Andrew, and Thomas Swiss, eds. *The World Wide Web and Contemporary Cultural Theory*. New York: Routledge, 2000.

Hermkens, Anna-Karina, Willy Jansen, and Catrien Notermans. *Moved by Mary: The Power of Pilgrimage in the Modern World*. Aldershot: Ashgate, 2009.

Hoover, Stewart. *Religion in the Media Age*. London: Routledge, 2006.

Howard, Michael, ed. *Aboriginal Power in Australian Society*. St. Lucia: University of Queensland Press, 1982.

Ingold, Tim. *A Brief History*. New York: Routledge, 2007.

Katz, James, and Ronald Rice. *Social Consequences of Internet Use*. Cambridge, MA: MIT Press: 2002.

Kaufman, Suzanne. *Consuming Visions: Mass Culture and the Lourdes Shrine*. Ithaca, NY: Cornell University Press, 2005.

Kitzmann, Andreas. *Saved from Oblivion: Documenting the Daily from Diaries to Web Cams*. New York: Peter Lang, 2004.

Kolig, Erich. *The Silent Revolution: The Effects of Modernization on Australian Aboriginal Religion*. Philadelphia: Institute for the Study of Human Issues, 1981.

Langton, Marcia. "Sacred Geography." In *Aboriginal Religions in Australia: An Anthology of Recent Writings*, edited by Max Charlesworth, Francoise Dussart, and Howard Morphy, 131–139. Aldershot: Ashgate, 2005.

McWilliams, Mark. "Virtual Pilgrimages on the Internet." *Religion* 32 (2002): 315–335.

Merlan, Francesca. "Do Places Appear?" In *Aboriginal Religions in Australia: An Anthology of Recent Writings*, edited by Max Charlesworth, Francoise Dussart, and Howard Morphy, 115–129. Aldershot: Ashgate, 2005.

Notermans, Catrien. "Loss and Healing: A Marian Pilgrimage in Secular Dutch Society." *Ethnology* 46, no. 3 (2007): 217–233.

Orsi, Robert. "Abundant History: Marian Apparitions as Alternative Modernity." In *Moved by Mary: The Power of Pilgrimage in the Modern World*, edited by Anna Karina Hermkens, Willy Jansen, and Catrien Notermans, 215–225. Aldershot: Ashgate, 2009.

Peelen, Janneke, and Marga Altena. "Voor altijd een stralende ster op het web. Digitale herinneringen aan vroeg gestorven kinderen." In *Rituele Creativiteit: Actuele Veranderingen in de Uitvaart en Rouw-cultuur*. Zoetermeer: Meinema, 2008.

Peterson, Nicolas, and Will Sanders, eds. *Citizenship and Indigenous Australians*. Cambridge: Cambridge University Press, 1998.

Radde-Antweiler, Kerstin, ed. "Virtual Worlds: Research Perspectives from Cultural Studies." *Online-Heidelberg Journal of Religions and the Internet* 3 (2008), http://www.online.uni-hd.de.

Rappaport, Roy. *Ritual and Religion in the Making of Humanity*. Cambridge: Cambridge University Press, 1999.

Sliggers, Bert, ed. *Naar het Lijk: Het Nederlandse Doodsportret 1500–heden*. Zutphen: Walburg Pers, 1998.

Smith, Jonathan Z. *To Take Place: Towards Theory in Ritual*. Chicago: University of Chicago Press, 1987.

Swain, Tony. "Australia." In *The Religions of Oceania*, edited by Tony Swain and Garry Trompf, 9–118. London: Routledge, 1995.

Tonkinson, Robert. *The Mardu Aborigines: Living the Dream in Australia's Desert*. Fort Worth: Holt, Rinehart and Winston, 1991.

Turner, Victor, and Edith Turner. *Image and Pilgrimage in Christian Culture: Anthropological Perspectives*. Oxford: Blackwell, 1978.

Venbrux, Eric, Meike Heessels, and Sophie Bolt, eds. *Rituele Creativiteit: Actuele veranderingen in de uitvaart—en rouwcultuur in Nederland*. Zoetermeer: Meinema, 2008.

Vries, Brian de, and Judy Rutherford. "Memorializing Loved Ones on the World Wide Web." *Omega* 49, no. 1 (2004): 5–26.

Widlok, Thomas. "Local Experts—Expert Locals: A Comparative Perspective on Biodiversity and Environmental Knowledge Systems in Australia and Namibia." In *Culture and the Changing Environment*, edited by Michael Casimir, 351–381. Oxford: Berghahn, 2008.

———. "Practice, Politics and Ideology of the 'Travelling Business' in Aboriginal Religion." *Oceania* 63 (1992): 114–136.

———. "Time, Death and Property in Australia." *Journal de la Société des Océanistes* 124, no. 1 (2007): 157–165.

6

Contested Rituals in Virtual Worlds

Simone Heidbrink, Nadja Miczek, and Kerstin Radde-Antweiler

When I enter the church, I step into silence broken only by the ringing of the bells. I am late for the service; the church is already packed and nearly all seats in the pews are taken. The building itself resembles an ordinary historical church in continental Europe, a Gothic-style structure with pointed arches, stained glass windows, and wooden pews in the nave. The sanctuary is traditionally equipped with a pulpit, lectern, and altar flanked by two large candles presided over by a golden cross. Behind the altar is the most prominent piece of art, a colorful stained glass window in red and blue. Along with a rather traditional organ, the aisle features a modern equivalent of the Stations of the Cross, showing religiously inspired works of art by various modern artists. I do not have time to linger. The service is about to start, so I hurry across the checkered stone floor to one of the few remaining seats.

Even though the church is crowded, there is a dearth of the usual coughing and murmuring, and I sit in utter silence. Then the minister, who is about to lead the short daily service called Night Prayer (reminiscent of Evensong in traditional Anglican churches), steps into the sanctuary and the hymns begin. Other than the music, I hear only the clicking of a keyboard—my own keyboard, since I am at my computer, typing the words of the hymn as a substitute for singing. Even if I were to sing, no one could hear me, since the church I am attending resides in virtual space filled with millions of bits and bytes. Those next to me in the pew are only present as virtual representations of themselves (so-called avatars chosen from a limited selection of gender, skin color, and clothing styles), sitting at their computer screens all around the world. Nonetheless, the whole experience feels somewhat real—not unlike being in a sacred place—a feeling I apparently share with many other visitors, some of whom have not entered a conventional church for a long time.[1]

Church of Fools

This recollection of a visit to the Church of Fools hearkens back to the early days of online Christian worship in 2004.[2] The Church of Fools was a project planned by the editors of *Ship of Fools*,[3] a Christian Internet magazine and bulletin board launched in 1998 with a strong and stable community. In 2003, after having successfully organized a 3D Internet reality game show called *The Ark*,[4] the participants' commitment to the virtual space led organizers to propose an online church that was realized the following year.[5] The project, launched as a self-contained, multiuser environment modeled after a real-life church, was initially limited to a three-month experience in which individual visitors could choose their avatars and then attend the service (see figure 6.1).

After the Church of Fools experiment ended in September 2004, a stable community of service attendants continued to keep in contact by way of a bulletin

FIGURE 6.1. Church of Fools service.

board Web site. With financial aid from the Methodist Church of Great Britain, this platform later evolved into what is now called St. Pixels, a community which, like its predecessor, defined itself as interdenominational.[6] Unlike the Church of Fools, St. Pixels is not restricted to a fixed period of time but is designed as a long-term project featuring blogs (which soon turned out to be one of its central applications),[7] discussion boards, chat rooms, and the like. To this day, live services are held in a separate worship area, a two-dimensional Java environment consisting of different virtual rooms for silent prayer and meditation, informal chat, and communal service.[8]

A major goal of the Church of Fools project was "to find out if online church is a viable way to 'do church.'"[9] The church itself was nondenominational but funded and supported by the Methodist Church. The bishop of London, who led the opening service on May 11, 2004, stated in his sermon that what was needed was "setting out into the cyber ocean aware that the Spirit of God is already brooding over the face of the deep."[10] The initial plan to run one service a week was quickly abandoned due to the huge visitor demand. Even though at least two services a day were conducted by a team of ordained pastors and laymen from various denominations in Britain and other primarily Anglophone countries, many visitors simply could not find room in the overcrowded church.

Visitors were divided in their opinions about the online church, and their voices ranged from bursts of outrage about substituting a virtual for a real church to insistence that the Internet was too important a cultural venue for the church to miss.[11] One conflict that did not openly arise in the Church of Fools, however, was serious debate about how best (that is, "correctly," "authoritatively," and "authentically") to conduct services.[12] One reason for the organizers' harmonizing, or conflict-avoiding, attitude about how to do ritual in such a new and undeveloped environment might have been the fact that the Church of Fools was a nondenominational project; nevertheless, it was exclusively designed for religious use and supported by two of Britain's main churches.

The fact that the Church of Fools used written chat and users' avatars only had a limited choice of gestures and movements at their disposal meant that the liturgy had to be adapted to these restrictive conditions. As it turned out, the most effective means of ritual adaptation was using short services with short sermons and encouraging audience participation by way of the written word and certain gestures. One of the central acts of the services quickly became that of reciting the Lord's Prayer, which visitors were invited to pray "in the language and version they knew best" by typing it line by line in the voice-chat window.[13] Soon gestures that had been partly designed as gimmicks also took on an important role. The "pull hair out" gesture, for example (originally meant as a quirky way of showing anger), became part of the liturgy as an expression of lament for suffering in the world, while the "shake hands" gesture became a way of showing sympathy with invisible visitors, those who, for technical reasons, could not enter the church as visible avatars (only as "ghosts") as well as with all people who were absent.[14] On the whole, these ritual adaptations were well accepted. As one visitor remarked on the liturgical use of the handshake gesture: "The whole ghost thing is rather beautifully symbolical, I think.... The fact that we're worshipping with unseen multitudes, while it's happening literally in [the] 'Church of Fools' would be good to remember in real life churches too!"[15]

The Internet and Religious Worship

However, apart from a majority of voices in praise and agreement, there arose a multitude of conflicts, both during and apart from the services. For one thing, the church suffered multiple attacks by hackers, rogue programmers who tried to gain control over the software behind the Church of Fools. Hacking forced the operators to step up security measures. Significantly, then, most of the disturbances and conflicts did not originate outside but rather within the virtual church environment. The main problem was a host of disruptive visitors, so-called trolls,[16] who forced the organizers to remove certain applications such as the "shout" function of written chat by which people could "speak" in the church. This modification was needed to quiet the place.[17] Officials also had to ensure constant control over the environment by church wardens, whose interface was equipped with a "smite" button that enabled them to ban troublemakers. Troll behavior ranged from uttering swear words and obscenities during services, disturbing others by shouting blasphemies or political slogans, and unauthorized preaching from the pulpit to misusing available gestures so they became sexually suggestive. In the worst period, organizers had to ban up to a hundred trolls per hour.[18]

One conflict that arose often and was extensively covered by the press was misusing the ritual space of the apse, especially by people claiming to be Satanists or even Satan himself.[19] According to a CNN article, "Bogus 'worshippers'... have logged in as 'God,' 'Jesus' and 'Satan.' They have greeted newcomers with: 'Satan loves you' and walked up to people praying, shouting four-letter words."[20] Simon Jenkins, one of the founders of the Church of Fools, recalls an encounter with a person who claimed to be Satan:

> Disguised as a normal worshipper, I came across him ranting in our pixilated pulpit. I was logged in as a church warden, who has a smite button capable of visiting an Old Testament-style logout on the unrighteous. "What are you doing?" I asked him. "Who is this who dares

approach the Evil One?" he demanded. Well ... "I'm the church warden," I replied, "with the power to smite you out of the church." "Ah ... " he said, before becoming disappointingly contrite.[21]

Indeed, conversations with church wardens, which usually preceded any forced action, proved especially effective for making disruptive visitors understand the serious religious nature of the undertaking, in which case they apologized and left voluntarily.[22] Simon Jenkins notes that one Satanist even apologized by e-mail for his many fellow believers who misbehaved in the virtual church: "'I have been Satanist all my life and would never have pulled any such thing,' he wrote. 'So, for all the immature twits within the Satanic community, you have my sympathies as I truly hope to see you fix the problem soon. Best of luck, sincerely, Satanist with a heart.'"[23] Jenkins recollects this incident as being "one of the most heartwarming offers of support during problems with disruptive visitors."[24] Strategies such as increasing the number of wardens authorized to smite troublemakers by forcibly logging them off and technically blocking certain areas of the church such as the pulpit were introduced to control the environment and avoid conflict. Nevertheless, a certain level of misuse of the environment could not be prevented.

These examples illustrate the wide range of users' actions and reactions in a virtual church. One reason for this broad spectrum of interactions is the fact that many disruptors perceived the Church of Fools as a mere game environment. Mistaking the church for a game was not restricted to trolls, however. A journalist for *The Guardian* noted, "One visitor looked around with her five-year-old son on her lap. 'Wow!' he said, 'Who's on your team and which ones do you kill?'"[25]

Unlike Second Life, the Church of Fools was constructed exclusively as religious space and aesthetically marked as such by traditional church architecture. Even so, divergent assumptions about Internet media influenced the ways individuals defined various places in the church, and these differences led to conflicts regarding the ritual dimensions of these spaces.

Weddings in Second Life

In our second case, that of the virtual world which is Second Life, conflicts surrounding rituals also proliferate. Thanks to widespread media coverage, Second Life is probably one of the best-known virtual 3D environments. This online 3D world was founded by a U.S. company, Linden Lab, and has been accessible to the public since 2003. Using free client software downloaded from Linden Lab's home page, people set up a personal account in order to enter the virtual world. These users, often also called residents, then move and communicate in this virtual world through the use of an avatar, whose design can be modulated according to individual preferences. Most use human characteristics, but animal shapes or "furries" are also options. The avatar is manipulated using a keyboard and mouse, and it can go from walking to flying, although traveling great distances is managed using a "teleport" function reminiscent of "beaming" in *Star Trek*. Most in-world communication is done by written chat. However, Linden Lab implemented a voice-chat option in August 2007, and this alternative has become more popular.

Once you have practiced controlling your avatar and using the communication devices, the entire world of Second Life is open to your exploration. One of the most popular activities is buying virtual land and creating a virtual home. You can build a gorgeous mansion, set up an office building, or found your own church, and every object you build in-world is yours. Since you own the property rights, you are also able to sell the items you have created to other people using the in-world economy system based on Linden Dollars, which, in turn, are linked to first-life currency exchange.

Since its earliest days, Second Life has been developing a rich social and cultural life, including a wealth of rituals, especially religious ones. Christian churches offer regular services that include prayers and sermons; Buddhist temples invite you to stay for a brief mediation, and New Age classes initiate you into Reiki healing. Indeed, the presence of so many rituals in Second Life makes it a compelling case study for examining conflict.

An example of recurrent ritual conflict in this world is the case of wedding crashing, a significant issue, since weddings are big business in Second Life. A lot of time and money are spent creating dream weddings. A host of wedding businesses flourish: everything from land rental and building or scripting wedding areas to acting as wedding planners. All such activities have sprung up or were invented by residents in order to earn money. A typical Christianized wedding follows the model of U.S. first-life weddings, which means a church is chosen and elaborately decorated with flowers. Perfectly dressed bridesmaids and groomsmen, together with glamorous guests, create a festive atmosphere for the anticipated rite. At the appointed time, the wedding couple steps in a dignified manner to the front of the sanctuary, where the celebrant—often the wedding designer—stands waiting. The vows are said or typed into the chat window, the celebrant addresses the required questions to the couple, and finally the celebrant's speech act declares the couple virtually married. Due to technical conditions, the exchange of rings is replaced by words that describe the act. The kiss, however, works perfectly (which is to say, a bit awkwardly) by using an "animation script" enabling avatars to perform certain actions. Afterward, both the couple and their guests enjoy a big party to celebrate the nuptials.

But, just as in real-life weddings, Second Life rituals are not without controversy. In fact, there is a lot of discussion about the role of rituals in Second Life.

Residents, for example, debate the on- and offline effects of such weddings. What does it mean to get married in a virtual world? Does such a marriage have any consequences for someone's first life? Accordingly, the need for a properly performed rite is also challenged. How important is it to have a "correct" ceremony? And what exactly does a correct procedure look like under the circumstances?

The recurring questions deal with the underlying conflict about whether critical life-passage rituals should be permitted in a 3D environment. Wedding-crasher groups sometimes disturb weddings specifically to prevent their performance. "Crashes" are behaviors considered inappropriate, for example, throwing fog bombs, making it impossible for ritual participants to see anything on their monitors. Another strategy for ritual disturbance is to overload the wedding site with so many avatars that the whole system breaks down. Because members of these groups think of Second Life as a game environment, they are not willing to accept serious rituals conducted in-world. By contrast, most people who have, or are planning to, wed in Second Life consider this virtual space as an inclusive online environment for all kinds of cultural activities and, therefore, viable rituals.

In the face of major problems, including threats to a lucrative business environment, many wedding designers have developed prevention strategies, such as restricting access to the wedding site to invited guests only, or instituting an enclosed nonpublic chat channel that can only be used by the couple and their guests. Such remedies, however, were not available to L.L. and R.D. when their Second Life wedding on September 19, 2006, was targeted by enthusiastic wedding crashers (see figure 6.2).[26]

The wedding designer had built a special wedding site, a pavilion festooned in white and pink. While guests were arriving and waiting for the bride, three avatars tried to gain access to the event by flying wildly on brooms around the elaborately staged scenery and shouting swear words at the groom and guests. The clergyperson tried to stop them, emphasizing the serious nature of the event, but finally the wedding designer—the person who actually owned the land and ran the wedding business—had to be informed offline. After logging onto Second Life and trying to deal with the intruders in a civilized manner, he finally banned them from the land.

Interviews with wedding crashers reveal that the motivation for such aggressive behavior was not the desire for gratuitous mischief making but a different basic understanding of Second Life. They regarded it as a game and thus an improper place for serious actions such as religious rituals or rites of passage. Second Life, then, is the locus of the same debates as the Church of Fools, namely, whether rituals can, or should be, part of an online environment and whether this environment is in fact a game or a genuine expression of online culture. Again, the same processes operate as in the first case study: conflicts over ritual occur when the medium is challenged or defined in divergent ways.

FIGURE 6.2. The Second Life wedding of L.L. and R.D. on September 19, 2006.

World of Warcraft

Life-passage rituals also occur in popular role-playing games such as World of Warcraft, a 3D online game that often features mourning rituals for players who have died in real life. World of Warcraft, like other famous online games such as Everquest and Final Fantasy, is a "massively multiplayer online role-playing game" that takes place in a virtual world accessible only by way of the Internet. Usually, these environments are populated by thousands of players who use their avatars to face numerous quests and enemies.[27] In most cases players have to pay a monthly fee to set up their characters on a server. Cost, however, is apparently no deterrent. With 11.5 million subscribers, World of Warcraft is one of the most successful online games on the market, perhaps because its host company, Blizzard, continually enhances the game world and frequently adds new content.

When you first enter the game, you must choose which warring faction you want to join: the Horde or the Alliance.[28] You can also decide whether you want to take advantage of the option of battling players from the opposite faction at any time. You then set up your character on a PVP (player-versus-player) server, or, if you prefer, limit opponent-bashing to certain areas such as battlegrounds or other sites designated for battle campaigns. If you decide to spend more time on quests (tasks to develop the skills of your avatar without the threat of being killed by other players), you will have to choose a PVE (player-versus-environment) server.[29] You then design your character by choosing from one of several races and classes, for example, Gnome Mages, Bloodelve Hunters, or Orc Deathknights. Now, you are set to enter the world at level 1, which means you can begin quests by killing computer-generated monsters in order to gain the necessary experience to graduate to successive levels. The aim of the game is in fact to "grow up," that is, reach the final level, which, at the moment, is set at level 80 (see figure 6.3).[30]

An important part of this level-attainment process is interacting with other players. Certain quests or dungeons, that is, areas with especially daunting monsters, necessitate building up small teams with complementary fighting and healing skills. Distinct from these temporary groups, another form of social affiliation is the guild. Members join together to manage guild property and help each other in game affairs. Social commitments within such networks often prove to be very

FIGURE 6.3. Level 80, World of Warcraft, Deathknight (right) fighting a monster (left).

strong. Players care for one another and cultivate friendships that often extend well beyond the gaming experience.

These sustained relationships can lead to the invention of in-world rituals. Close contact between players of World of Warcraft leads gamers to conduct in-game rituals for special occasions. Very popular, for example, are in-game weddings, which are often celebrated within a guild. Another example is mourning rituals, which, like Second Life wedding rituals, frequently become targets of concerted attacks.

A telling example of a crashed ritual in World of Warcraft was a disturbed memorial. In 2006 this incident sparked heated discussions in a variety of forums as well as on video platforms outside the game environment itself. A Horde guild had planned a memorial service on the PVP server, Illidan, for another guild member who had died in real life. The guild announced this performance in various forums, including an Illidrama Forum:

> Yanoa on March 3, 2006: On Tuesday . . . February 28th Illidan lost not only a good mage, but a good person. For those who knew her, Fayejin was one of the nicest people you could ever meet. On Tuesday she suffered from a stroke and passed away later that night. I'm making this post basically to inform everyone that might have knew [sic] her. Also tomorrow, at 5:30 server time March, 4th, we will have an in-game memorial for her so that her friends can pay their respects. We will be having it at the Frostfire Hot Springs in Winterspring, because she loved to fish in the game (she liked the sound of the water, it was calming for her) and she loved snow. If you would like to come, show your respects please do. Thanks everyone.[31]

Not surprisingly, since the service was held in a PVP area—a territory frequently contested between the two factions—the ritual was disturbed by a competing guild named Serenity Now. In contrast to crashed weddings, this memorial crashing provoked enormous debate about the morality of the contested behavior. The seriousness of this heated discussion is reflected in videos about the crashing, video responses, and ongoing written comments, which continue to this writing. The crashing was filmed and put online in various forums and video platforms, as was a video featuring the most contentious comments from the discussion forum as well as the reactions of opponents. What are these videos about, and why are the reactions to this crash so thrilling that, three years later, more than a thousand users are still reacting to the issue?

A video of the crashed funeral can be viewed on YouTube. "Wow Funeral Pwnage" was put online August 6, 2006, by a user called Irishlacrosse, who stressed that it presents a modified form of the original, that is, it has different music.[32] The video, which depicts events from the perspective of the crashers, nonetheless begins with a quotation from one of the bulletin board postings by an opponent of the crashing: "A day that will live in infamy in the WoW world." The video opens with walk-in music commonly used at the beginning of boxing matches, and a screen shot shows basic information about the reason for the memorial: "The CROM clan—holding a memorial for a team mate who had died in reality–were ambushed by the Serenity Now clan." Then the scene changes and the music quickens to a song with the refrain, "I ain't no son of a bitch."[33] What emerges is a typical gaming interaction. Various players band together to ride through Felwood Forest, while more players stream in from both sides so that the whole group swells. Meanwhile, riding through a tunnel, the Timbermaw Hold, bearlike monsters named furbolgs emerge to join the group. Then a white snowy area flashes onscreen as players from the Horde, the other faction, appear, marked in red. All the while, somber choral music underscores the tragic atmosphere of the occasion. Now and then the perspective changes so that viewers get a glimpse of the heated group, ready to fight, racing through the tunnel. In the meantime, the bereaved players are forming a line as the videographer's avatar queues up. We cannot see what is at the beginning of this line A memorial in the form of an avatar? A stone? As the horde rides, a map of the area appears, so we understand that there are mere seconds until the crashers meet the mourners head on. Back in the snowscape, more and more avatars are joining the mourners. The changing music and rapidly shifting scenes create mounting tension in anticipation of the clash. Then another tune sounds to mark the beginning of the fight. Spectacular lighting effects caused by the innumerable spells and weapons pop up all over the screen, while the death tally appears on the monitor. The lyrics of the song now playing include lines such as, "How come it ended up like this?" and "Who's gonna be there when I've lost control?" In two minutes the fight is over, leaving several corpses on the ground. Again, a black screen shot is shown stating, "Serenity Now thought it was damn funny. . . ." A second picture that ends the video includes the statement, "Several million gamers worldwide can't help but agree."

As the discussion posts show, this video was enormously popular. The number of downloads exceeded 185,000 by January 2009, and the number of comments stood at about 960. Despite being three years old—very old indeed for Internet material—the discussion persists, as do other videos featuring this same event, again, stressing its importance in the eyes of the players. The video, "So We Pwned This Funeral Today: Serenity-Now.org," put online on YouTube on July 8, 2006, by Vash12788, is described in such a way as to suggest that the author is criticizing the crash: "A person that played WoW died in real life, so the person's friends in WoW decide to have a funeral for him/her. But a guild full of nothing but assholes decides to invade the funeral [and] kill everyone."[34] The clip also includes comments from the first video: "Congratulations you have stooped lower than any other guild in MMO [massive multiplayer online] history," a remark taken from the original video by Byzon on March 4, 2006.[35] "So We Pwned" shows screen shots of forums and Web sites, while the Beatles song "Yesterday," stressing sincerity and seriousness, plays. After two minutes the crashing scenes appear, but the scenery is identical with the that in the other video, which tells the story from the perspective of the crashers. The final battle also features the song by Scatman John used in the first video, and the last screen shots end with, "Yes, we know we are assholes :D."[36] This line, shown along with the fading guild banner, makes it clear that the opening sequence was in fact an ironic twist on the opposing guild's critique.

While it is common to publish scenes of film fights on video-sharing Web sites, it is surprising in this case that morality and ethical assessments are the critical points. Remarks on the different video platforms, forums, and Web sites clearly show that, apart from the usual bashing between two factions, a serious discussion about the morality of in-world actions and the interconnections between off- and online life took place. The supporters of the funeral crashing, however, stress the total separation of gaming and real life:

> Naxir from the guild, Serenity Now, on March 5, 2006: I know what RP [role-play] means, I suppose it was a poor choice of words, but that doesn't change the fact you guys are complete t[u]rds for having a memorial for her in game. Personally, I have always thought that "memorials" were silly, but bringing it inside of a game is like someone having a wedding in game. I mean really wtf [what the fuck] is the point of gath[er]ing your digital characters up in a specified location? The only reason I can think of is because you want to do things "Face to Face." That implies that you consider your character to be an e-version of your self. IMO [in my opinion], that's similar to RP'rs trying to "live in the world of Azeroth." [Azeroth is the name of the game world of World of Warcraft.] So while it's not strictly RP'ing, since that would imply you are assuming the role of an Azerothian citizen, it does show that you want to act out an event that has no business in being in a video game.[37]

> Pagy on May 3, 2006: Again as it has been mentioned, it wasn't about her, it was about the players at that hotspring. It's as simple as that, for me at least. You may not be able to differentiate rl [real life] and what players do in a multiplayer video game, but some of us can. Now as you've maintained, a medium for a memorial doesn't matter, well that isn't an absolute. You can freak out all you want, but the fact remains

that they held a gathering in a pvp multiplayer game and announced it to the server. The event itself doesn't change the fact i pay my monthly fee to be able to target horde characters in contested zones for my own enjoyment. It all comes down to a point of view, and while i understand your opinion and your fe[e]lings, i don't understand your outward expression of righteousness over the subject . . . chillax.[38]

Summon on September 9, 2006: On a serious note, a life without introspection or philosophy is pointless. The game as a conduit simply fails for making real connections. If WoW is your base for friends or real emotional sol[a]ce. Then you sir are amazingly damaged person. Get out [and] live real life. Funerals are meant for people who really knew them. It's like all the retards who show up at celeb funerals. You didn't know this person to an extent that gives you a right to mourn them. If you did then it's another cookie cutter non person we are talking about. I would have supported my guild's actions out of idealism not just [because] I (we) like be amazingly huge e [electronic]-wangs.

Living through a game is fucked. Live a real life, stop making babies that shoot up schools because of video games, stop having a spouse you call a[t] night out raiding BRM [Black Rock Mountain, the name of a dungeon], stop being the vapid piece of shit that clutters my fucking university. I'm tired of the E-Knighting and pretending you feel any real genuine emotion. I agree my guild are retards for coming on the boards, they should have waited for the flames then brought the lol [laughing out loud]. In all honesty fuck Blizzard for making a MMO with such a low learning curve. Taco and most of all stop making my video games so FUCKING SERIOUS.[39]

On the other hand, those who felt the crashing was wrong emphasize that online identity, even in a game, cannot be separated from offline identity since both are part of one's identity; therefore a memorial for a dead person can be part of the game:

Rifter on May 3, 2006: Just because WoW is a game doesn't mean RL is not involved or can be ignored like it doesn't matter.[40]

Zoewe on April 3, 2006: I'm sorry this whole the internet =/= real life thing is flawed to me . . . yea killing someone in a game is not the same as killing someone in real life but the internet is still part of real life. People were sad about someone they knew dying and instead of saying "hey, sorry your friend died" you spit in their face just because you can and then argue omgz like [oh my God like] buts its pvp server kekeke. You're still assmonkeys in real life and on the interwebs whether you got "honor" points for your actions or not. Congrats on a new personal low. /golfclap[41]

Minus Sign on June 25, 2006: A classic case of in-game mentality intruding on real life emotions. In RL the people of Serenity Now would never dream of doing something like this (hazing a public function) because there are consequences to their actions. The RL versions of these victims would easily bend them—each and every one—over a knee and spank their butts red till bleeding. In game, I'm sure that SN's [Serenity Now's] days are numbered. If they aren't hunted down and camped to the point that their characters become useless to play, they should be hounded into outcast status by the WoW community at large. This, of course, can give no great solace to those players who still mourn the loss of their friend. To those who were affected by this, I offer empathy. Out of curiosity: those who were responsible for making the funeral intended to make their own video for the family of this young woman. Did they carry through?[42]

Ritual Conflicts and Virtual Worlds

These comments illustrate the range of interpretations regarding what is considered appropriate and inappropriate behavior within a game environment. When it comes to ritual authenticity or efficacy, discussions about the disruption of the mourning ritual in World of Warcraft focus on one main issue: whether virtual space is proper ritual space. This question arises in all three virtual environments—Church of Fools, Second Life, and World of Warcraft—regardless of their differing, explicitly stated purposes. Whereas the Church of Fools was constructed for the sole purpose of religious practice and is restricted to one building, World of Warcraft is an area explicitly designed for online gaming and role-playing, and Second Life is a vast environment comprised of different landscapes, countries, cities, and designated areas for specific activities and purposes.

According to Philip Rosedale of Linden Lab, the company that developed the software for Second Life and made the online environment publicly accessible in 2003, the vision that drove the company to build this online life sim (simulation) comes from the book *Snow Crash* by Neal Stephenson. The novel describes an Internet-based multiuser environment called Metaverse, a term still in use for 3D online environments, yet the idea can be traced back even further to science fiction and computer technology. Even so, none of the early examples of Internet life sims such as the Palace or Active World from 1995 and There from 1998 became as successful as the prominent successor Second Life, which, by the end of 2008, featured more than 15 million registered users.

The fact that in Second Life there is no predetermined goal or purpose means that it is entirely up to users to do their own meaning making and to find purpose in the ways they choose to play the game. Consequently, any given undertaking might differ greatly from one user to another, which can therefore be one of the main reasons for conflicts within this environment.

However, conflicts still occur even when an online environment provides a clear, uncontested purpose, as is the case with both the Church of Fools and World of Warcraft. The latter online environment represents a classic example of an MMOG (massively multiplayer online game), now the most widespread model of a virtual world. In fact, the category dates back to the late 1970s when the first text-based virtual game world, then called Multiuser Dungeon, went online.

What connects all three case studies, then, is the fact that, despite decades of history in some online environments, virtual worlds still involve a new kind of community building and social networking; thus the social-cultural purpose of these environments is not clearly, universally defined. In other words, since there is as yet no role model for how to behave in online environments, its users are free (and, in the case of Second Life, even obliged) to define their own personal raison d'être for inhabiting a virtual world and adapting their behavior accordingly. While on the World Wide Web certain rules of etiquette have been defined and are being enforced, certain activities even on traditional Web sites still prove to be blind spots and, accordingly, areas of debate and conflict. One of these blind spots is the area of ritual, especially ritual performance, which is found in a great variety of virtual domains as well as other sectors of the Internet, including the earliest examples of text-based electronic interchange.

Irrespective of these perpetually negotiated virtual worlds, what seems most remarkable is that conflicts occur particularly around and in rituals. Rituals, especially in a religious context, have been found online since the Internet became publicly available in the early to mid-1990s. From the beginning, this new medium has provided a broad variety of ritual resources, ranging from ritual prescriptions and descriptions on personal home pages to discussions about ritual in forums or mailing lists, and, very recently, audiovisual representations of rituals on photo- and video-sharing Web sites. Furthermore, opportunities for the online performance of rituals have been found in many different online forms. Indeed, from early on they became an important part of cultural, social, and religious activity in virtual worlds. It is noteworthy that many rituals, especially those performed online, bear such a high potential for conflict and heated discussion.

In any case, what is clear from this brief survey of virtual worlds is that mediated rituals often provoke conflict. What is less clear is whether the conflict is caused by the transfer of rituals from an off- to an online realm or provoked by the newly mediated ritual itself. In these case studies, the initial issue that provoked conflict was disturbance of the ritual or ritualistic space. In other words, the regular ritual structure was interrupted and the performance was interfered with or, in some cases, even fully terminated. An adequate answer assessment must include the broader context. Conflicts made visible by the disruption of rituals do not begin and end only with some disruptive incident; they have a prehistory as well as consequences. Thus we must inquire into the reasons behind the disturbing groups' provocations as well as into how conflicts are negotiated. Of course, we must also include in our deliberations the question whether and how ritual action changes as a consequence of disruptions.

Knowing all the reasons for any given provocation is difficult; they can only be inferred from the behavior of the actors involved. As for the World of Warcraft guild that crashed the mourning ceremony, we can gain a certain insight into their motives by means of their discussions and the videos posted to YouTube. For the crashers, apparently their aggressive actions fit perfectly into a game frame in which rival factions attack each other. As the video indicates, the crashers had a lot of fun. Since the mourning service had been announced on the discussion forums ahead of time, it became an obvious target for the disrupting guild. In the case of the Second Life wedding crasher and the "Satan" in the Church of Fools, deducing the motives of the actors involved is more difficult, but in both cases there are clear indicators that the disturbers did not assess the ritual performances as serious events.

It is important then to keep in mind that the root of conflict really amounts to disparate definitions of virtual space. For ritual practitioners, virtual space can serve as a location for conducting valid and efficacious rituals, while for disturbing groups a virtual environment is a space for testing the range of performative and behavioral options available in this new location. Either way, the different interpretations often include assumptions about the nature of ritual, game, and play that require further research.

As for which negotiations may resolve the conflict and what are the consequences for further ritual actions, the issue can be regarded several ways. On the one hand, negotiations may happen immediately after a disruption. For example, in the Church of Fools, when the ritual space was violated by "Satan," who climbed up to the pulpit and preached, the conflict-laden situation was resolved soon after. Another option is that the negotiations are delayed and may even transpire on another virtual platform, as is the case with World of Warcraft. The conflict-laden discussion did not arise immediately after the disrupted ritual but some time later, on a video-sharing platform. Here, the possibility of discussing the posted clips provided the space for negotiating the conflict.

What, if any, is the impact of conflict on the subsequent conduct of rituals after their initial disruption? The main trend, at least from the perspective of the actors involved, seems to be that the structure, performance, or meaning ascribed to the ritual is not changed; what the actors perceive as having changed is really only the external settings. As a consequence of wedding crashing in Second Life, for instance, designers changed the ritual setting. They built barriers to restrict entrance to the ritual area so that only invited members of the wedding party could participate. In the Church of Fools, access to certain areas was restricted and more church wardens were put in charge to keep the peace. In World of Warcraft, the ritual setting seems to have changed from public to private. (An exact assessment is not possible since the videos and discussions on YouTube lack reliable connections.) At least one video shows the likely repetition of the mourning ceremony held in a private circle of guild members and, consequently, without disruption.[43]

Contextualizing a conflict leads back to the question: is it indeed the transfer of a ritual into an electronic medium that provokes conflict? For now, we must say no. However, even though conflict in virtual worlds is not dependent on the specific characteristics of ritual, conflicts are undeniably commonplace when ritual action is transferred to an online environment. So, if it is not the ritual itself that is the source of conflict, what is the source, and is it detectable in ritual action within virtual worlds? We claim that it is indeed the media's indeterminate, or fuzzy, boundaries between virtuality and reality that is the reason for conflicts expressed in debates about rituals. Certainly in all three case studies, the interruption of a ritual performance ignited heated discussion between the parties involved. But subsequent to the discussions, what became obvious was that it was not the ritual space nor the ritual performance that was at the center of debate so much as the fact that the virtual space was not perceived by everybody in the same way.

The Church of Fools had numerous conflicts caused by disruptive visitors who misused the religious space for all kinds of inappropriate actions. Some visitors evidently saw the environment as a gaming place where they could play around in ways that would be prohibited in a real church by social and cultural boundaries. But "Satan," who climbed the pulpit and demanded worship, quickly relented and left after a warden announced the serious purpose of the space. Thus, it was not the ritual itself but different notions about the authenticity of the virtual church building—that is, whether it served as religious or game space—that was the real trigger of conflict. The same is true for the wedding crashers in Second Life. Whereas couples and designers claimed a virtual environment was a place for serious social interaction where rituals could be conducted efficaciously, the crashers claimed the environment as a game space and behaved accordingly.

Again, the different definitions of the environment—and not the ritual itself—proved to be the source of conflict. This issue is even more apparent in the case of the mourning ritual in World of Warcraft, in which one group was disturbed by opposing players—a phenomenon that is part of the game's intrinsic purpose. However, the fact that one group perceived the game environment as a space inextricably linked with the physical realm meant that conflicting notions of virtuality and reality led to an inevitable clash.

Conflict, then, does not arise as a consequence of transferring rituals to a virtual environment nor because the rituals are mediated. Rather, the cause of conflict lies in the indeterminate characteristics ascribed to virtual worlds and their unclear classification as authentic ritual space. Not surprisingly, then, contradictory ascription processes abound. Why do these processes play such an important role in rituals? Is there something special about ritual performance in virtual worlds that they so readily evoke conflict?

In general, identifying precisely which characteristics make ritual a special category of action is problematic, even for ritual studies scholars. For Thomas Lawson and Robert N. McCauley, ritual is primarily a religious action that differs from ordinary actions by the existence of so-called culturally postulated superhuman agents.[44] Or consider Rodney Needham's criteria, which distinguish "ordinary" from "ritual" action.[45] Axel Michaels describes ritual as a distinct form of action that can be distinguished from nonritual acts by its special formality, framing, elevation, and transformation processes.[46] Caroline Humphrey and James Laidlaw identify the "ritual stance" as the central characteristic of rituals.[47] Although these approaches have been criticized for claiming one or more characteristic as an exclusive, universally valid identifier of ritual, most ritual actors would agree that ritual does possess a quality that can be distinguished as extraordinary. Thus we keep asking if there is something distinctive that marks rituals in such a way that they attract conflict in the virtual realm. Our conclusion is that it is the ongoing process of defining virtual space rather than ritual performance itself that triggers conflict. Other kinds of events and actions trigger conflicts of equal frequency and intensity.

Rituals performed in an online scenario are actions that strongly affect the identity of a person. At least, users seem to imply that this is the case. The performance and efficacy of online rituals crosses the imaginative border between on- and offline realms and thus directly affects the person in front of the screen. For example, in the Church of Fools the operators and visitors perceive the virtual space as an environment for valid and efficacious rituals that concern not only their avatars but also the person behind the virtual representation. As one visitor stated in the (now offline) bulletin board of the Church of Fools, "Hi I have been into the church a few times and I feel more at home here than I do in any other church. I hope you can stay for a long time on the internet. [I]t means so much to pray with such good people from around the world even if there are some idiots who try to spoil it for the rest of us who believe in the Lord Jesus Christ."[48]

In Second Life it is evident that the efficacy of rituals cannot actually be limited to virtual space due to the fact that the avatars act on behalf of real persons. For instance, an Anglican priest from the United Kingdom who acts a wedding designer in Second Life was interviewed about the meaning of wedding rituals there. He stressed the influence of the offline realm on the ritual actors: "[A] ritual is an event that all parties involved perceive as a ritual. If you went to a rabbi and had him say a bunch of words in [H]ebrew and you were raised [F]rench and new [sic] no [H]ebrew . . . , this would not be a ritual. [T]he rabbi may think it is but the parti[c]ipants would not. [B]y the time my clients are marriend [sic] they know how real this day is."[49]

This strong connection between on- and offline realms is not unique to rituals. Indeed, other topics provoke conflict in virtual worlds. The most controversial and discussed events in Second Life deal with sex, drugs, and violence. An incident stressing the assumption that a strong connection exists between on- and offline identity was news of rape in this environment. The accusations of a crime committed in virtual space engaged Belgian police, since the alleged victim was said to be a Belgian citizen.[50] The main question that arose again and again in discussions was not whether the virtual rape of an avatar in an online environment was possible, but how much the user-victim might be traumatized by the event.[51] Debates about online sex and online rape resemble those about online ritual. Similar examples can be found in World of Warcraft where (apart from minor discussions on cheating or the selling of highly equipped avatars on platforms such as e-Bay) sexism, racism, and other forms of harassment play a substantial role.

In sum, what is obvious from the above case studies and examples is that actions triggering conflicts typically hinge on the interconnections between offline and online bodies and behaviors. Actions dealing with powerful, intimate matters such as sex, religion, and ritual strongly influence both the off- and online selves. If Internet users hope to resolve core conflicts, they must first find or construct a clear border between their offline and online identities, or they must step back and ask whether a such a border even exists.

NOTES

1. Simon Jenkins, "Rituals and Pixels: Experiments in Online Church," *Online— Heidelberg Journal of Religions on the Internet* 3, no. 1 (2008): 113, http://archiv.ub.uni-heidelberg.de/volltextserver/volltexte/2008/8291/pdf/jenkins.pdf.

2. The Church of Fools is still available as a single-user environment. See http://www.churchoffools.com/.

3. The Ship of Fools, http://shipoffools.com.
4. Ship of Fools Project, *The Ark*, http://ark.saintsimeon.co.uk/.
5. Jenkins, "Rituals and Pixels," 95–115.
6. St. Pixels, http://www.stpixels.com/.
7. Mark Howe, *Online Church? First Steps towards Virtual Incarnation* (Cambridge: Cambridge University Press, 2007), 3.
8. Java is an object-model programming language derived from C and C++ originally developed by Sun Microsystems; Java allows for easy implementation on different operating systems, software environments, and Web browsers.
9. Jenkins, "Rituals and Pixels," 100.
10. Richard Chartres, Anglican bishop of London, in his opening speech on May 11, 2004; see Jenkins, "Rituals and Pixels," 107.
11. Telephone interview with Simon Jenkins, one of the main organizers of the Church of Fools, on January 27, 2009; see also Jenkins, "Rituals and Pixels," 113.
12. Telephone interview with Jenkins, January 27, 2009.
13. Jenkins, "Rituals and Pixels," 109.
14. Jenkins, "Rituals and Pixels," 110.
15. Jenkins, "Rituals and Pixels," 110.
16. "Troll" is Internet slang for a person who provokes other users of an online community or an Internet forum into emotional responses, i.e., someone who posts inflammatory, controversial, or off-topic messages, or who uses other kinds of inappropriate behavior.
17. Rowland Croucher et al., "Profanity in the Pews," John Mark Ministries, May 20, 2004, http://jmm.aaa.net.au/articles/12812.htm.
18. Jenkins, "Rituals and Pixels," 112.
19. For example, "Online Church Blocks Satan Visits," BBC News, May 19, 2004, http://news.bbc.co.uk/1/hi/uk/3730807.stm.
20. Graham Jones, "Devils Hit Cyber Church," May 19, 2004. http://www.cnn.com/2004/WORLD/europe/05/19/uk.online.church/index.html.
21. "Satan Loses His Sulphur," The Church of Fools, May 15, 2004, http://www.churchoffools.com/news-stories/02_sulphur.html.
22. Telephone interview with Jenkins, January 27, 2009.
23. Jenkins, "Rituals and Pixels," 111.
24. Jenkins, "Rituals and Pixels," 111.
25. Randolph Kluver and Yanli Chen, "Virtual Ritual and Material Faith," *Online—Heidelberg Journal of Religions on the Internet* 3 no.1 (2008): 131, http://archiv.ub.uni-heidelberg.de/volltextserver/volltexte/2008/8292/pdf/Kluver.pdf.
26. Following our code of ethics, interviewees' names have been abbreviated to protect their anonymity.
27. Often several game environments are located on a single server. Every server contains an exact copy of the game environment and can host a certain number of players. This division is mostly done for technical reasons, so servers with a limited number of accounts can guarantee a frictionless gaming experience.
28. For more information, see T. L. Taylor, *Play between Worlds: Exploring Online Communities* (Cambridge, MA: MIT Press, 2006).

29. Both server versions can also be played in a role-playing style, so the language and behavior of avatars are suited to that particular environment.

30. The final level has been continually increased by Blizzard to keep up players' interest and to integrate new game content.

31. "Memorial to Fayejin," Illidrama Forums, http://forums.illidrama.com/showthread.php?t=1826.

32. Irishlacrosse, "WoW Funeral Pwnage," YouTube video, http://de.youtube.com/watch?v=oTSGUf1xbF8.

33. The song, by the Misfits, is called "Where Eagles Dare."

34. Vash12788, "So We Pwned This Funeral Today: Serenity-Now.org," YouTube video, http://www.youtube.com/watch?v=ewP1zfm_Yqg.

35. "Byzon Answers 'Memorial to Fayejin' Post," Illidrama Forums, http://forums.illidrama.com/showthread.php?t=1826&page=5.

36. The abbreviation ":D" is an emoticon that means "laughing out loud."

37. "Naxir Answers 'Memorial to Fayejin' Post," Illidrama Forums, http://forums.illidrama.com/showthread.php?t=1826&page=11.

38. "Pagy Answers 'Memorial to Fayejin' Post," Illidrama Forums, http://forums.illidrama.com/showthread.php?t=1826&page=14.

39. "Summon Answers 'Memorial to Fayejin' Post," Illidrama Forums, http://forums.illidrama.com/showthread.php?t=1826&page=18.

40. "Rifter Answers 'Memorial to Fayejin' Post," Illidrama Forums, http://forums.illidrama.com/showthread.php?t=1826&page=14.

41. "Zoewe Answers 'Memorial to Fayejin' Post," Illidrama Forums, http://forums.illidrama.com/showthread.php?t=1826&page=6.

42. "Post from Minus Sign," Guild Wars Guru Forum, http://www.guildwarsguru.com/forum/showthread.php?s=47fb1be252f61ea59a4e8b437663f835&t=306472. This post is no longer available online.

43. doofis333, "WoW Funeral Service for Estela," YouTube video, http://www.youtube.com/watch?v=3sPPC09Q81o.

44. Lawson, Thomas, and Robert McCauley, *Rethinking Religion: Connecting Cognition and Culture* (New York: Cambridge University Press, 1990).

45. Rodney Needham, "Remarks on Wittgenstein and Ritual," in *Exemplars*, ed. Rodney Needham (Berkeley: University of California Press, 1985), 149–177.

46. Axel Michaels, "Zur Dynamik von Ritualkomplexen," *Forum Ritualdynamik* 3 (2003), http://archiv.ub.uni-heidelberg.de/volltextserver/volltexte/2004/4583/pdf/Axel_Michaels.pdf.

47. James Laidlaw and Caroline Humphrey, "Action," in *Theorizing Rituals: Issues, Topics, Approaches, Concepts*, ed. Jens Kreinath, Jan Snoek, and Michael Stausberg (Leiden: Brill, 2006), 265–283.

48. The comment was posted on the bulletin board of the Church of Fools Web site in summer 2004. The board is no longer available online.

49. Interview conducted by Kerstin Radde-Antweiler, September 12, 2006.

50. See, for example, Regina Lynn, "Virtual Rape Is Traumatic, but Is It a Crime?" *Wired*, http://www.wired.com/culture/lifestyle/commentary/sexdrive/2007/05/sexdrive_0504.

Also see "Reader Roundtable: 'Virtual Rape' Claim Brings Belgian Police to Second Life," Virtual Blind Blog, http://virtuallyblind.com/2007/04/24/open-roundtable-allegations-of-virtual-rape-bring-belgian-police-to-second-life/.

51. See Lynn, "Virtual Rape Is Traumatic, but Is It a Crime?"

REFERENCES

"Byzon Answers 'Memorial to Fayejin' Post." Illidrama Forums. http://forums.illidrama.com/showthread.php?t=1826&page=5 (accessed March 4, 2009).

The Church of Fools. http://www.churchoffools.com/ (accessed March 4, 2009).

Croucher, Rowland, et al. "Profanity in the Pews." John Mark Ministries, May 20, 2004. http://jmm.aaa.net.au/articles/12812.htm (accessed March 4, 2009).

doofis333. "WoW Funeral Service for Estela." YouTube video. http://www.youtube.com/watch?v=3sPPC09Q810 (accessed March 4, 2009).

Howe, Mark. *Online Church? First Steps Towards Virtual Incarnation*. Cambridge: Grove, 2007.

Irishlacrosse. "WoW Funeral Pwnage." YouTube video. http://de.youtube.com/watch?v=0TSGUf1xbF8 (accessed March 4, 2009).

Jenkins, Simon. "Rituals and Pixels: Experiments in Online Church." *Online—Heidelberg Journal of Religions on the Internet 3*, no. 1 (2008): 95–115. http://www.ub.uni-heidelberg.de/archiv/8291.

Jones, Graham. "Devils Hit Cyber Church." May 19, 2004. http://www.cnn.com/2004/WORLD/europe/05/19/uk.online.church/index.html (accessed March 4, 2009).

Kluver, Randolph, and Yanli Chen. "Virtual Ritual and Material Faith." *Online—Heidelberg Journal of Religions on the Internet 3*, no. 1 (2008): 116–143. http://www.ub.uni-heidelberg.de/archiv/8292.

Laidlaw, James, and Caroline Humphrey. "Action." In *Theorizing Rituals: Issues, Topics, Approaches, Concepts*, edited by Jens Kreinath, Jan Snoek, and Michael Stausberg, 265–283. Leiden: Brill, 2006.

Lawson, Thomas, and Robert McCauley. *Rethinking Religion: Connecting Cognition and Culture*. New York: Cambridge University Press, 1990.

Lynn, Regina. "Virtual Rape Is Traumatic, but Is It a Crime?" *Wired*. http://www.wired.com/culture/lifestyle/commentary/sexdrive/2007/05/sexdrive_0504 (accessed March 4, 2009).

"Memorial to Fayejin." Illidrama Forums. http://forums.illidrama.com/showthread.php?t=1826 (accessed March 4, 2009).

Michaels, Axel. "Zur Dynamik von Ritualkomplexen." *Forum Ritualdynamik* (2003). http://archiv.ub.uni-heidelberg.de/volltextserver/volltexte/2004/4583/pdf/Axel_Michaels.pdf.

"Naxir Answers 'Memorial to Fayejin' Post." Illidrama Forums. http://forums.illidrama.com/showthread.php?t=1826&page=11 (accessed March 4, 2009).

Needham, Rodney. "Remarks on Wittgenstein and Ritual." In *Exemplars*, edited by Rodney Needham, 149–177. Berkeley: University of California Press, 1985.

"Online Church Blocks Satan Visits." BBC News, May 19, 2004. http://news.bbc.co.uk/1/hi/uk/3730807.stm (accessed March 4, 2009).

"Pagy Answers 'Memorial to Fayejin' Post." Illidrama Forums. http://forums.illidrama.com/showthread.php?t=1826&page=14 (accessed March 4, 2009).

"Post from Minus Sign." Guild Wars Guru Forum. http://www.guildwarsguru.com/forum/showthread.php?s=47fb1be252f61ea59a4e8b437663f835&t=306472 (no longer available online).

"Reader Roundtable: 'Virtual Rape' Claim Brings Belgian Police to Second Life." Virtual Blind Blog. http://virtuallyblind.com/2007/04/24/open-roundtable-allegations-of-virtual-rape-bring-belgian-police-to-second-life/ (accessed March 4, 2009).

"Rifter Answers 'Memorial to Fayejin' post." Illidrama Forums. http://forums.illidrama.com/showthread.php?t=1826&page=14 (accessed March 4, 2009).

"Satan Loses His Sulphur." The Church of Fools, May 15, 2004. http://www.churchoffools.com/news-stories/02_sulphur.html (accessed March 4, 2009).

The Ship of Fools. http://shipoffools.com (accessed March 4, 2009).

Ship of Fools Project. *The Ark*. http://ark.saintsimeon.co.uk/ (accessed March 4, 2009).

St. Pixels. http://www.stpixels.com/ (accessed March 4, 2009).

"Summon Answers 'Memorial to Fayejin' Post." Illidrama Forums. http://forums.illidrama.com/showthread.php?t=1826&page=18 (accessed March 4, 2009).

Taylor, T. L. *Play between Worlds: Exploring Online Communities*. Cambridge: MIT Press, 2006.

Vash12788. "So We Pwned This Funeral Today: Serenity-Now.org." YouTube video. http://www.youtube.com/watch?v=ewP1zfm_Yqg (accessed March 4, 2009).

"Zoewe Answers 'Memorial to Fayejin' Post." Illidrama Forums. http://forums.illidrama.com/showthread.php?t=1826&page=6 (accessed March 4, 2009).

7

Media on the Ritual Battlefield

Ignace de Haes, Ute Hüsken, and Paul van der Velde

For quite some time, the idea that rituals facilitate social cohesion has dominated thinking and writing about ritual.[1] This notion, based on Emile Durkheim's theories, stresses that rituals are created for the sake of solidarity and are central to social integration. Durkheim's theory is predicated on the view that religion is based on the classification of things as either profane or sacred and that sacredness extends to the symbols and representations of the sacred. The profane is associated with everyday existence, whereas sacred things are protected, isolated, separated, prohibited, and inaccessible, set apart from the mundane world and invested with special properties. Durkheim argues that there can be no society that does not regularly reaffirm its collective sentiments and ideas, and that this affirmation is the purpose of ritual.[2] Other scholars, such as literary critic Kenneth Burke, argue that the ritual construction of symbolic unity depends as much on creating differences as on identifying similarities.[3] If inclusion is one social function of ritual, exclusion is necessarily another; boundaries that include one group automatically exclude another.[4]

Sociologist Philip Smith goes one step further, examining aspects of ritual that emphasize difference instead of cohesion, in his interpretation of war and the ritual dimensions of armed conflict. Agreeing with Durkheim, Smith argues that rituals receive their special character from underlying semiotic structures that set concepts in binary opposition as sacred and profane. According to Smith, this binary opposition is characterized by a "violent hierarchy" in which one concept governs the other.[5] Two alternative and often extreme positions are presented in such a way that they seem the only possible—and mutually exclusive—options, while, in fact, there may be a spectrum of possibilities. Smith interprets wars as ritual events, because they are organized around binary oppositions represented as sacred and profane. Sacred qualities refer to one's own group, while profane elements represent the foe. Thus, the construction of the enemy is accompanied by the construction one's own sacred identity, which is in a dangerously antagonistic relationship with the profane identity of the enemy.

Smith's case study is the 1981 Falklands War, in which Argentina's invasion of the Falkland Islands was perceived as a threat to key values in British society. The fundamental opposition in this case is the distinction between dictatorship and democracy, a distinction that the British government reinforced by using other binary sets such as free/unfree and liberation/dictatorship. In contrast to the Argentine government, which was depicted as blind, stupid, incompetent, incapable, irrational, emotive, and unstable, the British government represented itself as rational and reasonable.[6]

As a ritual event, the war requires celebration and reaffirmation of the sacred side of the conflict, along with vigorous opposition to the profane side. The key to the ensuing, constructed reality is a rhetoric that defines, or rather redefines, the crisis. Thus, the Falklands War was not a "war" but a "conflict," and the British forces were not an "army" but a "task force." Accepted by almost all British participants, this kind of ritualized discourse set the necessity of war beyond doubt and soon became the dominant culture code.[7]

Generally, in times of national or international conflict the dominant discourse regarding a threat is embraced by a majority of the population, and ritual amplified by mass media plays a crucial role in the acceptance of such discourse.[8] Here, we explore the reasons why ritual features prominently in times of crisis and how its mediatization affects the conflict at hand.

Our case studies, the toppling of Saddam Hussein's statue in Baghdad on April 9, 2003, and street protests against Myanmar's ruling junta in September 2007, ask how rituals are used in conflict-laden situations and illustrate the role of media in these processes. While the particulars of the two cases differ widely, they have in common their antagonists' use of ritual actions surrounding national, political, and religious symbols and their media representations. Key symbols—a public statue, national flags, inverted bowls, white elephants, and miraculously appearing Buddha stones—seem an unlikely combination, and their representation to the outside world could not have been more different. Thanks to mass media, the toppling of Saddam Hussein's statue was known around the globe, while the protests of Buddhist monks and laypeople against the Burmese junta was underreported in international media, making the white elephants and miraculously appearing Buddha statues little known beyond Myanmar's borders.

Raising Ratings and Toppling Saddam

The toppling of statues is a widespread tradition going back to ancient Egypt. Statues of Roman emperors were toppled when they died. In England, toppling statues dates back to Henry VIII. Statue breaking reached its height during the English Revolution, in 1643, and there was even a law that demanded the reconstruction of statues. New Yorkers tore down a statue of George III in 1776, and French revolutionaries toppled one of Louis XV, melting it down and replacing it with a guillotine. In the eighteenth and nineteenth centuries the erection of statues increased dramatically in Europe and America, evoking a countertradition of damaging statues for political reasons.

With the development of mass media, damaging statues soon became world news; hence famous photographs of a toppled statue of Stalin in Budapest during the Hungarian revolt against Russian occupation in 1956. In 1958, the end of the monarchy in Iraq was marked by toppling the statues of the British general Stanley Maude and the last monarch of Iraq, King Faisal.

More recently, cities in Eastern Europe saw their Marx and Lenin statues toppled to mark the end of the communist regime. The same happened in Romania with the statues of Ceaușescu. The power of such an act is inherent in the fact that the material image of the ruler is understood to represent the entire political system. In no other ritualized political action is the power of images as apparent as in tearing down statues when power changes are at hand.

Saddam Hussein had erected many statues of himself, thus replicating his personal power and fusing it with the existing political system. As it happened, the statue on Firdos Square, which Saddam had dedicated to himself on his sixty-fifth birthday, stood near the Palestine Hotel, the site that housed the international media throughout the war. Not only did the statue's toppling become a key image in the American war narrative, there is also ample evidence that the event was actually stage managed by the U.S. military (see figure 7.1).[9]

On April 9, 2003, three weeks after the beginning of Operation Iraqi Freedom, U.S. troops entered Baghdad, the capital of Iraq. Following their entry, a crowd of Iraqis gathered on Firdos Square near a giant statue of Saddam Hussein. Iraqis first threw shoes against the statue, and a man with a sledgehammer began pounding at its concrete base before U.S. Marines moved in with armored vehicles and a chain. An American flag in hand, one soldier draped it over the statue's face, then suddenly pulled the flag away, replacing it with an Iraqi flag. The Marines then proceeded to pull down the statue with the chain.

Since the invasion of the Iraq had been a cable news affair from the start,[10] the scene of the statue's toppling was immediately circulated internationally via live

FIGURE 7.1. The toppling of the statue of Saddam Hussein in Firdos Square, Baghdad, Iraq, April 9, 2003. Photo courtesy of Goaran Tomasevic/Reuters.

coverage on the U.S. cable networks, Fox News, and CNN.[11] In the first Gulf War, CNN had enjoyed a monopoly on twenty-four-hour cable news, but by 2003 Fox News had more viewers. Fox could compete with its rival station because it offered a flashier, more patriotic television product—the outcome of a vicious branding war between the networks, each trying to project itself as more patriotic than its competitor. Fox had branded its news coverage using the American flag in the upper-left-hand corner of the TV screen, waving continuously. The Fox News logo stamped in red, white, and blue identified the network as essentially American. A banner at the bottom of the screen in red, white, and blue signified the Pentagon's code name for the invasion, Operation Iraqi Freedom. Clearly, the war in Iraq was also a war between the networks. Driven by a race for ratings, each network tried capturing war footage in the most sensational way.

The toppling of Saddam Hussein's statue was thus presented as a spectacular event on competing news networks. At 9:45 A.M., CNN reporter Bill Hemmer commented on people gathering in the square: "You think about seminal moments in a nation's history . . . indelible moments like the fall of the Berlin Wall, and that's what we're seeing right now. Regular Iraqis with their opportunity and their chance to take their own axe down Saddam Hussein."[12] David Asman on Fox had already begun commenting at 8:52 A.M.: "You are seeing history in the making right now." At 10:12 A.M. he continued, "This is one of those moments in history that we are privileged to [be] reporting on." This last comment was repeated by anchor Brit Hume, who added, "This transcends anything I have ever seen."[13]

The image of an American soldier draping the U.S. flag around the head of the statue was a visual reference to other historic images, including shots of U.S. Marines raising the American flag atop Mt. Suribachi at the end of World War II, arguably among the most famous photographs in American history. Raising the flag is considered a highly patriotic ritual. As the embodiment of sacrifice, the flag has transformative power. Soldiers are fused with their flags, and the nation is rejuvenated on the basis of their sacrifice. Even apart from war, the use of flags carries enormous symbolic meaning. Whether planting the American flag on the moon or burning a flag in protest, flags are used to make highly charged statements and to achieve patriotic and antipatriotic goals.

Given this kind of symbolic valence, it is not surprising that Marine Ed Chin's draping the U.S. emblem around the statue's head soon became known as the "flag incident." Deborah Lynn Jaramillo gives a detailed report of the event, showing how the cable news reporters set the stage for their viewers to grasp the historic impact of the scene.[14] At the moment of the draping, CNN reporter Christiane Amanpour said, "Oh there we have it, an American flag. Now this, I have to say, may look like fun, but a lot of soldiers have been told not to sort of do this triumphalism because it's not about American flags, but about Iraqi sovereignty and the Iraqi people."[15] When Ed Chin removed the American flag, Fox's David Asman immediately tried to reframe the situation: "Look who's holding the flag now. It's an Iraqi citizen waving the U.S. flag. That might do something to dispel criticism no doubt we are about to hear from with regard to the Al-Jazeera stations. You can understand these Marines who have put their lives on the line, sweated with blood and guts for the past three weeks, wanting to show the Stars and Stripes in this moment of glory. Understandable but no doubt Al-Jazeera and the others are gonna make hay with that."[16]

In fact, the interpretation of the scene by the Arabic-speaking networks was strikingly different. It should be noted that the three major Arabic channels' footage of the statue's toppling was virtually the same as that of the American networks, since all three networks were present at the same events and used the same international film originating from the same source. However, the Arab channels' comments on the American flag draped around the statue's head were entirely different, declaring, "That should have been an Iraqi flag!"[17] By the time the American flag was replaced by the Iraqi flag, moments later, the damage had been done. Al-Jazeera emphasized that it was not regular Iraqis but U.S. troops who tore down the statue, and that "the Americans succeeded in removing only half of the statue," noting that "Saddam's legs remained deeply rooted in the bronze base." Al-Arabiya made the media issue explicit: "This is the scene the U.S. TV networks have been waiting for.... Now we will know whether the U.S. was really after freeing the people of Iraq or after the Iraqi territories." All three Arabian networks emphasized that, locally, the "liberators" were perceived as invaders, and that resistance to occupation would never end. This commentary was supported by images of angry Iraqis, symbols of the ongoing resistance following the fall of Saddam Hussein's regime.[18]

These diverging interpretations were not due to different journalistic traditions or practices in media coverage. Most staff at the three Arabic channels—Al-Jazeera, Al-Arabiya, and Abu Dhabi channel[19]—had been trained and employed in Western media organizations, especially the BBC. In their coverage of pan-Arab and international politics, all three channels follow Western-style journalistic practices. Yet in Arabic-speaking media, the key image was not the toppling but rather the "flag incident." Arabic-speaking media did not frame the fall of Baghdad as the end of dictatorship and the advent of democracy but as yet another episode of Arab defeat and humiliation. Television coverage of the Iraq war had a strong impact throughout the Arab states. Writing about Egyptians' response, Hussein Amin, a researcher on journalism and mass communication, argues that the image of an American flag draped over Saddam Hussein's statue transmitted to tens of millions of Arabian viewers contributed to a sense of humiliation and fear of American imperialism.[20]

In contrast to Arabic-speaking media, the toppling of the statue immediately became the dominant news image in America and England.[21] On Fox the image was relayed an average of 6.83 times every half hour between 11 A.M. and 8 P.M., that is, every 4.4 minutes.[22] On CNN the shot ran an average of four times every half hour. Thus the image of the toppled statue achieved iconic status in America and its ally Britain. CNN and Fox also used the image to promote upcoming shows and to advertise their networks, making the image a branding device. Every time it was shown, the networks labeled the incident a "historic event" associated with "liberation." In this way, the "liberation" of Iraqis eventually constituted a full third of the American media's total narrative of the war.[23] The image was further promoted by selective editing, such as concentrating on close-ups. While reporters initially estimated "a small crowd" on the public square, both channels aired only dramatic close-ups in which celebrating Iraqis filled the frame, while news anchors spoke of "jubilant crowds." Viewers were thus left with the impression that countless Iraqis were present at the statue's demise. This reporting also led to the claim that Iraqi citizens were welcoming the Americans as liberators. Most explicit was ABC News, which described the decisive event as "a dream of freedom come true." In fact ABC opened their broadcast with this declaration: "Overjoyed Iraqis swarmed into the streets of Baghdad, dancing, celebrating, ripping up images of Saddam Hussein, and welcoming U.S. Marines with flowers and kisses."[24] The flag incident was entirely ignored. That same day, Donald Rumsfeld, secretary of defense, said:

The scenes of free Iraqis celebrating in the streets, riding American tanks, tearing down the statues of Saddam Hussein in the center of Baghdad are breathtaking. Watching them, one cannot help but think of the fall of the Berlin Wall and the collapse of the Iron Curtain. We are seeing history unfold events that will shape the course of the country, the fate of a people, and potentially the future of the region. Saddam Hussein is now taking his rightful place alongside Hitler, Stalin, Lenin and Ceausescu in the pantheon of failed, brutal dictators, and the Iraqi people are well on their way to freedom.[25]

Later, in September 2003, President Bush added, "Saddam Hussein's monuments have been removed and not only his statues. The true monuments of his rule and his character—the torture chambers and the rape rooms and the prison cells for innocent children—are closed."[26] Not only the media, then, but representatives of the U.S. government and the president insinuated that the war in Iraq had effectively come to an end. It certainly looked that way. The event was not only echoed in daily television reporting but also shown in later commemorations of events and thus became an obligatory part of every retrospective of the year 2003.

In June 2004, the *Los Angeles Times* reported that the U.S. military, not Iraqis, were behind the toppling of the statue.[27] The article stated that the U.S. Army's internal study of the war in Iraq had criticized efforts by its own Psychological Operations (PSYOP) units to produce memorable images of the invasion.[28] The army report stated that, as the Iraqi regime was collapsing on April 9, 2003, when U.S. Marines converged on Firdos Square in central Baghdad, it was a Marine colonel—not joyous Iraqi civilians, as was widely assumed from the TV images—who took initiative to topple the statue. And it was a quick-thinking Army PSYOP team that made the act appear to be a spontaneous Iraqi undertaking.[29] The event was not completely staged, however. Staff Sergeant Brian Plesich of the PSYOP team reported that "an American flag had been draped over the face of the statue. God bless them, but we were thinking from PSYOP school that this was just bad news. We didn't want to look like an occupation force, and some of the Iraqis were saying, 'No, we want an Iraqi flag!' So I said 'No problem, somebody get me an Iraqi flag.'"[30]

The American flag was replaced by the wrong Iraqi flag. The pre-1991 flag differs from the Iraqi flag of 2003 in one important detail: the older flag lacks the green Arabic script that reads, "Allahu akbar" (God is great). Choosing a flag that lacks this reference to Islam was the wrong message to beam to the hundreds of millions of Muslims who were already convinced that America's war was not against Saddam Hussein but against Islam itself. So, while the U.S. government was employing diverse strategies to defeat Saddam Hussein, media offered the public a binary model of reality that carved the world into good and evil.

In times of violent conflict, rituals that convey a strong, overt message are the ideal tools for communicating government discourse to the public. Although alternative news accounts are sometimes available in print and on the Web, mainstream media and government go hand in hand in times of crisis. Today there are plenty of critical sources about coverage of these events. Distortion of the news was later openly discussed by news reporters and editors. One of America's premier news anchors, Dan Rather of CBS, observed, "It is an obscene comparison . . . but you know there was a time in South Africa that people would put flaming tyres around people's necks if they dissented. And in some way the fear is that you will be necklaced here, you will have a flaming tyre of lack of patriotism put around your neck. Now it is that fear that keeps journalists from asking the toughest of the tough questions."[31]

In June 2008, Rather wrote about the failure of American media in the wake of 9/11 and in the run-up to Iraq, when news organizations in a climate of fear were perpetuating the narrative frame supplied by the White House. As we know now, there was no evidence that Iraq played a role in the September 11 attack. However, by March 2003 the inevitability of war was based on a seemingly perfect narrative that centered around a hero, a crime, and a villain. The villain, inherently evil and irrational, had to be defeated by the hero.

The *New York Times* was one of the few media organizations to apologize for its one-sided coverage.[32] Editor Daniel Okrent admits that in the months leading up to the invasion of Iraq, the newspaper's coverage was credulous, much of it inappropriately italicized in lavish fonts and headlines. "The failure was not individual, but institutional. War requires an extra standard of care, not a lesser one. But in The Times' W.M.D. coverage, readers encountered some rather breathless stories built on unsubstantiated 'revelations' that, in many instances, were the anonymity-cloaked assertions of people with vested interests. Times reporters broke many stories before and after the war—but when the stories themselves later broke apart, in many instances Times readers never found out."[33]

In March 2005, *Washington Post* journalist Philip Kennicott reflected on what was lacking in the war coverage:

> After two years and more than 1,500 U.S. casualties in a war that has been perhaps the best documented in history, no single photograph from the hostilities in Iraq has emerged as iconic. Images arrive, vie for our attention and are contradicted or superseded by other more immediate images. The red glare of shock and awe, the orange haze of sandstorms in the early weeks of war, the toppling of the statue of Saddam Hussein, the speech on the deck of an aircraft carrier—all of these moments, captured in photographs or video, belong to what feels like a prehistory

of what we have now, a long grind with continuing destruction and a failing attention span for the daily death toll. Only a few images from the prison scandal at Abu Ghraib have forced themselves repeatedly on our attention, and even those have faded (here) as our attention turns elsewhere and the U.S. government prosecutes a few low-level offenders. Despite heroic efforts of photojournalists to document the challenges and successes of the long grind of occupation, no one has captured a picture that has anything like the power of Nick Ut's photograph of a naked girl fleeing a napalm strike in Vietnam (could it be published in a "family" newspaper today?) or Joe Rosenthal's image of the flag raised on Iwo Jima. Those images captured—or helped crystallize—a consensus about the wars they represented, a consensus that has yet to emerge about the war in Iraq.[34]

Kennicott shows that, by 2005, the pictures were no longer iconic because the story was not perceived as simply as it was in 2003. The image of pulling down Saddam's statue was the climax of the visual victory frame. This frame was but one part of the process that U.S. forces employed, using media iconography to turn the fall of Baghdad from a merely symbolic act into an iconic image of the U.S.-led victory over evil that, in turn, would invite collective identification on a global scale. Yet as it turned out, this story had only temporary value. The war dragged on and the victory image lost its iconic status, as the story and the public memory of that story changed irrevocably.

Let's Go to War

Carolyn Marvin and David Ingle argue in "Blood Sacrifice and the Nation: Totem Rituals and the American Flag" that war has both strategic and ritual aims.[35] Strategically, the enemy is to be vanquished by killing. Ritually, protagonists sacrifice their own members to ward off perilous social frictions that threaten the group. A compelling external scapegoat is needed so groups can justify sacrificing their own members, dying "for the flag" and committing their children to do so without admitting that they are actually destroying members of their own group. In this sense, war is ritualized: its rules channel, shape, and legitimize violence and thus help to make killing appear civilized and humane, an expression of important values such as loyalty, freedom, and manhood.

The constructing an enemy was part of preparing for the Iraq invasion. Preparations began directly after the events of 9/11, when U.S. President George W. Bush set up an explicit binary opposition: "Every nation in every region now has a decision to make. Either you are with us, or you are with the terrorists."[36] In all fourteen national addresses George Bush delivered between September 11, 2001, and the invasion of Iraq in 2003, he used binary oppositions: "We are in a conflict between good and evil, and America will call evil by its name" (June 1, 2002).[37] "The doctrine that says 'Either you're with us or with the enemy' still holds. It's an important doctrine. It is as important today as it was 13 months ago" (October 2002). In his State of the Union address in January 2002, President Bush used the now-infamous phrase "axis of evil" to refer to Iran, North Korea, and Iraq. The reference to the Axis powers of World War II (Germany, Italy, and Japan) is as obvious as it is misleading, since it suggests a coalition between these states, whereas in fact Iran and Iraq had been at war with one another in the previous decade. Bush's speech used the word *evil* five times and *war* twelve times. Then, in his State of the Union address of January 28, 2003, Bush insisted that America could not afford to trust in the "sanity and restraint" of a dictator with access to "the world's most dangerous weapons," nor could it wait any longer to disarm him, especially with his history of using such weapons to kill and disfigure thousands of his own people. Saddam Hussein, the speech continued, was an "evil" man who tortured children and adults alike with electric shocks, hot irons, acid drips, power drills, amputations, and rape. "If this is not evil," Bush proclaimed, "then evil has no meaning."[38]

After September 11, 2001, George W. Bush painted the world in black and white. His distinguishing between "those who are good" and "those who are evil" was coupled with a distinction between "those who are for us'" and "those who are against us," and "those who love freedom" and "those who hate the freedom we love." By consistently using sets of binary oppositions to frame the issue, the Bush administration prepared the press and the public for the day when U.S. troops would be welcomed as liberators by Iraqis, ending their suffering by the defeat of the evil Saddam Hussein.[39] Ironically, while the liberation of Iraqis colored the war narrative in the American media, the idea only made sense if Iraqis did not figure prominently in their own liberation. As a result, they were rendered curiously absent, present only in the service of the act of liberation by American troops.

Ideologically loaded words such as *freedom* and *liberation* are ambiguous. They are also used in different contexts to signify rather divergent meanings. Rhetorical scholar and critic Michael McGee labels the terms *ideographs*, words generally perceived as having the same meaning for all people, but that are in fact used in certain rhetorical instances to evoke specific responses.[40] Those in power can redefine such words on a mass scale, using ideographs to include or exclude individuals or groups. The word *liberator* is significant insofar as it invokes historic imagery of American soldiers being greeted joyously by flower-throwing Italian and French citizens at the end of World War II. Materially, these ideographs are represented by powerful symbols such as the American flag, the Statue of Liberty, or by the toppling of Saddam Hussein's statue in Baghdad.

News in mass media is a social construct shaped by journalists and the organizations for which they work. Since neither journalists nor their news organizations operate in a vacuum, their work both reflects and shapes the societies and cultural contexts in which they operate. News production is a process shaped by a reporter's opinion and by the editorial policy of his or her particular news organization.

Sociologist Gaye Tuchman exposes the ideological and bureaucratic factors that play a shaping role in news manufacturing.[41] While a story must pass through the hands of journalists, editors, and managers before it is publicized, these stories are produced and framed by people with the same latent biases as anyone else. Framing is unique not to media but to human perception; it helps structure reality to make it manageable. Selection then is a necessary, indeed valuable, process. However, by framing an event one way or another, media also influence the way people think about an event and, later, remember it. Framing is a continuous process that begins with choosing which events to cover, selecting which pictures to take and how to take them, and then which ones to submit to senior editors. The process continues in the newsroom with decisions about which images to publish, in what size, and where to position them on the page or screen. Subjective and corporate realities, then, affect the final product, which reflects interpretations of an event. Thus, a news story or image is the bureaucratic and ideological result of both an organization and its members working in concert, ostensibly for the public good. Ideologically, news articulates what members of a society need to know, informing consumers who they are—and who they are not—as part of the collective. This need to know that is satisfied by news determines the frame and selects the content of the story.

This need to know also implies that viewers want the truth, want to learn about events as they really are, so news reporting conveys the message that objective truth is being presented. This impression is strategically achieved through certain routine techniques and procedures, such as putting verbatim statements in quotation marks and juxtaposing opposing ideas. These devices protect journalists from being criticized as subjective, thus lending them credibility. However, such procedures are in fact the result of selective perception, while simultaneously conveying the message that the facts speak for themselves.

Framing is inescapable, but it is used strategically. In framing, some aspects of a perceived reality are selected and made more salient, meaningful, and memorable for the audience.[41] What is excluded is as least as important as what is included, because the exclusions reinforce the inclusions by depriving the audience of information needed to forge alternative perspectives. Robert Entman suggests that a policy frame cascades from the administration downward and can, in a feedback loop, return to the top. The efficacy of such a policy frame in shaping press coverage depends on policy agreement among the elite. When there is disagreement among elite groups, there will be more dissent from and questioning of executive policy by the press. However, the war in Iraq had in 2003 a strong elite consensus, judging by the number of senators who voted to grant the president authority to declare war. A comparative study of media framing in television news broadcasts during preparations for the war in Iraq showed that the news coverage in Arab countries, Australia, Belgium, Bosnia, Canada, France, Germany, the Netherlands, the United Kingdom, and the United States was closely linked to the position of political elites and governments in each of these countries.[43] Despite freedom of the press, there is a solid relation between media framing and government positions.[44]

Professor of journalism Shahira Fahmy examined forty-three newspapers in thirty countries with regard to their visual representation of the event.[45] Most of the pictures that appeared in the United States belonged to what she calls a "victory frame," showing jubilant Iraqis jumping on a toppled statue, welcoming the soldiers as liberators. A victory frame selected narrative and visual information declaring that the United States won the war and that masses of Iraqis participated in the event.[46]

By contrast, the press in countries whose governments opposed the war used an "occupation frame." In accordance with the stance of the French government, Le Monde and Le Figaro were outspoken against the war. Arabic media used the occupation frame as well. In his article "Arab Media: Did It Cover the Same War?" Ahmed Gody, of the Modern Arts and Sciences University in Cairo, reports that the three Arabic satellite channels informed people about the other side of the "war of Iraqi freedom."[47] These Arab channels were not directly linked to Arabic governments and so differed from censored Arab daily newspapers, yet they covered the war in much the same way.[48] In the case of both newspapers and television, the fall of Baghdad, former capital of the Islamic caliphate, was not framed as the end of a dictatorship and the advent of democracy but as a momentous event, heralding yet another episode of Arab defeat and humiliation.

Irrespective of the frame chosen, the story within the frame is usually, if not always, dramatized. Anthropologists Elizabeth Bird and Robert Dardenne argue that news should be characterized as story rather than fact.[49] "In news making, journalists do not merely use culturally determined definitions; they also have to fit new situations into old definitions. It is in their power to place people and events into the existing categories of hero, villain, good and bad, and thus to invest their stories with the authority of mythological truth."[50] News is storytelling featuring "good guys" and "bad guys," conflict and uncertainty. News, like all human communication, may be framed as dramatic and morally binary. Film theorist Robert Stam concludes that the "fictive we" supports binary oppositions because "we" can speak warmly about "ourselves" and coldly about "them."[51] Sociologists Jeffrey Alexander and Ronald Jacobs point out that "media operate as a cultural space where actors and events become typified into more general codes (e.g. sacred/profane, pure/impure, democratic/antidemocratic, citizen/enemy) and more generic story forms which resonate with the society's culture."[52] Editorials in the twenty leading U.S. newspapers used the same binary oppositions as Bush did in his twenty national addresses between 9/11 and the subsequent invasion in 2003. Bush was depicted as the ideal protagonist and Saddam Hussein as the ideal antagonist. The media certainly did not invent the conflict, but they welcomed it and intensified its melodrama.

It is important to note that public memory of war, at least from the twentieth century onward, is created less from a directly remembered past than from an audiovisually manufactured past shaped by documentaries, feature films, television programs, and new media. Images are readily inscribed in collective memory out of a repository of stock images. Pictures of the Twin Towers in New York collapsing on September 11, 2001, immediately became iconic for those watching the catastrophe unfold on television screens around the globe, especially as they were repeated over and over again.

Iconic images are mixtures of actual events and stagecraft, even though they are believed to be definitive representations of political crises, motivating public action on behalf of democratic values.[53] Iconic images achieve a social status beyond their mere visual representation of fact, symbolizing whole historic themes. Once the association between a particular image such as the American flag and a value such as patriotism is created and internalized, the image becomes a symbol for the abstract value and can be used to trigger associated emotions.

Some images are routinely re-presented long past the time when they first emerged. People who did not witness history can engage in a replay of experience through the simulation of iconic photographs and other well-known images.[54] These images are then kept in circulation and used in conjunction with the grand narratives of official history. Their meaning and effects are likely to be established slowly, shifting with changes in context and use. Dana Cloud, a professor of communication studies, asserts that images are central to the constitution of meaning and should be considered as ideographs.[55] Images render the abstraction of an ideograph concrete. A visual ideograph is an even stronger inducement to national identification than its propositional counterpart. Images of the war in Iraq are based on a positive, Western self-identity and a projected negative identity of "the other." They are framed in terms of "our way of life" and perceived challenges to that way of life, thereby reducing a complex set of geopolitical motives, strategies, and outcomes to a clean, uncontested binary set.

Myanmar, September 2007

September 2007 saw shocking events unfold in Burmese society: Buddhist monks in the streets of Yangon with their begging bowls as usual, but refusing to accept any gifts.[56] Most important, they would accept no gifts from the government. Monks kept their alms bowls upside down in a ritual called *patta nikujjana kamma*, a strong act of protest made by the conservative Buddhist order (*sangha*) against the junta that has governed Myanmar for almost fifty years.[57] The government must have been horrified at the sight. *Patta nikujjana kamma* is, in their eyes, a brutal provocation. If the monks refuse to accept alms from the government, the act means that they also refuse to give their moral and spiritual consent or agree to support junta needs. Through almsgiving, government support of the *sangha* results in religious merit, which everyone needs, the junta included.[58] Suddenly, ritual refusal had turned the monasteries into a ritual battlefield.

Images of the protesting monks were broadcast around the globe, an event which is itself rare, since Western audiences seldom hear about Myanmar. For many years there have been worldwide protest movements against the Burmese junta, which is accused of violating human rights under a cruel, dictatorial rule.[59] Now, through images of the protesting monks, the global community focused directly on Myanmar. As soon as the monks were driven back into their monasteries, the laity took over, and the protest became severe and gruesome. The street became a ritual battlefield filled with symbolic gestures. Television news, and in 2008, *Burma VJ*, a documentary about the role of clandestine journalists,[60] showed young men approaching soldiers guarding the streets of Yangon, opening their shirts and baring their chests to the armed troops, inviting them to shoot. The soldiers could have done so, but they did not. Tellingly, these were almost the last public images of the escalating crisis. Shortly afterward, the Internet was closed and no more regular news data or broadcasts were allowed out of the country. Some rare images recorded on cell phones still made their way onto the Internet, but, by and large, the rest of the world was shut out shortly after the laypeople took over the protests. However, the protests continued. Although the trigger for the September uprising was the sudden rise of fuel prices, deeper reasons behind the protests were rooted in decades of frustration and suffering under the repressive junta.

Politics and Buddhist Animism

The monks' demonstration on the streets of Yangon, the *patta nikujjana kamma*, was not street theater but part of the canonical Buddhist ritual system.[61] Since its inception, the Buddhist order has been dependent on the laity, and the bonds between the ruler and the *sangha* have been very tight. Without monastic support the junta would lose its moral and spiritual ground, which is why the junta donates abundantly to the monasteries, individual members of the *sangha*, stupas, and temples, and Buddha images worshipped throughout the country. These practices are broadcast, and images of them are featured in magazines and newspapers. Large billboards are stationed in front of temples, showing members of the junta participating in or sponsoring the rituals performed there.[62]

While the cycle of donations and resulting merit is to be understood within the framework of orthodox Theravada Buddhist values, another parallel set of values seems to challenge the automatism that connects giving (*dana*) with religious merit (*punya*). Although Myanmar is a Theravada Buddhist country, it has long been deeply involved in what the Australian-Dutch anthropologist Barend Jan Terwiel calls "Buddhist animism," a synthesis of Buddhism with popular religious practices.[63] Not only average citizens but also Buddhist monks, the great kings of Myanmar, and the junta have been involved in these beliefs and rituals. The practices differ profoundly from place to place and from monastery to monastery, while the underlying principles remain similar. Even if the actual forms differ, everyone shares common assumptions and knows how the practices work. It is a given, for instance, that if a government rules unjustly, or practices unjust rituals, nature will lash out with disasters. For example, the government's gilding of the Shwe Dagon in 1999 stirred widespread dread: "The gilding of the spire was a high-risk ploy for an unpopular regime, an act permitted only to kings and legitimate rulers. When the two-ton, seven-tier finial was added and the spire was complete, the nation held its breath, waiting for the earth to send a signal of disapproval through lightning or thunder or floods, but nature remained indifferent."[64] The religious, social, and political importance of these rituals and their consequences—or lack thereof—can only be understood in the context of the dominant values and ritual codes.[65] Buddhist animism and Theravada Buddhism are part of the dominant culture not only because they are propagated by the government but also because almost everyone embraces them. For example, because the number 9 is the lucky number of the government, 8 is the lucky number of the opposition. Consequently, the revolt of 1988 was started on August 8, 1988, that is, 8/8/88.

White Elephants and Miraculously Appearing Buddhas

If Than Shwe, one of the central figures of the junta government, were asked what he considered the most significant events of the last few years, he could mention the protesting monks or Typhoon Nargis, but he would most likely point out three auspicious events at the dawn of the new millennium. In 2001 and 2002, three white elephants were found in the jungles of Arakan.[66] The first one, an eight-year-old male named Yaza Gaha Thiri Pissaya Gaza Yaza, meaning Glorious Elephant King, had such outstanding characteristics that he was anointed with gold, silver, and nine kinds of precious stones by General Khin Nyunt. A second white elephant, a nine-year-old female, appeared soon afterward and was named Rati Malar. The third, a twenty-six-year-old female named Theingi Malar, was found in Kainggyi Creek in Maungtaw Township. She arrived in Yangon on April 5, 2002.[67]

In Myanmar it is generally accepted that a white elephant found in one's kingdom is a rare, miraculous sign. All elephants caught in Myanmar belong to the government, but they are usually kept privately. Historically, however, a white elephant was offered directly to the government, and the person who offered the elephant was exempted from taxes.[68] Because a white elephant is considered a celestial animal, when one is discovered, well-being, riches, and proper rainfall are ensured.[69] Moreover, it is said that this celestial animal will only come down to earth if earth is a better place than heaven. According to one Burmese newspaper report:

> In Myanmar's history, only during the reign of just and virtuous kings was such a white elephant usually discovered, and the country prospered in peace and tranquility as a result. The emergence of the Royal Elephant at a time when Myanmar is striving towards building a peaceful modern state is obviously an omen for the emergence of a prosperous, peaceful and modern state. It is not known where the elephant will be kept, though it is certain the lucky albino will not be used in the jungles hauling timber.[70]

A white elephant is a powerful symbol not only in the world of Buddhist animism. In mainstream Buddhism, white elephants are also important, frequently appearing in connection with the Buddha. Before the Buddha Shakyamuni was born, his mother, Maya, dreamed of a white elephant. Indeed, there are stories about the Buddha himself living many of his former lives as a white elephant, excelling in profound wisdom and honesty.[71] Accordingly, everyone understands that the three white elephants that the junta owns are three signs from heaven signifying that Myanmar is on the right course.

The miracles did not end with the royal animals' arrival. In 2000 the Buddha appeared in the form of an enormous boulder of white jade found in a quarry where earlier Buddhas "have made themselves known," as the expression goes. Out of this boulder an enormous Buddha was carved and named Loka Chantha Abhayalabhamuni, "Moon to the World, the Wise Man Who Provides Freedom from all Danger." This image, which was enshrined in a glass case close to the small zoo where the elephants were now kept, is a seated Buddha with his right hand lifted in the Abhayamudra, the royal gesture for dispelling fear. A pamphlet distributed at the shrine in Yangon mentions how the stone was found in the quarry of Sakyin

Hill, in Madaya Township, in the Mandalay division of Upper Myanmar. While substantial boulders had been found in the quarry in the past, this one was the largest to date.

The image of 2000 thus fits into a long succession of discovered images. One such especially important miraculous image of Buddha from Arakan is said to have been made under the probably mythical king Candrasuriya. Today the image, called Mahamuni ("Great Sage") and venerated as the state spirit of Myanmar, is housed in the temple of Mandalay. Many kings tried to remove the image from its original site in Arakan to their own capital, because of the enduring notion that there is a strong connection between royalty and the Mahamuni; this particular image embodies both the state spirit and the sacred land of Myanmar.

In any case, the current ruling junta worships the Mahamuni, and the generals have themselves portrayed alongside the image. Large amounts of gold are given to the image, as are precious jewels and ointments during daily worship. Thus the junta shows itself worthy of ruling Myanmar by capitalizing on the interconnected symbols of state spirit, royalty, and sacred earth. Moreover, possession of the Mahamuni increases the power of one's position: "Its patronage by Burmese kings and the present government not only implied an analogy to its mythological patron, the Arakanese king Candrasuriya, but it also serves as a symbol of control over social groups. This fact explains why competition and patronage by policies over possession of this image—and others like it—was, on occasion, intensely contested."[72]

Not only is the military junta a Shinbyushin, an "owner of white elephants," but the Buddha has made himself known during this government's reign, effectively putting the junta on par with ancient kings such as Shuddhodana, the father of the Buddha, and with the ideal Buddhist monarch, Ashoka.[73] In sum, it appears as if the universe agrees with the policies of a government that represses its people, ignores election results, and imprisons opposition leaders or keeps them under house arrest. But if the universe agrees, not so the monks and laypeople, as their September 2007 protests show.

Media and Strategic Rituals: So Many Lucky Signs

In the world of Buddhist animism, the signs of nature are media, communicating how the natural order of the universe responds to the acts of individuals, groups, or the government. These signs derive their meaning from shared cultural values and a shared religious code. In the case of the wondrous Buddha and the white elephants, the profane and the religious are indistinguishable because of the culturally shared belief in a divine or semidivine kingship. The miraculous appearances are media, or signs, from another world, and both the junta and Burmese citizens agree on this interpretation. Parallels in Southeast Asian culture are manifold. The other world communicates with this world through mysterious beasts, sacred animals, and miraculous signs. This is one of the reasons they are so often depicted in shrines and temples, which are at the interface of this and another world.

The junta of Myanmar is so deeply involved with Buddhist animism, its good and bad signs, that no major decision is made without consulting astrologers or numerologists who know how to handle the signs of the time.[74] Another important aspect of this animism is the Junta's desire to possess powerful objects or people. Historically, governments, dynasties, and kings in Myanmar have focused on the possession of powerful objects in order to legitimize their government. Possession and control are achieved by donating gold to, and sponsoring rituals for, the stupas and the Mahamuni. Thus even the *sangha* is, in some respects, in the junta's possession because of its donations to the monasteries and members of the *sangha*. In this respect the present junta is actively imitating ancient Burmese regimes and establishing a connection between itself and ancient and just kings who did not seize objects but to whom powerful objects made themselves known.[75]

The cult of the Nats, local spirits, can help explain protesters' provocative behavior in the street riots of 2007. When King Anuwrahta (eleventh century C.E.) converted to Theravada Buddhism, he tried to wipe out the cult of the Nats, or local spirits, and their priests. Failing to do so, he allowed thirty-seven Nats to be worshipped, but under his strict control.[76] He imprisoned several of the images of the Nats as well as those of Hindu gods, in effect, possessing them. To this day, most Burmese, including many monks, are still deeply involved with Nats. Local Nats have limited powers, as they are restricted to certain regions or villages or to one particular house, but the main cult consists of the thirty-seven official Nats allowed by Anuwrahta. Nats can be helpful, but they can be dangerous as well, which is why they need to be propitiated or gratified by offerings. Above all, they need to be controlled, even suppressed; otherwise they can be quite violent and cause great misfortune. Such malevolence arises because many Nats originated from the spirits of people who were unjustly or violently killed, often as the victims of unjust rulers or kings who, threatened by the powers of these "future Nats," had them executed on a preemptive basis, ostensibly for everyone's benefit.[77] Even executions by just rulers can produce Nats, because violence changes a victim into a Nat. Dangerous Nats may, for instance, be born out of blood unjustly shed on the "golden earth," Suvannabhumi, of Myanmar.

Belief in Nats is widely accepted in Myanmar. For example, when Thibaw succeeded his father Mindon as the king of Mandalay in 1878, he and his paranoid wife Suppalayat and her equally suspicious mother had several hundred members of the royal family executed in the first years of his government. By stowing the victims in velvet sacks, then clubbing or drowning them so no blood would be spilled on

Burmese ground, the king ensured that no evil Nats could arise from the mass execution. This same idea of unjustly spilled blood may have been what motivated the young men to bare their chests to soldiers in 2007. While many protesters may have been shot afterward, shooting victims who offer themselves directly leads to great danger, since no one controls Nats that spring from spilled blood. Uncontrolled powerful objects, beings, or spirits are dangerous. Once a ruler or powerful person controls these entities, he can use their powers for his own good.

The Political Use of Symbols, Rituals, and Media

The donations of gold to monasteries, stupas, and the Mahamuni Buddha are strategic ritual acts performed to send an unequivocally clear message: the junta is directly in line with the ancient kings of Myanmar. When members of the junta have themselves photographed with white elephants or while sticking gold leaf on the Mahamuni image, these are strategic ritual gestures. So, too, the lavish expenditure for the marriage of Than Shwe's daughter. More money is said to have been spent on her tiara than on the entire health care of Myanmar for a year. This act too reinforces the junta's connection to ancient kings.

Lavish ritual gestures, indisputably understood in their cultural contexts, are clearly strategic, but they can be enacted by either party in a conflict. Buddhist monks' performing the *patta nikujjana kamma* and the young men baring their chests to the soldiers are counterrituals challenging those of the junta.

Not surprisingly, strategic messaging in Myanmar is managed by government control of official media. The only other voices come from outside the country or from the vehemently suppressed opposition, which in large part must work underground. Insofar as the junta decides what is admissible in the media, it also determines the standards for journalistic objectivity. Because the Burmese people share the same symbolic set of references as the junta, manipulative framing has serious consequences. If the junta is photographed with the elephants, while distributing alms to the *sangha*, or while donating gold for the Mahamuni image or for gilding a stupa, the Burmese people know what these rituals imply. The impact of these images is reinforced by the suppression of opposing images.

In addition to owning three white elephants and an enormous Buddha image, and exercising power over the Buddhist *sangha* through donations flowing to monks, stupas, pagodas, and Mahamuni, the junta enjoys a new seat of power, now that, like the kings of Konbaungset dynasty, the government has changed the location of the capital.[78] However, this idealized picture representing the junta in the media was tarnished in September 2007 when the images of religious and lay protesters were aired by international media. Soon the Internet was closed and hardly any news of what was happening inside Myanmar reached the outside world.

Myanmar virtually disappeared from international news, not because the world lost interest but because all access to information was blocked. News only came out through Sri Lanka and Thailand.

Myanmar returned to international news when the country was struck by Cyclone Nargis, which slammed southern Myanmar on May 2, 2008. As many as 150,000 people are thought to have died or disappeared. The number cannot be checked, however, because of media restrictions.[79] The junta refused any help from outside and only later reluctantly accepted some degree of foreign aid. Relief organizations reported that matters soon deteriorated, becoming even more horrifying as the government used violence to drive people back to the flooded areas without shelter or food with no hope of relief. Once more news was blocked. How the Burmese authorities accounted for the devastating cyclone is anyone's guess, since the West has no direct access to the country's media reports. Nothing has yet been published on the event, but likely explanations can be inferred on the basis of the worldview of Buddhist animists. Nargis with its devastating effects might have been interpreted as nature's response to the people of Myanmar's opposition to just and righteous government. This would be the junta's most likely stance. Another explanation for why the cyclone struck the country with such force could be that nature was avenging the folly of astrologers, who miscalculated the date chosen for the transfer of the new capital.[80] We will only know in hindsight the place Nargis is given in official and unofficial Burmese histories.

Surrounded as the Burmese people are by an abundance of lucky signs that seem to justify the ruling government and their own suffering caused by junta policies, their ambiguous fate may be best expressed by the following Burmese story. When the white jade boulder in the shape of the Buddha Loka Chantha Abhayalabhamuni was transported by river to Yangon, people gathered along the riverbank and lamented, "Lord Buddha, can't you do anything? Can't you see what they are doing to us?" The Buddha, bound as he was with strong ropes, replied through a spirit medium, "Can't you see what they are doing to me?"

White Elephants and Tumbling Statues

Investigating the interplay of rituals and media representations in shaping the perception of two very different conflicts, we conclude that rituals are both a means of exclusion and a way of creating social cohesion.[81] Staging and telecasting the toppling of Saddam Hussein's statue in Baghdad was aimed at uniting an American audience in believing that the capital had fallen, thus ending the war and liberating the Iraqi people. Momentarily, those opposed to the U.S.-led invasion were effectively silenced and excluded. This power to exclude is even more apparent in

Myanmar, where opposition forces are denied access to the media altogether. In times of war, there is a sharp rise in rhetorical and visual binary oppositions. In the 2007 Myanmar uprising, only one position was visible, since nongovernment media were prohibited from beaming images of the street protests around the world. Setting up binary oppositions in the Burmese press was not necessary, since the existence of opposition was simply denied. Meanwhile, the junta's legitimacy is continuously renewed and served by the country's media, which continuously report on the white elephants, the wondrous Buddha, and the junta's donations to religious institutions.

What is striking in the Iraq case is that, despite freedom of the press in the West, mainline media in the United States and Europe propagated their respective governments' positions on the war. The implication is a disturbing conclusion: Regardless of whether a political system is democratic or despotic, in times of crisis the dominant discourse is ritualized and broadcast by a country's mainline media and, consequently, embraced by the majority of the population.

Both case studies illustrate how key ritual images are disseminated through mass media. However, their meanings and messages depend on the beholder, which is the reason why, ideally, a targeted audience shares the same cultural code as those who propagate the images. This sharing is clearly the case in Myanmar, where the daily lives of both the members of the junta and the people are deeply embedded in cultural practices of Theravada Buddhism and Buddhist animism. There is no question, in other words, that the Burmese recognize that inverting alms bowls means the monks refuse to grant the junta access to religious merit; that exposing one's bared chest to armed soldiers is the equivalent of threatening to become a powerful, dangerous spirit or Nat; or that white elephants and images of the Buddha only become manifest if the government is ruling in a just manner.

If rituals are embedded in an international context—rituals such as planting flags and toppling statues—the messages they transmit are evaluated differently according to the dominant cultural code of the various audiences. Thus, wrapping an American flag around Saddam's statue may have signified the liberation of Iraq to a U.S. audience, while simultaneously dramatizing defeat, humiliation, and Western occupation to audiences in Arab-speaking countries.

In both case studies, the media play notably different roles. The war in Iraq was from the start a media affair, with American public opinion about the war shaped mainly through the country's dominant mass media. In Myanmar, mass media are less important than traditional ritual objects—wondrous Buddhas, white elephants—that function as the primary media for carrying cultural messages. In Myanmar's culture, a white elephant is itself a mass medium insofar as it is displayed wherever the ruler goes.

Yet both cases are similar with respect to the importance of media ownership.[82] Those who possess power over mass media in the United States shape public opinion, just as the ritual objects in Myanmar work in favor of those who possess them. Those with the power to shape the representation of a ritual also, in effect, own the ritual and thus control the version of the event that is repeated and inscribed in public memory.[83] Rituals are not only bearers of meaning but also commodities serving their owners' purposes.

News reporting is a social construct, and so are rituals, yet both are considered reliable. News is considered reliable because of its imputed objectivity. Ritual is reliable because of its imputed longevity or sacrality. Both are grounded in a social agreement that their messages are true, beyond strategic manipulation, but, as we have shown, this assumption is itself untrue.

Even though competition for ritual ownership is a power struggle, the outcome of such struggles is never simply predetermined. Although tearing down Saddam's statue in Baghdad was most likely staged and therefore "on message," the incident with the flag was not staged, and it was this infelicitous act that opened the door to widely diverging perspectives on the same events.[84] Even though very few pictures of the protesters in Myanmar were broadcast internationally, because these pictures were rare, they had enormous impact on international public perception. One powerful difference between the two conflicts remains: critical self-reflection about the role that dominant American news agencies played in covering—and failing to cover—the Iraq war has since emerged in the media, while in Myanmar, critical local discourse is not reported in the news but couched in the tale of the fettered Buddha being carried to Yangon against his will.

NOTES

1. See, for example, Philip Elliot, "Media Performances as Political Rituals," *Communication* 7 (1982): 115–130, who claims that ritual behavior marks membership in group or community. Gerry Phillipsen, "Ritual as a Heuristic Device in Studies of Organizational Discourse," *Communication Yearbook* 16 (1993): 104–111, defines ritual as a form for enacting and expressing a participant's close identification with the symbolic code of a group.

2. Emile Durkheim, *The Elementary Forms of Religious Life* (New York: Free Press, 1965), 427.

3. For Kenneth Burke, society is best studied through the symbolic content of culture. He would require an analysis not only of the linguistic framework but also of ceremonies and rituals. The drama of human beings, in conflict with selves or others, has its origin in rituals. Ritualization, through common language and common ceremony, provides the way in which the social order maintains and controls the hierarchy both of structure and of language. Kenneth Burke, *The Philosophy of Literary Form*, 3rd ed. (Berkeley: University of California Press, 1973 [1941]).

4. See also Adam B. Seligman, Robert P. Weller, Michael J. Pruett, and Bennett Simon, *Ritual and Its Consequences: An Essay on the Limits of Sincerity* (New York: Oxford University Press, 2008), 84.

5. See Philip Smith, "Codes and Conflict: Toward a Theory of War as Ritual," *Theory and Society* 20, no. 1 (1991): 103–138.

6. In the initial stages of the conflict there was sympathy with English football hooligans insulting Argentine players. Smith quotes an editorial in the *Times* (April 5, 1982): "Emotion is no sound basis for successful thinking.... [T]here must be no nonsense of burning effigies, irrelevant spite or public hysteria. The aim of all strategy is to fulfill clearly-stated political objectives by making the best of the recourses available. At the heart of the strategy is the art of applying forces so that it makes the most effective contribution towards achievement of the political objective." Another example is an article in the *Observer* (May 23, 1982) from the archbishop of Canterbury: "Christians have the responsibility to urge that the force deployed must be clearly subservient and proportionate to clearly defined and morally justifiable political objectives. It is a moral, not just a political duty. To count the cost of every stage." Smith, "Codes and Conflict," 117.

7. Philip Smith, *Why War: The Cultural Logic of Iraq, the Gulf War and Suez* (Chicago: University of Chicago Press, 2005) examines the justification of military action in these conflicts. Each nation, Smith argues, makes use of binary codes, good and evil, sacred and profane, rational and irrational.

8. One shortcoming of Philip Smith's approach is that, while he uses written sources to illustrate his position, he does not work out the role of the mass media.

9. Many researchers gave evidence of this. See David Miller, *Media at War: The Iraq Crisis* (London: Pluto, 2004); Justin Lewis, Rod Brookes, Nick Mosdell, and Terry Threadgold, *Shoot First and Ask Questions Later: Media Coverage of the 2003 Iraq War* (New York: Lang, 2006); and Sean Aday, John Cluverius, and Steven Livingstone, "As Goes the Statue, So Goes the War: The Emergence of the Victory Frame in Television Coverage of the Iraq War," *Journal of Broadcasting and Electronic Media* 49, no. 3 (2005): 314–331.

10. Seventy percent of Americans polled reported relying on cable news as their main source of information about the conflict. Sixty-seven percent of the Fox viewers thought evidence of a clear Iraq–Al Quaeda link existed, and 48 percent of CNN viewers held that belief. See Steven Kull, Clay Ramsey, and Evan Lewis, "Misperceptions, the Media and the Iraq War," *Political Science Quarterly* 118, no. 4 (2003–2004): 586.

11. Aday et al., "As Goes the Statue, So Goes the War," report on the American networks and the toppling of Saddam's statue.

12. Aday et al., "As Goes the Statue, So Goes the War," 321.

13. Moreover, dissenting voices were silenced. Lindsey Hilsum, the Baghdad correspondent for the United Kingdom's Channel 4, who was present during the toppling of the statue, felt its significance was limited. Her editors, however, overrode her judgment. According to Hilsum, "The statue was a tiny little thing that happened at the end.... We saw what happened, and it was an American tank recovery vehicle which pulled it down. A few Iraqis went up to get it down, and then it was the Americans who got it down, with a small crowd of Iraqis and a large crowd of journalists around it. It doesn't mean that the Iraqis weren't happy or pleased that it happened, but we took it as a small symbolic event

for American television.... We did a long piece that day, maybe nine minutes, and initially the statue was the last four or five shots.... But then, interestingly, in London, where they had been watching, they said, 'No, you have to make that section much larger.' And so ... that section of the report became longer, which was fine.... But what one has to understand is that this is what the Americans did for symbolic effect.... There were a lot more interesting things that we saw that day." Lewis et al., *Shoot First and Ask Questions Later*, 103.

14. Deborah Lynn Jaramillo, "Ugly War, Pretty Package: How the Cable News Network and the Fox News Channel Made the 2003 Invasion of Iraq High Concept" (PhD diss., University of Texas, 2006).

15. Jaramillo, "Ugly War, Pretty Package," 143.

16. Jaramillo, "Ugly War, Pretty Package," 144.

17. Mohamed Zayanai and Muhammad I. Ayish, "Arab Satellite Television and Crisis Reporting: Covering the Fall of Baghdad," *International Communication Gazette* 68 (2006): 473.

18. Ahmed El Gody, "Arab Media: Did It Cover the Same War." In *Global War— Local News: Media Images of the Iraq War*, ed. Stig A. Nohrstedt and Rune Ottosen (Göteborg: Nordicom, 2005), 182–183.

19. Qatar-based Al-Jazeera is the leading television news agency in the region.

20. Hussein Amin, "Watching the War in the Arab World," *Transnational Broadcasting Studies Journal* (Spring–Summer 2003), http://www.tbsjournal.com/Archives/Spring03/amin.html.

21. Justin Lewis examined the coverage on British television and concluded that the toppling of Saddam statue received more coverage on British television than every other event on April 9: twenty-three times on the five main evening news programs (BBC1, five times; ITV, five times; Channel 4, seven times; Sky, three times; BBC2, two times). The significance of the image was straightforward. It showed the liberated Iraqis "doing it for themselves with a little help from their American friends." Justin Lewis, "Television, Public Opinion and the War in Iraq: The Case of Britain," in *International Journal of Public Opinion Research* 16, no. 3 (2006): 306.

22. Aday et al., "As Goes the Statue, So Goes the War," 322.

23. Images of the toppling of Saddam Hussein's statue also suggested that the war was over, which, for a time at least, was the dominant theme in American news coverage of Iraq.

24. Lewis et al., *Shoot First and Ask Questions Later*, 152.

25. Jim Garamone, "'A Good Day' Rumsfeld Says, 'but More to Do in Iraq,'" American Forces Press Service, April 9, 2003, http://www.defenselink.mil/news/newsarticle.aspx?id=29134.

26. "President Bush Addresses United Nations General Assembly." Office of the Press Secretary, The White House, September 23, 2003, http://georgewbush-whitehouse.archives.gov/news/releases/2001/09/20010920-8.html. Two years later, on April 9, 2005, in his speech to the soldiers of Fort Hood, President Bush commemorated the toppling: "For millions of Iraqis and Americans, it is a day they will never forget. The toppling of Saddam Hussein's statue in Baghdad will be recorded, alongside the fall of the Berlin Wall, as one of the great

moments in the history of liberty." http://georgewbush-whitehouse.archives.gov/news/releases/2005/04/20050412.html.

27. This article is based on Gregory Fontenont, E. J. Degen, and David Tohn, *On Point: The United States Army in Operation Iraqi Freedom*, Center for Army Lessons Learned (May 2004), http://www.globalsecurity.org/military/library/report/2004/onpoint/.

28. PSYOP is part of the Department of Defense whose aim is to alter the behavior of the enemy using psychological means, a means also used in manipulating public opinion.

29. Some researchers even suspect that the Iraqi crowd on the square was not comprised of local citizens but of members of an exiled Iraqi militia flown into Baghdad by U.S. forces.

30. Fontenont et al., *On Point*, chapter 6. Staff Sergeant Brian Plesich, team leader, Tactical Psychological Operations Team 1153, 305th Psychological Operations Company, interviewed by Lieutenant Cononel Dennis Cahil, May 31, 2003.

31. Matthew Engel, "War on Afghanistan: American Media Cowed by Patriotic Fever, Says Network News Veteran," *The Guardian*, May 17, 2002, p. 4.

32. Daniel Okrent, "The Public Editor: Weapons of Mass Destruction? Or Mass Distraction?" *New York Times*, May 30, 2004, Week in Review.

33. Okrent, "The Public Editor."

34. Philip Kennicott, "Waiting for a Clear Picture to Emerge: After Two Years the View from Iraq," *Washington Post*, March 20, 2005, p. D1.

35. Carolyn Marvin and David W. Ingle, "Blood Sacrifice and the Nation: Revisiting Civil Religion," *Journal of the American Academy of Religion* 44, no. 4 (1996): 767–780.

36. George W. Bush, "Address to a Joint Session of Congress and the American People," Office of the Press Secretary, The White House, September 20, 2001, http://georgewbush-whitehouse.archives.gov/news/releases/2001/09/20010920-8.html.

37. George W. Bush, "President Bush Delivers Graduation Speech at West Point," Office of the Press Secretary, The White House, June 1, 2002, http://georgewbush-whitehouse.archives.gov/news/releases/2002/06/20020601-3.html.

38. George W. Bush, "State of the Union," Office of the Press Secretary, The White House, January 28, 2003, http://georgewbush-whitehouse.archives.gov/news/releases/2003/01/20030128-19.html.

39. By September 2003, 70 percent of Americans believed Saddam Hussein had been personally involved in the September 11 attacks. "Bush Rejects Saddam 9/11 Link," BBC News, September 18, 2003, http://news.bbc.co.uk/2/hi/americas/3118262.stm.

40. Michael Calvin McGee, "The 'Ideograph': A Link between Rhetoric and Ideology," *Quarterly Journal of Speech* 66, no. 1 (1980): 1–16.

41. Gaye Tuchman, "Objectivity as Strategic Ritual: An Examination of Newsmen's Notions of Objectivity," *American Journal of Sociology* 77, no. 4 (1972): 660–679.

42. Robert Entman, "Framing: Towards Clarification of a Fractured Paradigm," *Journal of Communication* 43, no. 4 (1993): 51–58.

43. Dietlind Stolle and Marc Hooghe, "Chronicle of a War Foretold: A Comparative Study of Media Framing in Television News Broadcasts in Preparation to the War in Iraq (March 2003)," paper presented at Political Communication Conference on International Communication and Conflict, Washington, DC, August 2005.

44. This holds true for pro-war and antiwar stances. In France the media, government, and public opinion were united in remaining outspoken against the war.

45. Shahira Fahmy, "They Took It Down: Exploring Determinants of Visual Reporting in the Toppling of the Saddam Statue in National and International Newspapers," *Mass Communication and Society* 10, no. 2 (2007): 143–170.

46. Aday et al., "As Goes the Statue, So Goes the War."

47. El Gody, "Arab Media," 165–186.

48. See Zayani and Ayish, "Arab Satellite Television and Crisis Reporting," 475.

49. S. Elizabeth Bird and Robert W. Dardenne, "Myth, Chronicle, and Story: Exploring the Narrative Qualities of News," in *Media, Myths and Narratives*, ed. James W. Carey (Newbury Park: Sage, 1988), 67–87.

50. Bird and Dardenne, "Myth, Chronicle, and Story," 80.

51. Robert Stam, "Television News and Its Spectator," in *Regarding Television, Critical Approaches: An Anthology*, ed. Ann Kaplan (Frederick, MD: University Publications of America, 1983), 39.

52. Jeffrey Alexander and Ronald Jacobs, "Mass Communication, Ritual and Civil Society," in *Media Ritual and Identity*, ed. T. Liebes and J. Curran (London: Routledge, 1998), 28.

53. Robert Hariman and John Louis Lucaites, "Public Identity and Collective Memory in U.S. Iconic Photography: The Image of 'Accidental Napalm,'" *Critical Studies in Media Communication* 20, no. 1 (2003): 35–66.

54. Hariman and Lucaites give an example: "the iconic photograph of an injured naked girl running from napalm attack provides a complex construction of the horror of the Vietnam war at that moment and conventions of liberal individualism such as personal autonomy and human rights that have become increasingly dominant within the public culture since then. These images become justification, proof of what we want them to become. That's the nature of iconic images." Hariman and Lucaites, "Public Identity and Collective Memory in U.S. Iconic Photography," 62–63.

55. Dana L. Cloud, "'To Veil the Threat of Terror': Afghan Women and the 'Clash of Civilizations' in the Imagery of the U.S. War on Terrorism," *Quarterly Journal of Speech* 90, no. 3 (2004): 285–306.

56. Doing research on the recent developments in Myanmar is a complicated matter. Myanmar is quite secluded from the outside world, having been governed for fifty years by a military junta. Although tourists can easily visit the country, doing research is tricky business. There is not only the risk of problems with the That Madaw, the army, there is also the risk of endangering those with whom one has been in contact. For this reason in some cases it is not possible to give exact dates of meetings and conversations that have transpired over the last ten years. Much of the information in this case study came to the West through Burmese monks studying in Sri Lanka and Thailand, countries from which normal contact through e-mail is possible. Because of this situation, I (Paul van der Velde) have sometimes had to speculate about what is going on or how to interpret facts. After the uprising of September 2007 and again after Typhoon Nargis struck, hardly any news came out of the country. Even today, contact about anything other than tourism is risky and complicated. My interpretation of the reactions of the junta is particularly speculative, a

fact that, at present, cannot be changed. I hope that one day the situation will change for the wonderful people of Myanmar, so their lives will improve and their marvelous culture will be accessible not only for researchers but also for the people of Myanmar themselves. Recently a longer study on this subject was published in Dutch: Paul van der Velde, "Generals en witte olifanten—voortekens en politiek in Zuidoost Azië," *Acta Comparanda* 20 (2009): 75–99. For a recent study of Burmese politics from a journalistic point of view, see Hans Hulst, *In de schaduw van de generals, hoop en wanhoop in Birma* (Amsterdam: Meulenhoff, 2008). For a comic book on life under the junta in present-day Maynmar written from a Canadian resident's point of view, see Guy Delise, *Chronique Birmanes* (Paris: Delcourt, 2007), in English: *Burma Chronicles* (Paris: Delcourt, 2007).

57. Myanmar's recent history consists mainly of constant interaction between the military junta and the opposition. Examples of the repressive politics of the junta are manifold. To name just a few: The renowned 888 uprising of August 8, 1988, ended in bloodshed. The elections of 1990, won by Aung San Suu Kyi's National League for Democracy Party, were simply denied. Many opposition leaders were imprisoned and Aung San Suu Kyi lives in confinement to this day. In March 2009, an American citizen swam across Inye Lake to her house, which resulted in her imprisonment by the junta. For the recent history of Myanmar, see Thant Myint-U, *The Making of Modern Burma* (New York: Cambridge University Press, 2001); see also Thant Myint-U, *The River of Lost Footsteps: A Personal History of Burma* (London: Faber and Faber, 2007); Roger Kershaw, *Monarchy in South-East Asia: The Faces of Traditions in Transition* (London: Routledge, 2001).

58. See Ellison Banks Findly, *Dāna: Giving and Getting in Pāli Buddhism*. Delhi: Motlial Banarsidass, 2003.

59. In November 2008, even the elderly comic Zarganar, who is exceedingly popular in Myanmar, was arrested and imprisoned for forty-five years just for making a few jokes about the government.

60. Anders Ostergaard, dir., *Burma VJ* (84 min., DVD, color, Denmark, First Hand Films, 2008).

61. This measure, which is available to members of the Buddhist order, is mentioned in the Pāli canon; see Oliver Freiberger, "Zur Interpretation der Brahmadanda-Strafe im buddhistischen Ordensrecht," *Zeitschrift der Deutschen Morgenländischen Gesellschaft* 146 (1996): 456–491.

62. The prominent newspapers in Myanmar, such as *Burma Daily, Democratic Voice of Burma, Myanmar News, Myanmar Times,* and *The New Light of Myanmar,* are state controlled. Access to the Internet is limited and extremely expensive for Burmese. The situation is sometimes different for foreigners who stay there. In the larger hotels, CNN can be found among the channels, but in December 2007 the screen turned black when an announcement was made on news coverage from Myanmar.

63. Barend Jan Terwiel introduces this term in his study *Boeddhisme in de praktijk* (Amsterdam: van Gorcum, 1977). For further studies on Buddhist animism, see Niels Mulder, *Everyday Life in Thailand* (Bangkok: Duong Kamol, 1979); see also Niels Mulder, *Inside Thai Society: Religion, Everyday Life, Change* (Bangkok: Duong Kamol, 1994); and Marlane Guelden, *Thailand: Into the Spirit World* (Singapore: Times Editions, 1995).

64. Ingrid Jordt in an interview by Seth Mydans in the *New York Times*, Week In Review, September 30, 2007; see http://www.nytimes.com/2007/09/30weekinreview/3mydans.html.

65. For an introduction on how Buddhism works in Myanmar, see Heinz Bechert, "To Be a Burmese Is to Be a Buddhist," in *The World of Buddhism*, ed. Heinz Bechert and Richard Gombrich, 147–159 (London: Thames and Hudson, 1984).

66. There are several criteria for recognizing a white elephant. One of the more paradoxical aspects is that they are not always white, nor is the white elephant the rarest of pachyderms.

67. All three have characteristics specific to white elephants. The list of characteristics is cited in a small folder, which is available from the zoo where the elephants are presently kept. The zoo is located near the airport in Yangon, close to the Ramada Hotel, and it is named the Near the New Pagoda Soo.

68. Shway Yoe (Sir J. G. Scott), *The Burman: His Life and Notions* (London: Macmillan, 1882), 486, 585.

69. The celestial nature of this exceptional animal can be seen in the fact that Indra, king of the gods, rides on Airavata, a white elephant.

70. "White Elephant Found, Good Omen for Myanmar: Newspapers," *Asian Economic News*, November 12, 2001, published by Kyodo News International, Yangon, http://findarticles.com/p/articles/mi_m0WDP/is_2001_Nov_12/ai_80881994.

71. See the complete Jataka collection published by E. W. Cowell, *Jataka or the Stories of the Buddha's Former Births*, trans. H. T. Francis (New Delhi/Madras: Asian Educational Services, 2002 [first published Cambridge, 1897]), 7 volumes. For accounts of Buddha's birth as a white elephant, see, for example, the Chaddantajataka: Jataka 514, H. T. Francis, 1905/2002, *Jataka or the Stories of the Buddha's Former Births*, part 5: 20–31; and the Matrposhakajataka, Jataka 455, W. D. House, 1905/2002, *Jataka, or the stories of the Buddha's Former Births*, part 4: 58–61.

72. Juliane Schober, *Sacred Biography in the Traditions of South and Southeast Asia*, 2nd ed. (Delhi: Motilal Banarsidas, 1997), 280.

73. In biographies of the Buddha, it is often stated that Shuddhodana's government was so just that the Bodhisattva preferred to live on earth instead of in the Tushita heaven and so came down to earth to teach the Dharma. This is found, for instance, in the Saundarananda of Ashvaghosha, chapter 2; see Paul van der Velde, *Nanda de Mooiste, Ashvaghosha's Saundarananda* (Rotterdam: Asoka, 2007), 127–135.

74. For example, Ne Win (1911/12–December 2002), former main general in the junta government, who had his private astrologer, Aung Pwint Khaung, at hand, changed all banknotes in Myanmar in 1987, since nine was his lucky number. Officially it was stated that this change was made to fight illegal practices and gambling; however, the main reason seems to have been the personal preference of Ne Win for the number nine. Moreover, the year in which the giant boulder of the Loka Chantha Abhayalabhamuni was found is 1362 in the Burmese era. This is considered an excellent number in that the year coincides with the year 2000 C.E., commencement of the new millennium.

75. For example, King Anuwrahta of eleventh-century Pagan had been converted to the Theravada Buddhism of Sri Lanka by a Mon monk named Shin Arahan. He then

requested that King Manuha, of the Mon capital of Thaton, hand over one of the thirty-two Pali canons that were kept in Thaton. When Manuha refused, Anuwrahta attacked the city in 1057 C.E. and had all thirty-two Pali Tipatakas transferred to his city, Pagan, on thirty-two white elephants. Manuha and his wife Mingaladevi were then taken into Anuwrahta's possession as prisoners. The relics of the Buddha that had been kept in the stupas of Thaton also "made themselves known" to Anuwrahta, spontaneously coming out of the stupas, as is proudly recalled by local Pagan monks to this day. Anuwrahta is also said to have owned a magical spear that had belonged to Ashvatthaman, one of the heroes of the *Mahabharata*. Thus the king had several magical, powerful objects that legitimized his rule and his state rituals.

76. For their legends and stories, see Maung Htin Aung, *Folk Elements in Burmese Buddhism* (Rangoon: Buddhist Sasana Council Press, 1959), 83–113.

77. There are traditional stories, for instance, that human sacrifices were made for the sake of large, official buildings in Southeast Asia in general. The victims were often buried alive, or after a violent death resulting from torture, beneath the building's foundation. As long as the body remains there, the owner or inhabitant of the building has power over this person, who can be ordered to protect the premises. For instance, some fifty-two people were allegedly buried alive beneath the walls of the city of Mandalay. Some traditions say that fifty bodies were buried underneath the throne hall of King Mindon in Mandalay, where the famous Lion Throne was installed. There are also many stories from the past that relate how kings executed powerful persons to have them thus installed as Nats or protectors. See Aung, *Folk Elements in Burmese Buddhism*.

78. In 2005 the capital was shifted from Yangon to the new city of Naypidaw, also named Pyinmana. This moving of the capital follows the example of the ancient kings of the Konbaugset dynasty, which ruled central Myanmar from 1752 to 1885. They moved their capital with virtually every coronation. In 2005 all ministries and other government-related institutions were relocated to Naypidaw, officially, it is said, because the city is more centrally located. Among themselves, however, the Burmese are reminded of the mass migrations ordered by the kings of old. Control was in those days a key issue behind these movements, and, according to many Burmese, little has changed. Naypidaw means "seat of kings" and, indeed, enormous statues of three important kings of the past have been erected there. Notably, they are the three greatest kings of the three most important dynasties to have ruled Myanmar. Needless to say, the ritual transfer of the capital was made on an astrologically auspicious day, November 6, 2005, at 6:37 A.M.

79. See "Cyclone Nargis, Wikipedia, http://en.wikipedia.org/wiki/Cyclone_Nargis; Adiële Klompmaker, "Cycloon Nargis vernietigend," Kennislink.nl, http://www.kennislink.nl/publicaties/cycloon-nargis-vernietigend; and "Birma getroffen door cycloon Nargis," NRC Handelsblad, http://www.nrc.nl/buitenland/article1891547.ece/Birma_getroffen_door_cycloon_Nargis. No source says how this estimation was made.

80. Paul van der Velde heard remarks of this kind in Myanmar in January 2005.

81. See Victor Turner, *Dramas, Fields, and Metaphors: Symbolic Action in Human Society* (Ithaca, NY: Cornell University Press, 1974).

82. On the ownership of rituals, see Simon Harrison, "Ritual as Intellectual Property," *Man* n.s., 27, no. 2 (1992): 225–244; see also Ute Hüsken, "Contested Ritual Property:

Conflicts over Correct Ritual Procedures in a South Indian Viṣṇu Temple," in *When Rituals Go Wrong: Mistakes, Failure, and the Dynamics of Ritual*, ed. Ute Hüsken (Leiden: Brill, 2007), 273–290.

83. See Leo Howe, "Risk, Ritual and Performance," *Journal of the Royal Anthropological Institute* 6, no. 1 (2000): 63–79.

84. See Ronald L. Grimes, "Infelicitous Performances and Ritual Criticism," *Semeia* 43 (1988): 103–122. On ritual infelicity see Ute Hüsken, "Ritual Dynamics and Ritual Failure," in *When Rituals Go Wrong: Mistakes, Failure, and the Dynamics of Ritual*, ed. Ute Hüsken (Leiden: Brill, 2007), 337–366.

REFERENCES

Aday, Sean, John Cluverius, and Steven Livingstone. "As Goes the Statue, So Goes the War: The Emergence of the Victory Frame in Television Coverage of the Iraq War." *Journal of Broadcasting and Electronic Media* 49, no. 3 (2005): 314–331.

Alexander, Jeffrey, and Ronald Jacobs. "Mass Communication, Ritual and Civil Society." In *Media Ritual and Identity*, edited by T. Liebes and J. Curran, 23–41. London: Routledge, 1998.

Amin, Hussein. "Watching the War in the Arab World." *Transnational Broadcasting Studies Journal* (Spring–Summer 2003), http://www.tbsjournal.com/Archives/Spring03/amin.html.

Aung, Maung Htin. *Folk Elements in Burmese Buddhism*. Rangoon: Buddhist Sasana Council Press, 1959.

Bechert, Heinz. "To Be a Burmese Is to Be a Buddhist." In *The World of Buddhism*, edited by Heinz Bechert and Richard Gombrich, 147–159. London: Thames and Hudson, 1984.

Bird, S. Elizabeth, and Robert W. Dardenne. "Myth, Chronicle, and Story: Exploring the Narrative Qualities of News." In *Media, Myths and Narratives*, edited by James W. Carey, 67–87. Newbury Park, CA: Sage, 1988.

Burke, Kenneth. *The Philosophy of Literary Form*, 3rd ed. Berkeley: University of California Press, 1973 [1941].

Bush, George W. "Address to a Joint Session of Congress and the American People." Office of the Press Secretary, The White House, September 20, 2001, http://georgewbush-whitehouse.archives.gov/news/releases/2001/09/20010920-8.html.

———. "President Bush Addresses United Nations General Assembly." Office of the Press Secretary, The White House, September 23, 2003,http://georgewbush-whitehouse.archives.gov/news/releases/2003/09/20030923-4.html.

———. "President Bush Delivers Graduation Speech at West Point." Office of the Press Secretary, The White House, June 1, 2002, http://georgewbush-whitehouse.archives.gov/news/releases/2002/06/20020601-3.html.

———. "State of the Union." Office of the Press Secretary, The White House, January 28, 2003, http://georgewbush-whitehouse.archives.gov/news/releases/2003/01/20030128-19.html.

"Bush Rejects Saddam 9/11 Link." BBC News, September 18, 2003, http://news.bbc.co.uk/2/hi/americas/3118262.stm.

Cloud, Dana L. "To Veil the Threat of Terror: Afghan Women and the 'Clash of Civilizations' in the Imagery of the U.S. War on Terrorism." *Quarterly Journal of Speech* 90, no. 3 (2004): 285–306.

Cowell, E. W. *Jataka or the Stories of the Buddha's Former Births.* Translated by H. T. Francis. New Delhi/Madras: Asian Educational Services, 2002 [1905].

Delise, Guy. *Chronique Birmanes.* Paris: Delcourt, 2007 (in English: *Burma Chronicles*, Paris: Delcourt, 2007).

Durkheim, Emile. *The Elementary Forms of Religious Life.* New York: Free Press, 1965.

Elliot, Philip. "Media Performances as Political Rituals." *Communication* 7 (1982): 115–130.

Engel, Matthew. "War on Afghanistan: American Media Cowed by Patriotic Fever, Says Network News Veteran." *The Guardian*, May 17, 2002.

Entman, Robert. "Framing: Towards Clarification of a Fractured Paradigm." *Journal of Communication* 43, no. 4 (1993): 51–58.

Fahmy, Shahira. "They Took It Down: Exploring Determinants of Visual Reporting in the Toppling of the Saddam Statue in National and International Newspapers." *Mass Communication and Society* 10, no. 2 (2007): 143–170.

Findly, Ellison Banks. *Dāna: Giving and Getting in Pāli Buddhism.* Delhi: Motlial Banarsidass, 2003.

Fontenont, Gregory, E. J. Degen, and David Tohn. *On Point: The United States Army in Operation Iraqi Freedom.* Center for Army Lessons Learned, May 2004, http://www.globalsecurity.org/military/library/report/2004/onpoint/.

Freiberger, Oliver. "Zur Interpretation der Brahmadanda-Strafe im buddhistischen Ordensrecht." *Zeitschrift der Deutschen Morgenländischen Gesellschaft* 146 (1996): 456–491.

Garamone, Jim. "'A Good Day' Rumsfeld Says, 'but More to Do in Iraq.'" American Forces Press Service, April 9, 2003, http://www.defenselink.mil/news/newsarticle.aspx?id=29134.

Gody, Abmed El. "Arab Media: Did It Cover the Same War?" In *Global War-Local News: Media Images of the Iraq War*, edited by Stig A. Nohrstedt and Rune Ottosen, 165–186. Göteborg: Nordicom, 2005.

Grimes, Ronald L. "Infelicitous Performances and Ritual Criticism." *Semeia* 43 (1988): 103–122.

Guelden, Marlane. *Thailand: Into the Spirit World.* Singapore: Times Editions, 1995.

Hariman, Robert, and John Louis Lucaites. "Public Identity and Collective Memory in U.S. Iconic Photography: The Image of 'Accidental Napalm.'" *Critical Studies in Media Communication* 20, no. 1 (2003): 35–66.

Harrison, Simon. "Ritual as Intellectual Property." *Man* n.s., 27, no. 2 (1992): 225–244.

Howe, Leo. "Risk, Ritual and Performance." *Journal of the Royal Anthropological Institute* 6, no. 1 (2000): 63–79.

Hulst, Hans. *In de Schaduw van de Generaals.* Amsterdam: Meulenhoff, 2008.

Hüsken, Ute. "Contested Ritual Property: Conflicts over Correct Ritual Procedures in a South Indian Viṣṇu Temple." In *When Rituals Go Wrong: Mistakes, Failure, and the Dynamics of Ritual*, edited by Ute Hüsken, 273–290. Numen Book Series 115. Leiden: Brill, 2007.

———. "Ritual Dynamics and Ritual Failure." In *When Rituals Go Wrong: Mistakes, Failure, and the Dynamics of Ritual*, edited by Ute Hüsken, 337–366. Numen Book Series 115. Leiden: Brill, 2007.

Jaramillo, Deborah Lynn. "Ugly War, Pretty Package: How the Cable News Network and the Fox News Channel Made the 2003 Invasion of Iraq High Concept." PhD diss., University of Texas, 2006.

Kennicott, Philip. "Waiting for a Clear Picture to Emerge: After Two Years the View from Iraq." *Washington Post*, March 20, 2005, p. D1.

Kershaw, Roger. *Monarchy in South-East Asia: The Faces of Traditions in Transition*. London: Routledge, 2001.

Kull, Steven, Clay Ramsey, and Evan Lewis. "Misperceptions, the Media and the Iraq War." *Political Science Quarterly* 118, no. 4 (2003–2004), 569–598.

Lewis, Justin. "Television, Public Opinion and the War in Iraq: The Case of Britain." *International Journal of Public Opinion Research* 16, no. 3 (2006): 295–310.

Lewis, Justin, Rod Brookes, Nick Mosdell, and Terry Threadgold. *Shoot First and Ask Questions Later: Media Coverage of the 2003 Iraq War*. New York: Lang, 2006.

Marvin, Carolyn, and David W. Ingle. "Blood Sacrifice and the Nation: Revisiting Civil Religion." *Journal of the American Academy of Religion* 44, no. 4 (1996): 767–780.

Maung Thin Aung. *Folk Elements in Burmese Buddhism*. Rangoon: Buddhist Sasana Council Press, 1959.

McGee, Michael Calvin. "The 'Ideograph': A Link between Rhetoric and Ideology." *Quarterly Journal of Speech* 66, no. 1 (1980): 1–16.

Miller, David. *Media at War: The Iraq Crisis*. London: Pluto, 2004.

Mulder, Niels. *Everyday Life in Thailand*. Bangkok: Duong Kamol, 1979.

———. *Inside Thai Society: Religion, Everyday Life, Change*. Bangkok: Duong Kamol, 1994.

Mydans, Seth. "Interview with Ingrid Jordt." *New York Times*, Week in Review, September 30, 2007, http://www.nytimes.com/2007/09/30/weekinreview/30mydans.html?scp=2&sq=Jordt&st=nyt.

Myint-U, Thant. *The Making of Modern Burma*. New York: Cambridge University Press, 2001.

———. *The River of Lost Footsteps: A Personal History of Burma*. London: Faber and Faber, 2007.

Okrent, Daniel. "The Public Editor: Weapons of Mass Destruction? Or Mass Distraction?" *New York Times*, May 30, 2004, section 4:2.

Ostergaard, Anders, dir. *Burma VJ*. 84 min., DVD, color, Denmark, First Hand Films, 2008.

Phillipsen, Gerry. "Ritual as a Heuristic Device in Studies of Organizational Discourse." *Communication Yearbook* 16 (1993): 104–111.

Schober, Juliane. *Sacred Biography in the Traditions of South and Southeast Asia*. Delhi: Motilal Banarsidas, 1997.

Seligman, Adam B., Robert P. Weller, Michael J. Pruett, and Bennett Simon. *Ritual and Its Consequences: An Essay on the Limits of Sincerity*. New York: Oxford University Press, 2008.

Shway Yoe (Sir J. G. Scott). *The Burman: His Life and Notions*. London: Macmillan, 1882.

Smith, Philip. "Codes and Conflict: Toward a Theory of War as Ritual." *Theory and Society* 20, no. 1 (1991): 103–138.

———. *Why War: The Cultural Logic of Iraq, the Gulf War and Suez*. Chicago: University of Chicago Press, 2005.

Stam, Robert. "Television News and Its Spectator." In *Regarding Television—Critical Approaches: An Anthology*, edited by Ann Kaplan. Frederick, MD: University Publications of America, 1983.

Stolle, Dietlind, and Marc Hooghe. "Chronicle of a War Foretold: A Comparative Study of Media Framing in Television News Broadcasts in Preparation to the War in Iraq (March 2003)." Paper presented at the Political Communication Conference on International Communication and Conflict, Washington, DC, August 31, 2005.

Terwiel, Barend Jan. *Boeddhisme in de Praktijk*. Amsterdam: Van Gorcum, 1977.

Tuchman, Gaye. "Objectivity as Strategic Ritual: An Examination of Newsmen's Notions of Objectivity." *American Journal of Sociology* 77, no. 4 (1972): 660–679.

Turner, Victor. *Dramas, Fields, and Metaphors: Symbolic Action in Human Society*. Ithaca, NY: Cornell University Press, 1974.

van der Velde, Paul. "Generals en witte olifanten—voortekens en politiek in Zuidoost Azië." *Acta Comparanda* 20 (2009): 75–99.

———. *Nanda de Mooiste, Ashvaghosha's Saundarananda*. Rotterdam: Asoka, 2007.

"White Elephant Found, Good Omen for Myanmar: Newspapers." *Asian Economic News*, November 12, 2001. Published by Kyodo News International, Yangon, http://findarticles.com/p/articles/mi_m0WDP/is_2001_Nov_12/ai_80881994.

Zayani, Mohamed, and Muhammad I. Ayish. "Arab Satellite Television and Crisis Reporting: Covering the Fall of Baghdad." *International Communication Gazette* 68 (2006): 473–497.

8

What's at Stake in Torture?

Werner Binder, Tom F. Driver, and Barry Stephenson

Although torture and terror are age old, they are also thoroughly contemporary. Political scientist Darius Rejali has shown that modern democratic states persistently use torture as a means of establishing, extending, or maintaining political, military, and economic power.[1] Torture occurs during periods of war but also in the internal struggles of nation-states and as a tool of foreign policy. In Stalin's Soviet Union, de Gaulle's Algeria, Pinochet's Chile, Suharto's Indonesia, Pol Pot's Cambodia, *Ceauşescu*'s Romania, Hussein's Iraq, and many other examples, including George W. Bush's diffuse, global "war on terror," torturers have had steady employment in the past few decades.

In the American-led war on terror, the practice of torture, as is now clear, is rooted in high-level policy decisions. In response to critical questions about prisoner abuse and torture at the Abu Ghraib and Guantanamo Bay prisons, George W. Bush repeatedly claimed, "We don't torture," but the facts reveal otherwise. Whether the U.S. government will completely abandon the use of torture under its new administration is unclear at this writing. Under President Obama, in spite of an executive order issued January 22, 2009, ostensibly banning the use of torture by government agencies, the matter remains unclear. The use of so-called mild forms of physical violence in interrogations continues, Guantanamo Bay is still open, and the attorney general has refused to launch criminal investigations against the Bush administration and the CIA. The worry among liberals is that, while front-stage politics give the appearance of change, customary practices will continue. In any case, the dynamic of torture as a social phenomenon seems to have been little understood. We offer this chapter hoping that it will aid a fuller comprehension of modern torture and, ultimately, contribute to its demise.

Torture is not simply violence but violence that is ritualized. Under modern conditions, the full effect of torture by the state also requires that it be photographed or filmed. This effect starts in the torture chamber itself and does not necessarily require that the images of torture be made public. The point is powerfully suggested by what Sr. Dianna Ortiz, a victim of torture in Guatemala, had to say about seeing the photographs from Abu Ghraib: "I could not even stand to look at those photographs.... [S]o many of the things in the photographs had also been done to me. I was tortured with a frightening dog and also rats. And they were always filming."[2] The far from accidental use of photography at Abu Ghraib was constitutive of the humiliation that was a key part of the torture conducted at the prison.

The media also contribute to the construction of state power by depicting torture in fictional stories. Whether as fact or fiction, torture images made by a camera implant the practice in the viewer's imagination. Torture becomes part of the public's image of the state.

Torture, like many initiation rites, is premised on asymmetrical relations of power. Most rites have officiants and celebrants with diverging degrees of status, knowledge, and responsibilities. In initiation rites, elders know, and novices come to know. In torture, the playing field is absurdly tilted. In combat, soldiers from both sides are armed, each able to kill the other. In torture, the power of the torturer in relation to the tortured approaches the absolute. Whether all power corrupts, as Edmund Burke famously said, we hold that the power at play in torture is malignant on multiple levels. Rooted in our capacity for cruelty, in the perverse pleasure that often accompanies the ability to arouse fear in another, in the desire for political hegemony—torture is a reprehensible, unjustifiable act that deforms the individuals who enact as well as suffer it, and also the societies that ignore or allow it to take place.

From Somalia to the Streets of Iraq

The similarities and links between initiatory practices and torture are exemplified in the Canadian Somali affair, which can be viewed narrowly, as the torture and killing of Shidane Arone, or widely, as we are doing here, to include the revelations of initiatory hazing that emerged after Arone's killing. In 1995, videotapes emerged that had been shot during initiation rites conducted by Canada's Airborne Regiment on their base in Petawawa, Ontario. The regiment was a commando, or special forces, unit modeled on the U.S. Green Berets. In the video of an initiation conducted in 1992 by the unit One Commando, we see about fifteen men passing bread to one another. They vomit and urinate on it prior to eating, an obvious perversion of the Christian liturgical act of consecration, which precedes communion. We see initiates do push-ups on a mat that has been smeared with feces. One initiate, the regiment's only black member, is on his hands and knees, being led on a leash like a dog, and tied to a tree. The letters KKK are written on his back, using human feces for ink. As the participants continue to drink beer, we see one of the elders pretending to sodomize the black initiate. Another fakes fellatio with a different initiate.[3] During the scene, the men continue to drink and spin around a stick or jump from tables blindfolded.

One aim of such transgressive acts is to inculcate submission to authority. Another is to build solidarity on a unique experience outside the bounds of social norms, an experience not to be revealed to a wider public.[4] In this regard, hazing has similarities to the violence and secrecies of domestic abuse, where the victim, paradoxically enough, often remains loyal to the abuser. In hazing, shame and disgust are generated and then transformed by the ritual process into a dark loyalty, trust, and esprit de corps. In gangs and in military contexts, another function of hazing is to create the willingness and dispositions necessary to kill human beings and perform acts of humiliation and, ultimately, torture.

In 1992–1993, two years before the release of the 1995 tapes, the Airborne Regiment, during peacekeeping duties in Somalia, had been disgraced for having beaten and killed a helpless Somali teenager, Shidane Arone. Photographs depicting the torturer posing with the body of the dead sixteen-year-old made their way into the public sphere. In one estimate, at least eighty soldiers inside the camp heard the screams of Shidane Arone one night as he was tortured to death over the course of several hours in a bunker. The torture and killing of Arone reveals how the use of violence against Somalis had come to be seen as an acceptable part of the mission. In the subsequent investigation of the incident, more cases of such violence against Somalis emerged and, eventually, the hazing and initiatory videotapes shot by members of the Airborne Regiment.[5]

The brutal torture and murder of Shidane Arone at the hands of Canadian forces was but one of many indiscriminate acts of violence against Somalis during the peacekeeping mission. Canadian, American, Belgian, and Italian troops were involved in beatings, torture, rape, and execution-style killings. Sociologist Sherene Razack has conceptualized such violence, perpetrated by forces sent to keep the peace, as acts of "colonial violence. That is to say, the violent practices in which peacekeepers engaged in Africa are intended to establish northern nations as powerful and superior, nations in full control of the natives they have come to keep in line."[6]

A similar scenario is playing out in Iraq and Afghanistan. American soldiers serving in Iraq posted the following scene on YouTube.[7] Thirsty children are seen running behind an American army vehicle. Clean water is scarce in Baghdad, and finding fresh water is a matter of survival. The soldiers have water; the children do not. The soldiers flash a bottle of water to the children, wave, and call them to follow the moving vehicle.

"Are they coming?" a soldier asks, chuckling.

"Film them. Film them," says another. To his comrade, behind the camera: "Are you getting it?"

"I'm getting it."

To the children: "You want some water? Water?" The bottle is waved for all to see.

"Come on, keep runnin.' Here, here." The truck rolls on, the children chase, encouraged by the soldier.

"Are you getting them?"

"I'm getting them sir." Some children fall off the pace, giving up hope for a bottle of water. A few persist in chasing the truck.

"Come on, you're almost there, hurry [laughing]. Here. Can you see him?"

"I can see him sir."

"Hurry up. Want it? This kid is gonna run like two miles. This kid is running forever. Come on. Look at this kid [laughs]. Look."

"He's chasing it, man." The bottle is tossed, and a child at the side of the road jumps out and grabs it.

"He didn't get it. Hah!" the soldier comments.

In this cruel little game, we see the impulse to ritualize power. The soldiers already have power; the game dramatizes it, enhances it, inscribes it in the minds and bodies of the soldiers, on the one hand, and the child victims on the other. The soldiers play with, toy with, their victims. Only by dancing the directed steps will the children receive the gift of the water they so desperately need. The message is, "I don't have to give the water to you, and if you want me to give it to you, you will do as I say. Obey my every whim, and then I will give you what you need. Or maybe not."

An important feature of this scene is the ordinariness of it, the sense of routine. The scene is part of a broader practice of inscribing power relations into the bodies of the ruling soldiers as well as the ruled Iraqis. As a message may be inscribed on a clay tablet, the power relation is laid down into the bodies and psyches of those who perform it. The filming and sharing of the game objectify that power.[8] Torture is a more structured, elaborated form of such street-level power plays. Torture rests on a bed of quotidian ritualizations that utilize physical pain, verbal abuse, humiliation, and abjection, not only to demonstrate but also to inscribe power relations.[9]

During training, soldiers typically experience lack of privacy and deprivation of sleep and creature comforts. They undergo hazing rituals, the stripping of personal identity, disorientation, and symbolic and sadistic violence. It takes a great deal of training to overcome normal social and psychological inhibitions against committing acts of violence upon others.[10] Jonathan Z. Smith defines ritual as a "means of performing the way things ought to be in such a way that this ritualized perfection is recollected in the ordinary, uncontrolled, course of things."[11] What is perfected in torture is domination and submission, expressed in radical asymmetries of power. We turn now to the role of mass media in this process.

The Abu Ghraib Photos

Distinguished investigative journalist Mark Danner, writing in 2008, has observed that "torture has metamorphosed, these past few years from an execrable war crime to a 'key issue.' From something forbidden by international treaty and condemned by domestic law to ... something to be debated. Something one can stand on either side of. Something we can live with."[12] He follows this remark with an account of how certain images from Abu Ghraib became iconic through replication in the media. Massive documentation by himself and others traces responsibility for the torture up the chain of command to the White House. The documentation has been published and discussed without any significant effect other than discussion.

For many American citizens, not only activists and intellectuals, the resolution of the scandal remained unsatisfying. The government was able to frame the Abu Ghraib tortures as isolated abuses, quite against the mounting evidence that torture had been institutionalized. A content analysis of *Washington Post* articles, CBS transcripts, and a sample of national newspapers showed that the word *torture* was quickly abandoned by the established press in favor of the seemingly more neutral and accurate term *abuse*.[13]

Renaming acts of torture "abuse" is a way of making torture more acceptable to the public. The Abu Ghraib scandal obviously failed to bring justice. How could this happen? Did the scandal have any other effect? Why did certain photographs become iconic? To answer these questions and understand the ritualized violence at Abu Ghraib, we need to take a closer look at the media scandal and the iconic photographs.

On April 28, 2004, the CBS investigative journalism show *60 Minutes* broadcast several photographs of American soldiers abusing Iraqi prisoners.[14] The pictures were taken in the notorious Abu Ghraib prison near Baghdad, the former torture center of Saddam Hussein.[15] The images shocked the public consciousness and posed an important question: "How did it come to this?"[16] Mark Kimmit, a military spokesperson interviewed in the original show, admitted that it was a bleak day for the American military, but insisted that the depicted acts were not representative of the military as a whole. Military statements and early reports framed the incidents as isolated abuses caused by individual pathologies and a failure in leadership.[17] This explanation was quickly adopted as the official position of the U.S. government. Secretary of State Donald Rumsfeld referred to the perpetrators of Abu Ghraib as "a few bad apples." The bad apple image quickly determined the public reception of the photographs. It was decisive in the trials against the accused soldiers and prevented the scandal from becoming an obstacle for the Bush administration in the presidential elections of 2004.

The notion, however, that the events depicted in the Abu Ghraib photos were isolated incidents was challenged by investigative journalists and public intellectuals; it was also challenged in the final report of the independent panel conducted by former Secretary of Defense James R. Schlesinger.[18] The Schlesinger report stresses the systematic and widespread character of abuse and torture at Abu Ghraib, and makes links between U.S. military practices in Iraq and government policies back home. In attempting to account for the torture conducted at Abu Ghraib, the report turned to psychological analysis, drawing on the much-discussed Stanford prison experiment in 1971.[19] The Abu Ghraib prison and the war on terror, it was argued, created a climate in which degrading treatment could flourish. Philip Zimbardo, who was conductor of the experiment and fictive prison director at Stanford, agreed with this explanation, and advocated a "good apple, bad barrel" theory.[20]

In public discourse as well as in some intellectual circles, the abominable acts of Abu Ghraib were given a variety of cultural explanations and interpretations. Some authors highlighted the role of American popular culture in the Abu Ghraib abuses, in particular fraternity hazing and pornography. Others have read the photographs as documents of U.S. imperialism and colonialism, or as expressions of racism and sexism in American society, or the army in particular. Our aim here is to add to these understandings by emphasizing the ritual dimensions of torture.

Ritual is not an immutable, eternal thing, but a series of special acts and utterances that are the end result of a good deal of prior work, the outcome of a process of selecting, compressing, reframing, and enacting ordinary ritualizations. Everyone is capable of violence, capable of abusive behavior, capable of humiliating or demeaning another person. When one child at school is singled out, becoming the object of insults, hits, pranks, and scorn, ritualization has set in. Behavior becomes repetitive, condensed, focused, physically and temporally framed (in the washroom, before and after school), and so on. In torture, a set of behaviors and acts that are fundamentally violent, abusive, and dehumanizing receive a high degree of formality and style. A special space and context is created (the torture room) where these acts are performed. Those who enact torture receive training and instruction in a shared repertoire of behaviors and techniques. These behaviors and acts are encouraged and legitimated by powers on high. The acts of which torture is composed, to borrow from Humphrey and Laidlaw's definition of ritual, are constituted not by the intentions of the actors, but by prior stipulation.[21] From inside the torture room, the torturers perceive, it would seem, their acts to be natural, fitting, right, true—even pleasurable. Torture is part of the ritual family, and it is the result of ritualizing violence and dehumanization.

A detailed interpretation of a few selected Abu Ghraib photographs reveals the ritualized and stylized character of torture, which verges on theatrical performance, and informed by the "grotesque imagination." Figure 8.1 is one of the many pictures taken at Abu Ghraib Prison in November 2003.

The seven detainees in the photographs were removed to the prison's "hard site" after a riot. They were brought into a corridor, forced to remove their clothes, and arranged in what would come to be popularly called a human pyramid. Although the photograph bears no sign of direct violence, we know from reports that soldiers threw themselves upon the pile of bodies, while other photos show the male soldier, Charles Graner, beating up the prisoners while they were still dressed.[22]

FIGURE 8.1. Human pyramid, Abu Ghraib Prison, November 7, 2003.

The vertical composition of the photograph is striking. The prisoners lie on the floor. The female soldier is above them, smiling, and giving a thumbs up. Behind and above her stands a male soldier with folded arms and wearing rubber gloves, also giving a thumbs up and standing in the posture of the protective male. The image is structured by binary oppositions: bottom and top, naked (the prisoners) and clothed bodies (the soldiers), clean and dirty, individuality and anonymity. The faces of the prisoners are hidden behind bags; their bodies form an amorphous mass; they cannot perform on their own, but are raw material for someone else's performance. They are stripped of their individuality, whereas the soldiers present themselves as distinct persons. The performance embodies the asymmetry between the triumphal torturers and their humiliated victims. It quickly becomes clear that the whole scene is arranged for the camera, the pile as well as the posing soldiers. The camera is constitutive of these acts, not merely a recording device, encouraging the striking of a "heroic" pose and the use of triumphal gestures.[23]

The rubber gloves of the male soldier may fulfill a medical-technical function (hygiene, disease prevention), but they are also clearly symbolic, referring not only to the medicalized ethos of modern torture but also the imagination of torture as dirty but necessary work. The gloves function as ritual paraphernalia, dividing the body of the torturer from the unclean bodies of his victims. The gesture used by both soldiers was known in ancient Rome as the "hostile thumb." Romans used the upright thumb as a threat toward enemies, but also as an apotropaic sign to ward off evil. Nowadays, thumbs up may no longer connote hostility, but it remains a gesture of triumph, a visual demonstration of power and self-confidence. At Abu Ghraib it was not only a gesture of domination dividing torturer from victims, but also a display of power—first of all to the torturers themselves,[24] and secondarily to a generalized audience embodied in the camera. If ritual communicates meanings, the Abu Ghraib photos place before our gaze one of the communicative messages of torture, namely, the fact of radical asymmetries of power and authority. Like the soldiers teasing children with the water bottle, the soldiers in the Abu Ghraib photos exercise a godlike power over their victims.

This performance communicates values. It also stages and embodies a worldview. The common values or the shared worldview belong not only to the posing soldiers but also to potential bystanders and of course to the photographer of the scene. The camera and the audience are made accomplices of the depicted soldiers. The soldiers stage themselves as heroes doing dirty and necessary work, exemplifying what New York University law professor Stephen Holmes calls the "quiet heroism of torture."[25] The understanding of oneself as a dirty or law-defying hero not only is common among professional torturers but has also a central place in American popular culture.[26] Torturers usually do their deeds in secrecy, like comic-book superheroes, but in this case the photos were leaked into public view, with controversial results. By staging themselves as heroes, the soldiers tell the viewer not only that they wield power over their victims but also that they are right to do so: they show themselves as heroes, not bad guys, though they may, like Batman, have a dark side.

Spectators often associate the pile of bodies with an orgy, and many of the Abu Ghraib photographs depict sexual acts. Pornographic readings of several Abu Ghraib photographs point to the male soldier with his rubber gloves standing behind the prisoners' backs and the female soldier as a dominatrix playfully pointing her thumb on the top of the pile of naked men. The image of the dominatrix appears also in other photographs; most famous is the photo of Lynndie England holding a naked prisoner on a leash. Still, it is rather misleading to equate the photographs with ordinary pornography, because here the pornographic iconography serves a ritual and political function.[27] Sexuality becomes a marker of impurity, stamping the prisoners with the status of animals. Some of the victims were even said to have been "ridden like animals" during their night of torture.[28] Ritualized violence turns the prisoners into subhuman creatures and political enemies, but at the same time, they become a neutralized and laughable threat.

The pile of bodies created and photographed by the American soldiers is grotesque, in the sense employed by Bakhtin: "If we consider the grotesque image in its extreme aspect, it never presents an individual body; the image consists of orifices and convexities that present another, newly conceived body."[29] According to Bakhtin, the grotesque body is characterized by nakedness, violence, sexuality, and the loss of individual features. In medieval folk culture, the lower body stratum was conceived as a connection between the opposite poles of life and death, thus symbolizing rebirth and re-creation. The medieval grotesque, by representing the unity of life and death, allowed participants to overcome their fear of supernatural forces by laughter. This view of the grotesque body belonged to a worldview and set of practices, such as carnival, that periodically blurred the boundaries between the sacred and the profane.[30] Contrary to the ambivalent and often positive understanding of the grotesque in the Middle Ages, Abu Ghraib is a modern perversion of the grotesque. "Modern indecent abuse and cursing have retained dead and purely negative remnants of the grotesque concept of the body," writes Bakhtin.[31] Unlike a carnival, in which everyone is part of the grotesque spectacle, in the Abu Ghraib tortures there is a clear distinction between the grotesque body pile and the individualized soldiers. Here the grotesque becomes a symbol of evil and an object of fear, even while being ridiculed. In the Middle Ages laughter was also part of the grotesque and was used to overcome fear. The laughter of the soldiers serves a similar function; it seems, among other things, to signal triumph over the unknown enemy lurking both outside and inside the prison walls. In the human pyramid of Abu Ghraib, the grotesque style aids the construction of "the enemy" in a ritual of degradation, drawing and creating clear lines between good and evil, purity and pollution, heroes and villains, the civilized and the savage, the strong and the weak, life and death.

The ability of torture at Abu Ghraib to communicate feelings and narratives of power was aided by their immediate recognition by an audience, namely, the photographer and surrounding comrades. The seven soldiers involved in the abuse rotated in their roles as performers, bystanders, and photographers; they encouraged each other to push the acts further and further. The camera itself was a placeholder for an undetermined audience. The photographs enlarged and multiplied the possible audience of these acts beyond the immediate witnesses. The photographs circulated first among the soldiers in the prison. Subsequent investigations revealed that some soldiers regarded what they saw as inappropriate, but only one soldier, U.S. Army Reservist Joe Darby, found it necessary to inform his superior.[32] Once broadcast, the images reached a global audience that responded to them in various ways. Importantly, the original intended message of the human pyramid was in part subverted. The national and international audience saw no heroes and no enemies, only sadists abusing their institutional power to humiliate helpless men. The intersection of ritual and media is crucial to understand how the acts of ritualized violence at Abu Ghraib had such an impact on conflicts on a global scale. The demonstrations and protests in Arab countries following the broadcasting and dissemination of the photographs, as well as their adoption on billboards and murals in Baghdad, Tehran, and Havana, bear witness to the power of media to shape narratives and understandings of global events.[33]

The importance of this shift to a global audience as well as the ritualized character of torture becomes even clearer when we consider the image that became the icon of the scandal (figure 8.2). It is not by chance that the philosopher and culture critic Slavoj Zizek mistook the "prisoner wearing a black hood, electric wires attached to his limbs as he stood on a box in a ridiculous theatrical pose," for "a piece of performance art."[34]

The victim's torturers placed him in the "stress position," a textbook technique approved by the American military. The victim was forced to stand on a box and threatened with electrocution should he fall. Again, we see a grotesque figure, a ridiculed enemy conjuring up a variety of associations—from Halloween to the Ku Klux Klan to crucifixion. The hooded man becomes the specter of terrorism, the embodiment of a faceless enemy. Although depicted as a scary and evil figure, the victim is helpless and subject to the laughter of the spectator. Again, the fear of the unknown enemy is met by the liberating power of laughter and amusement. Many viewers have been reminded of Jesus, hung on the cross and mocked by Roman soldiers.[35]

FIGURE 8.2. Hooded man, Abu Ghraib Prison, November 4, 2003.

The forced posture of the prisoner stops being an expression of his person and becomes a masquerade and a manifestation of the torturer's power-over. The stress position suits perfectly the requirements and purposes of modern state torture. It inflicts no wounds and leaves no scars. As the victim is forced to inflict pain upon himself, the body is turned against itself as a weapon. The violence at work here is concealed, but all too real. Though the U.S. Army considers the stress position legal and morally unproblematic, the photo led to disgust and outrage in the public sphere.

The reason this image became the dominant emblem of the scandal lies beyond the acts and their message directed at the immediate witnesses. To a Western audience, the hooded man appeared as "a figure from the Passion plays, the staging of the humiliation and torture of Jesus."[36] Due to this interpretation, the photograph profited from the conventions of Christian art in depicting the dignity of the humiliated and the sacredness of suffering. It remains unclear whether the torturers themselves intended or recognized this mimesis of Christ, but in any case it added to the public impact of the image.

Another reason for the popularity of this image was its lack of closure and its symbolic overdetermination. Besides the crucifixion, many other motifs were associated with the photograph—among them the Spanish Inquisition, lynchings, the Ku Klux Klan, and the electric chair. The image of the hooded man opened up a variety of associations with and discussions of the history of violence in America. The image was also picked up by a popular American television series, *Prison Break*. The series, begun in 2005, is about the rescue of an innocent prisoner sentenced to death by electrocution.[37] In episode 16 of the first season, we see a convict during his former military career in Iraq witnessing the torture of a hooded prisoner in a kind of electric chair. Here, the hooded man image provokes a critique of the electric chair as barbaric and the death penalty as inhumane; indeed, the series depicts prison life in general as barbaric and inhumane. The torture at Abu Ghraib, the episode implies, is very close to home, and its victims were probably innocent.

The hooded man image, then, functioned in some quarters like Rene Girard's account of the scapegoat, revealing the dynamic of the innocent victim. The Abu Ghraib scandal triggered a wave of critical imaginings, if not a clear change in policy. The Abu Ghraib abuses cannot be excused as "interrogation gone wild." Rather, they constitute representative acts of ritualized violence.

Having lifted up the photographed torture at Abu Ghraib as our primary case study, we turn now to analysis of torture in a wider social compass, especially its use by the modern state. We offer four propositions.

Proposition 1: Torture Is Not Primarily a Technique of Intelligence Gathering

Torture is widely seen as a specific, instrumental use of violence, a technique to inflict pain in order to achieve various goals. We can distinguish three ways in which torture is employed to achieve certain ends: as a form of corporal punishment, as a method to obtain confessions in legal matters, and as an interrogation technique.[38] Today, only the third use of torture, as a means of intelligence gathering, is deemed defensible by many people. While torture is widely recognized as a form of cruelty, the advocates of torture claim that it is even crueler to abstain from torture if we can use it to save innocent lives.[39] We hold that such a view is not tenable when the dynamics and effects of torture are better understood.

The most dramatic scenario in favor of the use of torture is the "ticking time bomb," the imaginary case of a terrorist who knows where a bomb is about to explode and is caught by a government that knows he has such knowledge. Before 9/11, the ticking-bomb scenario was considered to be merely a way to illustrate an abstract moral philosophical problem; afterward it became a basis for state policy.

The terrorist attack on the Twin Towers gave the scenario of ticking-bomb terrorism an apparent plausibility it never had before. It became a justification for intelligence gathering by any means necessary.

The ticking bomb had long been a favorite of popular culture and media.[40] After 9/11, in popular culture, the scenario of the law-defying hero-torturer regularly foiling the ticking-bomb terrorist captured the popular imagination. In public imagination, suggests Stephen Holmes, "the once scorned torturer now appears as a potential savior."[41] It was not only fictitious torture that became popular. In setting up the prison camp at Guantanamo Bay three months after 9/11, the United States openly declared its intention to use torture for the collective good, although it refrained from calling torture by name, preferring the term "harsh interrogation technique."

From the time of Aristotle, the notion that torture can produce reliable information has been questioned. "People under [torture's] compulsion," wrote Aristotle, "tell lies quite as often as they tell the truth, sometimes persistently refusing to tell the truth, sometimes recklessly making a false charge in order to be let off sooner."[42] Aristotle pointed out what much informed testimony today holds to be true: torture yields very little "actionable intelligence," that is to say, useful information.[43]

The modern world is replete with testimony to the same effect. Damien Corsetti, an interrogator and torturer at Bagram Air Base in Afghanistan, said:

> [T]orture doesn't work. One thing is losing your temper and punching a prisoner, another is to commit these acts of brutality. In Bagram we managed to find out about an al-Qaeda plan to blow up dozens of oil tankers across the world. We smashed the plot so well that they only managed to attack one, the French oil tanker Limburg, in Yemen in October 2002. And we managed to get a guy to tell us without laying a finger on him.... In Abu Ghraib and Bagram they were tortured to make them suffer, not to get information out of them. At times the torture had no other goal [than] to punish them for being terrorists. They tortured them and didn't ask them anything.[44]

The dubious value of torture for intelligence gathering should lead us to examine it from a different perspective.

Proposition 2: Torture Is a Ritualization of the Power of the Torturer

Violence is the doing of physical and psychological harm to a person. Torture is violence ritualized. As we use the term here, ritualized violence is bodily suffering (pain) intentionally inflicted, encoded with meanings, and used as a tool to communicate values, narratives, and beliefs.

The terms *ritualizing* and *ritualization* have variable meanings in the literature of ritual studies. In the usage of the present chapter, the stress is upon those characteristics of an action that make it either similar to ritual proper or the same as ritual in some respects but not in all. The principal reason it would be awkward to call torture ritual is that there is no cultural understanding of it as ritual. At the same time, torture cannot, we suggest, be adequately understood without attention to those qualities that it shares with phenomena people do call ritual. The pain experienced by victims of torture is all too real, yet also an enactment staged for communicative effect. In the discussion that follows, the word *torturer* refers not only to the individual who deliberately inflicts pain upon the body or psyche of the victim but also to any person or persons who may direct the torture session, as well as whoever may have authorized it. By *victim* we refer to the individual person who is tortured.

Having certain features that are like ritual, torture becomes useful in the construction of state power. Theologian William Cavanaugh, analyzing the practice of torture in Pinochet's Chile, describes it as a "kind of perverted liturgy,"[45] a notion to which we shall return. Indeed, torture shares many of the family characteristics of ritual. Torture takes place in set-aside places, at specified times often chosen for maximum psychological effect upon the victim. As Elaine Scarry points out, torture rooms have often been described as performance, production, or theatrical spaces: the "production room" in the Philippines; the "cinema room" in South Vietnam; the "blue-lit screen" in Chile; the U.S. government's "Black Room," the name given to the former detention and torture center of Saddam Hussein located on a military base near Baghdad and operated after the invasion of Iraq by an American Special Forces unit known as Task Force 6-26. Foucault called torture a "theatre of horror." Like theater and much ritual, torture is staged.

Torture is embodied physical enactment. As ritual is, first and foremost, a kind of physical action, so torture is something deliberately done with, to, and by bodies. Torture, like some rites of passage that involve pain and alteration of the body, uses the malleability of the body to articulate and inscribe values and a worldview. We can make the same point by saying that ritual is performance, in both senses of that word: it is something actually, physically done, and it is something done for show.[46] In premodern times, physical punishment and ceremonial killings were often done in public squares before large public audiences. In modern times, it becomes important for torture to be both invisible and visible.

Torture is patterned, stereotyped, repetitive, stylized. Its behaviors (techniques) exist within a tradition, or at least a known repertoire of such behaviors. Waterboarding dates at least to medieval Europe. The technique simulates drowning by spilling water over the cloth-covered face of the victim, leading to an immediate gag reflex that causes extreme pain and sometimes lasting physical and psychological damage. Torture manuals and training schools develop the repertoire of techniques and methods. Torture has been the object of scientific investigation, aimed at developing increasingly effective techniques for inflicting terror and pain. In recent years, an emphasis has been placed on the development and use of torture techniques that leave no physical trace on the body.

Torture, for all the very real pain involved, is symbolic and dramatic. In the human pyramid photo from Abu Ghraib, the rubber gloves connote the technical, medicalized ethos of modern torture and suggest a complex symbolic network of binary oppositions associated with uncleanliness and purity.

Torture, like some rites, involves a transgression, in which normal interactions, relationships, and values are suspended. Less broadly speaking, three qualities of torture suggest comparison with states of liminality that characterize some initiation rites:

- The deliberate infliction of bodily pain—circumcision, the cutting of scars into an initiate's flesh, forced nosebleeds, physical exhaustion—is essential to some initiation rites. Though modern torture utilizes so-called clean techniques that leave no visible scarring, bodily pain is basic to torture.
- The transgression of social norms in order to produce disgust, shame, and submissiveness. Hazing practices are prominent in some initiation rites and central to military culture. Torture is an elaboration of such practices.
- The secrecy that surrounds some initiation practices creates ambiguity in relation to the rite's audience. Initiations often include periods of sequestration and obligatory secrecy. In such cases, part of the excitement surrounding the rite is the fact that everyone in the community knows that something secret is going on. Similarly, modern torture is sequestered and secretive, albeit an open secret.

Proposition 3: To Commit or Authorize Torture Implies Making a Claim of Absolute Power

Torture is organized, systematized cruelty in which the exercise of one actor's power over another is extreme.[47] The theatrical and creative dimension of torture in a situation in which the victim's freedom is nearly zero reveals the torturer to be an agent in a bid for power that has no limits. Complex interpretations and explanations of the relations between violence, cruelty, and ritual are, from this perspective, superfluous. A mystique surrounds torture, lending it the aura of the sacred or the demonic.[48] "Sacred and profane activities," says Catherine Bell, "are differentiated in the performing of them." Ritualization, she adds, "gives rise to (or creates) the sacred as such by virtue of its sheer differentiation from the profane."[49] Precisely because the torture room is both a chamber of horrors and a theater of cruelty, it has the quality of a sacred space. Torture's sacrality is, as Bell's comment suggests, its sharp separation from ordinary life, its actual, symbolic, and psychological distance from the street, the mundane. The torture victim must be snatched away and transported to a forbidden space that, by virtue of the unspeakable things that go on there in sequestration, is a kind of inner sanctum of damnation.[50]

To speak of torture as being at the edge of human life, at the edge of law, is to recognize its liminal, sacred, or what we might prefer to call its demonic character. The torturer plays God, whether saying so or not. In the case of torture done by the state, the man conducting the torture session behaves like an emissary of God, a point that is suggested in the feature film *Rendition*. The torture chamber is in North Africa. The man in direct charge of the torturing is a North African civil servant. The session is observed on the spot by a U.S. intelligence officer unused to this scene and agonized by it. But the effective power is high above and far away in Washington, personified in the character played by Meryl Streep, a high-level functionary of the CIA who is determined to do whatever is "necessary." Looming silently in the background of several of the movie's frames are the U.S. Capitol and the Washington Monument. Torture comes from a power most high.[51]

Part of the perverse fascination of torture is that the violence it entails threatens to become its own end. Those who perpetrate torture and terror risk crossing over at some point from using them for a specific utilitarian purpose (which has been torture's rationalization) to the infliction of pain merely because it is possible and because it feels absolute in itself. The Abu Ghraib photos reminded us of torture's autonomous tendencies. The photos can be understood as tools in the creation and dehumanization of "the enemy," for example. But they also reveal the working of a sadistic pleasure; those who commit acts of torture are not merely willing to engage in acts of extreme violence, degradation, and humiliation, but seem to do so with gusto. Torturers, as photographs and testimony reveal, seem to relish what they do, or are driven to do what they do. In the film *Taxi to the Dark Side*, Damien Corsetti, one of the torturers at Bagram Air Base in Afghanistan, talks about how the torturers kept on torturing even though they knew there was no more information to be gained. If power is to be absolute, it will be embodied in acts that have their own autonomous being. Like persons, God, the universe, or some forms of art, torture does not exist for any reason outside itself. The torturer tortures because he can.

Proposition 4: The Game of Torture Is an Open Secret, Designed to Augment State Power While Constructing "the Enemy"

In his classic work *Discipline and Punish*, Michel Foucault opens with a description of the public execution in 1757 of a man named Damiens, whose punishment for attempted regicide included the burning of his flesh with molten lead and boiling oil, before he was drawn and quartered by four horses. The final act of this public spectacle was the burning of Damiens's dismembered body and the scattering of his ashes to the winds.

Within eighty years of this scene, changes in penal codes all over Europe resulted in "the disappearance of torture as a public spectacle." In its place came the modern penal system, in which those being punished are removed from public view. For a time, to be sure, convicts were put on display in chain gangs performing public labor, but that too has now largely disappeared. The "ceremonial of punishment," as Foucault calls it, went into decline. Punishment was turned into "a new legal or administrative practice," and in time became "the most hidden part of the penal process."[52] Public sentiment turned away from wanting to view the body in pain. To reduce the pain of execution, the gallows gave way to the guillotine, the hangman's rope to the electric chair, and the latter to injections. The courts are still hearing arguments that this or that method causes too much pain.

What has actually happened, let us observe, is a removal of physical pain from the sphere of judicial procedure and punishment and its relocation into the sphere of so-called interrogation. However, pain as spectacle has not entirely gone away. Its venue has for the most part moved from live action in public squares to photographs, television shows, and movies.

Torture today takes place at the edge of the rule of law, and to some extent beyond it. Jeremy Waldron, whose field is the philosophy of law, maintains that to permit torture is to undermine the moral basis of law itself. The prohibition of torture, he writes, "is not just one rule among others, but a legal archetype—a provision which is emblematic of our larger commitment to non-brutality in the legal system."[53] Torture by the state, standing at the boundary between the rule of law and the rule of tooth and claw, asserts the omnipotence of sheer power.

Torture's occurrence is not due to rage, derangement, or personal depravity. On the contrary, the more modern torture becomes, the more it is characterized by sophisticated techniques arrived at through research. This is one of the ways we know that the U.S. government's and army's claim that the Abu Ghraib atrocities were the work of "a few bad apples" is deceptive. The atrocities shown in the Abu Ghraib photos belong to a known repertoire of torture techniques, carefully elaborated and refined with the aid of insights from social psychology. There are antecedents to this science and art of torture in the premodern era. Foucault speaks of "the art of maintaining life in pain, by subdividing it into a 'thousand deaths,' by achieving before life ceases 'the most exquisite agonies.'"[54] That is a splendidly accurate name for waterboarding, the technique that has recently been the object of so much discussion and legal hairsplitting.[55] Moreover, contrary to popular assumption, the use of torture at Abu Ghraib was not a new departure for the United States, which has a legacy of practicing torture ever since the Vietnam War, if not longer.[56]

As we have already indicated, torture no longer belongs to a "liturgy of punishment." Its context is no longer that of a judicial process. Although ostensibly used now as a technique of interrogation, there is ample reason to doubt that torture is actually restricted to interrogation. The victim of torture well resembles the figure of the *homo sacer*. In the city-states of ancient Rome, the *homo sacer* was defined as a human being who could not be ritually killed or offered up in sacrifice—he did not belong to the liturgy of punishment—but who could be killed without his assailants incurring the charge or penalty of murder. The *homo sacer* was banned from participation in both the sacred and the political community, with the result that he was reduced to what Giorgio Agamben calls "bare life" or "naked life." The life of *homo sacer* was opposed to the "way of life proper to men";[57] that is, his was a life without rights, a life of exclusion from the polis. This exclusion, argues Agamben, is, however, a secret inclusion, since a sovereign power, to be truly sovereign, must be able to suspend the political and legal order that it instituted in the first place. The doctrine of "preemptive war," introduced by the Bush administration after the attacks of 9/11, the suspension of rights instituted through the Patriot Act, the violation of habeas corpus, and the practice of torture are the salient contemporary examples of what Agamben, following the political theorist Carl Schmitt, refers to as a political order rooted in a "state of exception."

Nowhere does the state of exception become clearer than in Guantanamo Bay, an exterritorial army base under American control, but not subject to American law. For Slavoj Zizek, the individuals indefinitely confined in the camps of Guantanamo are the modern *homo sacer*, subject to the "bare life" described by Agamben, par excellence. The perverse argument that the detainees were only those missed by the bombs places them between two deaths in a position where the American government can do with them what it pleases.[58] Guantanamo was from the very beginning no secret at all, but the official response of the U.S. government to the threat of terrorism after 9/11. As Stephen Holmes suggests, "torture is valuable, even if it does not work, *precisely because it defies the law*."[59] This would explain why the existence of torture and indefinite detainment has to be kept visible, while the concrete actions and conditions remain secret. Just as torture ritualizes and dramatizes the power of the torturers, so the authorization and open defiance of law by the state reveals the power of the state as a sovereign above the law.

Foucault had noted that medieval torture "must mark the victim: it is intended, either by the scar it leaves on the body, or by the spectacle that accompanies it, to brand the victim with infamy; ... it traces ... on the very body of the condemned man signs that must not be effaced."[60] Modern torture practice goes in the opposite direction. It becomes crucial that the victim not be branded, not left with any enduring marks on the body. That is why the psychological dimension of torture has become so important. The body is made to suffer excruciating pain, but not scarred. Deformation is now the fate of the mind if not the soul. In both a literal and metaphorical sense, torture has moved indoors, its worst effects lodged behind closed doors. With this internal scarring the direct victims of modern torture are, if possible, kept alive and returned to society. The indirect victims are the public at large, who are encouraged to go about business as usual. In this respect, as well as by the hiddenness of the torture chamber and prison, torture is made invisible.

Yet even though torture has moved indoors, it remains, mysteriously, a kind of theater. Torture is inherently a performance for show, requiring not only the tools and techniques of injury and terror but also spectators. When the torture chamber is hidden from public view, there is still a "chamber audience." The torture chamber becomes, as it were, a mirrored room, a place in which the performers become their own spectators. It is essential that the torturer dramatize himself before the victim, and that the victim be made to hear his own cries and see his own degradation. One of the principal aims, as Elaine Scarry has shown, is the production of shame.[61] Meticulous records are likely to be kept. Often audio and video recordings are made, or photographs taken. The torturer assumes a variety of roles in relation to the victim—now the friend, now the foe, now the intimidator, now the kind nurse, now the father confessor, now God Almighty who can do with you as he pleases. He is divine and you are shit. On the waterboard he controls your breathing, has your life literally in his hands. Off the waterboard, you are encouraged to take long, hard looks at yourself and to watch carefully how you behave. You become an actor in your own play, trying to improvise ways of acting within the severely limited options left to you. Your cries are designed to reach heaven. You are forced to listen to the silence that follows them, or else the false laughter of those around you. The play goes on. You pray for an intermission and are likely to do or say anything to get it. A theater may be a place with a proscenium and a velvet curtain, but it can also be an operating theater in a hospital, a theater of operations in war, or a torture chamber, in Foucault's keen phrase, "a theatre of horror."[62]

But there is more. The secrecy that surrounds torture today is an open secret. While you, the public, are not supposed to see it done, you are not to remain ignorant of its happening, which you are not to forget for a moment. We may speak, then, of the ambiguity of modern torture's secrecy. Although it is conducted out of sight, everyone in the community is made to know that horrible secret things are happening. The visible invisibility of modern torture enhances the mystique with which torture surrounds itself.

The bid for absolute power on the part of the modern state is enhanced by the open secrecy of torture. In order to remain at the edge of the law, and in order to continue to create and negotiate its power, the ritualization of violence that is torture must be hidden from plain view while at the same time the public must know of it and be shocked and awed. Hence it is better to "disappear" a victim than to arrest him or her. Disappearance causes more shock and awe to family, friends, and neighbors while simultaneously allowing deniability.

In the state's pursuit of the open secrecy of torture, audiovisual media have become vital. These media, whether showing torture as fact or fiction, lodge visions of torture in the public imagination. Since September 11, 2001, feature films and documentaries regarding torture have proliferated. Statistics from the Internet Movie Database reveal that the number of films featuring torture doubled between 2000 and 2002. By 2008 the number had multiplied by a factor of six (figure 8.3).[63]

The release of the photos from Abu Ghraib may not have had an entirely undesired effect from the perspective of those in Washington who favor working for "the dark side."[64] If the aims are the aggrandizement of the state's power, a certain amount of shock and awe are good for the general public as well as for the state's

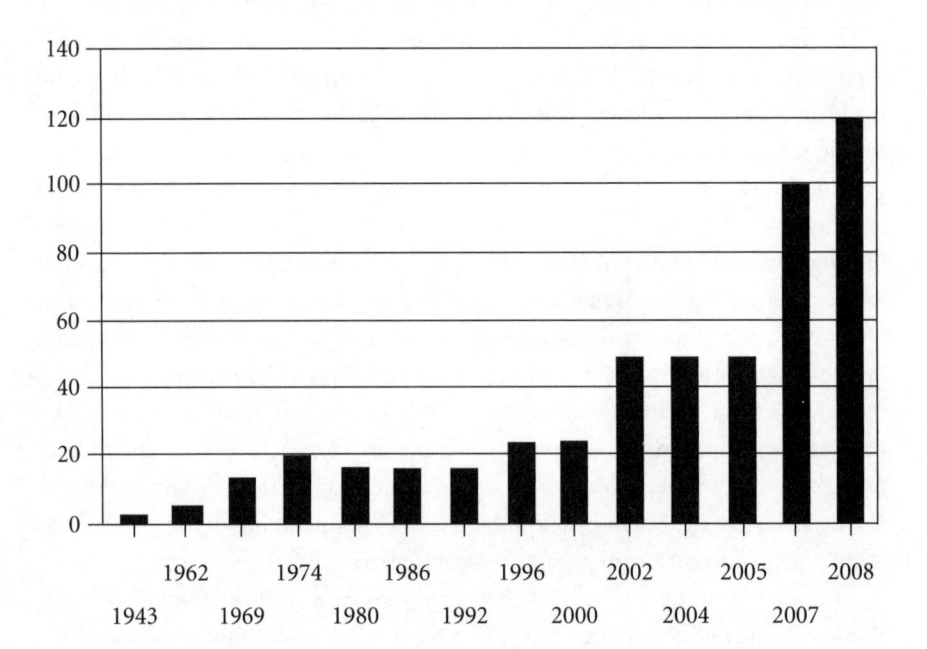

FIGURE 8.3. Torture films, groups of 100.

supposed enemies.[65] No human power can be absolute, but the aim to achieve it, and the illusion of having it, are all too human. In actuality, the state is unable to protect its citizens from ever becoming victims of terrorism, as it is unable to protect everyone all the time from becoming a victim of crime. For their part, many of the state's citizens become willing to sacrifice their own civil rights in order to be able to believe in an almighty state that will protect them from all danger. We take note of the irony that citizens of a democracy can become fanatically nationalistic in order to feel safe from religious fanatics.

One uses the word *dissemination* advisedly for the mass media—film, TV, video, and radio—which cast their seed everywhere. Who has remained ignorant of the atrocities of Abu Ghraib? The celebrated photos can be classed as documentary. So also such powerful film reportage and analysis as the Academy Award–winning *Taxi to the Dark Side* (2007) or *Ghosts of Abu Ghraib* (2007), both of which decry torture while making us more aware of it willy-nilly. There are also numerous feature films, including the fictional treatment of true stories such as *Rendition* (2007), all-too-plausible fictions such as *In the Valley of Elah* (2007), and fantasies glorifying torture or making it thrilling like the popular film *The Dark Knight* (2008) or the hit TV series *24*, which uses scripts based on the ticking-bomb scenario.[66] All of these lodge torture in the public imagination.

However, since all media, even documentaries, are but light, shadow, chemicals, and electronic bits, and since the media are notoriously subject to manipulation, they always leave the viewer unsure as to where the truth lies. In this way, the mystique of the open secret is compounded, the imagination of the populace is infected, and fear of the torturer becomes endemic, even among people who are neither criminal nor subversive.

The Abu Ghraib scandal and certain other critical representations of torture have led many people to see that torture is not an interrogation technique used in ticking-bomb scenarios to save innocent lives. Abu Ghraib showed torture as deeply offensive things done to powerless detainees by uniformed soldiers. Although this depiction has raised difficult questions for many people, it has not diminished the message of state power that torture carries. Right or wrong, the state did it. And the state itself, as embodied in its high-ranking officials, has not, as of this writing, been held accountable for the torture it authorized.

Torture, as William Cavanaugh has argued, is a bid for state power that involves the creation of an enemy and the tearing apart of all loyalties within the social body other than those directed toward the state itself. For this reason, Cavanaugh refers to torture as a "perverted liturgy." It is, he says,

> a ritual act which organizes bodies in the society into a collective
> performance, not of true community, but of an atomized aggregate of

mutually suspicious individuals. Just as liturgy is not a merely "spiritual" formation which then must be applied to the physical world, torture is not a merely physical assault on bodies but a formation of a social imagination.[67]

We may add that a rich density of bodily action, symbolic significance, and self-conscious performance is characteristic of torture as well as liturgy. "Torture," as Cavanaugh says, "is not meant . . . primarily for individuals but for whole societies." In Chile, under Pinochet, torture was "a central rite in the liturgy by which the Chilean state manifested its power." He tells us, "torture was used by the Chilean military regime to fragment and disarticulate all social bodies which would rival its power, especially the church."[68] Torture of this kind is not limited to Chile. Cavanaugh reminds his readers that torture "is very much a part of our [global] world, and we must make the mental effort, however uncomfortable, to put the ideas of 'governance' and 'torture' together."[69] In its gruesome way, torture comes close to sacralizing the state. In Cavanaugh's words, torture is a kind of perverse liturgy, for in torture the body of the victim is the ritual site where the state's power is manifested in its most awesome form. Torture is liturgy—or, perhaps better said, "antiliturgy"—because it involves bodies and bodily movements in an enacted drama which both makes real the power of the state and constitutes an act of worship of that mysterious power. In this way, "torture plays out the dream of a certain kind of state, the production of a type of power and knowledge," which Cavanaugh calls "the imagination of the state." At issue is "the scripting of bodies into a drama of fear."[70] In other words, torture exerts a claim not only over its victims' bodies, but also over their minds and emotions. It is a means of shaping body, mind, and emotion into alignment with a certain image of the state. Because it works powerfully upon the imagination as well as the body, it broadcasts its message far beyond the torture chamber. The image of the torture chamber, agent and symbol of an all-powerful state, travels through society.

If the public's imagination thus becomes schizoid, so much the better for the state. On the one hand, citizens in a democracy are educated to think of the state as the embodiment of society and the protector of our safety and our rights. If we are Americans, we carry within us something known as the American dream. In our imagination, the state offers us life, liberty, and the pursuit of happiness. On the other hand, the mediatizing of torture invites us to see the state under the aspect of its dark side. The image of the state in our heads is thus split—polarized between George Washington, on the one hand, who could not tell a lie and who, in fact, refused to torture the British soldiers his men captured,[71] and, on the other, the mysterious and evil Darth Vader. Hence, to our generalized fear of the torturing state is added the dismay and confusion of a state that, like many an image of God, occupies our aching heads as the author of both good and evil.

To study torture as ritual undercuts any view of torture as merely or even primarily a technique of interrogation. It brings us to view torture as a means of social control transgressing the rule of law. Torture is revealed as a threat to all freedoms and to the health of the human heart or soul. Concerted opposition to torture becomes both possible and necessary. We can also see that alternative liturgies, ritual processes aimed at building up the social body, or what Victor Turner has called *communitas*, are required if torture is to be resisted.[72] Torture rests on a seedbed of ritualization; we can ritualize cruel behavior and violence, and we can ritualize compassion and love: ultimately, the choice is ours.

To fight against state torture and torture states means to abandon a sometimes far too convenient state imagination—the illusion of an almighty state, able and obliged to protect us from every imaginable threat, including terrorism. There are sensible ways to minimize the danger to our societies from terrorism, but there cannot be absolute security. There can be, no doubt, relative degrees of safety, but torture does not enhance security. It merely helps us to believe in the illusion of a state that can save us from imaginary ticking bombs. To become cruel and inhumane is a price too high to pay for an illusion.

NOTES

1. Darius Rejali, *Torture and Democracy* (Princeton: Princeton University Press, 2007).

2. Dianna Ortiz, quoted by Naomi Klein in "'Never Before!' Our Amnesiac Torture Debate," *The Nation*, December 26, 2005, 12.

3. The symbolic or actual practice of anal rape has a long history in establishing hierarchies of dominance and submission within military, paramilitary, police, and gang culture. Missiles launched into Iraq by American forces during the Gulf War carried the painted-on message, "Bend over Saddam."

4. See Hank Nuwer, "Military Hazing," in *The Hazing Reader*, ed. Hank Nuwer (Bloomington: University of Indiana Press, 2004), 141–146.

5. For detailed discussions of the Somalia affair, see Sherene Razack, *Dark Threats and White Knights: The Somalia Affair, Peacekeeping and the New Imperialism* (Toronto: University of Toronto Press, 2004); and Donna Winslow, "Rites of Passage and Group Bonding in the Canadian Airborne," in Nuwer, *The Hazing Reader*, 147–170. The Canadian Airborne Regiment, following a parliamentary investigation, was disbanded in March 1995.

6. Razack, *Dark Threats and White Knights*, 55.

7. The video has been posted and reposted by numerous users of YouTube.http://www.youtube.com/watch?v=AmFj9vapVvs (accessed July 12, 2010).

8. YouTube, for example, contains dozens of videos depicting American soldiers interacting with Iraqi children in a fashion that embodies anything but "winning hearts and minds."

9. The term *ritualization* has a variety of meanings. The term draws attention to the fact that formal rites do not emerge full blown from nothing. Rather, rites are grounded in our ritualizations, sequences or patterns of behavior that serve as the elemental gestures which, through elaboration, stylization, periodization, and so on, eventuate in ritual. We humans, like our animal cousins, select certain behaviors, capacities, and powers to be developed into ritual. Ritualization, in this sense, is the basis for ritual, supplying the building blocks, gestures, and scripts that receive elaboration in more formal rites. To think of torture in terms of ritual means to see it as drawing upon ritualized forms of behavior and social relationships. See Ronald L. Grimes, *Ritual Criticism: Case Studies in Its Practice, Essays on Its Theory* (Columbia: University of South Carolina Press, 1990), 9–11.

10. See Dave Grossman, *On Killing: The Psychological Cost of Learning to Kill in War and Society* (New York: Little, Brown, 1995).

11. Jonathan Z. Smith, "The Bare Facts of Ritual," *History of Religion* 20, no. 1–2 (1980): 124–125.

12. Mark Danner, "Frozen Scandal," *New York Review of Books* 55, no. 19 (2008): 26–28.

13. Lance W. Bennett, Regina G. Lawrence, and Steven Livingston, "None Dare Call It Torture: Indexing and the Limits of Press Independence in the Abu Ghraib Scandal," *Journal of Communication* 56 (2006): 467–485.

14. The original report is available online: Rebecca Leung, "Abuse of Iraqi POWs by GIs Probed: 60 Minutes II Has Exclusive Report on Alleged Mistreatment," *60 Minutes*, April 20, 2004, http://www.cbsnews.com/stories/2004/04/27/60II/main614063.shtml.

15. A collection and a documentation of these and other photos from Abu Ghraib can be found at Salon.com: "The Abu Ghraib Files," March 14, 2006, http://www.salon.com/news/abu_ghraib/2006/03/14/introduction/index.html.

16. The question was posed on the cover of *Time* magazine, May 17, 2004, at the height of the scandal.

17. Karen Greenberg and Joshua Dratel, eds., *The Torture Papers: The Road to Abu Ghraib* (New York: Cambridge University Press, 2005), 449, 632.

18. See Seymour Hersh's series of articles in the *New Yorker* during 2004 and his book *Chain of Command: The Road from 9/11 to Abu Ghraib* (New York: HarperCollins, 2004). Also relevant here are Meron Benvenisti, ed., *Abu Ghraib: The Politics of Torture* (Berkeley, CA: North Atlantic Books, 2004); and Greenberg and Dratel, *The Torture Papers*, 909–975.

19. Greenberg and Dratel, *The Torture Papers*, 970ff. See also Philip Zimbardo et al., "Interpersonal Dynamics in a Simulated Prison," *International Journal of Criminology and Penology* 1 (1973): 69–97.

20. Zimbardo was approached by the attorney of one of the accused soldiers. He worked as an advisor of the court in this case and argued that in Abu Ghraib Prison the same situational factors were at work as in the Stanford Prison Experiment. See Philip G. Zimbardo, *The Lucifer Effect: How Good People Turn Evil* (New York: Random House, 2007).

21. "Action is ritualized if the acts of which it is composed are constituted not by the intentions which the actor has in performing them, but by prior stipulation.... In adopting the ritual stance one accepts ... that in a very important sense, one will not be the

author of one's acts," in Caroline Humphrey and James Laidlaw, *The Archetypal Actions of Ritual: A Theory of Ritual Illustrated by the Jain Rite of Worship* (Oxford: Clarendon Press, 1994), 97–98.

22. Other violent acts have also been reported: one of the prisoners was knocked unconscious and another was hit so hard on the chest that the medic had to be summoned. Seven soldiers participated in the abuse. For further details see George F. Fay and Anthony R. Jones, "The Fay-Jones Report," in *The Torture Papers: The Road to Abu Ghraib*, ed. Karen G. Greenberg and Joshua L. Dretel (New York: Cambridge University Press, 2005), 987–1131.

23. Sabrina Harman, who appears in the "body pile" picture and who took many of the infamous photos, told investigative journalists that her camera work was casual, not the result of any plan or torture technique. See P. Gourevitch and E. Morris, "Exposure: The Woman Behind the Camera at Abu Ghraib," *New Yorker*, March 24, 2008, 10–12, http://www.newyorker.com/reporting/2008/03/24/080324fa_fact_gourevitch?currentPage=all. Her account, however, is questionable. She may have wanted to downplay the importance of her picture taking in the prison, or she may have been less than conscious of its role in the torture process. The interpretation we give is based on analysis of the photos themselves and their subsequent history of dissemination.

24. This "self-referential" or self-informing aspect of rituals as communication is emphasized by Roy Rappaport, *Ecology, Meaning, and Religion* (Richmond, CA: North Atlantic, 1979), 52ff.

25. Stephen Holmes, "Is Defiance of Law a Proof of Success? Magical Thinking in the War on Terror," in *The Torture Debate in America*, ed. Karen J. Greenberg (New York: Cambridge University Press, 2006), 118–135.

26. Take for example the famous "Dirty Harry" played by Clint Eastwood, but also popular TV series such as *Dexter*, where a serial killer refers to killing bad guys as "taking out the garbage."

27. Dora Apel explores the visual and political links between the Abu Ghraib photographs and lynching photographs in American history. See her "Torture Culture: Lynching Photographs and the Images of Abu Ghraib," *Art Journal* (2005): 88–100. See also note 2.

28. See Fay and Jones, "The Fay-Jones Report," 1079.

29. Mikhail Bakhtin, *Rabelais and His World* (Cambridge, MA: MIT Press, 1968), 318.

30. In many societies, these occasions of liminality and antistructure reproduce or reflect social structure. See Victor Turner, *The Ritual Process: Structure and Anti-structure* (Baltimore: Penguin, 1974).

31. Bakhtin, *Rabelais and His World*, 28.

32. Darby handed over a CD of Abu Ghraib torture photographs to the U.S. Army's Criminal Investigation Command in January 2004. Darby appeared on the CBS investigative news program *60 Minutes*, December 10, 2006.

33. The importance of photography in modern torture goes beyond the dissemination of images to the public.

34. Slavoj Zizek, "Between Two Deaths: The Culture of Torture," *London Review of Books*, June 3, 2004, http://www.lrb.co.uk/v26/n11/print/zize01.html.

35. Luke 23:35–37.

36. W. J. T. Mitchell, "Echoes of a Christian Symbol: Photo Reverberates with the Raw Power of Christ on Cross," *Chicago Tribune*, June 27, 2004.

37. The script for the series was offered to Fox in 2003, but Fox was not interested. In 2004 they reconsidered, maybe because similar action-oriented series such as *Lost* or *24* were highly successful, but another explanation might be the cultural impact of the Abu Ghraib scandal. The scandal made it possible to depict innocent prisoners, abuse in prisons, and criticism of the death sentence.

38. See, for example, the following: Hans Joas, "Punishment and Respect: The Sacralization of the Person and Its Endangerment," *Journal of Classical Sociology* 8, no. 2 (2008): 159–177; Lisa Silverman, *Tortured Subjects: Pain, Truth, and the Body in Early Modern France* (Chicago: University of Chicago Press, 2001); John H. Langbein, *Torture and the Law of Proof: Europe and England in the Ancient Regime* (Chicago: University of Chicago Press, 1977); Michel Foucault, *Discipline and Punish: The Birth of the Prison*, trans. Alan Sheridan (New York: Pantheon, 1977).

39. Representative of advocates of torture is Alan M. Dershowitz, *Why Terrorism Works: Understanding the Threat, Responding to the Challenge* (New Haven: Yale University Press, 2002).

40. Jane Mayer, "Whatever It Takes: The Politics of the Man Behind '24,'" *New Yorker*, February 19, 2007, 66–82, quotes Rejali in tracing the ticking-bomb scenario to a French work of fiction at the time of the war in Algeria. Rejali's research yielded no evidence that this suggested link was based on fact.

41. Holmes, "Is Defiance of Law a Proof of Success?," 128. In Fox Television's series *24*, Jack Bauer is the heroic figure capable of doing the "dirty work" necessary to safeguard the state and its citizens, precisely because he has been hardened by his own experience of being tortured. Also see Madeline Hron, "Torture Goes Pop," *Peace Review* 20, no. 1 (2008): 22–30.

42. Aristotle, *Rhetoric*, book I, chapter 15.

43. Some of the testimony comes from former intelligence officers. Darius Rejali has demonstrated the deficiencies of torture as a means of intelligence gathering in his *Torture and Democracy*. Two months after September 11, 2001, John Derbyshire wrote in the *National Review Online*: "The first thing to be said about torture, as a means of discovering facts, was said by Aristotle in Book 1, Chapter 15 of *Rhetoric*: 'torture doesn't work very well.'" Robert Conquest, in *The Great Terror: A Reassessment* (New York: Oxford University Press, 1991), gives a figure of "one in a hundred" for those who failed to confess under the methods used by Stalin's secret police. However, most of those pulled in by the NKVD (the forerunner of the KGB) were ordinary people guilty of nothing at all. Dedicated resistance workers, fanatical terrorists, or revolutionaries would show better stats. In his memoir, *Nothing to Declare* (New York: Atlantic Monthly Press, 1994), Taki Theodoracopulos tells the story of a young World War II Greek resistance fighter named Perrikos, who blew up the German headquarters building in Athens on orders from Taki's father. Arrested and tortured to death by the Nazis, Perrikos revealed nothing, claiming to the end that he had acted alone, under no one's orders: "There were many such cases." See also Philippe Sands, *Torture Team: Rumsfeld's Memo and the Betrayal of American Values* (New

York: Palgrave Macmillan, 2008), who argues against the notion that torture provides useful information; and Vladimir Bukovsky, "Torture's Long Shadow," *Washington Post*, December 18, 2005, sec. 1.

44. Andy Worthington, "Former US Interrogator Damien Corsetti Recalls the Torture of Prisoners in Bagram and Abu Ghraib," Andy Worthington Blog, http://www.andyworthington.co.uk/2007/12/21/former-us-interrogator-damien-corsetti-recalls-the-torture-of-prisoners-in-bagram-and-abu-ghraib/. Also, see Worthington's *The Guantanamo Files: The Stories of the 774 Detainees in America's Illegal Prison* (London: Pluto Press, 2007).

45. William Cavanaugh, *Torture and Eucharist: Theology, Politics and the Body of Christ* (Malden, MA: Wiley-Blackwell, 1998), 12.

46. See Tom Driver, *Liberating Rites: Understanding the Transformative Power of Ritual* (Boulder, CO: Westview Press, 1998), 80–81.

47. Cruelty seems to be part of our species' inheritance. From her observations of a chimpanzee "war" at Gombe, Jane Goodall reports that chimpanzees are capable of cruel behavior. That is, they understand that certain actions cause pain, and they are capable of empathizing with the victim: "Chimpanzees are intellectually incapable of creating the horrifying tortures that human ingenuity has devised for the deliberate infliction of suffering. Nevertheless, they are capable to some extent of imputing desires and feelings to others and . . . they are almost certainly capable of feelings akin to sympathy. . . . The chimpanzee . . . stands at the very threshold of human achievement in destruction, cruelty, and planned intergroup conflict." See *The Chimpanzees of Gombo* (Cambridge, MA: Belknap Press, 1986), 533–534.

48. The phenomena of "the sacred" and "the demonic" are alike in that both stand in contrast to the mundane, and both evoke the twin qualities noted by Rudolf Otto as belonging to "the holy," namely fascination and awe. See Rudolph Otto, *The Idea of the Holy* (London: Oxford University Press, 1950 [1917]).

49. Catherine Bell, *Ritual Theory, Ritual Practice* (New York: Oxford University Press, 1992), 91.

50. This same quality of the forbidden holy, with its overtones of awe and fascination, is dramatized in Jean Genet's play *The Balcony*, trans. Bernard Frechtman (New York: Grove Press, 1960), which takes place simultaneously in a royal palace and a brothel while a revolution is brewing. The brothel is viewed as a house of imagination, which is necessary to the exercise of power in the state. See also Tom F. Driver, *Jean Genet* (New York: Columbia University Press, 1966).

51. Gavin Hood, dir., *Rendition*, New Line Cinema, 2007.

52. Foucault, *Discipline and Punish*, 7–9.

53. Jeremy Waldron, "Torture and Positive Law: Jurisprudence for the White House," *Columbia Law Review* 105, no. 6 (2005): 1681–1750.

54. Foucault, *Discipline and Punish*, 33–34; Foucault is quoting G. Olyffe, *An Essay to Prevent Capital Crimes* (London, 1731).

55. President Obama's attorney general, Eric Holder, broke with the Bush administration's attorney general, Michael Mukasey, over the question of waterboarding. During his Senate confirmation hearing, when asked whether he considered waterboarding torture,

Holder answered: "If you look at the history of the use of that technique, used by the Khmer Rouge, used in the Inquisition, used by the Japanese and prosecuted by us as war crimes. We prosecuted our own soldiers for using it in Vietnam. I agree with you, Mr. Chairman, waterboarding is torture." Holder's Senate hearing transcript was printed in the *New York Times*, January 16, 2009, sec. 1. It remains to be seen whether charges of war crimes will be brought against members of the Bush administration for authorizing the use of waterboarding.

56. See Klein, "'Never Before!,'" 11–12.

57. Giorgio Agamben, *Homo Sacer: Sovereign Power and Bare Life*, trans. Daniel Heller-Roazen (Stanford, CA: Stanford University Press, 1998), 66.

58. Zizek, "Between Two Deaths."

59. Holmes, "Is Defiance of Law a Proof of Success?," 131.

60. Foucault, *Discipline and Punish*, 34.

61. Elaine Scarry, *The Body in Pain* (London: Oxford University Press, 1985).

62. Foucault, *Discipline and Punish*, 63.

63. The authors created a chart based on a keyword search for *torture* in the Internet Movie Database as of December 18, 2008 (http://www.imdb.com/keyword/torture/). The database displays the search results in groups of 100 titles. The years shown at the bottom of the chart are the release dates of the last film in each group. The first group begins with a film released in 1912 (*Più che la morte*, a short Italian crime thriller) and ends in 1943. The second group begins in 1943 and ends in 1962, and so on. The number of films in each group (100) was divided by the number of years in each group to give the average per group. The calculations are thus imprecise. The database probably underrepresents the earlier years. Also, part of the rise in the number of films having to do with torture may be due to increases in the total number of films released over the years. Nevertheless, the steep incline since 2001 appears to indicate a dramatic growth in motion pictures involving torture after 9/11.

64. For the derivation of this phrase, see Jane Mayer, *The Dark Side: The Inside Story on How the War on Terror Turned into a War on American Ideals* (New York: Doubleday, 2008). See also *Taxi to the Dark Side*, directed by Alex Gibney (Jigsaw Productions, 2007).

65. See Naomi Klein, *The Shock Doctrine: The Rise of Disaster Capitalism* (New York: Metropolitan Books, 2007).

66. See Kathryn Reklis, "Prime-Time Torture: Jack Bauer as a Hero of Our Time," *Christian Century*, June 3, 2008.

67. Cavanaugh, *Torture and Eucharist*, 12.

68. Cavanaugh, *Torture and Eucharist*, 22.

69. Cavanaugh, *Torture and Eucharist*, 24.

70. Cavanaugh, *Torture and Eucharist*, 30–33.

71. Washington's prohibition of torture and inhumane treatment of prisoners of war during the American Revolution was in sharp contrast to the practice of the British. Some historians think the practice helped turn the tide in the Americans' favor by raising the morale of their soldiers while increasing the rate of desertion among the British. See Mayer, *The Dark Side*, 83–84.

72. Turner, *The Ritual Process*.

REFERENCES

"The Abu Ghraib Files." Salon.com, March 14, 2006, http://www.salon.com/news/abu_ghraib/2006/03/14/introduction/index.html.

Agamben, Giorgio. *Homo Sacer: Sovereign Power and Bare Life*. Translated by Daniel Heller-Roazen. Stanford, CA: Stanford University Press, 1998.

Apel, Dora. "Torture Culture: Lynching Photographs and the Images of Abu Ghraib." *Art Journal* 64, no. 2 (2005): 88–100.

Bakhtin, Mikhail. *Rabelais and His World*. Cambridge, MA: MIT Press, 1968.

Bell, Catherine. *Ritual Theory, Ritual Practice*. New York: Oxford University Press, 1992.

Bennett, Lance W., Regina G. Lawrence, and Steven Livingston. "None Dare Call It Torture: Indexing and the Limits of Press Independence in the Abu Ghraib Scandal." *Journal of Communication* 56 (2006): 467–485.

Benvenisti, Meron, ed. *Abu Ghraib: The Politics of Torture*. Berkeley, CA: North Atlantic Books, 2004.

Bukovsky, Vladimir. "Torture's Long Shadow." *Washington Post*, December 18, 2005, sec. 1.

Cavanaugh, William T. *Torture and Eucharist: Theology, Politics, and the Body of Christ*. Malden, MA: Wiley-Blackwell, 1998.

Conquest, Robert. *The Great Terror: A Reassessment*. New York: Oxford University Press, 1991.

Danner, Mark. "Frozen Scandal." *New York Review of Books* 55, no. 19 (2008): 26–28.

Dershowitz, Alan M. *Why Terrorism Works: Understanding the Threat, Responding to the Challenge*. New Haven: Yale University Press, 2002.

Driver, Tom F. *Jean Genet*. New York: Columbia University Press, 1966.

———. *Liberating Rites: Understanding the Transformative Power of Ritual*. Boulder, CO: Westview Press, 1998.

Fay, George F., and Anthony R. Jones. "The Fay-Jones Report." In *The Torture Papers: The Road to Abu Ghraib*, edited by Karen G. Greenberg and Joshua L. Dretel, 987–1131. New York: Cambridge University Press, 2005.

Foucault, Michel. *Discipline and Punish: The Birth of the Prison*. Translated by Alan Sheridan. New York: Pantheon, 1977.

Genet, Jean. *The Balcony*. Translated by Bernard Frechtman. New York: Grove Press, 1960.

Gibney, Alex, dir. *Taxi to the Dark Side*. Jigsaw Productions, 2007.

Goodall, Jane. *The Chimpanzees of Gombe*. Cambridge, MA: Belknap Press, 1986.

Gourevitch, P., and E. Morris. "Exposure: The Woman behind the Camera at Abu Ghraib." *New Yorker*, March 24, 2008, http://www.newyorker.com/reporting/2008/03/24/080324fa_fact_gourevitch?currentPage=all.

Greenberg, Karen J., and Joshua L. Dratel, eds. *The Torture Papers: The Road to Abu Ghraib*. New York: Cambridge University Press, 2005.

Grimes, Ronald L. *Ritual Criticism: Case Studies in Its Practice, Essays on Its Theory*. Columbia: University of South Carolina Press, 1990.

Grossman, Dave. *On Killing: The Psychological Cost of Learning to Kill in War and Society*. New York: Little, Brown, 1995.

Haggis, Paul, dir. *In the Valley of Elah*. Warner Independent Pictures, 2007.

Hersh, Seymour M. *Chain of Command: The Road from 9/11 to Abu Ghraib*. New York: Harper Perennial, 2005.

———. "Torture at Abu Ghraib." *New Yorker*, May 10, 2004.

Holmes, Stephen. "Is Defiance of Law a Proof of Success? Magical Thinking in the War on Terror." In *The Torture Debate in America*, edited by Karen J. Greenberg, 118–135. New York: Cambridge University Press, 2006.

Hood, Gavin, dir. *Rendition*. New Line Cinema, 2007.

Hron, Madeline. "Torture Goes Pop." *Peace Review* 20, no. 1 (2008): 22–30.

Humphrey, Caroline, and James Laidlaw. *The Archetypal Actions of Ritual: A Theory of Ritual Illustrated by the Jain Rite of Worship*. Oxford: Clarendon Press, 1994.

Joas, Hans. "Punishment and Respect: The Sacralization of the Person and Its Endangerment." *Journal of Classical Sociology* 8, no. 2 (2008): 159–177.

Klein, Naomi. "'Never Before!' Our Amnesiac Torture Debate." *The Nation*, December 26, 2005.

———. *The Shock Doctrine: The Rise of Disaster Capitalism*. New York: Metropolitan Books, 2007.

Langbein, John H. *Torture and the Law of Proof: Europe and England in the Ancient Regime*. Chicago: University of Chicago Press, 1977.

Leung, Rebecca. "Abuse of Iraqi POWs by GIs Probed: 60 Minutes II Has Exclusive Report on Alleged Mistreatment," *60 Minutes*, April 20, 2004, http://www.cbsnews.com/stories/2004/04/27/60II/main614063.shtml.

Mayer, Jane. *The Dark Side: The Inside Story of How the War on Terror Turned Into a War on American Ideals*. New York: Doubleday, 2008.

———. "Whatever It Takes: The Politics of the Man Behind '24.'" *New Yorker*, February 19, 2007, 66–82.

Mitchell, W. J. T. "Echoes of a Christian Symbol: Photo Reverberates with the Raw Power of Christ on Cross." *Chicago Tribune*, June 27, 2004.

Nuwer, Hank, ed. *The Hazing Reader*. Bloomington: University of Indiana Press, 2004.

Olyffe, George. *An Essay Humbl'y Offer'd, for An Act of Parliament to Prevent Capital Crimes, and prevent the loss of many lives; and to Promote a Desirable Improvement and Blessing in the Nation*. London, 1731.

Otto, Rudolf. *The Idea of the Holy*. London: Oxford University Press, 1950 [1917].

Rappaport, Roy A. *Ecology, Meaning, and Religion*. Richmond, CA: North Atlantic, 1979.

Razack, Sherene. *Dark Threats and White Knights: The Somalia Affair, Peacekeeping and the New Imperialism*. Toronto: University of Toronto Press, 2004.

Rejali, Darius M. *Torture and Democracy*. Princeton: Princeton University Press, 2007.

Reklis, Kathryn. "Prime-Time Torture: Jack Bauer as a Hero of Our Time." *Christian Century*, June 3, 2008.

Sands, Philippe. *Torture Team: Rumsfeld's Memo and the Betrayal of American Values*. New York: Palgrave Macmillan, 2008.

Scarry, Elaine. *The Body in Pain*. London: Oxford University Press, 1985.

Silverman, Lisa. *Tortured Subjects: Pain, Truth, and the Body in Early Modern France*. Chicago: University of Chicago Press, 2001.

Smith, Jonathan Z. "The Bare Facts of Ritual." *History of Religion* 20, no. 1–2 (1980): 124–125.

Theodoracopulos, Taki. *Nothing to Declare*. New York: Atlantic Monthly Press, 1994.
Turner, Victor. *The Ritual Process: Structure and Anti-structure*. Baltimore: Penguin, 1974.
Waldron, Jeremy. "Torture and Positive Law: Jurisprudence for the White House." *Columbia Law Review* 105, no. 6 (2005): 1681–1750.
Winslow, Donna. "Rites of Passage and Group Bonding in the Canadian Airborne." In *The Hazing Reader*, ed. Hank Nuwer, 147–170. Bloomington: University of Indiana Press, 2004.
Worthington, Andy. "Former U.S. Interrogator Damien Corsetti Recalls the Torture of Prisoners in Bagram and Abu Ghraib." Andy Worthington Blog, http://www.andyworthington.co.uk/.
———. *The Guantanamo Files: The Stories of the 774 Detainees in America's Illegal Prison*. London: Pluto Press, 2007.
Zimbardo, Philip G. *The Lucifer Effect: How Good People Turn Evil*. New York: Random House, 2007.
Zimbardo, Philip, et al. "Interpersonal Dynamics in a Simulated Prison." *International Journal of Criminology and Penology* 1 (1973): 69–97.
Zizek, Slavoj. "Between Two Deaths: The Culture of Torture." *London Review of Books*, June 3, 2004.

9

Refracting Ritual: An Upside-Down Perspective on Ritual, Media, and Conflict

Michael Houseman

The contributors to this volume have gone out of their way to make their intellectual lives difficult. In tackling the interplay of ritual, media, and conflict, they have taken on a humanities equivalent of the unresolved "three-body problem" in celestial mechanics: how to compute the mutual gravitational interaction of three masses. Getting a grasp on the ritual-media-conflict question, however, is complicated in a typically terrestrial, social sciences way. The bodies in question, far from being well-defined physical objects, are conceptual constructs, derived from the analysis of empirical events whose very nature is subject to debate. In the course of the project's history, the contributors entertained a wealth of partially contradictory propositions and queries: Ritual resolves conflict. Ritual disguises conflict, thereby amplifying it. Mediatizing conflict spreads it. If mediatization escalates, does ritualization follow suit, or does ritualization decline? When ritual and media interact, how do the patterns of conflict change? Such questions attest to the novelty and far-reaching character of their joint adventure but also to the conceptual difficulties it involves.

It is hardly surprising that Grimes's generous, even-handed introduction is largely devoted to unpacking the complex issues raised by these alternative touchstone statements, so as to better stake out a middle ground between unprovable generalities and ethnographic truisms. While tracing the project's collaborative history, he is mainly concerned with making explicit some of the authors' shared presuppositions regarding ritual, media, conflict, and the connections among them. The contributors are less preoccupied with identifying the boundaries of these concepts than in describing their interrelationships. However, as Grimes recognizes, definitional issues cannot simply be ignored, and addressing them will allow me to add my own two cents to the mix ("We're not just looking for polite words" was Grimes's admonition when inviting me to write this chapter).

Conflict

Conflict plays a somewhat special, all-encompassing role in this collection. It is at once the most pervasive and least conceptualized of the title's three terms. Dispute intervenes mostly as a context, as the regrettable yet recurrent state of affairs providing empirical situations in which ritual and media come into play. Precipitated or acted upon by one or the other or both, conflict's own distinctive properties remain largely unexamined. In short, conflict in these contributions intervenes more as a backdrop than as a "body."

One partial exception is described in the introduction and appears in several of the essays. A model of conflict advanced by sociologist Philip Smith holds that the essence of violent dispute (war being the prime example) is ritual, conceived as the source of an unquestionable polarization that sets a positively connoted "us" in opposition to a negatively weighted "them." As Grimes remarks, this view relies on an overly narrow understanding of ritual as "the mobilization of cultural symbols in the service of a sacralized we/they dualism." Alternatively, it implies an abusively comprehensive understanding of ritual as equivalent to symbolic practice in general. Following Gregory Bateson, for example, one might argue instead that polarization is an intrinsic, potentiating feature not of ritual but of conflict. From this standpoint, one should expect the discursive, iconic, and enacted representations called upon to advocate and justify the escalation of dispute, to make ample use of conflict's tendency to give rise to polar opposites. Such representations may include ritual events, but this is not necessarily the case. Thus, when Smith speaks of ritual (as opposed to instrumental) motivations for fighting, I would say that he is really speaking of something much broader, namely symbolism.

While the idea that symbolic polarizations are necessarily instances of ritual is highly debatable, it does have the merit of underscoring the fact that conflict and ritual are in no way antithetical. Indeed, one of the originalities of this collection is its insistence, "We do not assume that conflict is necessarily bad any more than we assume that ritual is always good." Thus, while recognizing that "ritual may be a means for peacemaking," the contributors have chosen to concentrate "on ritual as a factor in conflict rather than as a means for resolving it."

Old ideas die hard, however, and many of the chapters' analyses are implicitly built on the idea that conflicts are better resolved and that ritual has a role to play in this process. This important issue deserves clarification. The distinctive efficacy of ritual does not reside in its ability to provide answers to problems raised by social life. At best, it recontextualizes particular predicaments in a way that allows answers to be sought more easily elsewhere, by means of the myriad resources humans have at their disposable: intimidation, seduction, logical reasoning, secrecy, storytelling, negotiation, bluff, and so forth. On the other hand, ritual is particularly apt at transmitting certain fundamental questions in the light of which social life, including the problems it entails, may be defined. Ritual does not so much clarify identities or set things straight as it perpetuates, in a way that makes them particularly difficult to deny, the mysteries and unresolved issues that we hold dear. In other words and stated more positively, ritual promotes the ongoing relevance of certain axiomatic cultural values and ideas by packaging them, along with their attendant ambiguities and contradictions, in the form of somewhat enigmatic, yet highly memorable, enactments that are hard to argue with. Thus, while rituals are often occasioned by disputes or precipitated by transformative events in which unsettled concerns come to the fore, they remain decidedly ambivalent with respect to the resolution of these issues. Although they act to redefine particular contentions, at the same time, they corroborate and sustain the conceptual and relational grounds from which these contentions arise. In this way, ritual does somewhat less than what we might like to believe. However, what it does do, it does better than most anything else: provide an authoritative basis for the establishment, persistence, and incremental transformation of traditions geared to the organization of embodied action.

It is worth stressing that there are at least two clear advantages to having chosen conflict as a field of investigation. The first is that it anchors academic speculations regarding ritual and media to immediate, widely shared pragmatic concerns. The second is that it simplifies analysis in a realistic rather than purely logical fashion, thereby paving the way for fruitful comparison. Because of conflict's polarizing tendencies, the widely varying case studies can be easily grasped as being organized around issues having essentially two sides.

Ritual and Ritualization

In arguing for the specificity of ritual as a particular mode of symbolic practice with distinctive potency, I come up against what is perhaps the key concept in many of these chapters: ritualization. Indeed, the contributors speak of ritual but mostly of ritualization, thereby focusing attention on how events may be said to acquire certain ritual-like characteristics. This approach, as explicated by Grimes in his introduction, draws on a series of features that, while not definitive of ritual, are often associated with it. Ritual is deemed to be, among other things, "embodied, enacted, spatially rooted, temporally bounded, prescribed, formalized, and repeated or singularized." These are the qualities that are held to characterize ritualization. To the extent that they are present to a greater or lesser degree, a given activity may be said to be more or less ritualized. Thus, recapitulates Grimes, "No activity is a ritual, but any action can be ritualized." From a methodological point of view, this perspective is both appropriate and highly productive. Much of the material presented in this volume would be excluded if a stricter, more static conception of ceremonial activity were adopted. To be able to envisage works of art, acts of public vandalism, encounters over the Internet, protest marches, and political torture as instances of ritualization casts them in a new, unexpected light, allowing certain heretofore neglected aspects of these phenomena to come to the fore. However, every conceptual choice worth its salt has a price to pay, and it is useful to tease out exactly what that price is.

The problem is that ritual, as distinct from ritualization, doesn't seem to go away. This ambiguity is present, for example, when the latter notion is first introduced: "Ritualization, that is, activities that display fewer of the qualities normally associated with ritual." Normally associated by whom? Also, consider the following: "A ritual is what happens when someone notices ordinary ritualization and then compresses, reframes, and enacts it." The key word in this just-so story is *reframes*, which is a somewhat circular shorthand for "reframes as ritual," to be understood as that which makes "ordinary ritualization" recognizable as an instance of nonordinary ritual enactment. The question remains: Who is doing the noticing and the reframing? The answer would seem to be that it is the actors themselves: "ritualization," says Grimes, "refers to the process of increasing the extent to which something is pushed in the direction of socially recognizable ritual." Similarly, Binder, Driver, and Stephenson, while strenuously arguing in their contribution that torture is ritualized violence, nonetheless consider, "The principal reason it would be awkward to call torture ritual is that there is no cultural understanding of it as ritual." Thus, while ritualization is defined theoretically as the greater or lesser presence of particular qualities (embodied enactment, spatial and temporal delimitation, prescription, formality, and so forth), ritual is treated as a local (that is, ethnocentrically grounded) concept whose nature and extension vary from one cultural tradition to the next. In short, there is no such thing as ritual in general. However, I suspect, and Grimes's own formulations bear witness to this, that at least some of the contributors (I count myself among them) are less than satisfied with the impoverished, atomistic understanding of ritual that this position implies: ritual as a fuzzy set of typical features. Many of them, while espousing, in principle, a family-resemblance strategy that renders any distinction between ritual and ritualization superfluous, nonetheless hesitate to abandon this discrimination altogether, hence the feeling that beneath the surface of the analytical perspective adopted in this volume is the unacceptable desire to have one's ritual cake and eat it too.

The difficulty is that the alternative to this position also has its problems. To begin with, as Grimes shows, there is a variety of theoretical definitions of ritual to choose from. But more important, whatever the definition chosen, to the extent that ritual is held to be distinct from ritualization, the latter loses its tight connection to the former, regardless of how it is locally framed. Ritualization may be regarded as being like ritual, as evocative of ritual, as a metaphor for ritual, or what have you, but it is pointedly not ritual. While such a stance may be close in spirit to that taken by some of the contributors, it weakens the volume's overall argument considerably.

Trying to get out of this dilemma is daunting. As I see it, two things are required. On the one hand, it is necessary to provide a substantive account of ritual that, while sufficiently discriminatory, is able to subsume certain practices that depart significantly from canonical ceremonial forms. On the other hand, it is necessary to provide the grounds for an organic link between ritual and ritualization such that ritualization becomes simply the process whereby ritual is put into effect. This is fairly close to the approach favored by Grimes, but entails turning his proposal on its head: I am looking for a conceptual framework in which ritualization is soluble in a well-defined notion of ritual rather than the other way around. Let me briefly try to outline in the following two sections what such an upside-down framework might be.

Ritual as a Mode of Participation

Ritual, as Grimes remarks, is not a thing or even an event, but a way of partaking in an event. To springboard off Jonathan Z. Smith into more (inter)action-oriented waters, we might say that ritual is a particular way of paying attention to what one is doing (with others).[1] It thus pertains to the nature of the connection, as experienced by participants, between the actions they undertake and their intentional and emotional dispositions. This connection can take different forms, each of which may be said to define a particular mode of participation. One of these modes of participation, I suggest, is ritual. In ritual, participants' attention is focused less on how their actions may be construed as expressing their personal attitudes, feelings, and beliefs than on how their attitudes, feelings, and beliefs may be informed by the accomplishment of certain actions.

In this perspective, ritual is less a category of behavior than one among several possible pragmatic presuppositions that tacitly or explicitly govern people's participation in particular events. Another mode of participation is spectacle, in which, as in ritual, participants' attention is directed at how attitudes, feelings, and beliefs are affected by the performance of certain actions; however, in this case, it is not the performer's own intentional and emotional dispositions, but those of others that are purported to be affected by the actions undertaken. Still another mode is play, in which participants' actions are taken to express their personal feelings and motivations, all the while being pursued in conformity with what are perceived to be certain out-of-the-ordinary conventions. These different modes of participation are often combined in various ways.[2] They can be juxtaposed to each other or embedded within each other; they can oscillate from one mode to the other, and so forth. Indeed, the underlying idea of the model I am proposing is that most empirical events are not pure instances of any particular mode, but composite configurations giving rise to distinctive emotional, intentional, relational, and esthetic effects.

In any given performance, the ritual mode of attention is embraced by those concerned to a greater or lesser degree. Not only are some individuals less attentive to what they are doing than others, but what is resolutely ritual for some may be intuitively experienced by others as spectacle, play, or something else entirely. Moreover, an individual's mode of participation may vary in the course of the enactment. At the same time, however, the practical exigencies of ongoing coordinated interaction tend to minimize such disparities, orienting participants' perceptual and performative expectations along parallel lines. From this point of view, ritual, as one among a number of organizational principles governing the perception and patterning of social activity, is best understood as a statistical phenomenon not unlike a mathematical "attractor." In other words, ritual is a stable pattern of probabilities in the distribution of participants' attentiveness within a field of possible modes of participation. To qualify an enactment as ritual or ritualized thus amounts to the same thing. It is to entertain the hypothesis that the actors participate in this enactment by tacitly or explicitly attending to how their personal attitudes, feelings, and beliefs may be affected by their performance of certain actions. To speak of an event as a ritual is to estimate that this pragmatic presupposition is adopted by the participants in such a systematic fashion as to approach the theoretical limit of absolute ritualization.

We do not have direct access to how people attend to what they are doing. For this reason, and in order to avoid basing our analysis on local categorical schemes, analytical hypotheses and estimates regarding the ritualistic character of particular events, while fueled by the utterances of those involved, are founded on properties of the events themselves. Ritual is potentially present in any situation. However, what Don Handelman has called the "design features" of certain events favor a ritual mode of participation more readily than others.[3] Among these features is the use of distinctive designations, the evocation of authorities, as well as the morphological traits identified by Grimes (spatial and temporal delimitation, formality, repetition, etc.). All these features are concomitant qualities of ritual, ones that often contribute to the emergence and persistence of ritual activities, but which are not, strictly speaking, definitive criteria.

Foremost among these design features is the incorporation of a measure of structural indeterminacy or complexity that endows lived-through performance with a degree of self-reference, making it difficult for participants to make sense of what they are doing in other than ritual terms, that is, as exceptional enactments, meaningful in and of themselves, whose presumed significance is accessible solely by means of their performance. I have argued elsewhere that a privileged wellspring of such complexity is "ritual condensation," in which the simultaneous actualization of nominally contrary forms of relationship gives rise to highly evocative items of behavior that are difficult to account for in terms of everyday intentionalities and patterns of relationship.[4] This feature is indeed typical of events that anthropologists readily recognize as rituals, in which, for example, affirmations of identity are at the same time testimonies of difference, displays of authority are also demonstrations of subordination, the presence of persons or other beings is at once corroborated and denied, secrets are simultaneously dissimulated and revealed, and so forth.

Recent work on contemporary Western ceremonial, however, has prompted me to envisage another recurrent source of structural indeterminacy favoring a ritual mode of attentiveness. It relates less to the organization of the actions undertaken than to the definition of the agents who undertake them, that is, the participants themselves.[5] Taking this further design feature into account will allow us to envisage some of the cases in this volume in a new light.

Ritual Refraction

Consider the following example. In the course of her "first blood" ritual, largely designed by one of her mother's friends, Sonia, wearing a long hooded robe and carrying a basket of flowers, is led into the center of a circle formed by the participating women dressed in red. Standing close together, they "teach [her] who the Goddess actually is" by repeatedly singing: "Listen, listen, listen to my heart's song; I will never forget you, I will never forsake you; I will always love you, I will always be with you."[6] For the participants, I suggest, this performance does not so much proceed from their own private feelings and beliefs as it expresses the sentiments and convictions of beings (Orphic priestesses? Amerindian sagewomen?) deemed wiser and more natural than themselves whose attitudes they seek to emulate and whose ceremonial footsteps they do their best to follow. However, as the scene ends, each of the participants finds herself to be deeply affected: "For a long time [Sonia] only stares down at her feet. But we continue to sing, and after a while she raises her head, as if the spirit moves her to a place of strength. She then looks calmly into our eyes, one by one, as she slowly turns clockwise in the circle. To watch this shift from shyness to calm and conscious eye contact is a moving experience, and some of the women, including her mother, start to weep."[7]

And now, a second example. During Ken Cadigan's firewalking workshop, participants are led through a six-hour preparatory process that allows them to get in touch with their inner "fire of the heart" and to "be open to who [they] are" so as to be able to confront and overcome "fear and limiting beliefs." This involves praying, dancing, chanting, listening to stories and lectures, talking to themselves ("My intention is to have a healing experience"), "speaking from the heart" about themselves to others, visualizing their desires, writing down what they wish to abandon to the fire, and so on. Having thus revealed this unsuspected potential within themselves, the participants are ready to walk through the fire: "Let the coals invite you. Go in when you feel a big 'yes' in your heart." Their doing so is in large part upheld by a concerted effort on their part to become "extraordinary," that is, something other than what they usually feel themselves to be. However, it is as "ordinary" individuals that they come off the hot coals deeply moved, hugging each other and cheering "Yeah! All right! Way to go!"[8]

Enactments such as these are predicated less upon ritual condensation than upon what we might call "ritual refraction." The participants' personal attitudes, feelings, and beliefs are presumed to be affected by performances that do not consist of the pursuit of conventionally stipulated forms of behavior, but instead follow from an equally conventional emulation of what are held to be exemplary emotional and intentional qualities, often ascribed to non-Western, pre-Christian, or still more exotic others (Native American shamans, Celtic priestesses, Ascended Masters, etc.) or to more authoritative aspects of the participants themselves (one's inner child, one's spiritual self, the Goddess within, etc.). In other words, these rituals are organized less around the performance of archetypal actions, as discussed by Humphrey and Laidlaw,[9] than around the instantiation of archetypal agencies defined by a set of axiomatic intentional and emotional dispositions. Correlatively, the potency of these practices relates not to the special, mysterious character of the actors' behavior but to the exceptional, equally mysterious qualities taken on by the actors themselves. Indeed, ritual enactments such as these give rise to enhanced, refracted subjects spanning several contrary identities at once: the archetypal agencies the participants seek to emulate and the participants affected by the performances deriving from this emulation. The structural uncertainty intrinsic to this situation pertains not so much to what exactly is being done—typically, the actions carried out are rendered readily intelligible (by analogy, for example) in terms of everyday patterns of motivation and interaction—as to who exactly is doing it.

There are three particularities of identity-refracting ritual enactments that contrast markedly with more canonical ceremonial performances. First of all, self-conscious innovation and creativity are considered to be a necessary, pivotal feature of such practices, essential to their effectiveness. Existing or imagined religious traditions are taken to provide not models to follow but resources to be inventively explored with a view to their personalization, that is, their adaptation to the peculiarities of the situation at hand and the sensibilities of those involved. Thus, the practitioners' overriding concern is not to replicate antecedent ceremonies but rather to recapture, in themselves and in the performances they create, the spirit in which such ceremonies are presumed to have been performed.

Second, ritual enactments of this type are designed to be reflexive, the participants being made to relate to images, utterances, and somatic sensations that participants themselves deliberately generate. Such reflexivity is an essential feature that prevents the two opposing aspects of the participants' ritually engendered identities from collapsing into one. Thus, without calling their exceptional nature into question, many practitioners insist on the metaphorical significance of their performances, and few would maintain, for example, that they simply are, unequivocally, an Ascended Master or a Native American shaman.

This reflexivity is also closely connected with a third feature, the extensive use of immaterial props or devices. In more classical ceremonial events, ritual relationships among participants and between participants and nonhuman entities are generally, if not always, mediated by the manipulation of objects whose very physicality provides these difficult-to-grasp relationships with intention-laden material grounding. Here, however, although objects may be involved, the emergence of ritually constructed subjects is often mediated by immaterial representations that favor the ambiguities that these refracted identities bring into play. Visualization or creative projection, in which participants are affected by intangible, virtual performances largely of their own making, is a prime example of this.[10]

Personalized creativity, self-aware reflexivity, and the prevalence of immaterial representations, then, are among the concomitant characteristics of what I suggest is a largely undertheorized type of ritual activity.[11] As in all instances of ritual, the participants attend to how their pursuit of certain behaviors may impact upon their personal feelings, attitudes, and beliefs. The behaviors in question, however, rather than standing on their own (as archetypal actions), occur as actualizations of exemplary intentional and emotional qualities that are felt to be different from those of the individual participants who strive to emulate them. Participants are presumed to be affected by performances deriving from their attempt to assume these axiomatic qualities. Taking this refractive process into account should allow us to appreciate some of the events described in this book not as ritualized in the sense of having a number of ritual-like features (spatial and temporal delimitation, formality, repetition, etc.), but as enactments governed by the pragmatic presupposition (participants' dispositions follow from their actions) that defines a distinctly ritual mode of participation. To see how this might be the case, however, requires saying something about media and mediatization.

Media and Mediatization

"We use 'mediatization,'" says Grimes, "to denote the process that includes both constructing and receiving communications by way of a medium," the latter being "any means of communication that, metaphorically speaking, sits in a middle position thereby linking two parties." At different points in this volume, the contributors grapple with the question, what are media? As the above quotation suggests, the answer is, potentially, just about anything, including conflict and ritual activity itself. However, as Grimes and others make clear, the type of media that many of the authors are concerned with is what is often called mass media, addressed to a public audience: press, radio, television, Internet. Written, auditory, or visual representations communicated by mass media, by virtue of the distancing, technical processes that govern their production and because of the supposed anonymity of those to whom they are addressed, acquire a degree of autonomy with respect to senders and receivers. Such representations are capable of marshaling attention, inducing reactions, and being exploited in their own right. "Mediatization," denoting the construction, reception, and utilization of widely accessible depersonalized representations, thus goes far beyond the idea of information conveyed by a particular means. Rather, it is a cultural process geared to the production of and response to conventional, exemplary narratives, images, and sounds that do not so much portray the way things are as propose how things are supposed (in both senses) to be, untainted by the entanglements and irrepressible contingencies of personal relationships.[12]

Mediatization, as the creation and communication of such representative representations, is an increasingly banal feature of our contemporary social life. "For most people," say the authors of chapter 4, "their perception of the world is media based; their reality is media fed." It should thus come as no surprise that, as they go on to stress, "media representation [is] a powerful factor in identity making," and that, in general, people make privileged use of mediatized representations as benchmark references for their feelings, convictions, and behavior. Indeed, much of the time, most of us, consciously or not, are caught up in Alan Klima's far-reaching question that recalls the culture/nature perplexity (how can humans be part of nature and stand apart from it?) that Lévi-Strauss took to be the grain of sand around which the pearls of culture are formed: "How could the media be divested of 'real life,' when the media is, to some extent, our life?"[13] A case in point is provided by Grimes's discussion of "iconic" photographs such as those selected by World Press Photo: "An icon is any image that embodies itself in viewers with sufficient power that the viewers then echo, if not reproduce it." Grimes's use of the liturgically resonant term *icon* is no accident, and I would like to follow up on his observation that "ritual and media are not necessarily two separate things" by stressing how often mediatized products provide the basis for ritual enactments of the type described in the previous section. A number of cases analyzed by the contributors can be seen as self-affecting performances founded upon the emulation of mediatized representations exemplifying what are taken to be axiomatic attitudes, feelings, and beliefs.

In the perspective that I am proposing, the reflexive nature of many mediatized artifacts and entities, the fact that their ostensibly contrived nature encourages us to perceive ourselves perceiving them, in no way detracts from their aptitude to act as paradigmatic references for the organization of ritual events. On the contrary, this quality is consistent with what I have argued to be an essential feature of identity-refracting ritual: the unresolved tension between the participants as the extraordinary effecting parties and as those personally affected by the performances they undertake. This tension is the source of indeterminacy that sets such enactments apart from everyday intercourse and allows the participants to experience themselves as more than what they seem to be. The process becomes more circular and indeterminate when the mediatized representations concerned are, in part, of the participants' own making. There are a number of examples of this dynamic in the present volume. In such cases, the ritual performances in question follow from the reflexive emulation of archetypal others that are none other than the participants' mediatized selves. Ritualization is made to exploit the process of mediatization "by which the self recognizes itself by returning to itself, renewed and once removed."[14]

I have divided the chapters and the eighteen case studies they present into two groups, each implying a fairly different type of relationship between ritual and media. In the first group, ritual practices are seen as having been transferred to new, mass-mediatized performative contexts. In the second, they are shown to interact with mass media in a variety of ways.

Transfers

In many of the examples analyzed in this collection, ritual enactments or features pertaining to such enactments are drawn from their original, face-to-face context to be used in the creation of new types of performances involving the use of new media or contexts of communication. However, we need to distinguish between two quite different sorts of transfers. The one translates the enactments in question from one mode of participation to another, thereby giving rise to performative events whose purported effectiveness is altered accordingly. The other transposes ceremonial enactments to new, more widely accessible, video or online virtual environments.

The first, intermodal type of transfer is illustrated by the case studies presented by the authors of chapter 2. In them, minority group representatives assert both their cultural specificity and their collective autonomy by portraying, as artistic spectacles, components drawn from ritual enactments that the surrounding, dominant populations attribute to them. In Christian Thompson's commissioned piece *I Need You / You Need Me (The Fox)*, in Garo students' Wangala dancing during the televised annual Indian Republic Day Parade, and in the young people's staged performance of Burhdeva at a yearly national heritage festival, mediatization plays a peripheral role, acting as a neutral medium of expression (*The Fox*) or ensuring a widespread diffusion of the events. What is at stake is the potentially problematic transfer of elements from enactments undertaken as ritual to performances founded upon another mode of participation entirely, art or spectacle. Unlike Australian Aboriginal initiation rites, Wangala dancing in village harvest celebrations, and the presentations that punctuate pilgrimages of the Jakh and Chandikah deities, the distinctive effectiveness of these exhibited events is assumed to reside less in the impact they may have on the feelings and beliefs of those who undertake them than in how they may affect the feelings and beliefs of others, namely those who visit the Centre for Contemporary Photography's Black on White photomedia exhibition, those who attend Republic Day festivities, and those who take part in the Virasat national heritage festival.

In these cases, features of ritual performances are used to create what are consensually treated as artistic ones. Conflict occurs when a ritual mode of engagement is nevertheless entertained by some of the participating parties. It is clearly as a publicly mediatized symbol, and not as a ritual enactment, that students undertake Wangala dancing to showcase Garo culture in the Republic Day children's pageant. Because the non-Christian, poor village communities who still practice Wangala as ritual and the Christian, urban elite who perform it as spectacle do not overlap (Christians do not participate in village harvest ceremonies), there is little ambiguity and, consequently, little conflict. However, the potential for such conflict, as well as the preeminence accorded to ritual Wangala, is given conventional expression in pan-regional Wangala competitions, which the villagers always win.

The Burhdeva case is less straightforward. When undertaken to honor local deities, this event's undeniable theatrical qualities are subordinated to its supposedly ritual character. Night-long performances, entailing stringent sexual and caste-based divisions, need to take place whether there is an audience or not. However, when staged by mixed-caste young people of both sexes as an artistic display promoting their regional cultural heritage, this ritual dimension all but disappears. Conflict arose when some of these young people, to their teacher's alarm, began participating in the Burhdeva play as ritual by drawing attention to how they themselves were affected by their performance. It is important to emphasize that this short-lived bid for ritual (re)creation, in which the actors became the mouthpieces for gods demanding the exclusion of low-caste dancers, was not a return to usual Burhdeva practice, but a novel synthesis, combining the disparaging remarks the deities traditionally address to their villagers, the young people's dissatisfaction with their well-meaning teachers, and the teachers' determination to distinguish themselves from customary Burhdeva practitioners.

The Fox juxtaposes elements drawn from Australian Aboriginal ceremonial and from recent developments in contemporary indigenous art to make an aesthetic statement from the artist's perspective as both an Australian of European descent and as a member of an Australian Aboriginal community. Thompson describes his installation, which portrays a man being symbolically transformed into a nonindigenous animal, as a contemporary reenactment of a bygone initiation rite. In doing so, he comes up against the perceptions of others who, although excluded from such rites, have very different ideas about what they should be. Conflict is grounded in the artfully maintained tension between the explicitly fanciful content of the work (involving pink lederhosen, stylish pointy-tipped shoes, a long-nosed "neutral" mask, wide suspenders, and a foxtail) and the circular yet traditionally coherent claim that it derives from ritual knowledge whose nature, for ritual reasons (as "men's business"), cannot be revealed. In this way, in interesting counterpoint to the ambivalent attitude of the white Australian establishment toward Aboriginal people, Thompson, not content to both eat and have his profoundly marbled black-and-white cake, does his best to bed the (Australian) baker as well. The result is a highly provocative, somewhat disturbing presentation eliciting conflicting attitudes and understandings among the exhibition's visitors. And this disturbance is precisely what makes Thompson's installation a work of art and not ritual, regardless of what the artist's personal experience and knowledge might be. Art is above all presumed to induce complex emotional and intentional states in others.

Like many public events, the three artistic spectacles presented by DuBois, de Maaker, Polit, and Riphagen are capable of accommodating a ritual mode of participation on the part of at least some of their participants. This accommodation is what leads to conflict. However, I suggest that participants' aptitude to do so relies less on the presence of certain morphological features shared by ritual and spectacle (embodied enactment, spatial and temporal delimitation, formality, etc.) than on the potential these performances offer for ritual refraction, that is, the possibility of being moved by actions proceeding from the emulation of archetypal convictions and attitudes incarnated by exemplary others: Wangala-dancing non-Christian Garo villagers, Burhdeva-performing devotees of Jakh and Chandikah, secret-keeping Aboriginal initiates. The use of audio and video media plays an important role in the creation of such depersonalized, representative entities. Thus, the development of both showcased Wangala dancing and staged Burhdeva was largely founded on the study of locally made, state-financed documentary videos, and it is no accident that the young people's renewed ritualization of Burhdeva was precipitated not by observing actual customary practices but by watching a film of such practices. Likewise, it is significant that the purported source of ritual knowledge underlying Thompson's video installation is an audiotape of his deceased Aunt Carrie.

The cases described in chapter 6 entail two types of transfer. On the one hand, familiar rituals—church services, weddings, and funerals—are transposed to the medium of the Internet in which participants interact in a digitally rendered, three-dimensional visual space by means of virtual self-representations known as avatars. On the other hand, a degree of intermodal transference is involved as well. Because spaces such as these are often used as environments for multiuser role-playing, participation in these on-line ceremonies is as much predicated on the presuppositions of play as it is on those of ritual. This makes for a highly equivocal situation. Participating in an event as ritual means focusing one's attention on how one's behavior may affect one's feelings and convictions. Participating in an event as play, however, means attending, as one does in everyday interaction, to how one's behavior may be taken to express one's personal motivations and beliefs, and, at the same time, attending to how one's behavior is constrained by what are recognized to be unusual conventions (the rules of play). As one might expect, doing all this at once can pose problems, and it is difficult to imagine performing a ritual properly and engaging in good play (not just following the rules) simultaneously. Some of this ambiguity can be resolved by encapsulating ritual events, assigning their performance to particular niches within the virtual environment where the suppositions of play no longer apply. However, conflicts easily arise when encapsulations of this type are not recognized by all concerned, such that the ritual participation of some becomes undermined by the play participation of others.

The aggressive disruption by rival factions of a memorial service undertaken for a deceased teammate in the online game World of Warcraft offers a clear example. Whereas celebrants were committed to what they anticipated, and publicly announced, as a moving (ritual) ceremony for one well loved, their gaming opponents saw this gathering as a golden opportunity to inflict some serious (play) damage on the enemy.

The crashing of weddings in Second Life provides another, less obvious example. Second Life is a virtual world in which participants can engage in rich social interactions just as they are presumed to do in real life, but under out-of-the-ordinary conditions. One can choose how to appear to others, one can fly, one communicates mainly by typing, and so forth. In this respect, although Second Life is pointedly not a game, participation in it remains implicitly oriented by the pragmatic presupposition of play. Thus, elaborately orchestrated Second Life weddings, involving considerable effort and expense, sometimes become the object of disturbances by outsiders. Much as in the World of Warcraft example, the intruders seem to be motivated by the idea that a play-governed environment is not a legitimate setting for serious ritual activity. These disruptive interventions, while upsetting the wedding participants, may also comfort their conviction that what they are enacting is indeed a ritual (for if it were not, why would intruders react so negatively to it?). However, they also make such performances difficult to pull off, such that persons who wish to get married in Second Life are obliged to encapsulate their ceremonial performance still further by restricting access to the wedding site to invited guests only.

The Church of Fools, a three-month-long experimental online church constructed exclusively for religious worship and modeled on real-life churchgoing, is the most ambiguous example. Here, the premises of play were explicitly excluded. In many ways, the frequent recourse to stipulated, largely equivocal gestures (such as injunctions to "please use 'tear hair out' gesture as we think of them" or shaking hands with coparticipants who are invisible to all except themselves) made these online services close to what many would recognize as canonical ritual behavior. However, even here, ongoing, coordinated virtual ritual became difficult to sustain. The 3D multiuser environment itself, which many users associated with online role-play, led to the intrusion of numerous disruptive visitors who enthusiastically insulted parishioners, misused liturgical gestures, and engaged in parodies of worship, upsetting proceedings to the point that increasingly stringent encapsulating measures proved necessary.

Heidbrink, Miczek, and Radde-Antweiler note that in these examples, conflicts derive not from the online mediatization of ritual as such but from disparate definitions of the virtual space in which they take place. The implication is that ritual and play, when pursued simultaneously, are largely incompatible. This incompatibility comes out clearly, for instance, in the online debates that raged for three years following the massacre at a funeral in World of Warcraft. The solution that consists of isolating ritual within the overall context of play is possible, but, as these examples also show, poses ongoing problems. These difficulties arise because ritual, predicated as it is on a single, straightforward presupposition (attending to how the performance of actions affects the performer's dispositions), is pragmatically less complex than play, such that negotiating a move from a situation of greater to one of lesser complexity and back again is not easy. It is indeed no accident that, whereas instances of play or game embedded in or framed by ritual are commonplace (initiation rites are typical in this respect), the reverse is much harder to come by. The only example that readily comes to mind is when young people perform children's versions of adult rituals as part of (what is seen by adults as) conventional play.

One of the questions chapter 6 raises is the status of ritualizing in multiuser virtual environments. I argue that the funerals, weddings, and church services in their examples are not merely cases of play; however, nor are they merely instances of ritual. They are examples of something more subtle and less obvious, rarely found in real life but prevalent online: ritual embedded in play. I am tempted to suggest that it is not so much the recourse to the customary trappings of conventional ritual behavior as it is the mediatized refraction of those who participate in these activities that contributes to making their ceremonial enactments irreducible to mere playing. Participating persons, seated at their computers, are involved in creating exemplary, virtual avatars of themselves, defined by archetypal dispositions whose emulation leads to enactments (funerals, weddings, church services, etc.) whose performance is presumed to affect not the avatars' emotions and beliefs, but those of the persons themselves. The participants, at once their avatars and themselves, are made to feel, and to be felt by others, as more than what they ordinarily are. Awareness of the ambiguities inherent in such enactments contributes to rather than detracts from their effectiveness by helping to maintain the copresence of one's different selves. To my mind, the widespread development of ludic ritualization as a mode of participation experienced by those who pursue it as having value in its own right is a truly innovative development, the import of which has only begun to be explored. And therein lies the potential danger of encapsulation. If online ritual enactments are hermetically sealed off from their encompassing play context, ludic ritualizing becomes untenable. One is left with something simpler: ritual.

Online rituals that are nothing but rituals are the subject of chapter 5. The authors are explicitly concerned with the consequences of a single type of transference: rituals relocated to cyberspace. The three examples considered are Internet sites largely devoted to Australian Aboriginal smoking ceremonies, the Web site of the Marian sanctuary at Lourdes, and Weblogs created by the dying and the bereaved in the Netherlands.

One of the interesting findings of this chapter is that the first two sorts of Web sites don't really function well as venues for the ritual enactments they advocate. Smoking ceremonies, which consist of holding leafy branches over a fire and then over people, places, and objects to the accompaniment of words, song, or commentary, is customarily undertaken following death, during initiations, and on other ritual occasions. Smoking has gained widespread acceptance as an important public act in Australia for the inauguration of new buildings, mines, and civic events. Beyond the purifying effects these ceremonies may have, they mediate conflict-laden relations between non-Aboriginal and Aboriginal Australians, allowing the former to legitimate their presence on the continent by giving recognition to the latter as first occupants of the land. The Web sites that display and publicize such ceremonies, most of which are run by non-Aboriginal Australians to promote aspects of Aboriginal culture, also provide a variety of resources and testimonials. However, they do not include the possibility of online ritual enactments, and, according to the authors, at the present time, virtual smoking ceremonies are difficult to imagine.

The official Lourdes Web site is ostensibly intended for those unable to go to the shrine itself. It provides useful contact information and practical advice regarding various forms of devotion, allows online visitors to make a virtual tour of the shrine and access Webcam images, lets them send a prayer that is burned onto a CD and placed in the Virgin's grotto, and allows them to participate in a forum where they can leave messages and respond to those left by others. The highly commercialized, tightly managed, and aseptically reconstructed nature of the physical shrine notwithstanding, this online experience is apparently no substitute for the acts of intimate personal communication that, in spite of the regulations that prohibit them, constitute an essential part of what going on a pilgrimage is about: looking into Mary's eyes, touching her hands and feet, hiding handwritten notes, and entering into physical and emotional relationships with other pilgrims. In short, while virtual pilgrimages are possible, they prove to be less than satisfactory.

Death and mourning Weblogs, on the other hand, are highly successful and a source of great comfort and inspiration for their creators and visitors alike. In ongoing diaries and online memorials addressed to a largely anonymous audience, individuals or groups present material relating to their personal experiences of illness and bereavement: reflections, photographs, videos, poems, songs, and inspirational quotations, often accompanied by commentaries explaining the special meaning these items have for the persons concerned. In keeping with the spirit displayed by the Weblogs' creators, visitors provide feedback in the form of personal testimonies, condolences, comments, and advice for all to see. These sites are maintained for several years running, and the idea that Weblog authors' mediatized presence might continue to exist after death is an additional source of comfort to them. Mourners often continue to address messages and petitions to the deceased, adding further entries detailing new events and phases in their lives.

Is this kind of Weblogging ritual? The authors describe it as such mainly by virtue of its repetitive and symbolic character, and because managing such a site provides solace to those in distress. Moreover, while the authors stress the creative dimension of this activity in which the persons concerned exercise direct control over how they present themselves, the degree to which they do so by means of highly conventional images and texts should also be noted. However, I would consider such activities as ritual on other grounds.

In creating and contributing to Weblogs, people are not expressing themselves as they would in the context of ordinary face-to-face interaction, any more than authors may be said to be simply expressing themselves in producing books or songs. Potentially, they are doing something quite different. As Altena, Notermans, and Widlok remark, Webloggers are creating "a mediatized self-portrait," a distanced representation of themselves that is animated by their feelings about who they experience themselves really to be. When, in striving to live up to this exemplary self-representation, they engage in what are recognized as characteristic actions (maintaining the Weblog), the performance of which is presumed to have an effect on their personal sentiments and beliefs, they are participating in ritual refraction. This ritual process pursued by Weblog creators is upheld by the occasional cooperation of visitors who, in much the same way, are involved in creating and trying to live up to mediatized selves defined by what they consider exemplary qualities such as empathy, self-disclosure, and willingness to share. The personally lived-through, yet highly conventional type of emotional reverberation that this online dynamic sets up affords participants with a distinctive, out-of-the-ordinary experience in the light of which they are able to reassess their lives.

The study of these three types of Internet sites is framed by Altena, Notermans, and Widlok's interrogation regarding the basis of ritual effectiveness: does it depend mainly on qualities of space (as Jonathan Smith would have it) or on the entailments of embodied action (as Ronald Grimes has suggested), both of which may be missing from online ritualization. The answer is that it all depends. Recognizable location, bodily experience, degree of control, agency, and situated action all seem to matter. However, I would stress the importance of interactive coordination in the effectiveness of online ritualization. I suspect that individual-based online rituals, such as lighting a virtual memorial candle, digital prayer and spell casting, or electronically mediated soothsaying, are viable forms of online ritual. The presence and intervention of others (deceased persons, those to whom a prayer or spell is addressed, divinatory powers) are almost entirely contained within the individual's performance itself, with the result that a close degree of continuity between online and offline action (the link between my mouse click and the candle it lights on-screen) is easy to maintain. Problems arise, however, when the synchronization of one's own behavior with that of independent others in the pursuit of joint enactments is required. On the one hand, when coordination requires the use of virtual representations such as avatars, the situation tends to become one not of mere ritual but of ludic ritualization. When, on the other hand, one must collaborate with autonomous others directly, the deficits of current online environments with respect to the bedrock qualities of effective interaction—intentionality, responsiveness, adaptation, and personalization—become glaringly obvious. The Weblog case is particularly interesting, because it makes use of a ritual process that depends not on the joint performance of stipulated actions but on the creative coconstruction of refracted agencies. In this case technical shortcomings in no way detract from the effectiveness of ritual performance. Online virtuality, rather than undermining ritual experience, provides the latter with a privileged medium.

Interactions

A number of the chapters in this volume deal not with the transfer of rituals to new media or modes of participation (spectacle, play) but with the relationship between ritual enactments and mass mediatization. At one extreme are cases in which canonical ceremonial forms are given widespread media coverage, resulting in conflicts organized around minority/majority or local/global discriminations. At the other extreme are cases in which media and ritual are rendered interdependent to such a degree as to be practically inseparable, conflict itself becoming the object of mediatized ritualization.

The simplest types of interactions are those in which ritual, media, and conflict are seen as being connected to each other by external, causal relationships. In the situations described in chapter 4 by Langer, Quartier, Simon, Snoek, and Wiegers, for example, media intervenes to publicize a secret or little-known ritual: pamphlets are distributed detailing Masonic oaths; the Muslim call to prayer (*adhān*) in European cities becomes the object of radio and television broadcasts; Alevi congregation rituals in urban settings receive widespread media coverage; and a mass-distributed documentary film is made about evangelical religious training in the United States. In each case, increased exposure gives rise to controversies in which aspects of these ceremonial enactments come up against ideas and values holding sway in the larger social environment.

The interacting bodies themselves seem fairly clear-cut. The ritual character of the performances in question is unambiguous (evangelical summer camp activities, for example, include many eminently ritual acts, such as the washing of hands with "the water of the Word" or the breaking of labeled cups in the name of Jesus to "release the spirit"). While the selective and generalizing effects of mediatization are recognized and discussed by the authors, media are envisaged mainly as means of drawing attention to and transmitting heretofore restricted information to a wider audience. Finally, the conflicts occasioned in these cases derive from perceived value differences framed by a zero-sum (I-win-you-lose) rule as, respectively, a challenge to state and church sovereignty, a bid for Islamic ascendancy, a defiance of established orthodoxy, and an attempt at political and moral subterfuge. As the authors suggest, the issues involved are those typical of minority-majority relations in which a local community of celebrants enters into conflict with the dominant society that encompasses them.

These cases become less simple, however, when one takes into account the fact that the ritual-media-conflict arc is circular rather than linear, with media generating conflict that brings about changes in the ritual performances themselves. In some cases, the concerned parties abandon or alter their rituals to accommodate the dominant value system, thereby gaining a measure of their prior invisibility or acquiring new bargaining positions. The imprecations accompanying Masonic oaths have been for the most part dropped, and the muezzin's call has been either eliminated or made more discreet. In other cases, changes are introduced that make the minority group even more conspicuous. Intensely mediatized evangelical campaigns have become commonplace in ever wider arenas of American life, and increasingly public Alevi ceremonial has blossomed over the last two decades as a means both for advancing political agendas and for reconfiguring and consolidating Alevi identity.

In the case of Alevis and perhaps American evangelicals as well, something noteworthy has happened. Mass media images of ritual enactments on television or on Internet sites such as YouTube have become a privileged reference for the determination of proper ritual form. This is especially true of recently established Alevi commemoration rituals entailing protest marches and ceremonies at martyrs' graves, enactments that, according to the authors, "derived their standardized elements and general layout largely from mediatized sources." Within the context of such self-referential circuits in which ritual behavior is modeled on its own mediatized representation, media becomes an intrinsic feature of ritual practice. It intervenes less as a means of conveying information than as a source of inspiration, providing celebrants with depersonalized, archetypal rituals held to embody the feelings and motivations to which they aspire. In this way, the very nature of the ceremonies undertaken is transformed. They become increasingly dominated by a process of ritual refraction in which practitioners' affecting performances are predicated on exemplary images and narrations of their own making.

The situations described in chapters 4 and 3, while taking place on different scales, are roughly analogous. Whereas chapter 4 pertains to a majority population's adverse reception of minority groups' rituals, chapter 3 is concerned with local ceremonial initiatives and global-wide reactions to the "deviant" messages they imply.

In one case from chapter 3, largely through the personal initiatives of the revolutionary leader Francis Ona, rituals centered on the Virgin Mary, or Mama Maria as she is called locally, became an intrinsic aspect of Bougainville Island's bid for independence from Papua New Guinea. Collective prayer, propitiatory rites, pilgrimages, and the use of statues and rosary beads transformed a secessionist movement into a holy war and played a major role in the resolution of the conflict. Media coverage of these practices, however, sparked considerable protest both at the local level by church groups and globally by those who objected to the way the Virgin Mary had been made into an object of worship and exploited by the Bougainville Revolutionary Army to legitimate violent action.

In the other case, Graziano Cecchini, a Roman artist-activist dissatisfied with the city's cultural politics and with the exorbitant amount of money spent on a "lackluster" film festival, poured blood-red dye into the waters of Rome's "hallowed" Trevi Fountain. The extensive mediatization of this "counterritualistic" act of protest, which at once revived and challenged the fountain's traditional symbolic associations (the founding of Rome, Anita Ekberg's cinematographic frolicking, visitors tossing coins into the waters for good luck), raised wide-scale controversy. While most decried the performance as sacrilegious and potentially harmful, others applauded the "rediscovery" of Rome that it occasioned.

In the two examples presented by Hermkens and Venbrux, ritual, media, and conflict are integrated into tighter, more complex relationships than in most of the other cases. On the one hand, they are explicitly framed in terms of prior local conflicts from which the controversial ritual enactments arose, such that these small-scale disputes, along with the ritual enactments in question, are seen to be projected onto a global arena, prompting people from all over the world to position themselves negatively or positively with regard to the issues they raised. On the other hand, mediatization is shown to intervene both upstream and downstream with respect to the ritual events under consideration. Because these performances make use of "global icons," the Virgin Mary and Trevi Fountain, they become the object of the worldwide media coverage. The circular relationship implied between local and global levels goes both ways. The ceremonial appropriation of what the authors call "global ritual imagery" allows local conflicts to acquire the status of global events. At the same time, the ongoing relevance of such global ritual imagery is corroborated by its use in rituals undertaken in response to local conflicts that become the object of widespread mediatization. The ritualization of mediated representations (the Virgin Mary and Trevi Fountain) and the mediatization of such ritual practices (the Bougainville Revolutionary Army's Marian devotions, Graziano Cecchini's iconoclastic dye-pouring) go hand in hand, forming self-reinforcing circuits of meaning and action in which individual initiatives, conventional enactments, and collectively held ideas and values become the interdependent aspects of new, dynamic totalities. This is the way cultural traditions are begotten and sustained.

Consider one of the case studies in chapter 7. In September 2007, in spite of an impressive accumulation of auspicious omens (the appearance of white elephants and the discovery of large boulders of white jade whereby Buddhas "make themselves known") extensively mediatized by the Burmese junta to legitimate their regime, the conservative order (*sangha*) of Buddhist monks, accompanied by laypersons, engaged in a ceremonial protest by undertaking the ritual called *patta nikujjana kamma*. Parading in the streets with their alms bowls inverted, they indicated their unwillingness to accept gifts from the government, thereby displaying their refusal to give spiritual and moral recognition to the ruling junta. Young men undertook similar counterritual practices by baring their chests and inviting armed soldiers to shoot, thereby threatening the latter with the possibility of engendering vengeful spirits (Nats) such as those of persons killed by unjust rulers. This event brought about an escalating, violent national crisis, whose images were aired extensively over Western media channels until the regime closed down the Internet and stopped news transmissions, effectively shutting out the rest of the world.

In this case, as in the Bougainville and Trevi examples, rituals undertaken in response to a local conflict were given considerable global media coverage that led to international expressions of support for the protesters. However, unlike these examples, and closer to those described in chapter 4, the ritual enactments in question were entirely grounded in local religious practice. What is striking in this instance is the degree to which recursive circuits linking local and global levels and upheld by the interrelationship of ritualization and mediatization did not occur. As one might imagine, the absence of such circuits was due not only to the fact that the ritual events took place within the context of a local conflict whose media coverage was interrupted, but perhaps especially because only local ritual imagery (that is, of a type unfamiliar to Western viewers) was employed. In this respect, the Burmese case stands in stark contrast with another, well-known, extensively mediatized, local ritual event undertaken in a distant land in response to what was perceived as a global conflict making use of a global icon: the Afghanistan Taliban regime's destruction in 2001 of a UNESCO World Heritage Site, the twin Bamiyan Buddha statues (figure 9.1).[15]

Chapter 7's other case study concerns the pulling down of Saddam Hussein's statue on Firdos Square in Baghdad. Here, globally dominant parties, especially the

FIGURE 9.1. The twin Bamiyan Buddha statues, UNESCO World Heritage site, destroyed by the Afghanistan Taliban regime.

United States, are directly implicated, and ritual practice and media production are interrelated to such a degree as to be almost indistinguishable. De Haes, Hüsken, and van der Velde's detailed analysis shows how what was seen by many, especially American television viewers, as a highly emblematic ritual event was largely constructed as such after the fact through the intensive use of media representations and techniques such as image selection and framing, commentary, and sidebarring. Mediatization, in the hands of experts, transformed an off-the-cuff, partially fumbled attempt by the U.S. military to grandstand a handful of locals engaged in throwing shoes at the statue and attempting to smash its concrete base into an inspiring ceremonial performance in which the polarization of good and evil and the ascendancy of the former over the latter were dramatically "revealed" for all the world to see.

If ritual is understood in a canonical fashion, as the self-affecting performance of what are taken to be archetypal actions, it is plainly abusive to qualify the statue-toppling event, as it occurred, as ritual. Indeed, the only ritual act that actually took place was the Iraqi shoe throwing. On the other hand, to characterize the media presentation of this event as ritualization means either reducing the latter to a series of recurrent morphological features (repetition, formality, and so forth), or buying into the ritual-as-polarization thesis proposed by Philip Smith. This is close to the position taken by the authors, whose analysis aims to expose the procedures whereby truth is systematically distorted and reconfigured so as to marshal public support for American interference overseas. Such an interpretation, however, does insufficient justice to the subtleties of human agency, at least insofar as the news makers and their audiences are concerned. Whereas the former are made to appear as blatant manipulators, the latter are made to appear as mindless sheep.

To the extent that ritual is also understood as subject-refracting enactments proceeding from the emulation of archetypal dispositions, a somewhat different picture emerges. From this point of view, images and narrations pertaining to the event as it occurred acquire value not as facts to be accurately conveyed but as resources for the creative construction of distanced, mediatized figures incarnating exemplary sentiments and convictions whose emulation provides the basis for self-affecting actions. In this light, it is not the soldiers but the news makers who are engaged in ritual performance. Taking on the sentiments and convictions attributed to distanced, mediatized figures partially of their own making (oppressed Iraqis, liberating soldiers) leads them to embark on conventionalized activities (those of televised media production), the pursuit of which impacts their own feelings and beliefs. News makers' undertakings, as actions designed to affect others, are clearly instances of ideologically motivated spectacle. At the same time, however, to the extent that the news makers themselves may be thought to be personally moved by what they present, their performance acquires a ritual quality that is also appreciated by the viewing audience. In the same way that the allure of participating in online ceremonies derives from the fact that they are not instances of mere ritual but of ritual embedded in play, the attraction (one is tempted to say the enchantment) of watching televised news reports stems from the fact that the latter are instances not of mere spectacle but of ritualized spectacle. It is as the vehicles of such complex performances that, as the authors state, "iconic images [in news broadcasts] achieve a social status beyond their mere visual representation of fact." From this standpoint, the relationship between news makers and news viewers is not unlike that between Weblog creators and their visitors.

Binder, Driver, and Stephenson's contribution, the last of the volume, deals with political torture, specifically with the violent, abusive practices perpetrated by the American military at the prisons of Abu Ghraib and Guantanamo Bay. Their thesis is that "Torture is not simply violence but violence that is ritualized." By this they mean that while the practice of torture is not culturally understood as ritual and for this reason is not ritual per se, it is "similar to ritual proper or the same as ritual in some respects." Treating torture as a ritualized activity, also akin in many regards to theater or to a deadly game, allows them to better foreground its all too often overlooked performative, communicative, and symbolic entailments. Torture, they convincingly show, is above all a violent, unlawful bid for political hegemony, a terrifying demonstration of power for its own sake, not only played out in the shadowy confines of torture chambers, but also addressed to wider audiences as a means of inculcating submission to authority. While the existence of abuse at Abu Ghraib and Guantanamo Bay, for example, has been made known, the exact details and circumstances of these brutalities remain shrouded in mystery. Relayed by the mass media as an open secret, and increasingly picked up as a theme in fictional works, torture is implanted in the public's imagination as a regrettable, yet acceptable, necessity whose undertaking is delegated to law-defying, quasi-heroic state representatives whose infamous behavior—unavoidable drudgery laced with the exhilaration that comes from total domination—can be at once acknowledged and ignored. In this way, the systematic infliction of pain and humiliation upon others contributes to the construction of state power in several ways: by spreading fear among those who might oppose it, by providing the unavowable grounds for a secret solidarity among its immediate practitioners, and by making tacit accomplices of a general public willing to accept the legitimacy of a government whose authority resides in its capacity to act beyond the law.

The authors argue that torture is of little practical utility as a means of exacting valid information. Indeed, one of the hallmarks of modern torture is the extent to which the abusive practices it entails exceed the limits of fruitful interrogation. Victims are punished less for what they know than for who they are. This is so because torture's main purpose lies elsewhere, as a demonstration of the state's absolute ascendancy over the minds and bodies of its supposed adversaries. Such a display of power by the state's representatives strikes fear in the hearts of its actual or potential enemies and attests to the state's ability to act on the behalf of its citizens. At the same time, however, the brutal ferocity and the absurdly tilted playing field of torture, the lack of empathy of those who inflict or condone it, and the abject suffering and depersonalization of its victims constitute torture as an inhuman, transgressive act lying beyond the bounds of accepted social norms. As such, the practice of torture cannot but call into question the legitimacy of the government forces involved. This is the case not only from the "enemy's" perspective but also, more significantly, from the point of view of the citizens of the torture-practicing regime itself, especially when it lays claim to democratic, humanitarian ideals. In short, while providing incontrovertible evidence of state power, torture may also act to undermine state authority. In this respect, political torture is highly ambiguous. In order to be effective as a basis for affirmations of political hegemony, it requires special treatment in which it is both exhibited and obscured.

In prerevolutionary France, as elsewhere in Europe at the time, this special treatment consisted of spectacular public exhibitions of legally imposed suffering:

exposure, whipping, branding, scorching, amputating of parts of the body, dragging the body, drowning in a barrel, garrotting, hanging, and breaking on the wheel.[16] I have argued elsewhere that such relentlessly excessive, exaggeratedly elaborate inflictions of pain involved members of the onlooking public, less outside observers than full-fledged participants, in a network of contradictory relationships whereby their position with respect to those in power was ritually defined.[17] The greater the suffering imposed by the authorities, the greater the demonstration of the power the authorities represent, and the wider the disparity between these authorities and the condemned individual. At the same time, the more ferocious the punishment, the more the public at once detached itself from the suffering person to join forces with the authorities and dissociated itself from the punitive authorities to ally itself with the condemned person. In this way, a complex ritual relationship was constructed with respect to the powers that be in which citizens fully identified themselves with neither the people suffering nor those who caused them to suffer, but, on the rebound as it were, with both at the same time. The strange emotional mixture the spectators displayed on such occasions—at once intimidated and uninhibited, horrified yet strangely thrilled, at times urging the executioner on and at others rising up in revolt against him, alternately cheering at each new atrocity and moved to tears—can be understood as the emotional correlate of their paradoxical and inherently unstable position as defined by this ceremonial performance. These were ritual events in the usual sense of the term, in which the participating public were caught up in stipulated, exceptional enactments defying ordinary intelligibility and yet impacting on their personal feelings and beliefs.

Political torture, when undertaken by contemporary, democratic regimes such as in the cases of the Abu Ghraib and Guantanamo Bay prisons, also requires special treatment whereby it can become, as Binder, Driver, and Stephenson suggest, both visible and invisible. It too may become the object of ritualization, not in the analogical sense that the authors give to this term (as being like ritual in certain ways) but as a performance founded on ritual refraction.

As the authors remark, one of the salient features of contemporary political torture is the importance of the camera, both as a means of reinforcing the victim's humiliation and as an instrument for the objectification of state power. The images leaked to the media from Abu Ghraib are striking in at least two respects. First, they were clearly taken by the torturers for their own, collective gratification as they performed for an audience that was none other than themselves. Second, they are highly stylized, almost burlesque, portraying torture in a way that verges on theatrical performance and brings various religious, artistic, and pornographic associations to mind. While attesting to the reality of the abusive, depersonalizing treatment to which the prisoners were subjected, these images are at the same time

FIGURE 9.2. Detainees at Guantanamo Bay's Camp X-Ray.

dramatically overstaged. They contrast sharply, for example, with the quiet, anonymous horror recorded in the Wikipedia photograph of detainees upon their arrival at Guantanamo Bay's Camp X-Ray (figure 9.2).[18]

The Abu Ghraib pictures were produced as "iconic" images by and for the prison guards themselves, and their value resides not in their ability to depict torture as it is, but in their capacity to capture certain exemplary qualities to which these soldiers-cum-torturers may be thought to aspire. The photographs are distanced representations incarnating qualities they feel they need to embody: brutal yet fun-loving, heartless yet sexy, far from home yet regular folk, fiercely loyal to America yet not naive. To the extent that the prison guards drew on these mediatized selves to engage in further staged and photographed performances presumed to impact on the way they thought and felt, these images may be seen as the artifacts of a process of ritual refraction. Split between the exemplary personae they seek to emulate and their identities as individuals affected by the enactments occasioned by this emulation, the torturing soldiers are made to become, for a time, more than what they ordinarily are. It is perhaps regrettable, yet hardly surprising, that it was these mediatized, ritual representations of torture, rather than the actual practice of torture itself, that became the privileged basis for the American public's perception of Abu Ghraib. Shocked to recognize themselves in appalling images, partly of their own making, they could at the same time take comfort in the exceptional, outlandish, symbolic nature of the persons and enactments the photos portray.

Often the way of research in the social sciences is to proceed less by validating and applying general principles to empirical situations than by using empirical material to burst out of conceptual conventions in the hope of stumbling upon other ways of thinking. This is what the contributors themselves have done with respect to some of their own original hypotheses. While apologizing for any distortions I may have introduced in responding to their chapters, I am grateful for having had the opportunity to do a bit of bursting out of my own. In proposing notions such as ritual refraction, archetypal dispositions, and the emulation of mediatized others and selves, I am led to a single conjecture of my own: as ritual performances become increasingly dominated by processes of identity refraction in which mediatized representations play a central role, we should expect an accentuation of conflict and its characteristic tendency toward polarization.

The upside-down perspective on ritual and ritualization that I have tried to outline and apply to the material in this collection is, of course, not without problems. One of them, for example, concerns the limits of refracting ritual: where does it end? Should we consider reality TV, self-help workshops, Internet Weblogging, and other familiar features of current Euro-American life to be instances of this type of ritualization? I have no ready answer to this question. However, recalling the often encountered assertion that "traditional" societies are imbued with ritual, I wonder if, in changing our perspective, we might discover that the same holds true for "contemporary" Western culture. Imagine: a ritual-filled society of our very own.

NOTES

1. Jonathan Z. Smith, *To Take Place: Toward Theory in Ritual* (Chicago: University of Chicago Press, 1987), 103.
2. See, for example, Michael Houseman, "Vers un modèle anthropologique de la pratique psychothérapeutique," *Thérapie familiale* 24, no. 3 (2003): 289–312.
3. Don Handelman, *Models and Mirrors: Towards an Anthropology of Public Events* (Oxford: Berghahn Books, 1998).
4. Michael Houseman and Carlo Severi, *Naven or the Other Self: A Relational Approach to Ritual Action* (Leiden: Brill, 1998); Michael Houseman, "Relationality," in

Theorizing Rituals: Issues, Topics, Approaches, Concepts, ed. Jens Kreinath, Jan Snoek, and Michael Stausberg (Leiden: Brill, 2006), 413–428.

5. Michael Houseman, "Menstrual Slaps and First Blood Celebrations: Inference, Simulation and the Learning of Ritual," in *Learning Religion: Anthropological Approaches*, ed. D. Berliner and R. Sarró (Oxford: Berghahn Books, 2007), 31–48; Michael Houseman, "Des rituels contemporains de première menstruation," *Ethnologie française* 40, no. 1 (2010): 57–66.

6. Jone Salomonsen, *Enchanted Feminism: Ritual, Gender and Divinity among the Reclaiming Witches of San Francisco* (London: Routledge, 2002), 236.

7. Salomonsen, *Enchanted Feminism*, 236.

8. Loring M. Danforth, *Firewalking and Religious Healing: The Anastenaria of Greece and the American Firewalking Movement* (Princeton: Princeton University Press, 1989), 237.

9. Caroline Humphrey and James Laidlaw, *The Archetypal Actions of Ritual: A Theory of Ritual Illustrated by the Jain Rite of Worship* (Oxford: Clarendon Press, 1994).

10. Sarah M. Pike, *New Age and Neopagan Religions in America* (New York: Columbia University Press, 2004), 4–9.

11. Refracting ritual of this type has obvious congruencies with a number of aspects of contemporary Anglo-American culture, and I have yet to find a full-blown example it in non-Western traditions. However, this does not, in itself, invalidate treating it as ritual, any more than the fact that elaborate subsection marriage systems do not exist outside of Aboriginal Australia automatically makes them any less instances of kinship.

12. Marika Moisseeff, "Qu'en est-il du lien entre mythe et fiction: Réflexions à partir de l'ethnographie des Aranda (Aborigènes australiens)," paper presented at the CRAL conference, The Concept of Fiction: Towards an Epistimelogical Break, June 15, 2007, Paris.

13. Alan Klima, *The Funeral Casino: Meditation, Massacre and Exchange with the Dead in Thailand* (Princeton: Princeton University Press, 2002), 197, quoted in chapter 3.

14. William Mazzarella, "Culture, Globalization, Mediation," *Annual Review of Anthropology* 33 (2004): 357, quoted in chapter 3.

15. Taller Bamiyan Buddha statue, Wikipedia, http://commons.wikimedia.org/wiki/File:Taller_Buddha_of_Bamiyan_before_and_after_destruction.jpg.

16. Michel Foucault, *Surveiller et punir* (Paris: Gallimard, 1975).

17. Michael Houseman, "Quelques configurations relationnelles de la douleur," in *De la violence II*, ed. Françoise Héritier, 77–112 (Paris: Odile Jacob, 1999).

18. Detainees at Guantanamo Bay's Camp X-Ray, Wikipedia, http://en.wikipedia.org/wiki/Image:Camp_x-ray_detainees.jpg.

REFERENCES

Danforth, Loring M. *Firewalking and Religious Healing: The Anastenaria of Greece and the American Firewalking Movement*. Princeton: Princeton University Press, 1989.
Foucault, Michel. *Surveiller et punir*. Paris: Gallimard, 1975.
Handelman, Don. *Models and Mirrors: Towards an Anthropology of Public Events*. Oxford: Berghahn Books, 1998.

Houseman, Michael. "Des rituels contemporains de première menstruation." *Ethnologie française* 40, no. 1 (2010): 57–66.

———. "Menstrual Slaps and First Blood Celebrations: Inference, Simulation and the Learning of Ritual." In *Learning Religion: Anthropological Approaches*, edited by D. Berliner and R. Sarró, 31–48. Oxford: Berghahn Books, 2007.

———. "Quelques configurations relationnelles de la douleur." In *De la violence II*, edited by Françoise Héritier, 77–112. Paris: Odile Jacob, 1999.

———. "Relationality." In *Theorizing Rituals: Issues, Topics, Approaches, Concepts*, edited by Jens Kreinath, Jan Snoek, and Michael Stausberg, 413–428. Leiden: Brill, 2006.

———. "Vers un modèle anthropologique de la pratique psychothérapeutique." *Thérapie familiale* 24, no. 3 (2003): 289–312.

Houseman, Michael, and Carlo Severi. *Naven or the Other Self: A Relational Approach to Ritual Action*. Numen Books. Leiden: Brill, 1998.

Humphrey, Caroline, and James Laidlaw. *The Archetypal Actions of Ritual: A Theory of Ritual Illustrated by the Jain Rite of Worship*. Oxford: Clarendon Press, 1994.

Klima, Alan. *The Funeral Casino: Meditation, Massacre and Exchange with the Dead in Thailand*. Princeton: Princeton University Press, 2002.

Mazzarella, William. "Culture, Globalization, Mediation." *Annual Review of Anthropology* 33 (2004): 245–267.

Moisseeff, Marika. "Qu'en est-il du lien entre mythe et fiction: Réflexions à partir de l'ethnographie des Aranda (Aborigènes australiens)." Paper presented at the CRAL conference, The Concept of Fiction: Towards an Epistemological Break, June 15, 2007, Paris.

Pike, Sarah M. *New Age and Neopagan Religions in America*. New York: Columbia University Press, 2004.

Salomonsen, Jone. *Enchanted Feminism: Ritual, Gender and Divinity among the Reclaiming Witches of San Francisco*. London: Routledge, 2002.

Smith, Jonathan Z. *To Take Place: Toward Theory in Ritual*. Chicago: University of Chicago Press, 1987.

Index

ABC News, 194
Abhayamudra, 204
Aboriginals
    authenticity of, 41, 42
    Bidjara, 38, 39–40
    as corporations, 136, 137
    on Internet, 137, 138, 139, 141, 155
    land for, 140
    physical presence for, 138–39, 155–56
    smoking rituals of, 135–37, 139, 140, 154, 157, 271
abortion, 116, 118
Abu Dhabi channel, 194
Abu Ghraib, 197, 223
    grotesque in, 231–32
    hooded man in, 232–34, 233f
    human pyramid, 229, 229f, 232, 237
    lynchings and, 232–34, 233f, 247n27
    media of, 224, 227, 228–30, 229f, 232, 237, 238, 242, 243, 247n23, 247n32, 248n37, 280–82
    ritual of, 229–30, 229f
    secrecy of, 279
    sexuality in, 231
    Stanford prison experiment and, 228, 246n20
    torture techniques at, 239
    violence in, 247n22
Acqua Vergine, 68–69
Active World, 179

Adams, Eddie, 17
adhān, 101–2, 122
    in Germany, 103–4, 105–8
    in media, 125n28, 126n46
    as protest, 124n18
"Adhan al-Muhammadi," 124
Adorno, Theodor, 37, 57n3
affirmative action, 54
Afghanistan, 235, 238
Agamben, Giorgio, 240
AIATSIS. *See* Australian Institute of Aboriginal and Torres Strait Islander Studies
Airborne Regiment, Canada, 224–25
Alevis, 108–10
    martyrs of, 112–13
    mediatization of, 112–14, 123, 274
    ritual, 111
Alexander, Jeffrey, 201
Amanpour, Christiane, 193
American Airlines flight 11, 13
American Revolution, 250n71
Amin, Hussein, 194
Anatolia, 108
Andrew, Brooke, 57n1
Anglican Church, 100
animism
    Buddhist, 203–6, 208
    demonization of, 52
    Garo, 54

Anuwrahta (king), 206, 216n75
Apel, Dora, 247n27
Appadurai, Arjun, 50
appropriation, 83
Arabic, 101
"Arab Media: Did It Cover the Same War?" (Gody), 200
Al-Arabiya, 193–94
Arakan, Myanmar, 205
The Archetypal Actions of Ritual (Humphrey and Laidlaw), 49
Argentina, 190
Aristotle, 235, 248n43
The Ark, 166
Arone, Shidane, 224, 225
art, 268. *See also I Need You/You Need Me (The Fox)*
Ashoka (king), 205
Ashvatthaman, 216n75
Asman, David, 193
Association of Methodist Freemasons, 99
Âşûrâ, 113
Atta, Mohamed, 13–14
Augé, Marc, 146
Aung Pwint Khaung, 216
Aung San Suu Kyi, 215n57
Australia
    Aboriginals, 38–40, 41, 42, 135–37, 138–39, 140, 141, 154, 155–56, 157, 271
    Australian Institute of Aboriginal and Torres Strait Islander Studies, 58n22
    colonization of, 39
    Department of Education, Science and Training, 57n1
    Melbourne, 38, 40
    National Museum of, 135, 139
Australian Institute of Aboriginal and Torres Strait Islander Studies (AIATSIS), 58n22
"Avant-gardes and Totalitarianism" (Todorov), 82
avatars, 166, 168, 170, 173, 268
"axis of evil," 198
âyîn-i cem, 26, 109–12, 120–21, 123, 126n53

Baghdad, Iraq, 191–94, 192f, 195, 200, 213n29
Bagram Air Base, Afghanistan, 235, 238
Bakhtin, Mikhail, 231
The Balcony, 249n50
Bamiyan Buddha statues, 276, 277f

Baron, Don, 3
Batchen, Geoffrey, 16
Bateson, Gregory, 256
Bauer, Jack, 248n41
BBC, 194
Bektashi order, 112, 121–22
Belgium, 19, 183
Bell, Catherine, 55–56, 67, 238
Benso, Camille, 99
Bergkamen, Germany, 105
Bernadette. *See* Soubirous, Bernadette
Bettelheim, Bruno, 31n46
Bhattacharya, Kaustav, 17, 17–18
Bible, 97–98
Bidjara Aboriginals, 38, 39–40
"Bill of Public Manifestations," 103
binary opposition
    to Hussein, Saddam, 198, 201
    in Iraq, 197–98
    in media, 200–201
    of sacredness, 189–90, 249n48
    in war, 209
Bird, Elizabeth, 200
Birmingham, United Kingdom, 104
Black on White, 38, 40
Black Room, 236
Blizzard, 172, 185n30
"Blood Sacrifice and the Nation: Totem Rituals and the American Flag" (Marvin and Ingle), 197
Bochum, Germany, 105
body
    grotesque, 231
    location of, 156
    in ritual, 55–56, 57
Boswell, John, 102
Bougainville, Papua New Guinea, 70, 71f
    army of, 64, 71–74, 73f
    Virgin Mary, 64–65, 72–73, 74–78, 75f, 275
    women in, 74
Bougainville Catholic Church, 65
Bougainville Resistance Forces, 71
Bougainville Revolutionary Army (BRA), 64
    government's reaction to, 71–72
    holiness of, 73–74, 73f
Bourdieu, Pierre, 24, 51
Bowles, Eamonn, 119
Boyd, James, 56
BRA. *See* Bougainville Revolutionary Army

Bradford, United Kingdom, 104
brainwashing, 119
Breakcore, Miss Chiquita, 78
Brosius, Christiane, 51
Brussels World Fair, 1958, 19
Buddha Shakyamuni, 204
Buddhism
    animism in, 203–6, 208
    holy objects in, 204–5, 206
    Myanmar protest, 202, 209
    Theravada, 203, 209, 216n75
Buffalo, Rocco, 40
Buka, Papua New Guinea, 70, 71f, 76
bullying, 228
Burhdeva performance, 46, 50, 51, 52–53
    caste system in, 47–48, 49, 54, 55, 267
    deity possession in, 36, 48–49, 54–55, 56, 57, 267
    mediatization of, 268
Burke, Edmund, 224
Burke, Kenneth, 189, 210n3
Burma VJ, 202
Bush, George W., 114, 117, 198–99
    binary opposition of, 201
    on statue-toppling, 195, 212n26
    on torture, 223

Cadigan, Ken, 262
Canada
    Airborne Regiment, 224–25
    Indian Residential Schools Truth and Commission, 3
cancer, Weblogs about, 148–49
Candrasuriya (king), 205
Canning River Bridge, 137–38
cartoons, 63
caste system, 47–48, 49, 54, 55
Catholic Church
    Freemasonry and, 94
    holiness in, 74
    holy objects in, 77
    Lourdes, Sanctuary of Our Lady of recognition by, 141
    Virgin Mary in, 65, 70
Cavanaugh, William, 236, 243–44
CBS, 196, 228
Ceaușescu, Nicolae, 191
Cecchini, Graziano, 78, 81, 82, 275
cem. *See âyîn-i cem*
cemevi, 110, 112

Central Oxford Mosque, 103
Centre for Contemporary Photography, Melbourne, 38
Chamoli, 47, 48
Chandikah, 47, 48
Chapman, Allan, 103
children
    education of, 115, 116, 117, 120
    in Iraq, 226, 245n8
    in media, 197, 214n54
    memorials to, 151, 152
    preaching by, 118
    in religion, 114, 116
Chile, 244
chimpanzees, 249n47
Chin, Ed, 193
China, 17, 18
Christianity. *See also* Catholic Church
    Anglican Church, 100
    conflict and, 211n6
    evangelicalism, 114
    of Garos, 45, 52, 57
    mediation in, 8
    televangelism, 115
Church of Fools, 166–68, 166f, 180
    environment of, 178, 181, 183n2, 269
circulation, 83–84
clan, god of, 41
"Clarity and Good Neighborly Relations: Christians and Muslims in Germany," 125n28
Clement XII (pope), 99
clothing, 40
CNN, 192, 194, 211n10, 215n62
coin-tossing, as ritual, 66, 67, 69, 79–81, 84
Cole, Charlie, 16
Collins, Randall, 22
colonial violence, 225
colonization, 39, 51–52
communitas, 27, 245
community
    through Internet, 156–57, 173–74, 179
    through ritual, 210n1
Condon, Tom, 29n23
conflict. *See also* war; specific conflicts
    Christianity and, 211n6
    definition of, 22, 92
    explanation of, 67
    external, 93–94
    forms of, 95

conflict (*Continued*)
  internal, 93, 94
  on Internet, 26–27, 170–71, 174–78, 180–81, 182, 185n33, 269
  justification for, 211n7
  media and, 5–6, 107–8, 122
  mediation of, 7–8, 9
  from mediatization, 119, 123
  model of, 256
  polarization in, 256, 257
  religion in, 64–65
  ritual as factor in, 8, 26, 93–94, 120–21, 171, 174–75, 180, 256
  ritual impact from, 181
  ritual to mediate, 7–8, 9
  transformation through, 123
  Virgin Mary in, 64–65, 72–73, 74–78, 75f, 275
Conquest, Robert, 248n43
conspiracy theories, 121
Cooke, Hereward Lester, Jr., 69
copper mining, 71
Corriere della Sera, 78
Corsetti, Damien, 235, 238
Cranky Professor, 78
Criminal Investigation Command, U.S. Army, 247n32
cruelty, 249n47
culture
  funerary, 148–54
  intentional reproduction of, 50–51
  symbols of, 210n3
"culture wars," 7

D'Agostino, Roberto, 82
Damiens, 239
dancing
  semah, 127
  Wangala, 35–36, 42–43, 44f, 45–46, 51, 52, 53, 54, 267
Danner, Mark, 227
Darby, Joe, 232, 247n32
Dardenne, Robert, 200
The Dark Knight, 243
death. *See* funerary culture
dede, 109, 112
Dehra Dun, 46
dehumanization, 228, 229, 238, 279
de Maaker, Erik, 58n26
Derbyshire, John, 248n43

deritualization, 14
Der Spiegel, 126n46
Deuteronomy, 97
Devils Lake, North Dakota, 116
Dexter, 247n26
Di Francia, Silvio, 81
"Dirty Harry," 247n26
disappearance, 242
Discipline and Punish (Foucault), 239
dissemination, 243
DİTİB. *See* Turkish-Islamic Union for Religious Affairs
documentation, 20
La Dolce Vita, 66, 69–70, 79, 80, 81, 84
domestic abuse, 225
dominatrix, 231
Dortmund, Germany, 105
Douglas, Mary, 80
Dreaming, 38, 39, 40
Drew, Richard, 16
Duisburg, Germany, 105, 106, 107
Düren, Germany, 105
Durkheim, Émile, 41, 189

Eastwood, Clint, 247n26
Edinburgh, Scotland, 136
Edinburgh Resister House Manuscript, 96
education
  of children, 115, 116, 117, 120
  religious, 116
efficacy
  expectations about, 57
  of ritual, 37, 56, 57, 210, 257, 272–73
  of torture, 248n43
Eid al-Adha [ʿīd al-aḍḥā], 3
Ekberg, Anita, 66, 69, 79
elephants, white, 203–4, 205, 207, 209, 216n66, 216n67, 216n69
England, Lynndie, 231
Engle, Lou, 117
English Revolution, 191
entertainment, 37
Entman, Robert, 199–200
environment, virtual, 178, 181, 183n2, 269
Erbakan, Necmettin, 125n29
Erdoğan, Recep Tayyip, 112
evangelicalism
  in media, 115, 116

mediatization of, 118–20
ritual, 117
in U.S., 114, 121
Ewing, Heidi, 115
execution, 3
ex-votos, 159n33

Fahmy, Shahira, 200
Faisal (king), 191
Faith and Works Committee of the Methodist Conference, 99
Falklands War, 23, 23t, 190
"The Falling Man," 16, 18
fascism, 82
fatwā, 101
Fellini, Federico, 66, 69, 81
Festa del Cinema, 65, 66, 80
Firdos Square. *See* Baghdad, Iraq
firewalking, 262
Fisher, Becky, 115, 116, 118–19
flags, 191, 193, 195, 198–99, 209
Flickr, 17
Foucault, Michael, 236, 239, 240, 241
fox, 39, 41, 53. *See also I Need You/You Need Me (The Fox)*
Fox Television
News, 192–93, 194, 211n10
Prison Break, 248n37
24, 243, 248n41
framing, in media, 199–200
France. *See also* Lourdes, Sanctuary of Our Lady of
Islam in, 104
media in, 142, 214n44
torture in, 279–80
Frankfurt School, 37, 57n3
Franklin, Stuart, 16
Freemasonry, 25
arguments against, 95–96
Dutch, 98–99
English, 94, 98–99
French, 94, 99
interdiction on, 98
media and, 100
oath of, 96–99
papal bulls against, 94, 99
sovereignty claim of, 25, 98, 100
Freemasonry and Christianity. Are They Compatible? A Contribution to Discussion, 99–100

French Revolution, 191
Friday, 109, 127n55
FTM Azione Futurista, 80, 81
funerary culture, 148–54
futurism, 81–82

Garibaldi, Giuseppe, 99
Garo
animism, 54
Christians, 45, 52, 57
rice beer, 44
as tribe, 53, 54
Wangala dancing, 35–36, 42–43, 44f, 45–46, 51, 52, 53, 54, 267
General Assembly of the United Reformed Church, 100
General Synod of the Church of England, 99
Genet, Jean, 249n50
George III, 191
German Alevi Federation, 113
Germany
adhān in, 103–4, 105–8
Alevis in, 108
Islam in, 104–8, 125n27, 125n29, 126n41
Ghosts of Abu Ghraib, 243
Girard, Rene, 24, 234
Gody, Ahmed, 200
gold, donation of, 207
Golding, William, 31n46
Goodall, Jane, 249n47
gopeshwar, 48
Gospel of Matthew, 97–98
Graburn, Nelson, 79
Grady, Rachel, 115
Graner, Charles, 229
Great Architect of the Universe, 98
The Great Terror: A Reassessment (Conquest), 248n43
Grimes, Ronald L., 67, 68, 134–35, 147, 152, 156
grotesque body, 231
Guantanamo Bay, 223, 235, 240, 279, 281f
The Guardian, 81, 169
Gulf War, 192, 245n3

Hacıbektaş, 112
Hacı Bektaş Veli, 112
hackers, 168
Haggard, Ted, 118, 119

hajj pilgrimage, 3
Handleman, Don, 261
Haqqani, Nazim, Naqshbandi sheikh 124
Hariman, Robert, 214n54
Harman, Sabrina, 247n23
harvest festival, 43–44
hazing, 224–25, 237
Healing through Remembering, 3
Hemmer, Bill, 193
Herzfeld, Michael, 70
hijra, 101
Hilsum, Lindsey, 211n13
The Hindu, 42, 43f
Holder, Eric, 249n55
holiness, 249n48
  of Bougainville Revolutionary Army, 73–74, 73f
  forbidden, 249n50
  holy objects, 77, 204–5
  holy water, 69, 70
Holmes, Stephen, 230, 235, 240
Holocaust, 3
Holy Nation of Bougainville, 73, 77
home schooling, 115, 116
homo sacer, 240
homosexuality, 118
hooded man, 232–34, 233f
Hoover, Stewart, 120
hostile thumb, 230
human pyramid, 229, 229f, 232, 237
human sacrifices, 217n77
Hume, Brit, 193
Hume, Patrick, 138
Humphrey, Caroline, 49, 182, 229, 246n21
Hundred Drums Wangala Festival, 46, 53
Hungary, 191
Hüseyin, 109, 110
Hussein, Saddam, 3
  binary opposition to, 198, 201
  September 11 involvement of, 213n39
  statue of, 190, 191–93, 192f, 194, 195, 197, 199, 208, 209, 210, 211n13, 212n21, 212n26, 276–78
hymns, 165
ibâdet, 110
Ibn Jibrīn, 101

icon
  context of, 17
  as media, 68
  photograph as, 16–17, 196–97, 214n54, 265, 281
  religious, 66–67, 68–69
  in ritual, 15–16
  Twin Towers as, 201
Iconic Moments of the Twentieth Century, 16–17
iconoclasm, 16–17
identity
  through Internet, 182–83
  through media, 94
  mediatization and, 70, 264–65, 272
  refraction of, 28, 265, 282, 283n11
  torture and, 281–82
ideographs, 198–99, 201
images
  analysis of, 63
  communication through, 25
  purpose of, 84
inclusion, 48, 189
indexes, 16
India. *See also* Burhdeva performance; Garo
  affirmative action in, 54
  caste system, 47–48, 49, 54, 55, 267
  Chamoli, 47, 48
  Republic Day Parade, 35–36, 42, 46, 52, 54
  rice in, 59n27
  Uttarakhand, 36, 46, 48, 50, 51, 52–53
Indian Council for Cultural Relations, 58n26
Indian Residential Schools Truth and Commission, 3
indigenous people, 28n7, 40. *See also* Aboriginals
  authenticity of, 41, 53
Indra, 216n69
I Need You/You Need Me (The Fox), 35, 39f, 41
  at AIATSIS, 58n22
  authenticity of, 42, 56, 267
  as heritage, 38, 39–40, 50, 51, 52
In eminenti, 99
Ingle, David, 197
initiation rite
  modern, 35, 38, 50, 224–25
  torture as, 237
Institute for Social Research in Frankfurt, 37, 57n3
"Intentions de prières," 143, 143f
International Agile Manufacturing, 14

International Pilgrim Virgin Statue of Our
    Lady of Fatima, 75–76, 75f, 84
Internet. *See also* Second Life; Weblogs;
    Web sites; World of Warcraft
  Aboriginals on, 137, 138, 139, 141, 155
  church on, 165–68, 166f, 178, 180, 181,
    183n2, 269
  community through, 156–57, 173–74, 179
  conflict on, 26–27, 170–71, 174–78, 180–81,
    182, 185n33, 269
  funerary culture on, 148–54
  identity through, 182–83
  Myanmar on, 207
  prayer by, 143–44
  religion on, 4, 166–68, 166f, 178, 180, 181,
    183n2, 269
  religious icons on, 67
  rituals on, 133–34, 135, 137, 138, 139, 141,
    148–49, 152, 171–72, 179, 180, 181–83,
    268–71
  women on, 152
Internet Movie Database, 242, 250n63
In the Valley of Elah, 243
Iran, 198
Iraq
  binary opposition in, 197–98
  children in, 226, 245n8
  flag of, 195
  Kerbelâ, 110, 111, 113
  in media, 191–95, 192f, 196–97, 200, 201,
    208, 209, 211n13, 212n21, 212n23,
    212n26, 214n44
  mediatization in, 277–78
  missiles into, 245n3
  statue-toppling in, 190, 191–93, 192f, 194,
    195, 197, 199, 208, 209, 210, 211n13,
    212n21, 212n26, 276–78
Irishlacrosse, 174–75
Islam. *See also* Alevis
  adhān, 101–4, 105–7, 122, 124n18, 125n28,
    126n46
  âyîn-i cem, 109–12, 120–21, 123
  Democratic Party in, 111
  in Germany, 104–8, 125n27, 125n29,
    126n41
  in media, 105–8
  orientations of, 106–7
  prayers, 101–4, 105–9, 122, 124n18, 125n28,
    126n46
  protests against, 105–6

  symbols of, 125n34
  in Turkey, 125n27, 125n29
Islamophobia, 106, 122, 126n41
Islamrat, 105
Iwo Jima, 197

Jacobs, Ronald, 201
jade, white, 204–5
Jakh, 47, 48
Jaramillo, Deborah Lynn, 193
Java, 184n8
Al-Jazeera, 193
Jenkins, Simon, 168–69
Jesus Camp, 26, 115–20, 121
Jesus Christ, 114, 232, 233
"Jonathan Z. Smith's Theory of Ritual
    Space" (Grimes), 134
Jones, Dianne, 57n1
Juchtmans, Goedroen, 114
Judaism, 127n55

Kennicott, Philip, 196–97
Kerbelâ, Iraq, 110, 111, 113
al Khamlīshī, ʻAbdallāh , 102
Khin Nyunt, 204
Kids in Ministry, 119
Kids on Fire School, 116
Kimmit, Mark, 227–28
Kitzmann, Andreas, 148
Klima, Alan, 63, 68, 83, 265
Koningsveld, Pieter Sjoerd van, 104
Koran, John, 75, 76
Koromira Mission Station, 77
Kronenberg, Henk, 72, 77

Laidlaw, James, 49, 182, 229, 246n21
Landman, Nico, 103
Latour, Bruno, 77–78
laughter, 231, 232
Lawson, Thomas, 182
Le Corbusier, 19
lederhosen, 40
Le Figaro, 200
Leiden, Netherlands, 102–3
Le Monde, 200
Lenin, Vladimir, 191
Leviticus, 97
Lewis, Justin, 212n21
liberation, 111, 194, 198–99
Lincoln, Bruce, 4, 22

Linden Dollars, 170
Linden Lab, 169, 170, 178
Lion Throne, 217n77
liturgy, perverted, 236, 240, 243–44
Loan, Nguyen Ngoc, 17
location
  of body, 156
  of ritual, 134–35, 138–39, 140–41, 145–47
Loka Chantha Abhayalabhamuni (Moon to the World, the Wise Man Who Provides Freedom from all danger), 204, 208, 210, 216n74
Looking for an Icon (Batchen), 16
Lord of the Flies (Golding), 31n46
Lord's Prayer, 167
Los Angeles Times, 195
L'Osservatore Romano, 69
Louis XV, 191
Lourdes, Sanctuary of Our Lady of, 141
  location of, 145–47
  in media, 142
  pilgrims to, 142, 146–47, 159n33
  prayers left at, 144, 145*f*
  Web site, 142–45, 146, 147, 154, 155, 156, 157, 271
Lucaites, John Louis, 214n54
Lünen, Germany, 108
lynchings, 232–34, 233*f*, 247n27

Madaya township, Myanmar, 204–5
Magnolia Pictures, 119
Mahamuni (Great Sage), 205
Malburg, Carl, 75
Mama Maria, 64–65
Mandalay, Myanmar, 206, 217n77
Mannheim, Germany, 113*f*
Manuha (king), 216n75
Marianism. *See* Mary, Virgin
Marian Mercy Mission, 76, 77
Marian Mercy Movement, 72
Marian shrines, 144
Marines, U.S., 191, 193
Marinetti, Filippo Tommaso, 81
martyrs, 112–13
Marvin, Carolyn, 197
Marx, Karl, 191
Mary, Virgin. *See also* Lourdes, Sanctuary of Our Lady of
  appropriation of, 84
  in Catholic Church, 65, 70
  in conflict, 64–65, 72–73, 74–78, 75*f*, 275
  in media, 67, 68
  as religious icon, 66, 67
  shrines to, 144
  for women, 68, 74
Masonic Grand Lodges, 98
Masonry Dissected (Prichard), 96–97
Mastroianni, Marcello, 69
Maude, Stanley, 191
Maungtaw Township, Myanmar, 204
Mayer, Jane, 248n40
Mayakovski, Vladimir, 82
Mazzarella, William, 68
McCauley, Robert N., 182
McGee, Michael, 198
McLaughlin, Seán, 104
Mecca, 101
medallions, 14
media. *See also* photographs
  of Abu Ghraib, 224, 227, 228–30, 229*f*, 232, 237, 238, 242, 243, 247n23, 247n32, 248n37, 280–82
  adhān in, 125n28, 126n46
  bias of, 119, 122, 196, 199
  binary opposition in, 200–201
  children in, 197, 214n54
  conflicts and, 5–6, 107–8, 122
  context of, 18–19
  dissemination of, 243
  evangelicals in, 115, 116
  exclusion in, 208–9
  framing in, 199–200
  in France, 142, 214n44
  icon as, 68
  in identity making, 94
  interpretation by, 95, 193–95, 196, 199, 209, 211n10, 211n13
  Iraq in, 191–95, 192*f*, 196–97, 200, 201, 208, 209, 211n13, 212n21, 212n23, 212n26, 214n44
  Islam in, 105–8
  Lourdes, Sanctuary of Our Lady of, 142
  mediators of, 137
  in Myanmar, 190, 207–9, 210, 214n56, 215n62, 276
  ownership of, 210
  pain in, 239
  as real life, 64, 67–68
  ritual and, 4, 19–20, 68
  ritualization of, 20–21

Rome in, 66
September 11 in, 14, 196, 201
statue-toppling in, 191–95, 192f, 197, 199, 208, 209, 210, 211n13, 212n21, 212n23, 212n26, 276–78
stereotypes in, 107, 115, 120
of torture, 224, 241, 242, 242f, 243, 247n33, 250n63, 279
Trevi Fountain in, 67, 69–70, 78–79, 80, 84
of United Kingdom, 194, 195, 212n21
Virgin Mary in, 67, 68
weddings in, 20
medialization, 31n41
mediation, 7–8, 9, 137, 180
mediatization
of Alevis, 112–14, 123, 274
of Burhdeva performance, 268
conflict from, 119, 123
definition of, 21, 31n41, 264, 265
of evangelicalism, 118–20
identity and, 70, 264–65, 272
in Iraq, 277–78
reflexivity and, 265
of ritual, 25, 36, 56, 120–21, 273–78
of torture, 245
of Trevi Fountain, 275
Medina, 101
medium, 19, 68
Medusa, 19
Me'ekamui, 71, 72, 77
megachurches, 118
Meghalaya, 42, 46, 54
memorials, 150
to children, 151, 152
Weblogs as, 151, 152, 153–54, 271, 272
World of Warcraft, 174–78, 180–81, 182, 185n33, 269
metaphors, spatial, 6
Metaverse, 178
Methodist Church of Great Britain, 167
Metropolitan Council of Nyoongar Elders, 138
Michaels, Axel, 182
Middle Ages, 231
military
anal rape in, 245n3
Bougainville, 64, 71–74, 73f
torture by, 224–25, 226, 227–28
training, 227
U.S., 191, 193, 195, 213n28, 247n32

Millî Görüş, 125n29
minaret, 106
Mindon (king), 206, 217n77
Minus Sign, 178
Misfits, 175, 185n33
Mlak, Zdzislaw, 75, 87n53
MMOG (massively multiplayer online game), 179
morality, 176
Morgan, David, 75, 83, 84
mosques, 106, 107
Mt. Suribachi, 193
Mudéjar, 102
muezzins, 100–101, 105
Muhammad, Prophet, 63, 101
Mukasey, Michael, 249n55
Multiuser Dungeon, 179
musâhiblik, 111
musalaha [muṣālaḥa], 3
Museum Victoria, 136
Muslims, in Switzerland, 125n34
Mussolini, Benito, 82
Myanmar
Buddhism in, 202–6, 208
capital of, 205, 207, 208, 217n78
currency of, 216n74
holy objects in, 204–5, 206
Mandalay, 206, 217n77
media in, 190, 207–9, 210, 214n56, 215n62, 276
Naypidaw, 217n78
oppression in, 215n57
Pagan, 216n75
Thaton, 216n75
uprisings in, 202, 209, 215n57, 276
white elephants in, 203–4, 205, 207, 209, 216n66, 216n67, 216n69
Yangon, 202, 204, 208, 210, 217n78

napalm, 197, 214n54
Narad, 46–47, 48–49
Nargis, 208, 214n56
Natee, Albert, 72–74, 73f
National League for Democracy Party, 215n57
National Museum of Australia, 135, 139
National Review Online, 248n43
Nats, 206–7, 217n77
Naxir, 176
Naypidaw, Myanmar, 217n78

Near the New Pagoda Soo, 216n67
Needham, Rodney, 182
Neptune statue, 80, 81
Netherlands, 97–98
  funerary culture of, 147–54
  Islam in, 102–3
  religion in, 148
Netherlands Foundation for the Advancement of Tropical Research (NWO/WOTRO), 58n26
Netherlands Organization for Scientific Research (NWO/MAGW), 57
Ne Win, 216n74
New South Wales Health Department, 136
New York Times, 78, 196, 249n55
Nicoletti, Gianlucca, 81–82
Night Prayer, 165
NKVD, 248n43
Northern Ireland, 3
Nothing to Declare (Theodoracopulos), 248n43
numbers, lucky, 203, 216n74
NWO/MAGW. *See* Netherlands Organization for Scientific Research
NWO/WOTRO. *See* Netherlands Foundation for the Advancement of Tropical Research
Nyoongar people, 137–38

oath taking, 96–99
Obama, Barak, 20, 223
Observer, 211n6
Okrent, Daniel, 196
Old Testament, 97
"Olympic Torch Rally, London: Free Tibet Protest," 17–18, 17f
Ona, Francis, 71
  Marianism of, 72, 74, 75–77, 75f, 78
  status of, 87n53, 87n60
"100 Photographs That Changed the World," 16
Operation Iraqi Freedom, 191–92, 192f
Orsi, Robert, 145
Ortiz, Dianna, 224
Oss, Netherlands, 102
Otto, Rudolph, 249n48
Ottomans, 108
Our Lady of Mercy, 72
Over My Dead Body, 149

Pagan, Myanmar, 216n75
Pagy, 176–77
pain, 239
Palace, 179
Palestine Hotel, 191
Panguna village, 71
Papantonio, Mike, 118–19
Papua New Guinea Defense Force, 71
Patriot Act, 240
patriotism, 196
patta nikujjana kamma, 202, 207, 276
payback ceremonies, 135–36
Peirce, Charles, 16
Perrikos, 248n43
Petawawa, Canada, 224–25
Philips Pavilion, 19
photographs, iconic, 16–17, 196–97, 214n54, 265, 281
Pilgrim of Peace, 87n53
Pinochet, Augusto, 244
Pir Sultan Abdal, 112
Pisi, Father, 76–77
Pitjantjatjara Yankunytjatjara Media (PY Media) Aboriginal Corporation, 135
play, 260
Plesich, Brian, 195
Poe, Marshall, 16
Poème électronique, 19
polarization, 256
Polish Divine Word (SVD), 75
pornography, 231
possession, by deity
  aesthetics of, 56
  in Burhdeva performance, 36, 48–49, 54–55, 56, 57, 267
Povinelli, Elizabeth, 41
prayer, 29n23
  by Internet, 143–44
  Islamic, 101–4, 105–9, 122, 124n18, 125n28, 126n46
  Lord's Prayer, 167
  at Lourdes, 144, 145f
  Night Prayer, 165
  ritual of, 74
  for women, 143–44
preaching, 117–18
preemptive war, 240
presidential inauguration, 20
Prichard, Samuel, 96–97
Prison Break, 234, 248n37

privilege, 45
profane, binary opposition of, 189–90
promiscuity, 111
Psychological Operations (PSYOP), 195, 213n28
PSYOP. *See* Psychological Operations
puja, 49, 59n33
PY Media. *See* Pitjantjatjara Yankunytjatjara Media Aboriginal Corporation

Radboud University, 4
Rambos, 71, 86n39
rape, 183
    anal, 245n3
Rappaport, Roy, 134, 156, 247n24
Rather, Dan, 196
Rati Malar, 204
Razack, Sherene, 225
red carpet, 66
To Reflect and Trust, 3
reflexivity, 263, 265
Rejali, Darius, 223, 248n40, 248n43
religion. *See also* specific religions
    children in, 114, 116
    in conflict, 64–65
    definitions of, 4
    Durkheim on, 189
    education in, 116
    freedom of, 102
    icons of, 66–67, 68–69
    on Internet, 4, 166–68, 166f, 178, 180, 181, 183n2, 269
    minorities in, 122
    in Netherlands, 148
    public display of, 101–8, 120–21
    ritual as, 10, 55
    ritual in, 5
Rendition, 238, 243
Republic Day Parade, 35–36, 42, 46, 52, 54
res sacra, 105
rhetoric, 190
rice, 59n27
Rifter, 177
Ring of Fire, 118
Riphagen, Marianne, 57n1
ritual. *See also* specific rituals
    of Abu Ghraib, 229–30, 229f
    aestheticization of, 24, 50–51, 52–53, 56, 266–68
    Alevis, 111

alteration of, 35–36, 41–42, 50, 55, 56, 95
body in, 55–56, 57
boundaries of, 12
cleansing, 137, 141, 157
coin-tossing as, 66, 67, 69, 79–81, 84
commodification of, 37, 52, 210
community through, 210n1
conflict from, 8, 26, 93–94, 120–21, 171, 174–75, 180, 256
conflict impact on, 181
contesting, 120–21
criticism of, 15
definition of, 8–13, 182, 210n1, 258–59
disclosure of, 40
discourse, 190
dual properties of, 67
efficacy of, 37, 56, 57, 210, 257, 272–73
as embodied, 55–56, 57, 134–35, 138–39, 140–41, 155
etiquette of, 179
evangelical, 117
evolution of, 19–20
first blood, 261–62
formality of, 12
function of, 14–15, 56, 210
funerary, 148–50, 148–53, 154
global, 275–76
humans in, 11–12
icon in, 15–16
identity-refracting, 28, 265, 282, 283n11
importance of, 49–50
institutionalization of, 49
on Internet, 133–34, 135, 137, 138, 139, 141, 148–49, 152, 171–72, 179, 180, 181–83, 268–71
interpretation of, 7
invention of, 134, 156, 157
as irrational, 28n7
location of, 134–35, 138–39, 140–41, 145–47
meaning of, 49
media and, 4, 19–20, 68
mediation of, 137, 180
mediatization of, 25, 36, 56, 120–21, 273–78
mediators of, 137
modernization of, 51, 56
objects of, 77, 79–80, 117–18, 263
as outcome, 228
ownership of, 36–37, 50, 210
as participation mode, 259–61

ritual (*Continued*)
  as peaceful, 18
  physical presence at, 138–39
  of pilgrimage, 147, 159n33
  play and, 269–70
  of prayer, 74
  preaching as, 117–18
  protest, 202
  public, 138
  purpose of, 189
  for reconciliation, 3
  recordings of, 48, 133
  reflexivity of, 263
  as religion, 10, 55
  in religion, 5
  repetition in, 12–13
  right to, 122
  ritualization and, 259
  role of, 3–4
  sacrilege, 84
  in Second Life, 27, 170–71, 183
  self-referential, 247n24, 261–64, 265, 274–76
  smoking, 135–37, 139, 140, 154, 157, 271
  Sufi, 111
  as symbol, 121
  transfer of, 123n1, 266–73
  traveling, 140, 155–56
  of war, 22–24, 23t, 190, 197, 256
  Web sites as, 154
ritual commitment, 49
ritual condensation, 261
Ritual Dynamics Collaborative Research Center, 4
ritualization, 11, 13, 257
  animal, 29n20
  definition of, 21, 246n9, 246n21, 258
  of media, 20–21
  ritual and, 259
  of September 11, 14
  torture as, 27, 224, 228–29, 232, 234, 235–36, 238, 242, 245, 246n9, 278–79, 280
ritual refraction, 261–64, 274, 281–82
ritual space, 67
Rome, Italy, 64, 65, 65f
  history of, 68–69
  idea of, 66, 84
Rome Film Festival, 65, 66, 80
rosary beads, 74

Rose, Susan, 114
Rosedale, Philip, 178
Rosenthal, Joe, 197
rubber gloves, 230, 231, 237
Rumsfeld, Donald, 194–95, 228
Rutelli, Francesco, 79

Sabbath, 127n55
sacredness, binary opposition of, 189–90, 249n48
sacrilege, 84
sadism, 232, 238
Safavids, 108
ṣalāt, 101, 102, 124n18
Salerno, Nicholas A., 69
Salvi, Nicola, 69
Sanctuary of Our Lady of Lourdes. *See* Lourdes, Sanctuary of Our Lady of
sangha, 206
Satanists, 168–69
scapegoats, 31n46, 197
Scarry, Elaine, 236
Scatman, John, 176
Schechner, Richard, 37
Schlesinger, James R., 228
Schmitt, Carl, 240
Second Life, 19
  environment of, 178
  history of, 169
  ritual in, 27, 170–71, 183
  success of, 179
  weddings in, 170–71, 172f, 181, 183, 269
secrecy, 230, 237, 239–40, 279
semah dance, 127
September 11, 13
  binary opposition after, 197–98
  Hussein's involvement with, 213n39
  in media, 14, 196, 201
  ritualization of, 11, 14
  ticking-bomb scenario after, 235
Serenity Now, 174, 175, 176
şerîat, 110
Sermon on the Mount, 97
servers, 185n27, 185n29
Seventh-Day Adventists, 65, 77
sexuality, 111, 231
Shadid, Wasif, 104
shame, 225, 237, 241
Shiites, 101, 124n15
Shin Arahan, 216n75

Shinbyushin (owner of white elephants), 205
Ship of Fools, 166
Shuddhodana (king), 205, 216n73
Shwe, Than (king), 203, 207
Shwe Dagon, 203
Siegen, Germany, 105
Sivas, 113*f*
Siwes, Darren, 57n1
60 Minutes, 228
Smith, Jonathan Z., 67, 134, 152, 155, 227
Smith, Philip, 22, 189, 211n8, 256, 278
smiting, 168–69
smoking. *See* Aboriginals
Snow Crash (Stephenson), 178
socialization, 116
Soeterbeeck Study Center, 7
Solomon Islands, 72
Somalia, 225
Soubirous, Bernadette, 159n30. *See also* Lourdes, Sanctuary of Our Lady of
South Africa, Truth and Reconciliation Commission, 3
sovereignty, 25, 98, 100
"So We Pwned This Funeral Today: Serenity-Now.org," 175–76
spectacle, 260
St. Pixels, 167
Stalin, Joseph, 191
Stam, Robert, 200–201
Stanford prison experiment, 228, 246n20
State of the Union address, 198
Statue of Liberty, 199
statues
    Bamiyan Buddha, 276, 277*f*
    of Hussein, 190, 191–93, 192*f*, 194, 195, 197, 199, 208, 209, 210, 211n13, 212n21, 212n26, 276–78
    Neptune, 80, 81
    Statue of Liberty, 199
status
    of Ona, 87n53, 87n60
    social, 122
Stephenson, Neil, 178
stereotypes, 107, 115
Stoller, Paul, 79
strategy, 197, 211n6
Streep, Meryl, 238
stress position, 232, 233
Sufis, 111

Sulh [ṣulḥ], 3
Summon, 177
Sun Microsystems, 184n8
Sunnis, 108, 110
Suvannabhumi (golden earth), Myanmar, 207
SVD. *See* Polish Divine Word
Switzerland, 125n34
Sword of Sovereignty, 98
Symbolic Wounds (Bettelheim), 31n46
"The Synthetic Futurist Theatre: A Manifesto," 82

Tambiah, Stanley, 59n34
"Tank Man," 16, 18
tarîkat, 110
Task Force 6-26, 236
Tasmania, 141
Tasmanian Aboriginal Organization of the Lia Pootah, 136
Taussig, Michael, 79
tax, 54
Taxi to the Dark Side, 239, 243
Tekke ve Zaviye Kanunu, 111
televangelism, 115
television, 20
Ten Commandments, 97
terrorism, 27–28, 245
Terwiel, Barend Jan, 203
Thatcher, Margaret, 23
That Madaw, 214n56
Thaton, Myanmar, 216n75
Theingi Malar, 204
Theodoracopulos, Taki, 248n43
Theravada Buddhism, 203, 209, 216n75
There, 179
Thibaw (king), 206
Thompson, Christian Bumbarra, 39*f*, 42
    as artist, 51, 57n1
    criticism of, 35, 41, 56, 267
    heritage of, 38, 39–40, 50, 51, 52
thumbs up, 229*f*, 230
Tiananmen Square, 16
Tibet, *17*, 18
ticking-bomb scenario, 234–35, 248n40
Times, 211n6
To all godly people, in the citie of London (Winter), 100
Todorov, Tzvetan, 82

torture. *See also* Abu Ghraib; Guantanamo Bay
  Bush on, 223
  efficacy of, 248n43
  as heroic, 230–31, 235
  identity and, 281–82
  as initiation rite, 237
  for intelligence gathering, 234–35, 248n43, 279
  justifications for, 228, 234–36
  marks of, 233, 237, 241
  media of, 224, 241, 242, 242f, 243, 247n33, 250n63, 279
  mediatization of, 245
  by military, 224–25, 226, 227–28
  modern, 223, 237, 279
  opposition to, 27, 28
  power and, 224, 226, 227, 229–30, 229f, 237–38, 242, 243–45, 279, 280
  public, 224, 225, 227, 236, 239–42, 279–80
  renaming of, 227
  as ritualization, 27, 224, 228–29, 232, 234, 235–36, 238, 242, 245, 246n9, 278–79, 280
  room, 229, 236, 238
  secrecy with, 230, 237, 239–42, 279
  techniques of, 236–37, 239–40
  ticking-bomb scenario for, 234–35
  by U.S., 223–24, 240
  in Vietnam War, 240, 249n55
  waterboarding, 236–37, 240, 241, 249n55
Torture and Democracy (Rejali), 248n43
Toscani, Oliviero, 16, 82
To Take Place: Towards Theory in Ritual (Smith, J.), 134
tourists, 49, 82–83, 83f
Trafalgar Square, London, 18
traveling rituals, 140, 155–56
Traverse City Film Festival, 119
Trevi Fountain, Italy, 64, 65, 65f
  coin-tossing into, 66, 67, 69, 79–81, 82–83, 83f
  history of, 66–67, 68–69
  in media, 67, 69–70, 78–79, 80, 84
  mediatization of, 275
  as religious icon, 66–67, 68–69
tribe, 53–54
trolls, 168, 184n16
Trouw, 65
TRT, 113

Truth and Reconciliation Commission, 3
Tuchman, Gaye, 199
türbe, 127
Turkey, 102
  Alevis in, 109
  immigrants from, 125n27
  Islam in, 125n27, 125n29
Turkish Directorate of Religious Affairs, 110
Turkish-Islamic Union for Religious Affairs (DITIB), 104, 105
Turner, Victor, 27, 37, 245
Twelve Imams, 109
Twelver-Shia, 109
24, 243, 248n41
Twin Towers, 201

Unabali, Bernard, 72
United 93, 13, 29n23
United Airlines flight 93, 13
United Grand Lodge of England, 100
United Kingdom
  Channel 4, 211n13, 212n21
  Falklands War for, 190
  Islam in, 103–4
  media of, 194, 195, 212n21
unity, 189
University of Heidelberg, 4
U.S.
  evangelicalism in, 114, 121
  flag of, 193, 199, 209
  military, 191, 193, 195, 213n28, 247n32
  torture by, 223–24, 240
Ut, Nick, 197, 214n54
Uttarakhand, 36, 46, 48, 50, 51, 52–53

vandalism, 119–20
Varèse, Edgard, 19
Vash12788, 175–76
Vattimo, Gianni, 78
Veltroni, Walter, 79
Vietnam War, 17
  in media, 197, 214n54
  torture in, 240, 249n55
VIKZ (Association of Islamic Cultural Centers), 104–5
violence
  in Abu Ghraib, 247n22
  colonial, 225
  goals and, 95
  "good," 24

Virasat, 46–48
Virgin Mary. *See* Mary, Virgin
virtual pilgrimages, 144–45, 146–47, 155

Wadidge Web site, 136–37, 139
Waldron, Jeremy, 239
Wandoo Didgeridoo, 136–37, 139
Wangala. *See* Garo
Wangen, Switzerland, 125n34
war. *See also* individual wars
   binary opposition in, 209
   memory of, 201
   preemptive, 240
   ritual of, 22–24, 23*t*, 190, 197, 256
   symbols of, 197
war on terror, 223
Washington, George, 245, 250n71
Washington Post, 227
water, 226
waterboarding, 236–37, 240, 241, 249n55
"The Waters Run Red," 78
Web cams, 144
Weblogs, 26
   funerary, 148–53, 154, 155
   as interactive, 150, 151, 156, 271–73
   as memorials, 151, 152, 153–54, 271, 272
   as public, 152–53, 157
Web sites, 26
   Lourdes, Sanctuary of Our Lady of, 142–45, 146, 147, 154, 155, 156, 157, 271
   as ritual, 154
   Wandoo Didgeridoo, 136–37, 139
weddings, 20
   Second Life, 170–71, 172*f*, 182, 183, 269
   World of Warcraft, 174
"Whatever it Takes: The Politics of the Man Behind '24'" (Mayer), 248n40
"Where Eagles Dare," 175, 185n33
Widener, Jeff, 16
Williams, Ron, 56
Winter, M., 96, 100

women
   in Bougainville, 74
   inclusion of, 48
   on Internet, 152
   prayers for, 143–44
   Virgin Mary for, 68, 74
World of Warcraft (WoW), 172, 173*f*, 185n30
   community on, 173–74
   harassment in, 183
   memorial in, 174–78, 180–81, 182, 185n33, 269
   weddings in, 174
World Press Photo, 16, 18
World Trade Center, 13
World War II, 198
WoW. *See* World of Warcraft
"Wow Funeral Pwnage," 174–75
www.wadidge.com.au, 136–37

xenophobia, 105–6

Yangon, Myanmar, 202, 204, 208, 210, 217n78
Yaza Gaha Thiri Pissaya Gaza Yaza (Glorious Elephant King), 203–4
Yazīd Ibn Muāwiya;, 111
YouTube
   adhān, 124n18
   Iraqi children on, 226, 245n8
   WoW on, 174–75, 180

zâkir, 109
Zarganar, 215n59
Zentralrat der Muslime (Central Council of Muslims in Germany), 105
zikir, 110
Zimbardo, Philip, 228, 246n20
Zizek, Slavoj, 232, 240
Zoewe, 177–78
Zucker, Paul, 69